PERCEPTION AND PICTORIAL REPRESENTATION

PERCEPTION AND PICTORIAL REPRESENTATION

edited by ◇ Calvin F. Nodine
Dennis F. Fisher

Foreword by Rudolf Arnheim

PRAEGER

PRAEGER SPECIAL STUDIES • PRAEGER SCIENTIFIC

Library of Congress Cataloging in Publication Data
Main entry under title:

Perception and pictorial representation.

Bibliography: p.
Includes index.
1. Painting—Addresses, essays, lectures.
2. Visual perception—Addresses, essays,
lectures. I. Nodine, Calvin F. II. Fisher,
Dennis F.
ND1140.P38   750'.1   79-4613
ISBN 0-03-049816-3

Permission to reprint the illustrations that appear in this
book is gratefully acknowledged. Sources are indicated with
each illustration.

PRAEGER PUBLISHERS, PRAEGER SPECIAL STUDIES
383 Madison Avenue, New York, N.Y., 10017, U.S.A.

Published in the United States of America in 1979
by Praeger Publishers,
A Division of Holt, Rinehart and Winston/CBS Inc.

9 038 0987654321

Printed in the United States of America

What is pictorial representation?
How much does it depend on perception?
How much does it depend on cognition?
How do these ingredients combine to give one
a better understanding of the visual arts?

*To future experiments like this one
designed to foster communication
between the arts and sciences.*

Contents

PART I: WHAT IS A PAINTING?

PART II: THE ROLE OF PERCEPTION

PART III: THE ROLE OF COGNITION

PART IV: UNDERSTANDING PAINTINGS

LIST OF TABLES AND FIGURES

Visual Thinking in Overview

Rudolf Arnheim

In recent years, the notion of visual thinking has made its appearance everywhere. This cannot but give me some personal satisfaction (Arnheim 1969). But it also astonishes me because according to the long tradition of Western philosophy and psychology, the two concepts of perception and reasoning do not belong under the same bedcover. One can characterize the traditional view by saying that the two concepts are believed to require but also to exclude each other.

Perceiving and thinking require each other. They complement each other's functions. The task of perception is supposed to be limited to collecting the raw materials for cognition. Once the material has been gathered, thinking enters the scene, at a higher level of the mind, and does the processing. Perception would be useless without thinking; thinking without perception would have nothing to think about.

But according to the traditional view, the two mental functions also exclude each other, since perception, supposedly, can deal only with individual instances. George Berkeley extended this belief to mental images and insisted that nobody can picture in his or her mind an idea such as "man" as a generality: one can visualize only a tall or a short man or a white or a black one but not man as such. Thinking, on the

---

Originally, this foreword was intended to consider the subject of the Philadelphia conference in the broader context of visual thinking. An unforeseen absence from the United States, however, prevented me from putting my thoughts on paper in time for the conference. Instead, I formulated them in an address to the division on educational psychology at the 1978 meeting of the American Psychological Association. The overview thereby acquired a slant toward practical application that may seem to distract the discourse from its more general purpose. Nevertheless, I prefer to leave it in the form in which it was written, since theoretical statements and concrete exemplifications may be said to strengthen each other's case.

other hand, is said to handle only generalities. It cannot tolerate the presence of particular things. If, for example, to reason about the nature of man, any image of a particular man would lead me astray.

This supposed incompatibility of mental functions, which nevertheless cannot do without each other, has disturbed philosophers throughout the history of the Western world. It led to an underestimation of the senses and promoted thought to a splendid isolation, which threatened it with sterility. In education, it made for a strict distinction between the necessary and honorable study of words and numbers and the luxury of a slightly indecent concern with the senses. When nowadays, the budget for the teaching of the arts is the first to be cut, as soon as the school system of a city is in financial trouble, we are still heirs to the pernicious split that has hampered our educational thinking for so long.

In psychology, the mental image has returned from half a century of exile and enjoys an attention that cannot but help our efforts. But I have the impression that the best of these studies are still limited to mental imagery as a substitute for direct visual perception, that is, to experiments showing that some of the things done in direct perception are also attainable in imagery (Shepard 1978). This is useful enough, but theoretical and experimental psychology still has much to explore about direct and indirect perception as the principal instrument of problem solving.

Developmental psychology has been much impressed by attempts to distinguish three stages through which the child's mind passes as it grows from birth to maturity. There is in the beginning a motor stage, in which coping behavior relies on bodily action; there is, in the second place, a perceptual I try stage, during which the child manages his or her affairs by what he or she can see, hear, or touch; and there is the third stage, namely, reasoning, which operates at the level of abstract thinking. What matters for our purpose is to what extent the three types of behavior are assumed to be mutually exclusive and especially, what happens to the behavior mode of an earlier stage when the child progresses to the next. Let me illustrate the crucial theoretical point by a reference to the best-known demonstrations in this field, namely, the conservation experiments (Piaget and Inhelder 1962). Two basic approaches must be clearly defined before one tackles the less urgent task of finding out which psychologist believes exactly what.

One of these approaches has it that when the child is no longer fooled by the different shapes of the two containers into believing that they hold different amounts of liquid, he or she escapes from the appearance of things to the realm of pure reason, where he or she is not misled by perception. The other approach maintains that to judge the two columns of liquid by, say, their height is a necessary and legitimate first step toward the solution of the problem. To go beyond it, the child does not leave the domain of visual imagery—there is, in fact, no other place to go!—but proceeds to perceive the given situation in a more sophisticated fashion: instead of considering one spatial dimension only, the child looks at the interplay between two, namely, height and breadth. This is true progress on the scale of mental development, and it is not achieved by getting out of the perceptual situation but, on the contrary, by going more deeply into it.

The fact that thinking of this kind must take place in the perceptual realm because there is no other place to go is concealed by the belief that reasoning can only be done through language. I can observe here only briefly what I have tried to show more explicitly elsewhere, namely, that although language is a valuable help in much human thinking, it is neither indispensable nor can it serve as the medium in which thinking takes place (Arnheim 1969, chap. 13). It should be obvious that language consists of sounds or visual signs that possess none of the properties of the things to be manipulated in a problem situation. In order to think productively about the nature of, say, liberty, one needs a medium of thought in which the properties of liberty can be represented. Productive thinking is done by means of the things to which language refers— referents that in themselves are not verbal but perceptual. What else could they be?

As a further example, I would like to raise a question that is particularly relevant to psychology, namely, In what medium do we think about mental processes? Sigmund Freud in one of the few diagrams that accompany his theories illustrated the relation between two triads of concepts: id, ego, and superego and unconscious, preconscious, and conscious (Freud 1933). His drawing presents these terms in a vertical section through a bulgy container, a kind of abstract architecture. (See Figure F.1.) The psychological relations are shown as spatial relations, from which we are asked to infer the places and directions of the mental forces that Freud's model is intended to illustrate. These forces, although not represented in the picture, are as perceptual as the space in which they are shown to act. It is well-known that Freud made them behave like hydraulic forces—an image that imposed certain constraints on his thinking.

Note here that Freud's drawing was not a mere teaching device, used in his lectures to facilitate the understanding of processes about which he himself thought in a different medium. No, he portrays them precisely in the medium in which he himself was thinking, well aware though he was that he was thinking in analogies. Whoever hesitates to believe this is invited to ask himself in what other medium Freud—or, for that matter, any other psychologist—could have done his or her reasoning. If the hydraulic model was imperfect, it had to be replaced by a more suitable image, perhaps a more kinesthetic one. But perceptual it had to be. Unless Freud, instead of engaging in productive thinking, had

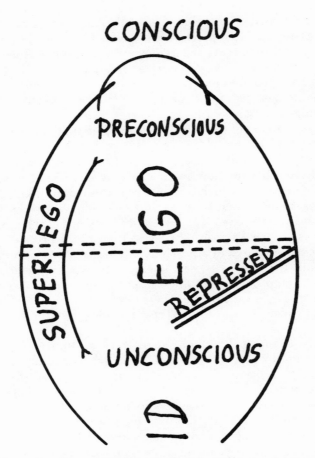

Figure F.1 Sigmund Freud's diagram of the relation between two triads of concepts: id, ego, and superego and unconscious, preconscious, and conscious (after Sigmund Freud) *Neue Vorlesungen zur Einführung in die Psychoanalyse.*

limited himself to trying out new combinations of properties his concepts already possessed, in which case an inexpensive computer would have done equally well.

In the beginning, I mentioned a basic objection that seemed to prevent visual images from serving as the medium of reasoning. Berkeley had pointed out that perception, and, correspondingly, mental images, could refer only to individual instances, not to general concepts, and was therefore unsuitable for abstract thinking. But if this is so, how can diagrams be used everywhere as vehicles for thinking at a highly abstract level? Take, as an example, the syllogism—that triumph of inferential logic. The device has been famous since antiquity because it permitted the thinker to draw a valid conclusion from two valid

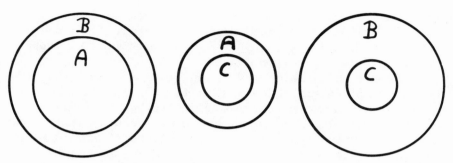

Figure F.2   Syllogistic diagram by Leonhard Euler from *Lettres à une princesse d'Allemagne sur quelques sujets de physique et philosophie.*

premises. One obtains a new piece of reliable knowledge without any need to consult the facts of reality for confirmation. Now, when the formula of the syllogism is recited in words, the listener experiences a fine case of scampering in search of a thought model. The listener hears: "If all A are contained in B, and if C is contained in A, then C must also be contained in B." Is this proposition right or wrong? There is no way of finding out, unless one resorts to the kind of image that turns up in Huttenlocher's splendid experiments on strategy in reasoning (Huttenlocher 1968). I want to refer here to the oldest syllogistic diagrams, introduced around 1770 by the mathematician Leonhard Euler in his book *Lettres à une princess d'Allemagne sur quelques sujets de physique et philosophie* (Euler 1770). Rather ungratefully, the device is called *Venn circles* in the English-speaking countries. One glance at Figure F.2 proves that the syllogistic proposition of the *modus barbara* is correct and must be correct not only in the present example but in all possible cases. In the drawing, the factual relations are shown as spatial relations, just as in Freud's.

Evidently, the syllogism uses concepts at a very high level of abstraction. They are despoiled of all particular characteristics, except the one of belonging under a superordinate category. The syllogism can serve to prove that Socrates is mortal or that cherry trees have roots, but neither Socrates nor cherry trees figure in the proposition. Visually, the circle is the most denuded shape we possess. But when we look at the drawing, we seem to find Berkeley's assertion confirmed: we see a particular instance of entangled circles and nothing else. How, then, do we reason so abstractly with particulars?

The answer comes from the psychological principle for which philosophers are searching when they discuss the problem of "seeing as" (Wittgenstein 1967; Hanson 1965). I would formulate this principle by saying that all perception is the perceiving of qualities, and since all qualities are generic, perception always refers to generic properties. Seeing a fire is always seeing "fireness," and seeing a circle is seeing "roundness." Seeing the spatial relations between three circles lends itself quite directly to seeing the range of enclosure. The topological aspects of enclosure are presented by Euler's images with the disciplined economy required by all good thinking.

By now it will be clear that the term "Visual Thinking" refers only to one facet of our subject. It fails to indicate that vision is only one of the senses that serve perception—kinesthesia being another important one. It also does not claim, as it should, that *all* productive thinking (as distinguished from the mechanical manipulation of data) must be perceptual. Once we acknowledge that thinking has a perceptual base, we must also consider the mirror image of this claim, namely, that all perception involves aspects of thought.

These claims cannot but be profoundly relevant to education, and I propose to devote the remainder of this foreword to a few more specific remarks on this subject. The teaching of the arts, an exclusively visual matter, seems to deserve a prominent place here. But this responsibility is not always clearly faced. We hear art educators say that the arts are needed to create a well-rounded person, although it is not obvious that being well rounded is better than being slim. We hear that the arts give pleasure but are not told why and to what useful end. We hear of self-expression and emotional outlets and the liberation of individuality. But rarely is there an emphasis on the art room or studio as a training ground for visual thinking. Yet every art teacher knows from experience that drawing, painting, or sculpture, properly conceived, pose cognitive problems worthy of a good brain and every bit as exacting as a mathematical or scientific puzzle.

How does one render in a picture the characteristic aspects of an object or event? How does one create space, depth, movement; how does one create balance and unity? How do the arts help the young mind comprehend the confusing complexity of the world it is facing? These problems will be productively approached by the students only if the teacher encourages them to rely on their own intelligence and imagination rather than on mechanical tricks. One of the great educational advantages of art work is that a minimum of technical instruction suffices to supply students with the instruments needed for the independent development of their own mental resources.

Art work, intelligently pursued, lets the student take conscious possession of the various aspects of perceptual experience. For example, the three dimensions of space, which are available for practical use in daily life from infancy on, must be conquered, step by step, in sculpture. Such competent handling of spatial relations, acquired in the art room, is of direct professional benefit for such activities as surgery or engineering. The ability to visualize the complex properties of three-dimensional objects in space is needed for artistic, scientific, and technological tasks.

So directly and indirectly connected are the exploration of perceptual space and the categories of theoretical thinking that the former is the best training ground for the latter. We noted that Freud, as well as Euler, used spatial dimensions to comprehend the interplay of forces of the mind or the hierarchy of a system of logic. It stands to reason that a person familiar with the intricacies of perceptual relations will be equipped to deal more imaginatively with the properties of theoretical concepts, such as inclusion, exclusion, dependence, interference, channels, barriers, sequence, random arrangement, and so forth.

What, then, are some of the desiderata of visual thinking for the various fields of teaching and learning? Let me mention the consequences for the use of language, an instrument needed by them all. If we look at language with some affectionate attention, we find that many so-called abstract terms still contain the perceivable practical qualities and activities from which they were originally derived. Words are monuments to the close kinship between perceptual experience and theoretical reasoning. They can promote the cross-fertilization between the two when in the use of language, attention is paid to the perceptual matrices from which intellectual terminology is derived. This is the specialty of poets and other writers. They know how to revive the fossils buried in words and, thereby, to make verbal statements come alive. Their services are needed for the survival of productive thinking in the sciences. When we remark regretfully that psychologists today no longer write like William James or Freud, we are not making a merely "aesthetic" complaint. We sense that the desiccation of our language is symptomatic of the pernicious split between the manipulation of intellectual schemata and the handling of live subject matter.

If I were asked to describe my dream university, I would have it organize itself around a central trunk of three disciplines: philosophy, the art studio, and the poetry workshop. Philosophy would be asked to return to the teaching of ontology, epistemology, ethics, and logic in order to remedy the shameful deficiencies of the reasoning now common in the fields of academic specialization. Art education would provide the instruments by which to carry out such thinking. Poetry would make language, our principal medium for communicating thought, fit for thinking in images.

A glance at the practice of secondary and higher education today indicates that imagery has its representatives in the classroom. The blackboard is the venerable vehicle of visual education, and the diagrams drawn in chalk by teachers of social science, grammar, geometry, or chemistry indicate that theory must rely on vision. But a look at these diagrams also reveals that most of them are the products of unskilled labor. They fail to transmit their meaning as well as they should because they are badly drawn. In order to deliver their message safely, diagrams must rely on the rules of pictorial composition and visual order that have been perfected in the arts for some 20,000 years. Art teachers should be prepared to apply these skills not only to the exalted visions of painters fit for museums but to all those practical applications that the arts have served, to their own benefit, in all functioning cultures.

The same consideration holds for the more elaborate visual aids—the illustrations and maps, the slides and films, and the video and television shows. Neither the technical skill of picture making alone nor the faithful realism of the images guarantees that the material explains what it is intended to explain. Here, it seems to me essential to get beyond the traditional notion that pictures provide the mere raw material and that thinking begins only after the information has been received—just as digestion must wait until one has eaten. Instead, the thinking is done by means of structural properties inherent in the image, and therefore, the image must be shaped and organized intelligently in such a way as to make the salient properties visible. Decisive relations between components must show up: cause must aim at effect, correspondences, and symmetries; hierarchies must be clearly presented—an eminently artistic task, even when it is used simply to explain the working of a piston engine or a shoulder joint (Arnheim 1974).

I would like to conclude with a practical example. Some time ago, I was asked for advice by a German graduate student of the Pedagogical Academy in Dortmund. Werner Korb was working on the visual aspects of classroom demonstrations in the high school teaching of chemistry; having discovered that Gestalt psychology has worked out principles of visual organization, he asked for my permission to send me his material. From what I saw, I received the impression that in general school practice, a classroom demonstration was considered to be doing its duty when the chemical process to be understood by the students was made physically present. The shape and arrangement of the various bottles, burners, tubes, and their contents were determined by what was technically required and what was cheapest and most convenient for the manufacturer and the teacher. Little thought was given to the visual shapes and arrangements that reached the eyes of the students and to the relations between what was seen and what was understood.

A small example is shown in Figure F.3. The diagram shows the arrangement suggested for demonstrating the synthesis of ammonia. The two component gases, nitrogen and hydrogen, each in its bottle, combine in a single straight tube, from which a short connection takes off with a sharp, right-angled break and leads the two gases to the container in which they form the ammonia. The single straight vertical tube is the simplest and cheapest way of making the connection, but it misleads the visual thinking of the students. It suggests a direct connection between the two components and bypasses their merging

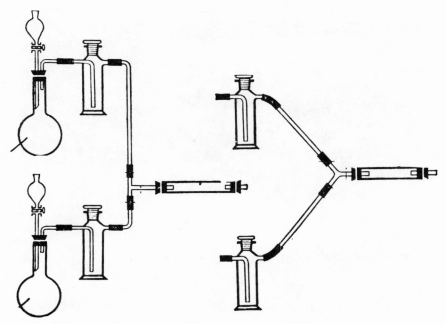

Figure F.3 Diagram showing the arrangement suggested for demonstrating the synthesis of ammonia.

for the synthesis. A y-shaped combination of two tubes, perhaps a trifle more troublesome for the teacher, leads the eye correctly.

My last illustrations, also taken from Korb's material, show first a typical classroom demonstration of the production and demonstration of hydrochloride. (See Figure F.4.) The array of bottles on the shelf in the background has nothing to do with the experiment. It is the teacher's storage space, supposed to be ignored by the students. But the visual discrimination of figure and ground does not obey nonperceptual prohibitions. In perception, whatever is seen is supposed to belong. Since the crowded shelf is a part of the sight but not of the experiment, the contradiction threatens to sabotage the teaching.

There is no need to comment on the virtues of the counterproposal illustrated in Figure F.5. A sense of well-being and order distinguishes the image. The eye is securely led, even before one has any conception of the particular nature of the chemical process.

As my modest examples will have indicated, visual thinking is inevitable. Even so, it will take time before it truly conquers its place in our education. Visual thinking is indivisible: unless it is given its due in every field of teaching and learning, it cannot truly work well in any field. The best intentions of the biology teacher will be hampered by half-ready student minds if the mathematics teacher is not applying the

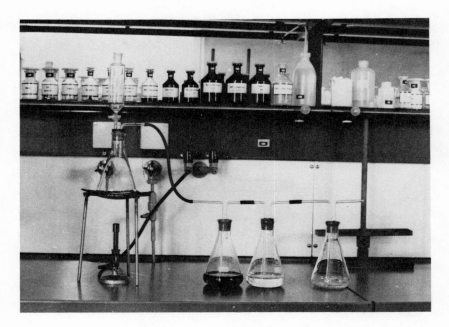

Figure F.4   A typical classroom demonstration of the production of hydrochloride.

Figure F.5   A more effective version of the same classroom demonstration as shown in Figure F.4.

same principles. We need nothing less than a change of basic attitude in all teaching. Until then, those who happen to see the light will do their best to get the ball rolling. The seeing of the light and the rolling ball are good visual images.

REFERENCES

Arnheim, R. *Visual Thinking*. Berkeley: University of California Press, 1969.

_____. *Art and Visual Perception*. Berkeley: University of California Press, 1974.

Berkeley, G. "Introduction." *A Treatise Concerning the Principles of Human Knowledge*. 1710.

Euler, L. *Lettres à une princesse de'Allemagne sur quelques sujets de physique et philosophie*. Leipzig: Steidel, 1770.

Freud, S. "Lecture 31." *Neue Vorlesungen zur Einführung in die Psychoanalyse*. Vienna: Internationaler Psychoanalytisches Verlag, 1933.

Hanson, N. R. *Patterns of Discovery*. Cambridge: Cambridge University Press, 1965.

Huttenlocher, J. "Constructing Spatial Images: A Strategy in Reasoning." *Psychological Review* 75 (1968): 550–60.

Piaget, J., and Inhelder, B. *Le Développement des quantités physiques chez l'enfant*. Neuchâtel: Delachaux & Niestle", 1962.

Shepard, R. N. "The Mental Image." *American Psychologist* 33 (1978): 125–37.

Wittgenstein, L. *Philosophische Untersuchungen*. Pt. 2, sec. 2.227. Frankfurt: Suhrkamp, 1967.

Preface

This volume contains the edited proceedings of the First Interdisciplinary Symposium on Pictorial Processing, entitled "What Is a Painting?," sponsored by the U.S. Army Human Engineering Laboratory. The symposium was held at the Philadelphia Museum of Art, Philadelphia, Pennsylvania, on April 17–19, 1978.

We wish to thank the U.S. Army Human Engineering Laboratory for sponsoring this interdisciplinary symposium. To John D. Weisz, Director of the Human Engineering Laboratory, we express our deep appreciation for his patience, encouragement, and support, which helped make our idea a reality.

We wish to thank Ted Katz, Director of Education of the Philadelphia Museum of Art, who gave his support by providing the appropriate setting for a symposium that brought artists, psychologists, and philosophers together to talk about the very objects that surround them. We thank John Fisher and the members of the Institute for Aesthetics, Temple University, Philadelphia, Pennsylvania, for their support of our idea, which helped make this a truly interdisciplinary symposium. We also wish to thank Ruth Lehrer Fine, of the Alverthorpe Gallery in Jenkintown, Pennsylvania, who corrected some of our misconceptions about art and artists. Ruth, John, and Ted formed a sounding board against which we tested many of our ideas as we planned the symposium.

The contributors addressed their ideas to questions that we thought would be of interest to artists, psychologists, and aestheticians. We hope their answers will bring the reader closer to an understanding of how different disciplines see a painting. The symposium follows the lead provided by Gombrich, Hochberg, and Black in *Art, Perception, and Reality* (Baltimore: Johns Hopkins University Press, 1972). Although Rudolf Arnheim could not attend the symposium, he agreed to submit an essay, which we have chosen to serve as a foreword to this volume.

We gratefully acknowledge the assistance of Diane Barnette and Michele E. Cohen for contributing endless typing and proofreading skills so critical to the completion of this volume. Although this volume represents an incomplete account of the informal interaction at the symposium, much has been added to the individual chapters to reflect that interaction as closely as possible. We hope the ways these contributors view a painting will serve as a basis for our readers so they may form their own answers to the question, "What is a painting?"

Introduction

An unusual experiment took place in April 1978 at the Philadelphia Museum of Art. The experiment was a symposium designed to bring together artists, psychologists, and philosophers to exchange their ideas about pictorial representation (note, we did not say *agree with* but, rather, *exchange* ideas). The controversies that arose during the symposium, evidenced in the chapters contained in this volume, are from our viewpoint the most important result of such an interdisciplinary symposium. The theme of the symposium was, "What is a Painting?," and that theme is carried throughout the volume and, most particularly into the first section, as addressed by a philosopher, a psychologist, and an artist.

The participants, in some sense, represent the subjects in our experiment and the chapters their response to our questions. Psychologists talk about art, artists talk about perception, and philosophers talk about both, but they seldom have the opportunity to come together and explore the question of how perception and art are related. For the artist, perception says something about the process of seeing and interpreting the visual world, which is the primary source of pictorial representation. Perceptual principles derived from the experimental psychology of perception not only help the artist understand how he or she sees the visual world as he or she does but also how he or she translates that three-dimensional world onto a two-dimensional canvas plane.

Perception is also important to the philosopher, but perhaps in more subtle ways than it is to the artist. The philosopher is certainly interested in the process of seeing, but the emphasis falls on the interpretation of what is seen and the nature of the visual world. The argument shifts from one that makes use of things seen to one which examines the nature of visual representation and its meaning when applied to pictorial representation. Thus, we already have the makings of a controversy between the philosopher, who focuses on the meaning of terms like *representation* and *abstraction*, and the artist, who focuses on the process of translating visual experiences of things seen into visual images. It is clear that the psychologists' views of visual perception provide some important links between the concerns of the artist and the concerns of the philosopher.

The psychologists' views of perception are not limited to the visual experience, learning, and other cognitive considerations. Most psychologists believe that cognition, loosely defined as knowledge of the world derived through empirical or rational means, and perception go hand in hand. The question then becomes, How do these two processes work together? This question has been and still remains a central issue in experimental psychology. Perhaps this defines a point of departure where perception ends and cognition begins, and this issue certainly has relevance to painting regardless of whether one accepts the view that pictorial representation mirrors or constructs reality. It therefore follows that perception and cognition serve as major sections in this volume.

The final section of this volume concerns the way in which researchers are attempting to examine appreciation, understanding, and interpreting of paintings, as well as an artist's and psychologist's approach to the development of the creative process. It is here where experimental aesthetics meets with artistic creativity.

It is our hope that by presenting the topics in this volume, subsequent conferences will emerge from the beginnings here, so that such interdisciplinary communication may be used to explore similar topics, that bring the arts and sciences together.

PART I

WHAT IS A PAINTING?

Introduction to Part I

Our purpose in the first section is to illustrate differences in perspectives between the philosopher, psychologist, and artist as they address the general question, What is a painting?

Danto is concerned with distinguishing artworks from artifacts. The problem arises because avant-gardists are dedicated to testing the limits of artform. A replica of the 1978 Manhattan telephone directory is not an artwork even though its producer may have intended it to represent the 1978 Manhattan telephone directory. But Lichtenstein's copy (replica?) of Erle Loran's diagram of Cézanne's painting of Mme. Cézanne is an artwork. Why? Because Lichtenstein's painting is more than a diagram; it is Lichtenstein's statement about the way Cézanne perceived and represented the world (or, in this case, Mme. Cézanne). This use of a representational vehicle (a painting of a diagram) to create a meaningful statement (about Cézanne's art) is what Danto defines as style. Perhaps it is these stylistic considerations that contribute to artworks but consume artifacts.

Hochberg distinguishes between paintings that attempt to achieve optical fidelity, using a scene as the reference point (for example, Leonardo da Vinci's windows) and paintings that are designed to simulate optical equivalences, using the perceptions of the viewer as the reference point (for example, Impressionism). In order to produce simulations rather than surrogates, artists became more analytical about their perceptual experiences and experimented with painting techniques, such as chiaroscuro and pointillism, which depend for their effects on the way the visual system operates. Thus, the concerns of modern art belong as much to the psychologist as to the artist and philosopher.

"Art is real fiction" claims Day, because the art world defines the *what* and *how* of art. To illustrate his point, Day traces the beginnings of modern art back to the middle of the nineteenth century. Art of this period was stagnating under the conventions dictated by the Academy, which were regulated more by social tastes than artistic intuitions. There were some dissidents. One of them was Gustave Courbet, whom Day singles out as sowing the seeds of the new paradigm—modern art.

Courbet believed that it was time to put art back into painting. What a more fitting way to transmit this message than through a painting of the artist in his studio. The painting takes the form of an allegory, in keeping with the style of the art of the period. The characters in the allegory represent Courbet's ideas about what a painting should be. It is a commentary on art, a painting about painting.

Chapter One

Pictorial Representation
and Works of Art

Arthur C. Danto

DISTINGUISHING ARTWORKS FROM ARTIFACTS

When endeavoring to understand the philosophical structure of entities of kind E, it is always useful to imagine counterparts to given instances like them in every observable respect but belonging to some ontologically different kind (E')—for then, what is distinctive of the instance of E cannot lie in whatever they may have in common with the instances of E' and must be sought elsewhere. This method is conventional enough in philosophy, where, for notorious instance, we are asked often to imagine a suite of experiences that exactly resemble what we would have had, had we been awake and responsive through our senses to the surrounding world, living in public time and history, but which instead compose the fabric of a dream. That there is no internal way allowed through which differentiation of the two counterpart suites can be achieved—and if it *can* be achieved, we have botched the design of our epistemological experiment—is less a matter of skeptical entrapment (which is only a kind of puerile sport) than of raising to conceptual prominence those factors, necessarily external to the experiences matched to one another, which after all make the deep differences between waking and dreamt life. Thus, if I believe my experiences now to be of dream, I have, for just that reason, no grounds for supposing them to continue in one direction rather than another, whereas to suppose I am justified in making claims on the future is exactly to reject the classification of them as dreamt.

It is always possible, wherever the subject matter is philosophical, to generate similar examples, and I am here simply supposing routinized what comes close to being a method of experiment in philosophy in order to bring out what separates artworks from the order of real things, however much in any given case instances from either order may resemble one another. After all, the problem of illusion and deception, the danger and triumph of mimetic art in ancient times, bears some structural resemblance to the problem of the skeptic's dream in modern times, where, again, the issue is less one of how to avoid being duped than of what conceptual differences divide seemingly twinned entities, which have, nevertheless, extraordinarily different ontological identities. Thus, it is not in the least difficult to imagine what one would have supposed was a novel, or an historical painting, or a symphony, or a dance, but which fails to be one of these just because it has the wrong sort of causal history to have been so classed; similarly, it is possible—*grace a l'avant-garde!*—to imagine that however little one would have supposed a certain thing to be a novel, or an historical painting, or a symphony, or a dance, it nevertheless has a history which requires it, surface outrage notwithstanding, to be dignified as an artwork after all. Imagine an entity that is an artwork though it resembles exactly the Manhattan telephone directory for 1978. Different criteria for appreciating it arise, depending upon which artistic genre it happens to belong to—whether it is a piece of papersculpture, a folio of prints, a novel, a poem, or, perhaps, the score for a musical composition—done, say, by Lusiano Berio—in which the names are to be chanted. We can lament the exiguities of plot if it is a novel, but hardly if it is sculpture; we can applaud the poet's achievement in having used not one single verb, though this is certainly irrelevant if we are appraising a folio of prints we would have taken for a routine telephone directory had we not been otherwise instructed—though now we respond to the fact that the artist has eschewed fancy paper in favor of commercial pulp and has forgone the richness of etched lines in favor of the banalities of cold type.

It is tempting to say that the fact that there should be such a novel (or sculpture or whatever) is quite interesting without it following that either the novel or its indiscernible counterparts are interesting as exemplars of their genres. It is true that the purpose of such works is often connected with what interest the very idea of them must have philosophically. Consider just the novel whose title is *Metropolis*. As a novel, we observed, it has little by way of plot, far too many characters in search of whatever plot there is, and scant suspense of at least the sort appropriate to the conventional novel. The sole temptation one can imagine the reader of it to have (if there is a reader of it)—to look at the end of the book "to see how it all comes out"—would be to determine whether the novelist adhered to what his intention may be conjectured to have been and ended his oeuvre with a ladder of Zs. So we would be surprised, just as if it had been the gardener rather than the butler who did it, if the last page gives us some Ms and As. We would want an explanation, the form of which would be determined by the generic identification of the object as a novel, that is, some reference to narrative ordering. Just to class it as novel is to make such explanation (that is, narrative ordering) appropriate, however little success we might have in getting it. Let it end, however, with Zs, which gives it a kind of classic form; as the churlish author points out: it has a beginning in the As and an ending in the Zs and a middle in the Ms. It also has suspense, for by the time we get to the Ms, we may have built up a sense of fatality so great as to bear comparison with Hardy, and we marvel at the author's ruthlessness in driving us with an iron necessity on to the Ns and thence through the Os and the Ps. It is true, he concedes, that his novel lacks romantic interest and description, but these are bourgeois excrescences anyway, which he is delighted to sacrifice in the interests of achieving a piece of pure art: an absolute novel of abstract narrative. Alas, we tell him, he perhaps remains infected with a certain *esprit conservateur* in retaining so classical a format and is a slave to narrative time and—Who knows?—a bourgeois linearity of historical conception, supposing just that structure of past, present, and future to have deep social determinants. Our author may decide to respond by rewriting the work in such a way that the pages are dealphabetized—destroying, he says, the last remnants of a rotten artistic culture. "Read it any way you want," he says, having invented participatory fiction: "The beginning is where *you* begin, the ending where *you* end." All of this can happen, perhaps does, but it is of less interest to protract these aesthetic conversations than to draw attention to the fact that the artistic experiment is *defined by the rules of the genre* and that beginning and end, for example, remain as attributes of the work, whereas were we to turn to the papersculpture indiscernible from this novel, beginning and end would give way to front and back, and a quite different schedule of artistic experiments would open up.

In "Artworks and Real Things" (Danto 1973), I invented a work of art that it pleased me to suppose to have been done by Picasso, simply because I was able to respond to the frequent challenge that "My child could have done that" by inventing an indiscernible object (from a Picasso work of art)—and this one indeed had been made by a child. The purpose of the experiment was to bring out the fact that one thing which makes the difference between an artwork and a mere artifact is that the question of what does it mean, of what it is about, *can* arise in the case of the artwork, even if it is not about anything, whereas the question is logically inapplicable in the case of a mere thing. It is in this spirit that we can raise, of the degenerate experimental novel just described, what its story is, and though it may not have one, its lacking a story is of a different logical sort than the telephone directory lacking one, for it belongs to a genre defined through the fact that just this question has application. There is a difference between allowing a question but giving a negative answer and giving a negative answer because the question itself is rejected. It would be pedantry to spell out here the structures of the distinct artistic genres: I refer to them simply to specify the logical boundaries that set the horizons for possible artistic experimentations and because the avant-gardist is committed to probe these boundaries by seeing to what extent he or she can produce something that remains within the boundaries, though lacking one or another of the traits conventionally thought to define the genre. Hence, we have abstract art, plotless novels, atonal music, and free verse, to mention some of the monuments to this mode of categorical exploration, whatever the merits of the works that actually exemplify them. Consider, finally, the musical composition whose score might be taken as just another copy of our directory. The composer, whose pretentiousness is Wagnerian in virtue of the insupportable length of his opus, may be told by a friendly critic that such work cannot be performed. Well, it could have been one of the composer's intentions to write an unperformable work ("Heard melodies are sweet and those unheard are sweeter still")—I have no idea—but even so, it is in the relevant sense unperformable only if it is classed to begin with as *music*. There is an irrelevant sense in which the Manhattan telephone directory is not performable, namely, because it is not music, is not a composition. Most of what the world is made up of are things that logically cannot be played.

Confusable counterparts from distinct ontological orders have philosophical interest only because at least one of the indiscernibilities is subject to a representational predicate or is of the right ontological sort to be about something or have a subject, or content, or meaning. A good example might be inscriptions, which consist of shapes it is in principle possible to read only against the assumption that they are written. Most pieces of writing look like pieces of writing and like very little else, but it is obviously possible to imagine a set of shapes indiscernible from any given inscription but which arrived on its relevant surfaces through historical circumstances of a sort that disqualify it as writing, and so, though it looks as though it is to be read, in fact, it cannot be. The inscription will obviously possess properties of a sort lacked by its noninscribed counterpart, simply because of its status: it may be in Latin, exhibit faulty syntax, contain a mispelled word, or simply be a sentential fragment. These are not *just* false, mere shapes: they are categorically false. One may be moved or stirred by what one reads in an inscription; but not, or at least not in the same way and for the same reason, by mere shapes, which happen not to be told apart from an inscription. These considerations apply exactly to artworks: to be an artwork is to fall under the structures of the artworld, and without some understanding of what these structures are, one cannot respond to these things as art. Artworks are at least like inscriptions in the respect that certain things are true of them that are categorically false of mere objects which are indiscernible from them. The *Brillo Box* of Warhol has perhaps an impoverished iconology, but even if it has degree zero of iconological richness, the mere proletarian Brillo box of supermarket identity is off the scale entirely.

There nevertheless arises a problem at this juncture that is central to the philosophy of art, namely, that it is all well and good to contrast artworks with mere things lacking representational properties in principle, but representationality can be but a necessary condition for the status of the artwork, lest we be prepared to assign that status to any scrap of writing, to any sign or drawing, to any simple snapshot, or to any map. But what must we then add to the concept of representationality that makes the difference between those entities which satisfy representational predicates but are not artworks from those which satisfy even the same representational predicates but are logic? It is this question that will principally occupy me in this chapter.

STYLISTIC PREDICATES FOR PERCEPTUALLY SIMILAR OBJECTS

Late in *Languages of Art*, Goodman (1968, p. 29) effects a striking juxtaposition: he asks us to compare the curve of a graph made by an electrocardiogram with a drawing by Hiroshige of Mount Fujiyama. One of these is certainly a work of art and the other a vehicle of representation, inasmuch as graphs represent relationships between sets of numbers through sets of points having coordinates defined by that relationship. It is certainly no aim of mine to say that there cannot be artworks consisting of graphs. But I take it as noncontroversial that not every graph is an artwork, and let us suppose the wiry jag congruent with Hiroshige's drawing is not one. For the sake of neatness, let the graph itself represent the gradients of Mount Fujiyama's slope itself, so that neither form nor content vary between our pair of curves. Goodman observes that all that is relevant to the determination of points on the graph is the assignment of numerical values for the x and y variables in the pertinent equation, and it may be admitted that Hiroshige did not arrive at his curve by overt calculation. How many Fourier series his highly developed brain may have had to resolve in order to make the subtle changes in direction registered here is not to the point: these stand to draftsmanly motion as retinal images do to perception, and Hiroshige is doubtless as unaware of what goes on in his brain as we are in general as to what goes on in our eyes. "I draw what I see," we may suppose him to say, in the blunt idiom of the artistic mystic. We may applaud Goodman's spontaneous effort to enlist historical considerations in differentiating the curves, but this still does not answer the philosophical question of why one of them is an artwork. This problem is exacerbated by the possibility of an artist, who, typically of the surly breed, sets out to expunge just these factors of dexterity, synaptic wiring, *maniera*, and sensitivity that set Hiroshige apart as a master and to work out a scheme of art which "anyone can follow." Enlisting the aid of analytical geometry, he plots the locus of points that describe the slopes of Mount Fujiyama and connects them up in a drawing, the mechanicality of which is just what he is after, part of his aim being to purge art of "all that hand-and-eye crap." I am willing to admit that he has produced a drawing, even if by nonacademic or counteracademic devices, and will go on to admit that it is an artwork, though perhaps I would withhold that accolade from a drawn curve generated by just the principles he ideologizes (commissioned, let us suppose, by the Japanese Bureau for the Preservation of the Ancient Profile of Mount Fujiyama).

Goodman is not especially helpful in eliciting a differentia, though he introduces a special term, namely, *"repleteness,"* and speaks of the Hiroshige as being "relatively replete." I am not wholly certain I understand what either repleteness or its anyonym, "attenuation," mean, but Goodman at least sketches the difference between the diagram and the drawing this way: "Some features that are constitutive in the pictorial scheme are dismissed as contingent in the diagrammatic scheme" (1968, pp. 229–30). This summarizes the somewhat more extended gloss:

> The only relevant features of the diagram are the ordinate and abscissa of each of the points the center of the line passes through. The thickness of the line, its color and intensity, the absolute size of the diagram, etc. do not matter. . . . For the sketch, this is not true. Any thickening or thinning of the line, its color, its contrast with the background, its size, even the qualities of the paper—none of this is ruled out (Goodman 1968, p. 230).

Relevant, one wants to know, to *what*. For Goodman, as nearly as I can tell, the issues have to do with synonymy, so that any line specified coordinately, as the diagram is, is synonymous with that diagram, all other features notwithstanding, whereas this is not true for the picture, where, I suppose, some decision has to be made as to what features of the object are constitutive and what features are contingent—not an easy decision in contemporary art when we have to reckon with such works as a legendary one of Rauschenberg's, in which the passing shadows on a canvas contributed to its repletion. The differences in any case are matters of degree, so that the diagram is not "attenuated," and attenuation, I would surmise, would only characterize just real things—things that do not happen to satisfy any representational predicate or do not conform, in Goodman's idiom, to any character. For just that reason, however, reference to repleteness leaves our problem just where we took it up, all the more so in view of the fact that we have succeeded in imagining a *drawing* in which all that matters is the locations of the points the curve passes through and which in point of repleteness would be indiscernible from Goodman's graph. Accordingly, Goodman's observation serves less to mark the difference between drawing and diagram than to identify two styles of drawings. But then it may very well be under the concept of style itself that we might look at our various visually indiscernible curves: the graph itself lacks any stylistic characterization just because it is a graph, whereas the analytically generated drawing might be stylistically characterized as *mechanical*—which is almost an aesthetic appraisal—while the drawing by Hiroshige is perhaps just disciplined and controlled, like a sword sweep by a samurai. To be sure, it may be objected that it is only because we know the histories of these curves that we ascribe stylistic predicates to works that are perceptually not to be told apart: but if it is in terms of differential histories that to begin with we discriminate between those things in principle susceptible to stylistic ascription but not to be told apart by immediate perception, it is far from plain that differential histories may not be just the tool we are seeking. Let me try to bring this out by examining an actual case.

RELEVANCE OF STYLISTIC FACTORS TO IDENTIFICATION OF ARTWORKS

In a quite respectable book (*Cézanne's Composition*), the critic Erle Loran (1947) worked out some of the deeper formal structures of the master's paintings. The book itself is illustrated with some quite helpful diagrams. One diagram in particular has become notorious. It diagrams a painting of Cézanne's wife, itself a celebrated portrait. It is just what a diagram should be, with arrows, dotted lines, and labeled areas, and it reveals just the variations in direction and proportion it was Loran's intention to make explicit. The notoriety of the diagram is due to the fact that some years after the book appeared, Roy Lichtenstein produced a canvas entitled *Portrait of Madame Cézanne* (1963) that differed in scale and substance from Loran's diagram but was so like it by criteria of optical indiscrimability (as between, say, photographs of the two) that Loran brought charges of plagiarism, and a minor controversy swept the art journals of the time (Loran 1963a and 1963b). Now of course during this period, Lichtenstein was "plagiarizing" from all over: a picture of a bathing beauty from an advertisement that still appears for a resort in the Catskills, various Picasso's, and a number of things often so familiar that the charge of plagiarism is almost laughably irrelevant—the Campbell Soup Can, to cite an artifact that has a parallel artistic correlate, is simply incapable of being plagiarized in a relevant way (an irrelevant way is that in which a soupmaker pastes Campbell labels on his or her product, exploiting familiarity and induction to save the expense of marketing his or her own mulligatawny under an unknown name). The moral issues, however, are really not interesting. The interesting issue concerns the serious philosophical difference between the diagram of an artwork and an artwork that consists in a diagram; in at least these cases, the point is pretty clear. Loran's diagram is about a specific painting and concerns the volumes and vectors of it. Lichtenstein's painting is about the way Cézanne painted his wife: it is *about* the wife, as seen by Cézanne. It is fitting and interesting to show the world as it appeared to Cézanne as so many labeled areas, as so many arrows, rectangles, and dotted lines: we have the famous conversations with Emile Bernard, in which Cézanne speaks of nature as so many cubes, cones, and spheres—a kind of Pythagorian vision of the ultimate forms of reality, never mind what the senses say and conventional paintings show. Not many years after these geometrical speculations, the Cubists were painting the world in pretty much those terms. But then, how singularly apt to apply this geometrizing vision to Cézanne's *wife*, treated as though she were a Euclidian problem! For we know the sexual side of this man, in whom prude and satyr warred, and we know the passion and violence of his relationship with this woman, with whom he lived out of wedlock and by whom he had a son. If the source and focus of all this affect should be reduced to a kind of formula, how much must this tell us of the final triumph of the artistic impulse in his soul, even if it entailed a certain dehumanizing transfiguration of the subject: as though the person were so many planes, treated with no more (and no less) intensity and analytical subversion than a wax apple. One is reminded of Monet's anguished discovery that sitting by the body of his late wife, Camille, his model, love, support, angel, that creature of sacrifice and devotion, he had, instead of grieving, been studying the purple on her eyelids! And he wondered what manner of monster he had become. Lichtenstein shows us the sort of monster Cézanne had become, if the parallel is allowed, but his in any case is a work of depth and wit, concerned with the way the world was perceived by the greatest painter of modern times, whereas Loran's is not a work of art at all, but just, after all, the diagram of a painting. The issue of plagiarism is silly, inasmuch as the objects belong to radically disjoint categories, though both may be allowed to stand classification as vehicles of representation. But what I want now to propose is that Lichtenstein's has a style (Loran's just uses the conventions of the diagram) in the sense that *the means it uses to represent its subject are determined by what statement about that subject is meant.* In the case of the Lichtenstein, one cannot separate what is shown from the way it is shown and still be talking about the work. Lichtenstein uses the idiom of the diagram rhetorically. The Loran does not use the idiom of the diagram to make some point about what it shows: it *is* a diagram, and it shows what it shows diagrammatically. That, in the end, will enable us to distinguish the two diagrams, one of them a special sort of drawing, of the slopes of Mount Fujiyama. The graphic style has a rhetorical force in the one case, inasmuch as the drawing is not just of Fujiyama but of how Fujiyama (or anything) is to be drawn. But the mere diagram of Mount Fujiyama is merely a diagram, and *logically* styleless.

WHAT THEN IS A WORK OF ART?

It is the relevance of these stylistic factors to the identification of the artwork that makes clear some familiar facts about artworks as a class. It helps explain, for instance, why we cannot substitute a paraphrase of a work for the work itself. A novel is not simply a story, for a story can be paraphrased. All that is required of a paraphrase is some sort of semantica equivalence with the original. Paraphrasing concerns only content and leaves out style; when *style* becomes a factor, it is no longer paraphrase but reconstitution, as in an artistic translation. It helps explain, moreover, the sorts of factors that enter into artistic criticism. We can criticize representations only from the perspective of truth and falsity or completeness and incompleteness. If we think of artworks in purely mimetic terms, there is nothing save such semantical criteria by which a work is to be judged. But stylistic considerations force a critic first to understand the work, which entails but does not consist exclusively in identifying what the work is about. There is the further identification of how the work makes the statement it makes, and then the question of how this relates to the statement made. This, in turn, raises questions of explanation, which can hardly be separated from criticism. I have sought to explain, for example, why Lichtenstein used the rhetoric of the diagram, but that required me to say that the painting was not just about a painting but about Cézanne's wife and about Cézanne's way of seeing and painting the world (and his wife). No such explanations arise in connection with Loran. Loran is diagramming; Lichtenstein is not. The activity of diagramming has criteria of success and failure and felicity. The activity of painting, which in special instances may utilize the diagrammatic idiom, has very much more complex criteria, which have to be worked out from case to case. However, it would be an evasion of philosophical responsibility not to press past this to see what general principles may be involved, even if no formula is ever going to be forthcoming (any more than a formula is possible that makes the generation of art works themselves a mechanical production), which may make the critical task mechanical.

I offer the thesis that in works of art, in contrast with representations indiscernible from them but which are not artworks, the means of representation play a role in the work as a whole that is not exhausted by their representational role. This may be especially perspicuous when the means of representation are, as it were, not used to represent, as in abstract painting so-called, but there is not in that connection the interesting sort of structure representational art yields us, and I shall consider it for present purposes only as something to be noted and tabled. Lichtenstein represents Mme. Cézanne by means of a diagram, but the diagram does more than represent Mme. Cézanne. Let us say that it *expresses* something about Mme. Cézanne, and it is its double role, as representation and expression, which would have to be worked out in an identification and establishment of the work. I shall suppose that diagrams represent without expressing anything about what they represent and that this will generally be true of representations which are not artworks. But expression itself is so ill-understood a concept that we scarcely can have gone very far in our understanding of artworks by enlisting it as we have done.

Goodman (1968, pp. 86–89) proposes an analysis of expression as metaphorical exemplification, and though I am not at all certain that he would wish to agree to what use I would make of this suggestion, I regard it as a very useful thought. Exemplification is one of the simplest sorts of representation (where I draw a sample from a class and then use it to stand for the class it is drawn from). Exemplificatory representation may be widened to include such cases as arise spontaneously in connection with mimetic art generally: a curve can be used to denote a curve congruent with itself; a color can be used to denote just the local color of the thing represented; a shape can be used to denote a shape of the same sort as it (in sculpture); motion can be used to denote motion, as in the moving picture or kinetic sculpture; speech can be used to denote speech, as in drama, where gesture is also used to denote gesture. For the most part, it is enough to characterize exemplificatory representation as follows: a exemplificatorily represents b if (1) a and b instantiate the same predicate and (2) a denotes b. I suppose areas in the diagram denote areas in Mme. Cézanne and instantiate the same predicates, whatever these may be. But at this level, there is little to choose between a diagram of Mme. Cézanne and a work such as Lichtenstein's. The difference must then arise over the metaphorical constituent of expression. *Metaphorical* exemplification is doubtless consistent with, though it need not entail, failure of condition (1): which is, in effect, the same as saying that a metaphorical truth need not entail a *literal* falsity. But I am unable at this stage of my thought to offer a theory of metaphor. I nevertheless believe that the diagrammatic mode is a metaphor for Mme. Cézanne as seen by her husband and that we grasp this painting, as I think we grasp any, by grasping the metaphor at its heart, after grasping what it represents. Cézanne's subjects are usually easy enough to identify: they are apples, peaches, vases, card-players, mountains, and so forth. It is the active metaphors with which Cézanne represents these things, and which explain the means he uses to represent them, which make Cézanne the great artist that he is.

As usual, the mimetic theory of art, whatever its failings, is philosophically instructive in the present case, for it generated an extremely interesting program, the purpose of which, as I see it, was to reduce to zero just those factors of representing I deem so crucial in the metaphor of a work in favor of producing something that cannot be told apart from what it represents. The medium is to be rendered so transparent that one, as it were, sees through it to the subject, enabling observers to believe they are in the presence of the things itself—a woman to embrace, as in the case of Pygmalion, or a bunch of grapes to be eaten, as in the celebrated birds of Zeuxis. So a painting of a beautiful woman would ipso facto be a beautiful painting, since it would have no properties of its own beyond the properties of what it showed: it *is* what it is about, and it aims at that sort of transparency which Proust celebrates in the actress Berma, who performed in such a self-effacing way that one was never aware of *her* but rather of Phedre, whom she represented. In a way, such representations, like beliefs, are said to be from the perspective of those who hold them: to hold a belief is less a matter of knowing that one holds that belief than of holding the *world* to be a certain way: to believe that p is to believe that p is true.

Nothing is more transitory than such transparencies. Giotto's contemporaries may have felt themselves in the very presence of the personages he painted. Vasari, for whom such remarks are standard praise, singles out a picture of a man drinking "portrayed with such marvelous effect, that one would almost believe him to be a living man drinking." *We* would hardly be tempted to such beliefs, for Giotto has, as it were, and this largely through the evolution of art he did so much to impel, become opaque; though we usually know what he was representing, we are more immediately fixated on the manner of representation and the great Giottoesque metaphors. Alas, we shall never see Berma performing Phedre. But I am certain that were we to do so, she would not be transparent to us. She would be opaque, a performative artifact of the Belle Epoque, whose style of acting had so thickened and dated that we would be far more aware of it than of Racine's heroine. And this is, I think, very generally the case. Van Meegeren's contemporaries were unable to perceive the differences between his work and Vermeer's because they saw, so to speak, *through* a style *we* are able to identify as very much of the 1930s—the vocabulary of Art Deco. My feeling is that if they could not see the difference between the two painters, I have no idea how they *saw anything*: which I offer not as a criticism of them but as a deep fatality of their historical period, and of historical periods as such, defined through the fact that people perceive the world in a certain way without being aware of anything *except* the world, it only being those who come after, like ourselves, who can identify the metaphors of their representation, just because we exist historically outside the period that was theirs.

It would be an attractive as well as a congenial thesis to argue that the true stylistic properties of a work of art become visible only when the historical period they serve to define is past and that when the stylistic properties indeed become opaque in this way, they can henceforward be used only in artistic acts of self-conscious archaism. This is attractive but tenuous, I am afraid and, in any case, requires better argumentation than any I can think of at the moment. I fortunately require no such thesis here, for the examples were marshaled to give drama to the thought that the transparencies enjoined by mimetic theory, however brilliantly and prestidigitationally achieved, will in all likelihood become an obstacle to illusion when the perceptual presuppositions they exploit are no longer shared by the viewers of the artworld. So the most transparent artworks cannot escape the stylistic considerations for which they will become cherished and in consequence of which they may be deep and to which, in any case, they owe their status as works of art rather than as mere pictorial representations. It is obvious that those features in which the concepts of metaphor, expression, style, and taste intersect are not likely to be analyzed and, as it were, put on ice in the last sentences of a chapter that means to carry one step further the subtraction formulas I have exploited so often in the philosophy of art (Danto 1964, 1973, 1974, 1976): to expose this crucial and ill-understood space that is left over when, from an artwork which is a picture of x, we subtract the fact that it is a picture of x.

REFERENCES

Danto, A. "The Art World." *Journal of Philosophy* 61 (1964): 571–84.

———. "Artworks and Real Things." *Theoria* 39 (1973): 1–17.

———. "The Transfiguration of the Commonplace." *Journal of Aesthetics and Art Criticism* 33 (1974): 139–48.

———. "An Answer or Two for Sparshott." *Journal of Aesthetics and Art Criticism* 35 (1976): 80–82.

Goodman, N. *Languages of Art*. New York: Bobbs–Merrill, 1968.

Loran, E. *Cézanne's Composition*. Berkeley: University of California Press, 1947.

——. "Cézanne and Lichtenstein: Problems of Transformation." *Artforum* (September 1965): 34.

——. "Pop Artists or Copycats?" *Art News* (September 1963a): 48.

——. "Pops or Robbers: The Big Question." *Newsweek* (September 16, 1963b).

Chapter Two

Some of the Things
That Paintings Are

Julian Hochberg

INTRODUCTION

Whatever else they are, paintings are, of course, made objects. They are made and bought and kept for various purposes. We cannot sensibly discuss the objects without discussing their purposes.

A gross classification of the purposes that paintings serve might run as follows: communication of information about some real or imaginary event (a factual description) or of evaluative attitudes about the event (inspirational or propaganda pictures); to achieve or indicate socioeconomic status or breeding; as a decoration; to provide feelings of identity as an individual (sometimes called self-expression, for example, "I am an informed admirer of or expert about . . .") or as a member of some class or group; as entertainment and as a conversation piece; and—most important of all—to provide a livelihood for maker and dealer and (more indirectly) critic and scholar.

These factors are not trivial in determining the perceptual characteristics of paintings. There is simply no way that consideration of paintings solely as informative stimuli can bring perceptual psychology to bear on the nature of paintings. Let me expand on that point.

Most perceptual study of pictures has been in terms of pictures as *surrogates*, by which I mean an object that is optically equivalent (from some specified viewpoint) to some three-dimensional scene, that is, a trompe l'oeil (compare Gibson 1954; Hochberg 1972 and in press a). For the past 80 years, however, trompe l'oeil painting has not been even a marginal concern of most important art. Paintings have not been made with the purpose of being surrogates (except for the minor resurgence of "figurative" art) for a very long time. Although a perceptual theory will not suffice as a theory or explanation of *non*surrogate pictures, a perceptual theory of pictures that deals only with surrogates would be peculiarly truncated, and quite obsolete.

Throughout history, but especially for the past 50 years, *the subject matter of paintings has been largely to provide visual comments on the properties of paintings, as objects.* I believe that neither those properties, nor the painters' (and collectors') concerns with them, are accidental. Both the properties themselves, and the concerns with those properties, can teach us something about perception in general and about picture perception in particular.

Part of what is important about pictures as flat objects is that they cannot, in general, be optically equivalent to three-dimensional scenes, even from a single station point. Because of these limits, even trompe l'oeil paintings usually rely on simulation in addition to, or instead of, optical equivalence. Because simulation is not optical equivalence, we almost always see pictures in two modes—as objects and as scenes. This is by no means a new point. We will see that Leonardo da Vinci's instructions to artists rest on it. But it is a point that is important to an understanding of perceptual theory and which interacts strongly with the set of purposes that I listed above.

In this chapter, I will try to spell out what I mean by simulation, as distinguished from optical equivalence; I will try to make the point about the different modes of picture perception at least one stage more concrete and less metaphorical; and I will undertake these two tasks within the framework of a general theory of perception, applied to the problem of picture perception. The approach can be briefly stated as follows.

The perception of pictures, whether as decorated objects or as represented scenes, consists of fitting *schemas* (a term loosely equivalent to *images*) to what is given by each momentary glance. The different modes by which pictures can be perceived probably depend (1) on the schemas that one elects to fit to the momentary glance; (2) on the peculiar characteristics of the fovea and periphery of the retina of the eye; (3) and on the way in which we deploy our eyes across successive glances.

I hope that this theory will become clearer by the time I have finished. First, I will briefly review how one makes a surrogate and the limited uses such an enterprise has for the professional painter, collector, or investor. Second, I will consider some of the technical limits of making surrogates. These include limitations on the luminance ranges that can be represented and limitations on the information about depth and distance of the scene being portrayed. Both sorts of limitations are very important to understanding the subject matter of *non*trompe l'oeil paintings. The expedients that painters have used to overcome the limitations themselves, in later paintings, become the elements of design, of expression, and of order; they become the cultural background, the terms of discourse, and the occasion for expertise, self-expression, and *signature*; they even become the bases for entire aesthetic programs. Most of these purposes are really the concerns of sociosemioticians—and I am surely not one. But it *is* the concern of the perception psychologist to see where these elements come from and how they are perceived in the first place. If the perception psychologist does not elucidate them, no one else is likely to, and an understanding of the sources of these pictorial elements should probably be helpful to any theory of art. Closer to home, I think that that study of these elements will help us to understand some of the apparent paradoxes of pictures and picture perception—such as why subjects think that parallel projections look better than "true perspective" (Hagen and Elliott 1976) and why anything was gained when Leonardo advised students of painting to trace the scenes before them on glass picture planes.

PICTURES AS TROMPE L'OEIL SURROGATES: THEIR MAKING, THEIR LIMITED USES, AND LIMITS

The Task

Imagine a single eye viewing the scene at A in Figure 2.1 from a fixed position in space. Assume also that the eye does not change its focus, that is, its accommodation is fixed. Then, it is clearly true that we can prepare an object, B, which can present to the eye precisely the same array of light as does the scene, A. The two objects of viewing, A and B, are then *optically identical*, and the fact that they will look alike is both guaranteed and uninteresting. The two do not, however, need to be identical in order for B to serve as a surrogate for A. Because our eyes only contain three different kinds of color receptors, we can duplicate the appearance of any of the myriad colors in the spectrum with just three wavelengths of light (short, which looks violet or blue; middle, which looks green; and long, which looks red). Because our eyes cannot resolve details below a certain size, we can replace any solid expanse of color with a field of dots too small to be individually discerned. We can therefore replace any scene (A) with a surrogate that is composed of a large number of tiny red, green, and blue dots—that is, of course, what a color TV screen is. It is possible to make one with dots so small and match the colors of the scene so well that the viewer cannot tell which is scene and which is surrogate *if* the viewpoint is controlled. Surrogate B' in Figure 2.1 represents such a screen of dots.

Although A, B, and B' all look exactly the same to a viewer, B' is *not* optically identical to A and B. *In fact, the light presented to the eye by B' is physically completely different from the light presented by A and B. The two arrays are equivalent only in the sense that they produce the same effects in the visual system of the*

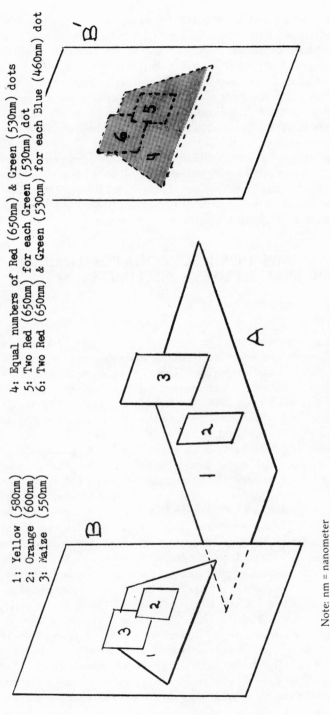

1: Yellow (580nm)
2: Orange (600nm)
3: Maize (550nm)

4: Equal numbers of Red (650nm) & Green (530nm) dots
5: Two Red (650nm) for each Green (530nm) dot
6: Two Red (650nm) & Green (530nm) for each Blue (460nm) dot

Note: nm = nanometer

Figure 2.1 A) A scene to be represented, with colors as shown. B) A picture that is *optically identical* to the scene, when regarded from the proper viewing point, presenting the same pattern of light to the eye as the scene itself. B') A picture that is *optically equivalent* to A and to B: it is composed of dots that are too small to be discerned at the distance from which it is viewed, and none of the dots are of the same color as any part of A or B; nevertheless, taking into account the nature of the normal eye, each small region of B' will look like (that is, is optically equivalent to) the corresponding small region of A and B—and the same is true for the overall scene and pictures.

viewer who has normal acuity and color vision, but not in terms of any physical similarities. Here is a *weak* version of what I mean by *simulation*, then: B′ is a surrogate for B and for A because it produces the same effect as they do, that is, it *simulates* A and B.

This point is essential in relating the present approach to pictures to the approach of Gibson and his colleagues (Gibson 1971; Kennedy 1974), which I regard as a necessary first step, but only as a first step. We might study the physical descriptions of B′ and of B for millennia without seeing their relationship to each other or to A; it is only when we are told that they are equivalent in appearance that we can use their similarities and differences to discover the facts of color vision. In general, *visual information simply cannot be defined except in terms of the sensory and perceptual characteristics of the viewer.*

This point is a simple one in the present context. It will become increasingly important, both to the understanding of paintings and to the understanding of perceptual psychology, as we deliberately make the array of light more unlike that from the represented scene in order, first, to improve and, then, to go beyond the simulation of a scene by a painting. I noted that the situation in Figure 2.1 was only simulation in a weak sense. That is so because B′, B, and A still look alike when viewed patch by patch, that is, they look alike not only when viewed naturally as a whole but also when examined and compared piecemeal. Thus, we can therefore always transform B into B′ and vice versa by translating each small patch of B into an appropriate mixture of tiny red, green, and blue dots (or whatever trichromatic system is being used) in a totally automatic and mechanical fashion. That, of course, is what a video or film camera does. More important to the present argument is the following consideration: unless the viewer looks through a magnifying glass (or moves much closer) or views B and B′ under special illumination or through a set of special color filters, B′ and B look alike—no shift in the viewer's attitude or mode of viewing will make them look any different from each other, and no special pictorial expertise is acquired by studying B′ and comparing it with B and A. Though the physical differences between B and B′ are profound and technically important to printing and to video, they are both pictorially and *perceptually* (but not *sensorially*) trivial.

The same is not true of the differences that the painter deliberately introduces to overcome the limitations of paintings as surrogates. Before we can discuss these differences, we must consider briefly the procedures by which artists produce surrogates.

Leonardo on the Production of Surrogates

Leonardo's instructions to painters, as we all know, were to trace scenes on panes of glass and to study the tracings. By observing the

characteristic patterns that three-dimensional scenes produce on the two-dimensional picture plane—the patterns that psychologists now call the *depth cues*—the artist learns what shapes to put on canvas that will produce the same pattern of light at the eye as does the scene itself. Close equivalents are provided by the study of other artists' notebooks and by exercises based on copying other artists' paintings, anatomical drawings, and perspective constructions. Add to these textbooks and optical devices (for example, the camera obscura), and instruction in representation of form and space becomes both exhaustive and effective.

Color Mixing

Given the tracings of the scene, the painter need only learn how to mix colors in order to produce a surrogate for any real or imaginary scene. A great deal in the way of trade secrets concerned the depth cues and the tricks of color mixing. By the end of the nineteenth century, visual science had caught up with, and surpassed, the painters' practical color theory (Helmholtz 1881) and provided for a deeper understanding of the techniques by which the inherent limitations of paintings as surrogates might be partially overcome. Those techniques and limitations will be of primary concern in this chapter.

Let us for the moment assume, however, that there are no limitations on how well a surrogate can be prepared—that once the laws of perspective and the use of the other depth cues, as well as the rules for color mixing, are thoroughly understood, perfect trompe l'oeil surrogates can be produced at will. The camera, which I have been ignoring, merely accentuates this point by increasing the dispersion of the ability to produce such surrogates, both by making its own brand of surrogates readily available and by making available to artists a profusion of "Leonardo tracings" more accurate and varied than they could hope to accumulate otherwise. How does the widespread ability to prepare surrogates fit the purposes for which paintings are made?

The Limited Uses Served by High Fidelity Surrogates

Given the marketplace of art dealers, museums, and galleries (they emerged as an international market toward the end of the nineteenth century) and given a widespread understanding among professional painters of the means of producing high fidelity trompe l'oeil paintings, what constraints confront the ambitious painter? What can an artist do in order to be a financial success, to be singled out and sought after?

The Artist's Requirements

First, the artist needs to achieve *signature* that is, some recognizable technique or subject matter. Without this, there is no demand that only this artist can satisfy. Note that to the degree that a picture is a perfect surrogate, that is, optically identical to its object or scene, the artist's technical freedom to achieve a unique signature is restricted. Second, the artist's work cannot be so different from that of other artists that it is totally unacceptable in an existing market—it must have some relationship to what has gone before, as well as to established taste. Third, the artist must produce a large body of recognizable work; otherwise, there is no worthwhile investment in it for the dealer or collector. This means that the signature cannot be so restrictive that only a single painting embodies it. Fourth, the artist must show signs of "growth" and must pass through definite periods that retain some of the previous signature but which do not render previous work obsolete. Without such change, the artist's market soon is satiated; with it, the value on the work as an investment cumulates, perhaps multiplicatively, as the need for filling out any collection of the artist's work is given subgoals.

Granted, the preceding vulgar materialistic analysis says nothing at all about aesthetics (although there are some implications concerning constraints on taste and interestingness implicit in the analysis). There is clearly more to the painter and more to the training of the viewer that makes the painter more or less enjoyable or acceptable, more or less of a master; the constraints listed above can all be fulfilled and the painter still be quite worthless. There must be more to the painter, but there cannot be much less to one who is to be successful and whose paintings are themselves to influence subsequent painting.

Trompe l'oeil Paintings Fitting These Requirements

How do trompe l'oeil paintings fit these requirements? They do not fit very well as long as there are major improvements in the technical preparation of surrogates to be achieved, as well as new ways in which to overcome the limitations of the medium (improvements that do not automatically teach themselves on sight to the artist's competitors), the production of high fidelity surrogates is itself a path to success, and one in which the viewer needs little or no tutoring to appreciate. Otherwise, there is a curious conflict between the "photographic painting" and the four purposes I described above: given the scene and the station point from which it is to be painted, there is really only one veridical painting to be made. One can change the scene, the actors' costumes and expressions, the colors, and the lighting, but given these, the picture is fixed. The variations that can be made are therefore in a sense all literary or theatrical, unrelated to the particular craft of the painter. How many new scenes from the Bible or new ways of posing Cato the elder addressing the Senate can be found? How many Gerômes does it take to make all the great and prototypical paintings the Western world will bear? Note that I am not talking about the itinerant painter who will peddle the same paintings, or very minor variations of them, from door to door, a topic for a very different study to explore. I am talking about the major paintings around which the lowly itinerants will cluster their exemplars.

How can signature and productivity be reconciled?

The Limitations of the Medium to the Rescue

We are in fact saved from seeking an empirical answer to the preceding rhetorical question by the fact that it is indeed not possible to make accurate trompe l'oeil paintings of just any scene at all. Much of the history of Western art is conditioned by the steps that must be taken to overcome the limits of paint and canvas, although the perceptual purposes served by those artistic innovations are not generally understood (and perhaps less understood by art critics than by perception psychologists, for a change). The limitations are important for two additional reasons, over and beyond the fact that they bound what can be portrayed. First, the techniques for overcoming the limitations of the medium provide a subject matter that is purely visual and nonliterary in nature for subsequent pictorial art to deal with. Second, except in very special circumstances, the limitations on the medium cannot be fully overcome, making each painting two very different objects (that is, the painter's product and the scene it represents); this enforces two modes of perception on the viewer and provides an inherent alienation (in Brecht's sense), which is essential if most of the purposes for which paintings are made, outlined at the beginning of this chapter, are to be served. Only in the case of the architectural trompe l'oeil, in which the viewers are to be deceived into believing that they are in a larger and more ornate structure than is true by painting additional rooms, balconies, and stories on walls and ceilings (Pirenne 1970) is full illusion desirable. We consider next the major limitations of the medium, as well as some of the ways of dealing with them.

The Technical Limits on the Possible Success of High Fidelity Surrogates

A painting can only be optically equivalent to a very restricted set of scenes because of the inherent limitations of pictures per se and because of the limitations of pigments that can practically be used.

Limits of Color and Brightness

The amount of light reaching the eye from scenes in the world can vary over an enormous range: a spectacular highlight on a wave or a spot of dew on the grass, reflecting the sun, and a deep shadow next to it, can vary by a factor of many thousands to one. Pigments have a much more restricted range: approximately 40 to one. This fact means that only scenes with muted ranges of light and shade can be accurately portrayed—that is, scenes that are high key low key or grisailles. Overcast scenes, the indoors, and nonmetallic and other nonspecular surfaces define the limits of what can be portrayed with accuracy. Without such restrictions on subject matter, accurate surrogates cannot be produced. Painting out-of-doors—*en plein air*—simply cannot be done by straightforward application of paint to canvas. Of course, steps were taken to overcome such limitations, and these steps will be important to this chapter.

The Limits of Using a Flat Surrogate for a Three-Dimensional Scene

Leonardo knew that the picture inevitably informs the viewer in many different ways that it is a flat object (see Figure 2.2 [B]) and is not a tridimensional scene (see Figure 2.2 [A]). Unless special precautions are taken (for example, monocular viewing with a fixed head from a distance at least six yards or so), the very strongest sources of spatial information are all optimally available at normal viewing distances to assure the viewers that what confronts them is a flat, pigment-daubed piece of canvas, that is, such information as that potentially available in motion parallax and stereoscopic vision, aided by the weaker information given by accommodation (that is, the fact that the eye does not have to be refocused when looking from one part of the picture to another, whereas it does have to be refocused when looking at different parts of the depth scene which is being represented). Nothing that the artist can do, under normal viewing conditions, can change these facts. *Nor can the perception psychologist choose to ignore the fact that viewers are responding to a pigment-daubed piece of canvas about which they have full sensory information as to flatness, as though it were a very different set of objects and distances in space.* This set of limitations on paintings as surrogates has received the most attention over the years. In the present chapter, my primary concern is with the color and brightness limits, because I think it is easier to make the distinction between optical equivalence and simulation in that context, as well as to show how the techniques of dealing with color limitations came to provide the subject matter, or pictorial content, of "modern painting." In a subsequent work (Hochberg in press b), I will try to do the same for spatial limitations. Here, the latter are only of concern insofar as they make the picture-as-pigmented-object noticeable even to the viewer who is untutored in art technique and history and who is interested only in the represented scene.

OVERCOMING THE LIMITATIONS OF PIGMENT: FROM REMBRANDT TO POST-IMPRESSIONISM

Pigment on canvas poses two separate problems: brightness range and saturation. By brightness range, I mean the ratio of light reflected

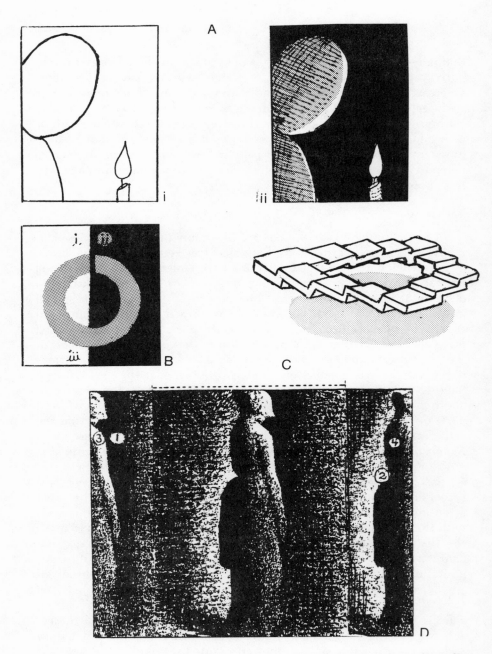

Figure 2.2   A) Enhanced brightness through contrast. B) Contrast as a local phenomenon: the gray ring at i looks darker than it does at ii, althogh no clear difference between the two halves appears at iii. In general, a contour is needed to make the local effects of contrast visible. C) Because of the phenomenon noted in C, portrayed lightness or brightness can progressively increase, from one region to the next, without exceeding the reflectance limitations of pigment and paper or canvas. This is analogous to the local

to the eye from the lightest place on the canvas to the darkest place; by saturation, I mean how much color there is on a scale running from colorless or gray through browns and pastels to a pure hue. These two sets of problems are touched on in turn.

Brightness Range

As noted earlier, a highlight on polished metal, an eyeball, or a wheatstalk or a ripple in a pond may be many times as bright as nearby shade. The artist has two major techniques for trying to capture such ranges: chiaroscuro and pointillism.

Chiaroscuro and Local Contrast

Artists learned very early to heighten the apparent brightness of, say, a candle flame by placing darks immediately adjacent to light (see Figure 2.2 [A]—after LaTour). The effect depends on two phenomena: simultaneous and successive contrast. Simultaneous contrast rests on the following principle: when two small adjacent paths of the retina in the eye are stimulated by light, each patch not only responds to the light but also *inhibits* the response of its neighbor. By providing a dark surround to any patch, we reduce the inhibition it receives, and its response to the same amount of light is increased. Figure 2.2 (B) shows two things about this phenomenon; *first*, that it is a *local* affair—although the gray ring at point i looks darker than at ii even though no step appears in the rest of the ring to provide the transition between them. It is in that respect like the modified Penrose and Penrose (1958) figure shown in Figure 2.2 (C): we can keep ascending and still remain in the same place. Second, without some line, gap, or contour to divide the gradient of contrast (as at i and ii in Figure 2.2 [B]), the effect is usually not noticeable (as at iii in Figure 2.2 [B]). Using these characteristics of local contrast, there is no theoretical limit to the number of increasing brightness steps that we can produce in any picture (compare Figure 2.2 [D], modeled after Seurat's *The Black Bow*). There is more to the story, however.

Masters of chiaroscuro, like Rembrandt and Eakins, usually com-

---

nature of the cues for depth-at-an-edge, which similarly permit progressive increase in height with no net gain (the figure is suggested by one by Penrose and Penrose 1958). D) These facts lie at the heart of chiaroscuro. The central panel is a simplified sketch of Seurat's *The Black Bow*. The right half of the figure has been duplicated at the left, and the left half of the figure has been duplicated at the right. Note the similarity to C. Note too that the surface colors represented by 1 and 2 are equal, as are those of 3 and 4. In the original, the shading is more gradual, making the difference between 1 and 2, 3, and 4 less evident unless a line is drawn dividing the figure (compare with B).

Figure 2.3 Sketch of Rembrandt's *Noble Slav*.

bine use of local contrast with an unequal distribution of detail. In Rembrandt's *The Noble Slav*, schematized in Figure 2.3, four extremely important features of this process are visible. First, the interval between dark and light is not evenly divided: there are extreme darks, extreme lights, and the remainder of the scale is used for a set of middle lightnesses. Second, the middle lightnesses are concentrated in one or two focal regions—those having the greatest interest (face, eyes, and so on). Third, fine detail is present in the focal region; progressively less detail is presented outside of that region. Finally, large swatches of color, and particularly contrasting patches to represent the brightest highlights, are placed nearby, outside of the focal region of fine detail.

Why Did Rembrandt and Eakins Do What They Did?

How does a chiaroscuro with focal concentration exploit the differences between fovea, parafovea, and periphery? The four characteristics described above are not an unrelated set of idiosyncracies, or aesthetic decisions, or deliberate departures from "realism." These characteristics are intended to exploit a set of differences between central and peripheral vision that are absolutely essential to any understanding of pictorial art and of picture perception. The center of the retina, the fovea, resolves fine detail and enjoys full color vision; as the distance from the fovea increases, that is, in peripheral vision, acuity decreases drastically, and a detail must be much larger in order to be visible. Consequently, looking at some point b on the picture, outside of the focal region, the viewer can see no detail visible anywhere on the picture in Figure 2.3. The focal region (a) falls in his peripheral vision, which cannot discern its detail, whereas region b, which the viewer happens to be looking at with his fovea, has no detail to be discerned. If the viewer stands at the right distance and keeps his gaze in the focal region, however, the scene then looks perfectly normal. His fovea, which can discern detail, receives it from a; the region b, which offers no detail, falls in that part of his vision, outside of the viewer's fovea, which is incapable of noting that there is no detail. *With the viewer's gaze directed at the focal region, therefore, the painting can be made indistinguishable from one that is uniformly detailed, as well as from the scene itself.*

Why do this? Why not simply paint in the detail in the remainder of the picture, as so many of Rembrandt's predecessors did?

One cannot say, of course, *why* artists really did what they did. We can, however, consider what they gained, perceptually speaking, by the use of this method of painting, and we will see that they gained a great deal, and opened the door to a great deal more.

First, the focal area becomes an extremely potent compositional factor. For reasons just considered, the viewer's gaze is constrained largely to the detailed region. Eakins, particularly, used this procedure to determine where one would concentrate one's gaze within large and crowded canvases. Second, the "rightness" of the painting, along with the fact that it *is* painting rather than reality, is emphasized by the "discovery" each time one's gaze wanders to some nonfocal region, b, that the "blob" then seen is just what it should be in order for the picture to look normal when the gaze returns to the focal region; that is, it is a little miracle that attests to the artist's skill and control over what the viewer will perceive. (Actually, it is really something of a trick, that is, by itself, this does not really require any particular genius.) Third, the constraint of the gaze to a single focal region, as well as the absence of detail elsewhere, probably helps to help conceal the information that the painting is flat. This is a tentative proposal; I know of no research with regard to this point, but I think that a good case can be made to support it (Hochberg in press b). Here, let us merely note that possibility.

Finally, highlights and regions of maximum contrast are placed outside of the focal region. This is an important fact for three reasons. First, it means that brushstrokes placed next to each other, which would be perceived as separate when viewed in foveal vision, are added together, that is, they are averaged over a single receptive field (see Jameson and Hurvich 1975). Additive mixtures can therefore be achieved in a manner similar to that of the tiny dots in Figure 2.1 (B'), a point to which we will return shortly. Second, outside the fovea, the enhancing effects of simultaneous contrast appear to extend over greater distances. In Figure 2.4, for example, dark blobs appear at the intersections of the white grid lines because there is more contrast from the black squares along the lengths of the white bars than at their intersections, leaving the latter less enhanced by contrast and, therefore, darker than more enclosed regions. If you keep your gaze fixed on any one of the intersections, however, you will see that the intersection you are looking at does *not* have a dark blob, because the enhancing effects of the black squares on the white bars is much less in the region of the fovea, so the difference between the bars and the intersection is also much less. Third, because large swatches of contrasting color are

Figure 2.4 The effects of simultaneous contrast are less in foveal vision than in parafoveal and peripheral vision.

used outside of the focal area, minor eye movements will change the borders between them, so that successive contrast occurs on the margins between the swatches. It is only with successive contrast that the maximum in saturation and brightness can be achieved. As an example of successive contrast, if you stare at point x in Figure 2.5 for a few moments and then change your gaze to point y, you will see a disc that is brighter than the paper itself. Similar effects occur with color (that is, if the paper at y were red and the disc at x were green, subsequent to staring at x, a super-red disc would appear at y).

I do not mean to imply that Rembrandt knew these technical facts of vision, or their physiological explanations (which have not been discussed here, for that matter), or that exploiting these facts will automatically generate a Rembrandt painting. But subsequent painters were indeed aware both of the consequences of these departures from optical fidelity and of Helmholtz's (1881) detailed discussion of the limitations of pigment and of the use of contrast to overcome those limitations. (I do not know, however, of any discussion prior to the one in this chapter and the one by Jameson and Hurvich [1975] that explicitly considers how the perception of paintings is affected by the relationship between distance from fovea, color patch size, and contrast.) I believe that the factors I have described, plus some few additional techniques, prescribe what is needed to extend the range of scenes that can be painted.

Illumination, Saturation, and Colored Shadows

At very low light levels, all is gray. As illumination increases, darker and lighter areas segregate within the visual field. With moder-

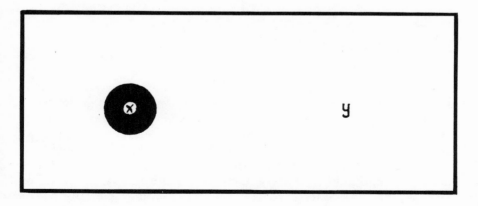

Figure 2.5   Successive contrast enhances brightness and saturation.

ate light levels, colors appear with increasing saturation. With full sunlight, saturation again decreases in the brightest regions, but the transition between full light and deep shadow now exhibits evident hue contrast in addition to brightness (or lightness) differences. Painters do not in general have available to them a gamut of saturated pigments for all of the colors they wish to employ, so they must mix the pigments. Mixing paints on a palette is, of course, a subtractive procedure, inevitably lowering the saturations that can be achieved. Additive mixtures can be obtained by placing tiny dots close together (as in Figure 2.1[B']) or—in black and white work—by using stipples and crosshatches that are below the power of the eye to resolve (look at a postage stamp or a dollar bill from a couple of feet away). To the pointillist painters, this promised a more scientific procedure than mixing pigments. It will not, of course, really solve the 40 to one problem nor achieve maximum saturations (any mixture, even an additive one, reduces saturation, and the bare canvas between the dots contributes to that reduction). However, it does serve to make viewers tolerant of the painter's use of adjacent patches of color, and that will, for reasons we have seen already at work in Rembrandt's technique, work to stimulate the experience of sunlit scenery.

One more ingredient is needed: *colored shadows.* Shadows are needed for modeling; shadows are also needed for contrast in chiaroscuro. They are not essential to painting, but they are close to essential for trompe l'oeil painting. Shadows are not merely dark regions, however, to be achieved simply by adding dark pigment to the mixture that otherwise represents a particular surface. As Corot discovered in Italy, shadows are blue or violet in sunlight. There are two reasons why that should be so. The first, understood by painters of the late ninteenth century, is that the blue light, scattered from the sky, is reflected to the eye by the intervening haze. A second, which was probably not quite as well understood but which had been well discussed by Helmholtz and Hering, to which painters (and, particularly, the early Impressionists) paid considerable attention is the effect of contrast, which we have already discussed: surrounded by yellow sunlight, a shadow will look blue or violet even when there is no blue light present.

By using colored shadows (for example, blue or violet) in sunlit scenes, three effects are obtained. First, the same effect is made visible in the reduced range of luminance in a painting that occurs more strongly in sunlit conditions, and even if the viewer does not consciously notice them, they contribute to the simulation of the experience of sunlit landscapes (Helmholtz's discussion is very close to this point). Second, colored shadows increase the saturations, "liveness," or vibrancy of the borders of objects in the paintings by marginal or successive contrast, described above. Third, and most important for the purposes of the present discussion, *blue or violet shadows in a painting of a sunlit scene permit modeling and contrast to be obtained without using areas of darkness that lower the overall lightness of the canvas.* In the far periphery, which is relatively color-blind, the eye gathers the impression only of an overall light and dappled scene; near the fovea (in the parafovea), luminous edges to the shadows, as well as their visible color differences, provide whatever modeling and contrast that is necessary; thus, something that is the opposite of chiaroscuro is thus made available to the painter.

Impressionism: Painting for Parafoveal Viewing

We now come to the heart of this chapter, and to a watershed in the relationship between painting and the study of visual perception. It is the early part of this century: all the strands of Western art are drawn together. The economics of the "star" system and of the fashion world move visibly into the machinery of painter's purposes. Finally, the simple relationship between painting and perception psychology (which was never as simple as the practitioners of either discipline pretended) dissolves just as the era begins (which continues today), in which painters freely call themselves perceptual researchers. I will discuss the late Impressionists' purposes and how those purposes were served by perceptual devices, the opportunities for the development of other "schools" (and purposes) of painting that were opened up by the Impressionists' products, and the successes and the specific and general implications for perceptual theory of these events.

Purposes

The late Impressionists' published purpose was, of course, to use optical science to produce paintings that would provide the same impression or perceptual experience as does the light in a (usually outdoors) scene. In order to see what this might mean, let us compare what they actually did, at the height of this attempt, with what was open to them to do.

The Possible Surrogates for Sunlit Scenes. Refer back to Figure 2.1. If we could provide a surrogate B or B′ that were large enough to enclose most of the viewer's peripheral vision and if we could duplicate the luminances of A, the experience obtained with painting and with scene would be identical, whether the scene were *plein air* or not. Using electronic displays or transparencies today, we could probably come very close to doing just that. Would that have made Impressionism unnecessary? I think not, because I believe that the stated purposes cannot be taken at face value. What Impressionism really means to the perception psychologist is, I think, a complicated amalgam. First, the patchwork technique characteristic of Impressionist painters permits higher *apparent* saturations and brightnesses, when viewed from appropriate distances, because of the factors already discussed in connection with the Rembrandt in Figure 2.3 (simultaneous and successive contrast, particularly in peripheral vision and with moving glances). There are other special sources of "liveliness" in these paintings. One of them is of the same sort that we have been discussing: pointillist paintings, seen from within a critical viewing distance, are vibrant in a way that has nothing to do with additive color mixture: it has to do with the fact that in peripheral vision, we have larger receptive fields, and at the appropriate distances of viewing (see Jameson and Hurvich 1975), we experience an alternation between dots and solid color areas. Moving the viewer's eye back and forth so that the fovea falls nearer to or further from some region of dots changes discernible dots into continuous colors and edges, and vice versa, as the dots come into and out of regions of higher acuity. Moreover, with each eye movement, afterimages left by the previous view "moire" (see Oster 1977) introduce a visible movement into the scene, which results from the shifting and trembling of the viewer's gaze, but it is not readily identifiable to the viewer as eye movements.

Years later, short-lived Op Art focused on these factors and made them the design elements of the painting; this brief flurry thus had its roots in chiaroscuro, colored shadows, and pointillism.

There is thus a sense in which the pigment reflectances are indeed enhanced beyond their stimulus values in Impressionist technique (and in a long line of predecessors), simulating something closer to what is experienced when viewing sunlit landscapes.

Second, we have noted that the same kind of enhancements had been achieved by users of chiaroscuro in earlier centuries, with several critical differences: Rembrandt had few focal regions in his paintings; his indoor scenes were spotlit; his outdoor scenes were crepuscular. El Greco used multiple foci with contrasting adjacent regions (see Taylor 1964), but they are separate islands, purchased at the expense of an impression of fitful gloom. Out-of-doors, in sunlight, we expect to find high illumination almost everywhere we look. Fragonard and Watteau provide more even illuminations, but brightness and saturations both seem low. The large patches of the Impressionists, on the other hand, permit contrast, high saturation, and high luminance throughout the field of view, where it is desirable to maintain them, all at once. Moreover, the use of colored shadows, as well as the orientations of the patches themselves (like the crosshatching in woodcuts and engravings) to produce the modeling that is normally achieved by the use of shadows, provides a light field of view that is as large as the picture itself, rather than a few or many areas of light, as in a traditional chiaroscuro setting.

Third, we should remember that Impressionism is not restricted to sunlit scenes: it is Impressionist *and* largely *plein air* painting, not Impressionist just because it deals with sunlight. Consider, for example, the stuffy Victorian interiors of Renoir and Degas and the often gloomy scenes of Lautrec. An Impressionist painting is, in a sense, a depleted—in a sense, an inverted—version of the Rembrandt in Figure 2.3. In the latter, when the glance is kept in the focal region, both foveal and peripheral vision appear normal. In an Impressionist painting, when it is viewed from a normal distance, there are no places at which the fovea can pick up fine detail. To peripheral vision, on the other hand, the Impressionist painting looks veridical, as it does when viewed with deliberately out of focus ("abstracted") gaze and when viewed from a distance that is considerably greater than normal. As Harmon and Julesz (1973) showed, the perceptibility of the object represented by a patchwork picture, like those most characteristic of Impressionist painters, is increased when the perceptibility of the small details or "high spatial frequencies" (provided by the edges of the brushstrokes) is reduced, as in peripheral viewing or viewing from an increased distance. At a normal viewing distance, the scene dissolves into patches wherever the fovea falls, patches that take on meaning only when the fovea leaves them and they are reclaimed by peripheral or parafoveal vision.

Fourth, with large brushstrokes or patches, only gross volumes and masses can actually be represented on the canvas. It had long been noted (see Corot's watercolor sketches) that quick studies captured the "impression" of the out-of-doors better than finished paintings. In this sense, Impressionists intended to convey the first fleeting impression by a minimal notation. Like a Japanese pen and ink, the viewer must complete the picture himself or herself, with all the "freshness" that act has been noted to entail. In the viewer's first glance at a real scene, all but the small part of the scene that falls on the fovea is devoid of detail; this provides information about the gross volumes and masses around the viewer. A similar overall impression of form and masses is provided by the Impressionist canvas, that is, the Impressionist picture simulates the abstracted or contemplative gaze or it simulates the momentary impression, leached of the accidental details provided by the relatively few places on which the fovea happens to be poised. It can simulate the experiences being dazzled by more than one can grasp, of trying to grasp the scene as a whole by defocusing the gaze and not regarding any part of it specifically, of being afforded only a single momentary glimpse. There is more to be done in terms of the perceptual conse-quences of the Impressionist technique (for example, I believe that the use of gross color patches sidesteps much of the conflict between the flatness of the painting and the tridimensionality of the represented scene), but I think this is enough for a start. There are two main points that can be drawn at this time.

The first point is that the Impressionist painting simulates, and is not optically equivalent to, the scene it represents. With respect to the purpose of evoking the same experience as is evoked by an out-of-doors highly illuminated scene, the Impressionist painting rests on *local* contrasts of lightness and hue. This is *not* merely a matter of preserving the *ratios* of lightnesses of the original scene with different absolute levels (since Fechner, Helmholtz, and Hering to Wallach and Land, it has been noted that preserving the ratios of brightnesses preserves the ratios of reflectances, regardless of illumination [see Hochberg 1978]): in order to profit from the effects of contrast, we must take advantage of the fact that they are largely local (see Figure 2.2(D)—after Seurat) and take into account the sizes of patch that will best suit particular distances from the fovea, and the probable distance from which the picture will be viewed by an observer with normal vision. There is no physical transformation that relates the picture to the scene without taking into account the characteristic inhomogeneities of the retina, the different sizes of receptive fields, and the viewer's choice of viewing distance.

With respect to evoking the momentary, sketchy quality of a first glance or of a dazzled glance, and with respect to using brushstrokes or patchwork that will model the surfaces to be depicted, again, there is no direct automatic transformation that will derive the picture from the scene without knowledge about what size of detail will smooth out in peripheral vision to be perceptually equivalent (although not optically equivalent) to the objects in the scene.

The second point is that Impressionist paintings as objects provide familiarity with painterliness. Patches of color that are unabashedly strokes or pats of impasto paint on canvas, blue or violet shadows, and daubs of red and green (when viewed foveally) that turn to yellow sunlight when viewed peripherally (Monet's poplars) force even the untutored viewer to see the painting as object—as deliberately daubed pigment on canvas—as well as seeing the picture to be a window on a scene. Viewers of the *Noble Slav* (Figure 2.3) may be so transfixed by the focal area of the sitter's face that they never notice that the hands are impressionistic blobs. But there is no way in which they can avoid seeing that the Impressionist, unlike Rembrandt, has given them only bits of pigment on a flat surface, which somehow, magically, also work as parts of a picture. Each piece of an Impressionist painting is, in a way, a bit of found art. This forced education had, I believe, consequences that are essential to understand what other kinds of things paintings started to become almost immediately thereafter.

ARTISTIC CONSEQUENCES

Because a painting is an object that provides the eye with full information as to its flatness, the viewer can see the techniques by which painting and scene have been brought into even approximate optical equivalence. This is the point of Leonardo's prescription that is illustrated in Figure 2.1: Aspiring painters can see that the road converges to the horizon in a painting, even if they could not see that in looking at the scene itself. Innocent consumers exposed to pictures must also slowly gain familiarity with converging lines in pictures, whether verbalized or not and whether useful to them or not. I do not mean by this that even without special attention, the viewers will learn in any verbalizable fashion that linear perspective is a depth cue, but only that they will be familiar with the appearance of converging lines on canvas in scenes that look, from the right vantage point, like a scene in depth.

Similarly, were viewers exposed to enough of Rembrandt, they would gain familiarity with blurs outside the focal region; familiarity with Impressionism would make blatant a host of technical devices, some of which we have been considering. Initially, they mainly serve their purposes in representation. If they become familiar as patterns of pigment on canvas, however, they offer the raw material for elements of decoration, for developing individual signature, or (when rationalized by programmatic aesthetic manifestos, which have not been scarce in the early years of this century), they may provide the boundaries of a new self-conscious "school." Each and every one of the technical devices we have discussed has become the subject matter, in this way, of some school: Van Gogh's elongations of the patches into elements of expression and signature or the blue shadows that start out as Corot's transcriptions of reflected sky and, in the service of induced or simultaneous contrast in the Impressionists, become, in turn, Cezanne's modeling on his wife's face, Derain's theatrical sidelight in his portrait of Matisse, pure mood note in Kokoshka's self–portrait, and simple design element in Matisse. The volumes and masses of Pissarro, Monet, and Renoir become, through Cézanne, the Cubism of Picasso and Braque. The dancing afterimages of successive contrast, first in Impressionism and then in the Fauves, become the elements of Op Art design. In all these cases, the reference is not to a scene or to an event: it is to the techniques themselves, which were introduced for quite different purposes—purposes of simulation—in earlier paintings. What has happened is that the logjam of subject matter has been broken: painters are freed from the necessity of making recognizable surrogates of recognizable scenes, and can pick and choose from among the variety of now-familiar "side effects" of simulation those phenomena that will provide their visual topics and métiers.

The Da Vincian analysis is now quite inappropriate, and has been so for almost a century, precisely because its central assumption—that the subject matter of a painting is some scene—is simply no longer even partially true. The process of representing a scene may itself become the topic of a painter's concern, but the painting is then a comment on preparing a surrogate, not a "naive" trompe l'oeil in itself. The perceptual psychologist who is concerned with paintings cannot remain fixated on surrogates. Let me spell out in more detail the implication of the previous pages for perceptual theory.

PERCEPTUAL IMPLICATIONS

We started with pictures as trompe l'oeil surrogates, objects optically identical to the scene they represent (Figure 2.1[A] and Figure 2.2[B]), with fidelity defined in terms of the light each—scene and surrogate—sends to the eye. Even a trompe l'oeil picture *need not* be optically identical to its scene, however, because of the limitations on the wavelengths and the details the eye can resolve, so optical *equivalence* will suffice. Equivalence can be defined in terms of a point-by-point comparison of surrogate and scene, taking into account the characteristic color vision and acuity of the viewer.

Paintings as surrogates are severely limited in the range of light they can reflect to the eye. Using the facts of simultaneous and successive contrast, a particular region can be made to appear brighter than it actually is by making the adjacent parts of the surrogate darker than their corresponding regions in the represented scene. Reflectance limits can be partially overcome in this limited sense, and the picture then produces an experience that is more like the experience that the viewer would obtain from the scene itself. The use of chiaroscuro, brought to perfection by Rembrandt centuries ago, makes the optical equivalence of paintings and scene an obsolete criterion inasmuch as such manipulations work by departing from that optical equivalence.

The relationship between surrogate and scene is made still more remote by Rembrandt's procedure of restricting detail to one or two focal regions and filling the remainder of the painting with impressionistic strokes that look normal to the viewer's peripheral vision, and which maximize the effects of simultaneous and successive contrast, but which can be related to the scene itself only if we can take into account both where the viewer will look and the characteristic differences between foveal and peripheral vision.

By exploiting these factors further and by eliminating the detailed focal region entirely, the Impressionists left little to painting that can be phrased in terms of *equivalence of information* between painting and scene. Using local contrast and saturated colors, which made the light to the eye from picture and surrogate grossly unlike each other, and using patches of color that were far too large to be fused as they are in Figure

2.1(B) by the acuity limitations of the viewer, the Impressionists strove to simulate the greater range of luminances presented to the eye in sunlit scenes, and to simulate as well the initial overall experience produced by any scene—to recapture the "freshness" of the incomplete sketches by which more "photographic" painters had made their notes to themselves. In pursuing these goals, they removed the picture from even a rough optical equivalence: an Impressionist picture and scene do not look alike when compared point by point, nor will any overall transformation of the stimulus provided by the scene result in the stimulation provided by the picture. My reading of their methods is that in addition to the use of contrast factors to enhance saturation, they eliminated the focal region of detail characteristic of Rembrandt (or, with multiple regions, of El Greco) to provid *patterns of light that are intended to be comprehensible only when viewed through the "low-pass" filters of peripheral vision and capable of providing only gross surfaces and volumes without at the same time providing foveal information to indicate that only such simplified masses are being used.* (Thus, some of the Cubists, like Léger, are merely *inverted Impressionists:* in the work of the latter, all of the simplified volumes are painted with clear and hard-edged contours, so that under normal viewing conditions, there is never any doubt that the objects are cylinders, spheres, and cubes; it is only after experience with the work of the Impressionists that the viewer can see any point to such pictures, either in a historical sense or relating to his or her own perceptual experience.)

Since at least the time of Rembrandt, painters clearly do not intend to present the eye with the same light as does the scene. The pattern actually presented by an Impressionist painting only makes sense in relation to the represented scene if you can surmise the effect that the artist intended to achieve, the limitations of the medium, and the characteristics of the visual system. When painting took the next major step, past Impressionism and into the varieties of Cubism and Expressionism, which have comprised the bulk of significant painting for most of this century, its subject matter no longer refers at all to a scene to which the term *stimulus information* can be meaningfully related. We must then turn instead to the things a painting is made for (signature, ordered variation of culturally accessible elements, and so forth), when it is not intended to provide a trompe l'oeil surrogate, for an understanding, evaluation, and perceptual analysis of what the paintings are about. The attempt to make "photographic" paintings has occupied only a very small corner of humanity's artistic enterprises—indeed, only a short span of Western pictorial art. I believe that what I have attempted to show here for the use of color and detail is true as well about the representation of form and space—that in order to overcome the limitations of the medium, a picture which is intended to have the same effect as a scene must depart in important ways from optical equivalence with the scene, with departures that cannot be understood without taking into account the characteristics of the perceptual system. Even if we only consider the first level of analysis, that is, the pigment to be applied to the surface that makes the canvas into a painting, we can see that the "optical" criteria of artistic purpose, which is all that Leonardo's prescription addressed, is always insufficient and often unnecessary in the attempt to understand the painting as a perceptual object.

REFERENCES

Gibson, J. J. "A Theory of Pictorial Perception." *Audio Visual Communication Review* 1 (1954): 3–23.

―――. "The Information Available in Pictures." *Leonardo* 4 (1971): 27–35.

Hagen, M. A., and Elliott, H. B. "An Investigation of the Relationship between Viewing Condition and Preference for True and Modified Linear Perspective." *Journal of Experimental Psychology: Human Perception and Performance* 2 (1976): 479–90.

Harmon, L. and Julesz, B. "Masking in Visual Recognition: Effects of Two-Dimensional Filtered Noise." *Science* 180 (1973): 1194–97.

Helmholtz, H. "On the Relation of Optics to Painting." In *Popular Scientific Lectures* translated by E. Atkinson, pp. 73–138. New York: Appleton, 1881.

Hochberg, J. "Art and Perception." In *Perceptual Ecology*, edited by E. C. Carterette and M. Friedman. New York: Academic Press, 1978.

―――. "Pictorial Functions and Perceptual Structures." In *What Is a Picture?*, edited by M. A. Hagen. New York: Academic Press, in press.

―――. *Perception*. 2d ed. New York: Prentice-Hall, 1978b.

―――. "The Representation of Things and People." In *Art, Perception, and Reality*, edited by E. H. Gombrich, J. Hochberg, and M. Black, pp. 47–94. Baltimore: Johns Hopkins University Press, 1972.

Jameson, D., and Hurvich, L. "From Contrast to Assimilation: In Art and in the Eye." *Leonardo* 8 (1975): 125–31.

Kennedy, J. *A Psychology of Picture Perception*. San Francisco: Jossey-Bass, 1974.

Oster, G. "Moirée Patterns in Science and Art." *Advances in Biological and Medical Physics* 16 (1977): 333–47.

Penrose, L. and Penrose, R. "Impossible Objects: A Special Type or Visual Illusion." *British Journal on Psychology* 49 (1958): 31–33.

Pirenne, M. *Optics, Painting and Photography.* Cambridge: Cambridge University Press, 1970.

Taylor, J. *Design and Expression in the Visual Arts.* New York: Dover, 1964.

Chapter Three

Painting as Paradigm

Larry Day

A painting is a complex image made up of many complex images that may be seen in a variety of ways; associated with each way is a particular nomenclature. A painted image is not necessarily a closed, continuous form but may include the areas adjacent to the form or may include a group of closed and open forms and adjacent areas. We talk of forms and areas as having rhythmic qualities, as stressing patterns of recognizable character, and as having attributes of balance and order. An image is a visual unit of intelligibility.

One cannot view an image as if it were the first image. An image approaches us with a history made up of resemblances, borrowings, personal memories, biases, inclusions, and exclusions that a part of us cannot ignore. An image is cultural to a greater extent than it is physiological. A rendered drawing of a complex object would betray the age in which it was done to any knowledgeable eye. An image is made with the skills that the artist was taught or persuaded to develop. The skills of the artist belong mainly to the artist. What the artist is skillful about belongs to the age.

Image is related to imagination and to imitation. One can think of an image as a concretion of an imaginative act, or as a residue, or as a refining (but when the image acts as a refining of the imagination, it is never as a passive servant but as an aggressive contributor to its ultimate direction and shape). An image grows out of past images confronted with present imagination.

If an image has a history—that is, a linear nature—there is also a nonlinear aspect, a multitude of image potentials within the image proper—variables of the image that retain the image's recognizability and force while, at the same time, destroying the notion of singularity. An image of the crucifixion includes all the possible images of the crucifixion, and the cross of the crucifixion becomes an ideogram of man or a template that man may fit into, that waits for man.

All images are teleological by nature. The artist's choice of image may be direct, that is, the image may be chosen because of its normative associations, or it may be chosen ironically by means of displacement, re-emphasis, deconstruction, or the like. Whatever the choice, it is always rhetorical by nature, concerned with persuading, seducing, and influencing the viewer—and the artist.

Painting is an art of representation. It always represents a subject, the artist's sensibility, idea, experience, and so on. Painting lends itself to four major categories: mimetic, paradigmatic, ideogrammatic, and specific, as well as mixtures of the four. Mimetic art is concerned with the nature of credibility. The subject is not mimesis, but mimesis is used to make the subject believable. Paradigmatic art is concerned with parallels and analogs, and the subject is revealed as the parallel or analogy is revealed. Ideogrammatic art is concerned with signs: the subject is the synthesis of these signs. Specific art is concerned with the painting as object and the object as subject. Prior to the twentieth century, paintings evidenced each of these characteristics almost equally. In our time, it has been possible to experience paintings as emphasizing one characteristic over others. On the current art scene, Gabriel Laderman and Sidney Goodman (for instance) would be mimetic or primarily so, Willem DeKooning and Richard Diebenkorn would be paradigmatic, Jasper Johns and Juan Miro would be ideogrammatic, and Kenneth Noland and Jules Olitsky would be specific. Even so, very few artists are ever wholly anything unless they are consciously attempting to start a school or uphold one—usually the very young and militant or the old and crotchety.

My concerns in this chapter are with one of the subdivisions of mimetic art ("realism"), paradigmatic meaning, one specific painter, and one specific painting. In talking about art, all generalities, categories, and concerns that one wishes to discuss must appear in individual works and in some way illuminate an individual work.

Realism, it may be argued, was a shift from the archetype to the specific. It may also be argued that realism was the use of the specific as archetype. The images of Poussin, even the image of Poussin himself (the famous self-portrait in the Louvre), gain power by their ability to be received as typical. The stress in classical art was always on the permanent—on what continues, on what prevails, and on what makes itself known. The archetypical reveals itself, assured of its complexity and its complicity. The artist depends upon the typical for whatever depth the image is to have. If the uniqueness of the image is necessary to justify for the modern sensibility yet another version, it must also satisfy the expectancies that surround the image's concerns. At this time in our awareness, it is impossible to think of an image without a history; seldom does art of the present invent images—rather, it finds new uses for, or new juxtapositions of, the seen.

A central concern of the modern sensibility lies in the sources of the image and how these sources manifest themselves in the image itself. Are the sources in things and spaces—in our masteries and confusions before them—or are they in our awarenesses, our replacements, our arts, so to speak? There is a great difference between trying to paint something as it is, independent of our will, and painting our response to something (not only in the act of painting but in the act of viewing the painting as well). Different modes of credibility are established, and the hierarchical patterns of concern are altered, when a work commits itself to the artist's particular sensibility.

What is important and what is possible within an area of involvement? Art has always been concerned with sorting out the trivial and the irrelevant—with making the work justify its look. At the same time, few works are ever wholly pure because the spirit of making them includes exuberance, with its frivolousness and joy in being—its awareness of, and dependency on, momentum.

One of the questions raised as one confronts an unstable world has to do with the presence of multiplicity, the apparent possibility of two (or more) correct choices and the inescapable awareness that reality may be an indeterminate issue. The problem of belief might be the central problem of our time, and the various attempts to draw upon the power that belief has in the past given the artist shows in both the troubled and complex motivations and simplistic forms which make up so much of current art.

If reality as a single awareness or state cannot be located and if the only things that we can accept without anxiety are fictions *as* fictions, then the emphasis must be on the maker of the fiction *as* maker and on the sharer of the knowledge of that fiction *as* sharer. The fiction has become objective fact. Art has ceased to describe reality (reality is not describable) and has settled for being merely real (along with everything else). Art is a real fiction.

But a fiction in the past was about something: "Once upon a time there was a Princess"; "Once upon a time there were Gods"; this is a painting of the finding of Moses; or this is a painting of the Garden of Eden. One moved into the story as one moved into the painting—with one's eyes, the way one moves with one's eyes into a room before physically entering the room. A painting was as a room seen from its threshold with familiar and unfamiliar things beckoning and repelling, shaping the space by their power and being shaped by the space when they had none. Things were capable of having power and of being known. All things had proper names and proper forms—essences—and a fiction to be accepted had to know the right names and the right forms, and so the motivations could be simplistic but the forms could be complex. Then that changed. With the gradual demands on our awareness, experiences that could not be suppressed, and knowledge that altered or seemed to alter everything, we slowly and at first almost imperceptibly dropped the stance that said there were correct forms. After correctness as a vital force disappeared, there was for a while nothing but memory and a sense of loss. We knew too much, too many things: all the gods and their representatives, all the myths and all the tales, and the inevitable laws of the natural world and the arbitrary laws of the human world. We knew what caused us to react in a specific way, and because we knew the cause, the response lost its meaning.

With the disappearance of God and with the taming and domestication of heroes, painting became a thing-in-itself, answerable only to its chosen conventions. It lacked a subject. It had nothing to point to. The paintings commanding the attention of those people interested in art were paintings depicting violent (unambiguous emotions in extreme situations) situations clearly calling for specific responses, situations chosen for their clarity of extension—that is, situations abstracted from experience, complete in themselves.

As the act of painting and the act of viewing become codified, the chief characteristic recognizable in the art world became what might be called *expectancy*, and when expectancy prevails, everything from process to mode becomes stabilized. Whatever the manner, when formalization sets in, no matter how chancy its inception, then that manner becomes *the manner*. Decorum, the art of knowing how to act and how to react, can be frozen and, if not tempered with empathy and understanding, can be trivialized. Romanticism, the dominant mode of the early part of the nineteenth century, lost its most powerful quality—the questioning of conventions—when it became answerable to a series of conventions that both artists and the art public found necessary for the continuing activity of painting.

Painting stressed both clarity and emotion, and obviousness was not considered too high a price to pay for their dual existence. A typical highly praised painting of the period, Ary Scheffer's *St. Thomas Aquinas Preaching during a Storm*, exemplifies the situation. St. Thomas is depicted as an Apollo-like figure in robes, and the cowering lay figures clearly portray either fear or hope. The large (11½ foot high) canvas deals in strong contrasts and rhythms. There is no attempt at specificity or historical accuracy. What is there is an abstract presentation of noble emotion and courage through faith. The fact that the painting's form is a pastiche of styles shows which styles were considered appropriate for serious art now that codification had been established. It may be that this is the nature of artistic aging. It had certainly happened before and has certainly happened since.

The main issue, however, is that since its inception, the art world at any given time defines not only its major preoccupations but also the manner or manners deemed most suitable for presentation. What is to be looked at and what one must bring to it in order to see it correctly defines not only the way a contemporary painting looks but how a past painting looks as well. We certainly see a Vermeer differently today (after Cézanne, Mondrian, photography, and everything else) than the cultured public of seventeenth-century Holland (including Vermeer). It is a point we must start from if we are to accept the evidence of our own eyes. Not only are objects passive until we invest them with our concerns, but in terms of art, it is our concerns that make us see objects at all. We all know of works capable of moving us in the highest and profoundest way that were at one time considered valuable only for their historical, social, or psychological documentation.

At the same time, art is always art. That is, in spite of the vagaries of our concerns and experiences, there is a continuing demand for the imaginative and aesthetic forming of those concerns. If what we consider to be art keeps changing—certainly a great deal of what we consider serious painting today if it could have appeared in the eighteenth century would have been considered madness—if art or what passes for art keeps changing, the need for art within a society does not. Art is and always has (with few exceptions) been considered essential for a complete society.

We have, then, two things; a continuing concern for art and a changing notion as to what constitutes the art that has meaning. Added to these, we have the self-destructive course that art takes when it is treated seriously. Art activity moves from trial and error, lucky guesses, and inspirations to awareness, analysis, and mastery over the forms. Once mastery is achieved, then irony is necessary to maintain meaning, and after irony is exhausted, cynicism and denial mark time until a new force, a new innocence, appears.

It seems to me the midnineteenth century was such a period. Romanticism has lost its innocence (and by innocence, I mean its sense of forward movement, its belief in its vitality and freedom). Romanticism had become codified: the moves were regulated by good taste and critical standards. The great original forces still worked in an artist such as Delacroix for instance, but they were individual forces, ambiguous, inward, outside of the codifications, only partially understood, only partially understandable—even to themselves. What was understandable was confined to the popular works of the time. Few sensed what was missing—an art public is almost always optimistic and pleased with itself. Indeed, few sensed that anything was missing, and of the few, fewer still were painters.

Painters generally do not consider themselves thinkers; painters think of themselves as doers, makers. Most of their thinking is done between paintings, and it is usually some external force in their lives that forces them to think about abstractions—that is, something other than the next painting. Some force, like rejection, usually sends a painter theorizing, taking sides with issues that heretofore were allowed to seep into the work unawares. Few painters feel that the success they achieve is ill-deserved. Few painters reject praise until they have had a great deal of it. (Perhaps this is why most revolutionary movements are started by the rejected young and the overly praised old.)

It was at this time that a painter appeared on the scene who to us, with our "extraordinary" gifts of hindsight, seemed to possess all the necessary qualifications for bringing new life to a cultural arena apparently dominated by ennui. A mere listing of some of the facts about him is like an explanation of why he was the right person for the times.

Born in 1819 (the same year as Walt Whitman), his father was a small landowner and farmer and more influential on his life than his mother. He was very close to his sisters, and they served as representatives of Woman for him both in his paintings and his life. He was committed to the land: he loved hunting and fishing and the pleasures of outdoor life. He had great empathy for animals (the hunter's vision), the weather, essentials. He disliked school, considering it abstract, antinature, and a distancing from experience. His art training was classical (what happens rather than what is happening), he copied paintings—Venetian, Spanish, Dutch, Flemish. He was aware of an ending and the loss of the sublime. He loved the sea and saw it as a reaffirmation of vision, vitality, and the continuing presence of grandeur. He was narcissistic and saw the self as mediator and an extension of the natural world. He loved to drink (he ended life as an alcoholic) and eat and talk and sleep. He loved workers, intellectuals (he called Proudhon "my compass"), poets, and people who liked his work. He was larger than life—at times, amazingly simple and, at other times, exceedingly complex. He was, of course, Gustave Courbet, and he painted what some people, myself included, believe to be the central painting of Western art in the nineteenth century.

The painting is *The Studio of the Painter: A Real Allegory of a Seven-Year Phase in My Life as an Artist,* a huge work over 11 1/2 feet high (359cm) and approximately 19 1/2 feet wide (598cm). (See Figure 3.1.) It was shown in 1855, and it now hangs in the Louvre, for which it was acquired in 1920.

So much has been written about the painting and so much that is valuable that there seems little reason for adding to the literature except for the light shed on other issues and the encouragement it gives to certain stances.

Many scholars have contributed theories as to the sources of the painting: from popular imagery (cartoons) to Dutch genre painting. Certainly, Velasquez's *Las Meninas* stands behind the painting (as do all artist's studio paintings) as a sanction. It was also a way of celebrating what one was doing and a pitch for painting's inherent value. But a work of art is not to be understood solely by an uncovering of its sources. As Nietzsche pointed out (and every artist knows), "Origin and purpose are separate—and ought to remain separate." What interests me more than the sources or the sanctions is the painting's presence as a reaction—and reaction as aim.

The climate of painting at the time of its conception was dominated by academia. The great themes were being trivialized time and again. The sublime, the highest and most ambitious of concerns for the artist, had lost what seemed to be its most pertinent component—the scene of awe or the act of awe. Since the defeat and gradual disappearance of revolutionary heroes and the domestication of the land, the wealth of the bourgeoisie, and the emergence of security and order as dominant virtues, the sublime ceased to be a possible experience except in dream and in nostalgia, itself a creator of distance and irreparable loss.

With the sublime no more than a distorted memory, the ambitious artists concerned themselves with reproductive skills, which at least guaranteed them a kind of respect and financial success.

The point that has always interested me about the Courbet painting is that he tackled, head on, the problem of the sublime and in a way that differentiates his studio painting from all other paintings in the genre. He made the creative act the heroic act—the place of creation, the scene of instruction. He justified, thematically, the scale of the painting, the explicit and the implicit forming, the cluster and openness of space, the specificity and the ambiguity. His painting was and can be understood as a reaction to the challenge of past sublimity and the present absence of it.

The sublime has been characterized as an experience growing out of the confrontation of an overwhelming presence in the form of a scene or an event, a presence so powerful that one's past qualifications are felt to be inadequate to meet or understand it, and one feels a terror that is ambiguously divided between a void in the self and a presence in the world, a terror demanding that one must change one's life.

The sublime had traditionally been linked with God's presence, but the revolutionary demands for personal bravery and human loyalty extended its scope—and, of course, made it more vulnerable when the challenges to bravery evaporated and were replaced by the entrenching concerns of the newly successful.

But to share in those great experiences, to be overwhelmed, to be in the presence of forces greater than oneself but, at the same time, forces that made the self greater than it was, these were, and always are, the concerns of the truly ambitious. It is to these concerns that Courbet's painting addressed itself.

First, there is the scale. Again, traditionally, one of the characteristics of the sublime is the sense of vastness—a sense of limitlessness. All the great images of the sublime in some way included this element. Limits signify order, and order signifies control and understanding. In this sense, Claude served as a more useful model than Poussin. Only Poussin himself knew how to invest his order with subversion, his triumph with defeat. But Turner (for one) could take Claude and twist him into what he needed. A Turner is often a Claude scene on a different day (and enlarged).

Courbet, accepting his predecessors' concern for vastness, knew the dimensions he had to work with—they were, perhaps, the first given. The painting is the size it is—there is no arguing that. In terms of the number or approximate number of figures he wanted to include, the length of the painting seems a necessity. The height is more arbitrary—or seemingly so. He could have made it a proportionally low rectangle, like the *Burial at Ornans*, which is twice as long as it is high—10 feet 3 1/2 inches by 21 feet 10 inches (one only has to think of the painting in that shape to realize how wrong that would have been). The reason for the height would have to be the sense of import that transcends the real. *The Burial* is directed to the real—the emphasis is on the actors in the event and the movement (the sanction for which comes from friezes). In *The Studio*, the place must share the priority with the artist. Its space must be felt: it must be *a* place, but at the same time, it must give the feeling of limitlessness. It seems perfectly right that the walls lose their corporeality as they rise to the top of the canvas. In fact, the ambiguity of the air was felt right from the beginning: Delacroix standing alone before the painting had "the impression of a real sky in the middle of the picture"—a quality he felt to be a fault in an otherwise remarkable painting. The walls and the relationship between the walls and the paintings hung on them is one of ambiguous substances, almost transparent, never confining. The most unwall-like of walls, they seem the only kind that make sense if the place is a place of allegory.

The huge curtain on the right maintains the sense of ambiguity. It draws apart from the wall; it helps us to conceive of the wall, but in the center of its mass, it is, like the wall, not definable in terms of space. Looking down from the top, the painting seems to have no surface—or a surface that retreats from physicality.

The vast studio is, in a sense, a response to the forms that inhabit it—as much a response as a generator of activity. Its permissive atmosphere and dimension are in turn what is permitted by the theme. How the studio became as it did is not the issue but rather that it is capable of directing our vision and rounding out our awarenesses.

The figures are organized into three groups, each group having its own kind of space. The group on the left seems lower and moves back in a manner suggesting a slightly different eye level than the central or right-hand group. The floor plane seems less steep, and the figures in the background are related to the wall less distinctly. Courbet was never greatly concerned with consistency but rather organized his paintings in terms of units. The left-hand group or unit, representing the world of memory—of paintings and experiences—is in a sense absent, possibly hallucinatory, but, at the same time, part of the painter's imagination—his reality. The figures are painted solidly in clothes that reveal their identities and their demands on the painter. They form smaller units within their larger one, but do so sometimes for the sake of visibility (because of the nature of vision and memory) and not because of iconographic connections. A hunter, a hired hand, and a reaper make up a unit. A textile peddler shows his wares to an undertaker's helper while a strong man and a clown watch. At the edge of the canvas that Courbet is working on, a woman and child—a memory from a trip to England—form a solid, compelling apparition, while to their left is a skull on a journal that championed official art. The skull is the ever-present memento mori of the romantic consciousness (and the death of official art); the woman is direct experience. The two images together form a unit, with a figure representing, simultaneously, a martyred saint and the art of the past. Free association and trust in the priorities of memory seem to establish connections, and we view what was once a faith in the artist's options as psychologically sound or believable.

On the right side of the canvas, the figures seem more ordered, perhaps because they are fewer in number but also because the spatial shift from the woman in the shawl to the figure in the background (a portrait of a musician friend, named Promayet) is a clear and direct diagonal. There is some sense of symmetry, each side having its seated figure facing the center, the hunter on the left, Champfleury on the right, but the dominant figure visually is the woman with the shawl—although Baudelaire, because of his subsequent fame, commands our attention today.

The right-hand group consists mainly of portraits but not exclusively so, for the lovers seem to be there because of what they are rather than who they are. Indeed, the groups are not tidy: there are two hunters on the left, which does not make sense symbolically unless one of them is a poacher (the seated hunter was not mentioned in Courbet's letter describing the painting), and the boy drawing on the right is clearly a role-oriented figure, while the man and the woman in the shawl bridge both systems. But the fact remains that the left-hand side of the painting encourages us to view the figures and objects as representatives of roles: they are hierarchical figures—but hierarchical figures from life made resonant by the artist's imagination and by their placement in the painting. It was necessary to have recognizable figures—figures advanced in identity and individuality elsewhere—to make those solid, memorable figures on the left stand for ways of life. We must see other possibilities of recognition before we can believe in the roles assigned to those figures. When the specific persons on the right become recognizable, another symbolic system is made possible, and of course, the same process happens in reverse. The groups differentiate themselves but depend on each other for possible meaning within the painting. They also support and extend the central group of Courbet painting a landscape while being watched by a small boy (the future) and a nude model (Courbet's muse) and a playing cat.

Courbet is painting a landscape from memory. It is a landscape of an actual place. Courbet was as much concerned with memory as Proust. It was the source and liberator of his imagination. *The Studio* was painted at Ornans, but it was, he insisted, his Paris studio. The figures on the left, notably the Jew at the far left and the beggar woman and child, were figures, images, seen and remembered, figures that demanded formal realization.

Memory cannot exist overtly in a painting, because what is there is always in the present, is always present. Memory if it is to exist must do so in actuality; it must establish the act of remembering in the viewer. Memory always stands outside of the painting, filtering our vision, and for this reason can never be accurately described, because we can never wholly distinguish what comes from the work and what comes from us.

The problems of representation are also problems of possession. The figures on the left—the absent, the remembered—stand out unequally from the atmosphere, which is intangible throughout the painting. The remembered are the products of will, but will tempered by pain and pleasure and unrealized significations. The figures on the right are present, but they are depicted as inactive, waiting. The central group is self-sufficient.

The central group is really the key to everything. A painting about painting, a representation of the act of representing, the artist as the subject of art. But the choice of what image was to occupy the center of the painting's breadth was not the artist's face but the palette and brushes (and palette knife)—the tools, the symbol of art itself. Courbet, the vainest of men, in his role as conqueror, as Assyrian king (in profile, as the Assyrian kings made themselves known), conquering nature through the act of painting, drawing nature into being through memory—the artist's mind; Courbet, the man, chooses not to be the center.

Next to him, the muse appears as a model, as an inhabitant of the studio. She is not posing but is in her natural state as model; she is also in her natural state as muse: seeing what the artist sees, approving what the artist paints, closer to him than any other. She is a real muse— an image, as Harold Bloom has pointed out, of instruction but also an image of pleasure.

The boy is the future, naturalness, innocence, but the boy is also a figure that serves to heighten the self-portrait and the act of painting. It is not just that youth is being represented but that a particular figure in a particular place has an existence to be considered and understood and that a unit moves toward a definition of the whole. The little boy is the future, but the future is a time without the artist; thus, the future is also death, just as the model/muse is erotic existence, a touching and a not touching. The small cat is play and domesticated nature, as the painting on the easel is nature itself and a manifestation of the painter's powers. Forms and identities merge and separate and merge again, and new identities are formed; the act of painting becomes the act of sensing.

Robert Warshow once said that the hero is someone who looks like a hero. The hero meets our demand for image as well as act, and in part, the act is altered because the image is potent. Courbet saw himself as both image and act and stressed both equally: the image, by the light coat and striped trousers and the resonating reference to kingliness, and the act, by the strength and complexity of gesture—the thrust arm (dynamic) and the drawn back torso (reflection). His immediate background, the landscape on which he is working, signifies his loyal ties and the source of his strength (it was a difficult feat to show himself in profile and the painted canvas in full view without awkwardness). The hero's strength comes from the land.

With all the explanations, nothing is fully explained. What the painting is about is only part of any painting: a painting must also be seen as a thing-in-itself, a presence—even a mimetic painting. For a representation to be accorded fullness of response, one must acknowledge, as a positive point, its difference from its source. Each representation seeks autonomy before it can adequately point to something outside of itself. *The Studio* was and is a vast presence to us—on one level denying explanations and on another inviting them. It was obviously unfinished when it was exhibited (it was shown once again—in the same state). There are examples of haste, of sudden revisions, such as the painted-out but still visible head of Jeanne Duval, Baudelaire's estranged mistress. There is the visually commanding image of a plaster cast, seemingly hanging on a painting, looking at times like a cold, flat moon. The painting is exactly what Courbet said it was—a real allegory. The figures and stuffs are persuasively painted. The interpretations are many, and it seems meant to be so. Courbet obviously painted it to

Figure 3.1 Gustave Courbet's *Studio of the Painter: A Real Allegory of a Seven-Year Phase in My Life as an Artist* (Paris, The Louvre).

show people something. He never tried to finish it and, as far as I know, never tried very hard to sell it.

What Courbet did, in my mind, was to define the stance artists were to take if they were to maintain high ambition. With the death of the hero, the creative act became the heroic act and the celebration of being; the true subject of art would be art itself. The creative life would be the only significant life. The painting could have been subtitled *The Growth of the Artist's Mind* (after Wordsworth), or it could have been called *The Song of Myself (Leaves of Grass* appeared the same year as the painting). It was, in short, the clearest and most exhaustive statement that painting was to make about where painting was going and what painting would be about for the next 100 years.

Reference

Warshow, R. "Essay on the Western." In *Sincerity and Authenticity*, edited by L. Trilling. Cambridge; Mass.: Harvard University Press, 1971–72.

PART II

THE ROLE OF
PERCEPTION

Introduction to Part II

This section is concerned with two questions. First, what does perception mean to the artist, philosopher, and psychologist? Second, what role does perception play in pictorial representation? The artist's viewpoint is represented by Finkelstein. He talks about how the process of seeing, which should not be confused with the term *perception*, is related to the way the artist paints. His distinction between seeing and perceiving is based on the notion that scientific approaches to the study of perception are directed at finding the material causes behind the phenomenon. Finkelstein's thesis holds that the scientist's assumption that the givens of perception rest on a material cause outside the viewer is artifactual and creates a distorted view of the role of perception when applied to art. For Finkelstein, seeing is a distinctly individual affair, called *individuation*. The individuation process of seeing affects how the artist pictures reality in painting in much the same way as tacit knowledge (Polanyi 1967) affects how the scientist pictures material or psychological reality. However, the focus of individuation is on the variance in experience, while the focus of tacit knowledge is on the invariance in experience. It is here where artist and scientist part company.

Haber is concerned with the psychological reality of three-dimensional pictures. For him, perspective is the most important device for representing the third dimension. However, perspective theory assumes a fixed station point between the eye of the artist (and viewer) and the scene. Yet, we perceive depth in pictures without aligning ourselves with the artist's station point. Haber explains this dilemma by saying that we compensate for the misalignment by using information about distance and orientation derived from the picture surface. Thus, we have, in effect, learned the rules for distorting three-dimensional scenes to two-dimensional pictures.

Yonas is also interested in how the artist represents the layout of objects in space on a flat canvas; however, his focus is on whether young children recognize such representations as three dimensional. Painters as far back as Leonardo have used two techniques to inform the viewer of the shape and location of objects in space. To give objects solidity, painters depend on attached shadows, which are represented by highlights and shading. To locate objects in space, painters depend on cast shadows, represented as shaded silhouettes falling on a three-dimensional spatial layout. One especially important cue for determining whether or not an object is resting on a surface is the gap on the picture plane between the object and the shadow that it casts, which has been used effectively by trompe l'oeil artists. There is growing evidence that children as young as three years of age begin to understand the logic of how light is structured by objects and surfaces in the world, although the ability to predict the shape of a shadow cast by an object from various orientation with respect to a light source comes later—around seven to eight years of age.

According to Wheelock, perspective was used in the seventeenth century by Dutch painters to bring the viewer into closer contact with the realities of the physical world. Their painting methods were rooted in the (linear) perspective traditions of Italian Renaissance art. The Dutch painters knew, however, that if they painted strictly according to the laws of linear perspective their works would appear distorted to the viewer unless viewed from the proper station point. Thus, they experimented with the laws of linear perspective by violating (modifying) them in order to bring the images in line with the perceptual reality of natural perspective. The standard for judging reality thus became the eye. Optics played an important role in their experimentation, because the eye was still the ultimate judge of reality. Wheelock proposes that Dutch artists produced images with optical devices such as the concave lens and camera obscura to reinforce and expand their naturalist view of reality. Thus, although we commonly think of Dutch painting as the ultimate epitome of realism, (using the standard of visual appearance), Wheelock demonstrates that the Dutch brand of realism moved away from the geometric view of reality handed down from the Italian Renaissance toward an optical view of reality.

The influence of scientific discoveries on the art of the times is given a more modernistic flavor in the chapter by Vitz. He argues for a kind of conceptual parallelism between research on visual perception in the late nineteenth and early twentieth century and developments in modern painting. To support his argument, he draws on numerous examples in which scientist and artist explored similar visual phenomena and produced similar conceptual schemes for solving them. The visual phenomena centered on the role of experience and its relevance to perception. The conceptual schemes were largely (although not exclusively, thanks to the Gestaltists) analytical and reductionistic. The results are documented pictorially, as, for example, the use of texture gradients by James Gibson and Bridget Riley to create the illusion of depth or the use of pointillism by Charles Blanc and Georges Seurat to create impressionistic forms.

Kennedy examines in detail one visual phenomenon that Vitz failed to mention, subjective contours, and shows how it has been and can be useful to the artist. Subjective contours are of interest to both the psychologist and the artist because of their unreal existence. Understanding how they are produced will not only give Op artists an expanded world to paint but will also satisfy the inquiring mind. Kennedy is not happy with the theories that have been advanced to account for subjective contours. They are not simply a matter of closure or figure–ground effects (Gestalt explanations). Nor are they responses to depth cues in the display, which give the impression of overlapping or stratified surfaces because the phantom shapes are also subjectively brighter than the background. Kennedy believes that subjective brightness is the key to understanding subjective contours. He proposes that subjective contours are partly dependent on perceived brightness differences induced by local visual effects (contrast and assimilation), which respond to the ends and sides of lines or dots (the usual background), and partly dependent on grouping processes attributed to the nervous system, which respond to shape, symmetry, and other Gestalt principles.

The final chapter in this section, by Hagen, returns to the issue of pictorial representation and its relation to psychological theories of perception. After pointing out the shortcomings of major theories of pictorial representation represented by the constructivist approach theory of Ernst Gombrich, the Gestalt theory of Rudolf Arnheim, and the perspectivist theory of James Gibson, Hagen offers her own theoretical solution. The problem with each of the former theories, and perceptual theories in general, is that there is too much emphasis on a single aspect of perception. All three theories are ultimately concerned with meaning, but meaning is derived differently in each case. For Gombrich, meaning is constructed from a knowledge base derived from sensory experience (the traditional sensation–perception paradigm). Thus, according to Hagen, pictorial representation in art for Gombrich depends on the ability of the artist to make images look convincing or real. Meaning for Arnheim resides in the *visual concept*, which is the Platonic idealized, multifaceted universal form (that is, prototype) of objects. Representation in art, both from the standpoint of making and viewing, depends on the achievement of the visual concept. Gestalt principles of perception are responsible for making this achievement possible.

For Gibson, meaning resides in the invariant properties of light to the eye, which characterize objects in their environmental context. Representation in art depends upon the artist's ability to capture invariant features of the object on canvas. The artist, however, is limited in his or her ability to represent invariant features of the object by the infinite number of potential perspectives (station points), which are associated with momentary transformations (variant features) of the object. In other words, the object appears to be different from different perspectives, and what the artist must capture is the enduring (invariant) properties by which the object is known.

Hagen proposes a solution to Gibson's theoretical approach, which she calls the *generative theory*. She proposes that pictorial representation can be described by rules of projective geometry. These are generative rules, which describe changes in variants relative to invariants as a function of station point. Thus, pictorial representation can be understood in terms of the way the artist uses these generative rules in executing a painting. The solution depends on the choices the artist makes with respect to station point and the relative emphasis on variant versus invariant features in two-dimensional or three-dimensional space. Hagen demonstrates how this theory can be applied to rock art and Egyptian art. But how can nonrepresentational art be analyzed with Hagen's theory?

REFERENCE

Polanyi, M. *The Tacit Dimension*. Garden City, N.Y.: Anchor, 1967.

Chapter Four

On the Unpicturelikeness
of Our Seeing

Louis Finkelstein

Quite recently, an experimental psychologist said to me, "I would very much like to see the way you painters see." The remark raises two points: first, that the demands of painters and psychologists may be different, and second, that individual visual experience is in some sense irreplaceable by the visual experience of another individual. Such considerations are germane to a general inquiry into how we see in that various approaches regarding seeing may be fruitfully critical of each other. The principle of the nonsubstitutability of individual vision implies that, in principle, all scientific approaches to vision which reduce it to those properties that are shared by all viewers may be distorting the phenomenon they propose to be investigating, unless, of course, it is understood in advance that the ultimate character of seeing is that it does individuate experience and that it is the actual mechanism whereby this takes place which makes seeing possible at all.

Such a stipulation is not likely to please scientists, since it negates the prospect of scientific inquiry. Without arrogating to myself the role of speaking for all painters (since this, in any event, would be precluded by my major premise), I must maintain that it is methodologically necessary for any useful colloquy between the arts and the sciences on the subject. From the artist's viewpoint, the scientist in a laboratory creates a series of artifacts by the process of cutting apart the living, continuous, individually intentioned process of seeing into its presumed components. Aside from those art objects that are deliberately made by the slavish application of conventional formulas, artists know, by many tokens—by their own direct experience; by analysis and reflection on the variables that characterize works of art and most particularly, the most superior works of art; by reflection on their own learning processes, as well as the experiences of teaching painting or drawing; and by reflection, even on the variations of what is seen in a number of viewings of the same art object over a period of time, that the individuation of seeing is irremovable. To hold that there are so many invariants in seeing that what differences might be found by the artist should be ascribed to some later process of selection presents two shortcomings. The first is that the invariant elements which the scientist usually refers to are at critically far too coarse a scale of discrimination than that which the artist habitually makes. The second is that displacement of individuation to some logically or temporally subsequent process to that of seeing is a possibly false characterization of seeing (it is, at any rate, false to a good number of experiences). It also begs the question of where and how such individuating decisions, which pervade our whole sense of being in the world and all the mystery and difficulty of touching other minds that goes with it, are made.

An interesting nexus of the problem is the question of pictures. To scientists, the demonstration that certain sorts of pictures (they are usually thinking of mid-nineteenth–century academic paintings or, what does not resemble them at all, color photographs) can be read to convey a variety of detailed information and, at the same time, conform to certain mechanical requirements, such as perspectival consistency and a smooth scale of tone and color variation, convinces them that our seeing proceeds along normative rules according to a fashion of picturing. An important part of the program here is that a picture is a static fact, which, although we may scan it in time is, if read according to those normative rules, everywhere consistent, whereas our seeing is instead ineluctably dynamic—and besides, the question of its consistency is problematical.

What is usually not examined in speculations about spatial perception is the role that is played by movements of the eye. From a neurophysiological point of view, the linkages that are involved are extremely complex, and knowledge about their interaction is quite incomplete. Some inkling as to the character of what is involved can be obtained, however, by contrasting our spatial sensations with what is experienced during a single fixation, which constitutes the model for perspective theory.

A simple experiment will suffice. First, we establish what a cone of focused vision is. This is done by stretching out our arms in front of us with our two thumbs touching so that we see the surface of the two thumbnails. We then focus on the thumbnails by imagining a small word to be printed on each. The trick is then to see how far apart we can move the thumbs while keeping both imagined words in focus. From this, we will see that the cone of focused vision is very narrow, about three degrees.

What has this got to do with the perception of space? This is shown in the following way. We fixate this now-observed-to-be narrow cone at a near point to ourselves in space, say, a point on the floor, about four feet away if we are sitting down. Care should be taken that the gaze is not directed directly frontally, in which case, we could then use our sense of axiality of our body as a kind of prestructuring information; care should also be taken that we do not look directly at a wall or other structure perpendicular to our line of sight for the same reason. If we then attempt to describe the angle off from us in space of any objects that may be casually located about this fixated point (I often have a few books or papers lying on the floor), this becomes quite difficult, especially if, while still fixating on the same point, we attempt mentally to define a relationship between two such objects. Moving our gaze then to but a very slight distance away in space, say, a matter of four to six inches, will produce entirely different estimates of these relationships. Not only will estimates change, but feelings that have to do with our sense of physical copresence in the space with them will also change. It is this sense of copresence that makes space meaningful to us, which makes it touch us affectively, and which is the basis of the artist's use of space as affective and meaningful. It is the range of natural confusions that the invention of linear perspective, with a fixed picture reference plane, as well as a fixed point of view, was designed to allay, although even before its introduction, there was a clear recognition of the difference between *perspectiva naturalis* and *perspectiva artificialis*. It was only by standing *outside* the conditions of direct experience with its attendant confusing flux of competing sensations that Leone Battista Alberti was able to hit upon a formula for a consistent set of proportional and occluding relations within the projective pyramid of the visual "rays," which make one point perspective, a perspective we never experience even through the most rigorously constrained setups, since even in these, we cannot focus uniformly in depth and angle throughout the visual field.

An instructive range of examples of what is at issue is contained in the body of work, over the past 15 years, of Philip Pearlstein, one of the most serious and accomplished of what are called *realist* painters (although the term *realist* causes some difficulties) now working (see Figure 4.1). Pearlstein's paintings, for the most part, are studio interiors with one or two figures seen from quite close and meticulously painted somewhat over life-size. Because he works at a viewing distance much closer than that contemplated by Albertian perspective (Leonardo believed that this should be about ten times the represented width of the scene), and because everything is in sharp focus, including the interruption of contours, as if from fixed station point of viewing, there exist numerous anomalies when such a painting is viewed as a whole. These are more or less glaring, depending on the particulars of the

Figure 4.1 Philip Pearlstein's *Female Model on Ladder* (Frumkin Gallery, photo: eeva-inkeri).

setup and the kinds of conflict of visual cues that are involved. Parts of the figure seem grossly out of proportion—the floor plane rises vertiginously, while other forms are maintained in strict elevation; objects or parts of objects appear to float, while some cannot be located in space at all. At the same time, the continuity of surfaces, the consistency of tone, and, perhaps, most importantly, the enumeration of details makes the paintings, by some standard, "look real."

An essential part of the problem is that when we mean *space*, we mean something that is completely the contrary to the enumeration of items which may be contained in it. Space as such is at every instant continuous, logical, noncontradictory, and convincing, as the matrix in which we find both our own and other bodies, even though at any given moment, we have no direct evidence of this in terms of the pattern of visual stimuli. This contradiction is at the root of all the pictorial conventions that replace the actual visual experience with something more controllable. Eventually, these are chosen or discovered, as Gombrich (1960) has pointed out, according to the "purpose and requirements of the society," and, we might add, by way of extension and articulation, the intentionality of the artist, through which they take place.

The critical focus of examination necessary for explicating the unfitness of the pictorial scheme is at those instances where the conventions or the means, however well rationalized, do not serve to satisfy some requirement, usually of the individual artist—a requirement, which, because it is so elusive, we can only guess at. Leonardo, when he painted the *Last Supper*, was certainly in touch with the most advanced perspective theory. Yet the problem of how to read the sharp convergence of the side walls of the room in the painting has challenged interpretation. Leo Steinberg (1973) has suggested that what is represented is not a rectangular room at all but, rather, with the back wall, three walls of a chapel of polygonal plan, which he then goes on to show would have a certain iconographical aptness. Taking liberty from Steinberg's observation that masterpieces may be explained by a range of intentions not necessarily consistent with each other, I would like to suggest another interpretation. The ideal viewing place as determined by Leonardo's own rules for perspective would be, in the setting of the refectory of Santa Maria delle Grazie, where the mural is located, not at a point that could be plausibly occupied by any of the monks for whom it was painted. Neither can we assume that the picture was painted for the sake of the photographic reproductions through which we commonly know it. Rather, the picture is located somewhat above eye level and in a relation to the observer such that were it to be looked at at all carefully would require either a lateral displacement of the gaze or a lateral displacement of the position of the observer, or some combination of these, which are the usual conditions that one produces when going to look at it today. In the course of so viewing it, I happened to notice that some tension between an oblique glance toward either group of apostles at either side—and, therefore, comparing them with the plane of the receding wall behind them, which placed them phenomenally within a room one felt oneself to be in, rather than on a plane one was looking at—and the memory of the immediately prior moments of viewing the laterally extended rest of the space of the room endowed the apostles with a voluminosity not achieved by any other painting of which I know, and only approached by a very distinguished few. That this was a temporal product was confirmed by repeated passages, either of gaze or of position, always with the result—most appropriate for the theme of the Eucharist, since it deals with the question of real presence—of an overwhelming impression of the physical presence of the figures which so strong that it overcame the countering, antiillusive effects of the deplorable condition of the painting's surface.

Another case is that of Rembrandt's *Syndics of the Cloth Guild* (see Figure 4.2). If we sit on the bench in front of it in the Rijksmuseum in Amsterdam, there is again the question of eye levels, which cannot be resolved, since we do not know its original hanging conditions. More examinable is the question of the represented depth of the painting. Almost anybody's first notion is that it is a predominantly lateral picture, with the figures arranged more or less side by side, in a manner that is not too dissimilar to Leonardo's *Last Supper* and the way it appears on the lid of Dutch Masters cigars (which is also the way Larry Rivers painted it). Subsequent to this, one gradually gets to see that the picture is deeper than it is broad. The gradual unfolding of the depth dimension endows the figures and their gestures with unusual presence, intimacy, and warmth, so that the glances of them to the observer, itself a fairly attainable device, establishes a kind of mutuality of human awareness and sympathy, for which the painting is noted. One observes further that the table at the right, at first seen as predominantly lateral to the picture plane, recedes sharply in depth, that one's glances to each of the people stationed about the table follow sharply different and yet hard-to-resolve vectors in space, and that the front edge of the table, instead of descending to the same eye level as the receding edge, *rises* to the right in defiance of any law of perspective. Somehow, these visual experiences are related: that the clues to depth are only gradually realized, that they have an expressive effect, that the expressive effect is more effective than virtually any paintings where the normative scheme is "correctly" followed, and that the scheme is indeed violated. It suggests that Rembrandt's intentions, however these are to be described, were such as could not be satisfied by the clear projective scheme, which is thought to be the bearer of veridicality.

Figure 4.2 Rembrandt Van Rijn's *Syndics of the Cloth Guild* (Amsterdam, Rijksmuseum).

The differentiation of vectors, as I have expressed it, seems to me an important clue to both the process and content of seeing, since it makes intriguing contacts with some of the material of scientific investigation of the dynamics of seeing. These, for the moment, I can only hope to place *suggestively* alongside the issues raised by paintings, since fundamentally, we switch over at this point from an examination purely of seeing to an examination of the dynamic nature of *mental processes in general*, of which seeing is a feature, and that is a task which lies beyond the scope of this chapter.

The study of eye movements is just such an instance where dynamic factors of some sort are at work. Noton and Stark (1971) have analyzed eye movements to show that the sequence of fixations plays a part in recognition of two-dimensional figures and that in some significant measure, the "scan path," or repeated pattern of fixations, is particular to a given individual in viewing a given pattern. This means that there is neither a rule-governed sequence given by the display nor a repeated habit on the part of the individual for scanning any pattern whatever. Further, since it takes time to scan, whether to learn, to recognize, or (which is least surprising) to disconfirm a target image, the pattern of activity during that time must be constitutive of the particular mental act which gives definition to that particular visual experience. We might ask, Just what is it which is going on during that time? Here, the question of language is an embarrassment because the usual testable means that are languagelike, either by indicating a match in the case of a nonrepresentational configuration or naming it if it is representational, fail to resolve the nuances of approximate definition in the critical time before or during which a new visual phenomenon is given definiteness. The definiteness—by naming, by metaphor, or by description—the moment it takes place may itself guide the content of the perception. This distinction is important, because it involves the coming-to-understand process on which all visual conventions are based and, in particular, the artist's and the art student's grasp of how such metaphors, or, as Gombrich would have it, "relational models" (1960), are meant. How we move from the state of not knowing a thing to knowing, the elusive event that Clark (1960) refers to in relation to seeing Velasquez's *Maids of Honor*—now the brushstroke, now the illusion, but never the transition from one to another—is an important and difficult-to-portray key to our understanding of vision, and, indeed, all mental acts. James (1890) in this connection raised the question of *transitive*, as distinguished from *substantive*, parts of consciousness, and this is the subject of a long analysis by Gurwitsch (1964), who concludes that the development of determinability within the thematic field (that is, of consciousness) proceeds according to a principle of unity by relevance according to *sense and meaning*. Since sense and meaning will vary according to individuals and their histories, as well as to the conditions of presentation, I am suggesting that the temporal processes of the scan path involve a probabilistic testing of meanings for the individual which are either confirmed, disconfirmed, or nuanced in previously undefined ranges of reference.

The studies of the contribution of finer movements of the eye, such as the fixation experiments of Pritchard, Heron, and Hebb (1960) indicate that dynamics are built into the system here as well. Their studies showed that when images were fixated onto specific cells of the retina, so that the small, rapid, habitual tremors of the eye at orders of 100 (plus or minus) per second and very fine amplitudes were stilled, intelligibility broke down either completely or to be unstably succeeded by partial and usually more stereotyped approximations of image characteristics. This finding suggests not only that it is the variation of energy pattern that makes perception possible but, also, that seeing proceeds from a rapid testing and reproposing of—what for lack of a better term I would call *mental fixes*—visual content.

One other area of research into visual dynamics deserves mention, and that is the analyses by Hubel and Wiesel (1962) of relations between receptor fields and hypercomplex cells of the visual cortex. These data suggest that perceptual processing selects for lines and contours of certain order of size, of certain orientation, and in certain ranges of rate and direction of movement along with position in the retinal field. Such findings nullify the utility of explaining the eye as a camera, since the aforementioned characteristics are not those typically distilled in a camera or picturelike operation, particularly the element of motion.

Physical motion along with geometrical positioning in space are only two of the possible characteristics of vision that are variable in time in ways which are recognized by the artist but not always by the scientist. I return to the question of vector, or the path of the eye through space. By this, I mean not the literal eye movement, in either the sense of the saccadic leap or the small involuntary tremor, but, rather, the sense of looking, or perhaps comparing, *from here to there* as a content of seeing in space that changes the sense and meaning of the other contents. Baroque art, as I have already indicated in its exemplification by Rembrandt, expanded greatly the relative weighting of how the spaciousness of space, as against the enumeration of its contents, was apprehended. Seeing something as "seen toward" or "seen past" or "seen through" or "seen at" mark somewhat objectifiable differentiations of spatialization, which change the apprehended contents of the space itself. The whole process of learning to draw and paint from direct experience involves finding uncontemplated and, often, incompletely understood metaphors for such contents. This is what was meant by one contemporary critic of Turner saying that he painted "pictures of nothing and very like." Turner's radicalism consisted equally in finding new modes of handling painting materials, most evident in his late watercolors, and in thereby making available new modalities of what I have termed *mental fixes*, visual metaphors that could direct and sustain attention and delectation to new qualities of experience.

The shift (mainly in the nineteenth century) of attention from the *items* of experience to the *qualities* of experience marks an important stage both in cultural history and the history of vision. As long as society shared common values and a collective estimate of reality, experiencing was thought to have the same content for everyone. This is nowhere more manifest than in the late eighteenth-century doctrine of the universality of judgments of taste. The movement that we call the *Romantic Revolution* placed a premium on individual experience, particularly as it was differentiable from that which was held in common. The immediacy of any direct experience became valuable, because through it, the sentient individual was asserting personal reality and uniqueness as the source of all value. Public painting, whether historical, religious, moralizing, or sentimental, indicated, through the shared ability to read the meaning of the items depicted, the entire range of shared values and assumptions about reality. The world of sensibility, heralded by Baudelaire and so remarkably consummated after the turn of the century by Proust, was problematical precisely because it dealt with those qualities of experiencing that are in principle not intersubjectively shareable. It is through this schism that are generated all the gaps in the understanding of art between artist and public. On the one hand, the normative vision flourishes in the anecdotal "academic" art of the century, which asserts that all is well and all is well-understood, according to rational and cozy standards. On the other hand, there is the artist from Constable through Giacometti, who continually doubts himself and who feels his artistic language inadequate to express his private intimations of reality, who feels even while using conventions from the past that these are in need of continual revision and adjustment. Although artists are perceived by the misunderstanding public as eccentrically and even arrogantly inventing new styles, trying to startle or amaze, artists finds themselves more and more anxiously involved in the quest for veridicality.

The gap is characterized by the public's failing to get the intentional sense of the metaphors through which the new qualities of experience are being registered. Constable's *Water-Meadows Near Salisbury*, now in the Victoria and Albert Museum, was rejected from the Royal Academy exhibition of 1829, with one of the members of the committee calling it "a nasty green thing" (see Figure 4.3). There are several reasons for this. Not only did it lack an ennobling subject matter, which would qualify it as a serious painting, but also, it almost literally could not be

Figure 4.3   John Constable's *Water–Meadows near Salisbury* (London, Victoria and Albert Museum).

seen. We cannot appreciate that it was difficult to see because our visual culture has been formed by the shift in sensibility which it was itself involved in bringing about. There is no doubt, because there is plenty of evidence on this score, that the very greenness of the painting was painful to many viewers. Moreover, what is now the delight of the appreciative eye—the many subtle rhythms, intervals, and vectors through the space and across the surface; their mutual adjustments and relations, which give in every part of the canvas fresh anticipation and discoveries of the way space *feels*; the translocal and transtemporal characteristics, which give to the work its unique distillation of a sense of being in the world, even to this day—fall very far outside the capacities of the experimental psychologist to identify or test. That such qualities (although they might be "fixed" diversely by diverse individuals) authentically exist in the painting, that they are in vision and yet not in any way amenable to the requirements of a scientific treatment indicate something of the gap which exists between the actualities of vision and their grasp by experimental psychology, which was observed at the beginning of this chapter.

Earlier, I stated that the point at which a pictorial scheme proved unfit for a given experience was a critical one. It is possible to show this in a positive way, that is, the moment when a new pictorial modality is coming into being. This fortunately exists in a very clear form in that painting which most appropriately gives its name to the most radical of all modern art movements—Monet's *Impression–Sunrise* (of 1872) (see Figure 4.4). As perhaps nowhere else, we see here the distinctive feature that made of Impressionism something at first so problematical and then so delightful. Most people's estimate of *plein air* painting is that it is involved with catching the transient qualities of light and weather at a particular moment. While this is true enough, it is only one-third of the story. The basic quality of a work that unlike a preparatory sketch is *finished* out-of-doors rests on the fact that the outdoors, in principle, has no structure; it does not conform (even though Claude and Ruysdael and others have made it seem so) to any a priori schema of framing or focus or guiding of one's eye through the space or any particular strategy of part-to-whole relationships, which, in effect, would constitute a weighting of various competing qualities of experience—not only perspective, light, and focus but various more private qualities—of rhythmicity, relative multiplicity versus relative consolidation, opticality versus tactility, openness, weightedness, obviousness, ambiguity, and the like. All these have to be decided not by memory or appeal to working methods or past models but by direct comparison on the spot of the efficacy of the collective set of metaphors that make up the painting structure against the immediacy of the motif which constituted, at least in anticipation, the reason for the painting being painted

Figure 4.4   Claude Monet's *Impression–Sunrise* (Paris, Marmottan Museum).

at all. From this process emerges another quality: that it is not merely those moments of outward, meterological, and geographical time that are involved but those moments of mental time wherein takes place the dawning realization of the efficacy of those mere blobs of paint, which by the very objectification in those actual blobs *endows the world* with qualities of experienceability, there being for which no language hitherto, it had not been suspected of possessing. But a very few moments before it was completed, Monet's *Impression* was nothing but a greyish-pink smear. Only the last strokes, the impasto weight of the sun or the relative tonal contrasts of the two boats, or maybe even a few extra dashes on the foreground water, which made it lie down, or a couple of touches in the sky, which made it full and overarching, gave at one and the same time the full and shimmering plenitude of the space itself, with all its precisions of internal nuance, which could never be obtained by systematic analysis and construction.

Monet was not "only an eye" but a serious constructor, who entertained, during his lifetime, many and various modalities of description. This is seen in another painting of the same year, the *Luncheon in the Garden* (in the Louvre), of which Andrew Forge (1976) has so well observed that it makes of the space something of which every part seems to be looking at every other part (see Figure 4.5). This is a large work, almost 80 inches wide, and it was worked on over a long period of time. Here, we have a problem in seeing not altogether dissimilar to that posed in Pearlstein's paintings—that of various paths of the eye comparing and making subject matter out of different intervals and relations in space. Whereas Pearlstein maintains the strict continuity and completeness of all seen surfaces and edges as if they were fixated simultaneously, Monet's art consists of making a synthesis, entirely intuitive and empirical, between many competing states of mind, and it is only through this act of what appears to be will but is more like the discovery and affirmation of a complex intentionality, referring both to the experience and to the painting means, that the picture is established at all. Another way of saying this is that there are various themes (the word *theme* here going back to Gurwitsch's treatment of James's transitive states of consciousness). In principle, all such themes are what I have previously characterized as *polyreferential*. They refer not only to the objects at hand but also to an assumptive world—a world of reveries, reminiscence, and anticipation, a world of imaginative construction built of all the poems and legends one has ever read, all the symphonies one has listened to, all the delights of the table and the bed, all the awe of the drama and the church projected into the living moment—and, at the same time, refer to language itself and all the experiences of language—Rembrandt's glow, Courbet's weight, Titian's fleshiness, Veronese's voluptuousness, Corot's silver calm, the transcendental

Figure 4.5 Claude Monet's *Luncheon in the Garden* (Paris, Louvre).

vibrations of the stained glass of Gothic churches, and, of course, more. The themes are cast into the picture because they are findable there.

Nobody makes manifest this character of the picture more than Cézanne. We revere him; we are in awe of him; he is for us the *fons et origo* of all modernism, not simply because he invents a style of working or imposes certain requirements on the picture plane but, rather, because he is so through-and-through phenomenological, because he shows the world as so much the creation of individual consciousness. He is the climax of the romantic revolution and the founder of a new dispensation, a dispensation that instaurates language as the molder of reality and which casts in concrete and analyzable form, at the same time, the evidences of the nature of mind's working processes and the serious issues of modern metaphysical thought.

While it is convenient for the sake of discussion to analyze Cézanne's paintings in terms of form (that is, in this case, shape and location) and color, as it is indeed for the work of any artist, it is important to emphasize that such a circumscription of reference is an expedient of description and demonstration. What is called *form* is not, particularly for Cézanne, an end in itself. Rather, it is a way of pointing at feelings, of which they are the vehicle. How can this be demonstrated? Hardly at all, but that does not mean the issue is not there. Since Fry (1958), there has grown up a body of interpretation of aesthetic ends as complete in themselves without respect to emotion (and, through Fry, specifically focused on Cézanne). On logical grounds, such a separation is open to question, since we do not have a clear warrant for discriminating where reasoning or analysis of visual events leaves off and feeling takes over. It is even more questionable on neurophysiological grounds. I refer here to merely two lines of speculation—Pribram's (1969) work on the participation of associative areas of the brain in perceptual processes and MacKay's (1961) suggestion of an *arbiter function*, which pervades and qualifies all cortical activity. The notion of an arbiter function, a mechanism that guides and discriminates thematic choices of attention and interpretation, is very close to what in ordinary language we call *feeling*. For while when we speak of emotion, we may intend the gross, nameable forms of psychical experience, such as love, fear, rage, despair, our everyday continuity of feelings are much more nuanced and less amenable to such clear classification. The best method which has so far been found to objectify them is that which is exemplified in the literary technique of Proust. In his writing, feelings are shown to be transient states of multiply linked associations that *register*, and which *qualify*, the whole state of awareness of the individual at any given moment. While this definition may prove to be a little primitive, it suffices (at least for the moment) to indicate a quality that is implicit in all perceptions, as well as also to suggest *neural mechanism*, that is, the regulation of whole-brain functions by vertical linkages between the cortex and lower brain centers, and, hence, in the area ascribed to emotions, which is ingradient in all processes usually thought of as transcortical, and, therefore, analytical only.

For Cézanne, the processes of feeling cannot be divorced from the processes of analysis because there would be no basis for making those choices that are called, variously, *formal*, *design*, or *compositional* without recourse to such holistic states of affect that make seeing *thematic*, in exactly the way in which it is used by Gurwitsch, that is, of being specific by *sense and meaning*. A still life by Cézanne (Venturi 735) in the National Gallery in Washington, D.C., provides an example of the thematicity of the process of seeing that is rooted in feelings (see Figure 4.6). The usual view is that Cézanne distorted objects for the sake of design, and his dealer Vollard recounted that he placed coins under still life objects to tilt them from their normal positions. This, at first glance, appears to be what is happening here. The dish containing the fruit seems to have its rear right edge elevated above the plane of the table. I would have accepted the Vollard interpretation (which may be a vulgarization of something Vollard did not quite understand about Cézanne) as having been done to provoke a rhythmic linkage between the contours of the fruit and the dish. This would mean that Cézanne produced or invented the theme, antecedently, to painting the picture. The painter Charles Cajori pointed out to me, however, that if one looks at the right-hand third of the picture only, the dish does not appear elevated but rather gives the appearance of lying back into a space which is apprehended by the movement of one's gaze (what I have referred to as a *vector*) into the depth of the upper right-hand corner. When this vector is compared with the left-hand two thirds, the effect is strikingly similar to that which I related of Leonardo's *Last Supper*. The fruits become enhanced in volume: they bulge in the space, causing one's glance to twist and turn around the volumes and transforming scalar and vector relations into what in mathematics are treated as tensor or quaternion relations, that is, which cannot be accounted for by reference to the three common orthogonal axes. Space, in this sense, is no longer what "scientific" perspective pretends it to be, neutral and homogeneous with respect to near and far, in front of and behind, above and below, but rather filled with all sorts of motives, what Merleau-Ponty (1964) calls, "an oneiric universe of carnal essences." The formal themes are not simply rigged up to achieve a harmonious pattern but are rather the compounding and intersection of many emergent awarenesses of meanings that are registered in the course of seeing. The unfolding of the consequences of spatial relations in this more elaborated universe has more the character of the musical development of thematic material in time than of the snapshot. Against

Figure 4.6 Paul Cézanne's *Still Life* (Washington, D.C., National Gallery of Art).

this, the flattening fracturing of Cubist practice, which is supposed to derive from Cézanne, has the aspect of a series of overhasty judgments.

All the components of the picture conspire to reveal continually new and unique meanings in the flow of sensuous experience. It is typical of the late works of Cézanne as it is for all authentic works of art (consider as a model of the same our ability to discriminate one authentic musical performance of a notable work from another) that a small increment of physical change occasions great displacements of overall sense and meaning.

Small differences in location within the rectangle or variations in the weight of stroke or color in relation to other strokes or colors give entirely different meanings not only to the forms they directly represent but to all the other forms in the visual field—and, more importantly, to the visual field itself and its dynamics, which constitute the largest class of meanings of the work. This is shown particularly by Cézanne's late methods of drawing and watercolor, which leave large areas of the page untouched. The openness of the page indicates a space, a field already charged with meaning although not filled with items or specifications—like the field of consciousness, filled with themes and with an implicit structure of mutual relevancies that is always changing potential into new awarenesses. What is true of these paintings must also be true of vision itself, but in a larger and more labile sense.

The juxtaposition, in the fall of 1977, of two great Cézanne landscapes at the Museum of Modern Art in New York brought this fact into sharp relief. *Mont Sainte-Victoire* (1902–6, Venturi 799) (from a private collection in Switzerland) and *Mont Sainte-Victoire Seen from Les Lauves* (1902–6, Venturi 798) (from the George W. Elkins Collection of the Philadelphia Museum of Art) are but very slightly different in size and proportion and show the same scene from essentially the same position. (See Figures 4.7 and 4.8.) Many of the objects depicted— houses, roads, masses of foliage, masses of the mountain, and so forth—occupy approximately the same location in each canvas. Yet, when any of these are compared, the *felt effects* of movement and emphasis of how the perceiving body finds itself in space as a copresence of the things perceived is altogether different. Even the meanings of the paint as designating modalities of transforming experiences into a conventional language are completely diverse from one painting to another. As one continues to look, one is enveloped, not in design or aesthetics but in the plenitude of an assumptive world coming into concrete awareness and specification. Rather than invent abstraction (which is merely the lame evasion of those who have not yet learned to see the lability, the plasticity, of space itself), Cézanne at every point thrusts toward a deeper veridicality. While both paintings are clearly

Figure 4.7 Paul Cézanne's *Mont Sainte-Victoire* (private collection).

Figure 4.8 Paul Cézanne's *Mont Sainte-Victoire Seen from Les Lauves* (Philadelphia Museum of Art, from the George W. Elkins Collection).

and identifiably in the late Cézanne "style," the style itself in its depth consequences is made over anew at each moment. "The landscape," he said, "thinks itself in me; I am its consciousness."

From this we may ask, Where is the picture that is the model of how we see? and What is its style? The answer would be: no place and any style. For that which takes place through which we take the world to be what it appears to be is nothing other than (paraphrasing Sherrington 1941) the contrast of transient electrical potentials on the occasion of coming to believe that something is the case.

REFERENCES

Clark, K. *Looking at Pictures*. New York: Holt, Rinehart and Winston, 1960.

Eccles, J., ed. *Brain and Consciousness*. New York and Berlin: Springer, 1966.

Finkelstein, L. "Gotham News." In *The Avant Garde*. New York: *Art News Annual* 34 (1968): 114–23.

Forge, A. *Claude Monet*. New York: Acquavella Gallery, 1976.

Fry, R. *Vision and Design*. New York: New American Library and Meridian, 1958.

Gombrich, E. H. *Art and Illusion*. New York: Pantheon Books, 1960.

Gurwitsch, A. *The Field of Consciousness*. Pittsburgh: Duquesne University Press, 1964

Hubel, D. H., and Wiesel, T. N. "Receptive Fields, Binocular Interactions, and Functional Architecture in the Cat's Visual Cortex." *Journal of Physiology* 160 (1962): 100–54.

James, W. *The Principles of Psychology*. New York: Henry Holt, 1890/New York: Dover Publications, 1950.

MacKay, D. M. "Interactive Processes in Visual Perception." In *Sensory Communication*, edited by W. A. Rosenblith. Cambridge, Mass.: MIT Press, 1961.

Merleau-Ponty, M. "Eye and Mind." In *The Primacy of Perception and Other Essays*, edited by J. M. Edie, pt. 2, chap. 5, pp. 159–90. Evanston, Ill.: Northwestern University Press, 1964.

Noton, D., and Stark, L. "Eye Movements and Visual Perception." *Scientific American* (June 1971): 34–43.

Pribram, K. "The Neurophysiology of Remembering." *Scientific American* (January 1969): 73–86.

Pritchard, R. M.; Heron, W.; and Hebb, D. O. "Visual Perception Approached by the Method of Stabilized Images." *Canadian Journal of Psychology* 14 (1960): 67–77.

Sherrington, C. S. *Man and His Nature*. New York: Macmillan, 1941.

Steinberg, L. "Leonardo's Last Supper," *Art Quarterly* 36 (1973).

Chapter Five

Perceiving the Layout of
Space in Pictures:
A Perspectve Theory
Based upon Leonardo da Vinci

Ralph Norman Haber

A three-dimensional scene is normally perceived as three dimensional. It does not look like a painting. It has a three-dimensional reality.

A representational picture of a photograph has two realities. It has the two-dimensional reality of a flat picture surface, set in a frame, attached to a wall. It also has the three-dimensional reality of a scene in depth: we recognize all the objects and know their respective locations in space, that is, we perceive an accurate layout of space in a representational picture.

Probably, the most important device that gives pictures three-dimensional reality is perspective. According to perspective theory, which accounts for our perception of the layout of space in pictures, we perceive the three-dimensional reality correctly because the information in the light reflected from a properly painted picture to the eye (that is, a one-eyed, motionless, correctly placed observer) is the same as from the scene that the picture represents.

By the late fifteenth century, a number of treatises had been published designed to train painters in the use of perspective, for example those by Dürer (Panofsky 1948) and by Alberti (Grayson 1972), and, most important of all, the *Notebooks of Leonardo da Vinci* (Richter 1970). Each of them describe rules for producing patterns on canvas that will project the same pattern of light to the eye as will the scene being portrayed.

The rules are based upon what we now know as geometrical optics. When painting a landscape while viewing a scene, the artist choses a station point, which is the position of his eye as it receives light reflected from the surfaces in the scene. Leonardo recommended that, initially, the artist use a plate of glass on which to sketch instead of a canvas. If the glass is placed between the eye and the scene so that the artist sees the scene through the glass, then, with head held still, the artist can sketch the scene on the glass so that each line on the glass corresponds exactly to a visual edge in the scene. In this way, the artist can create on the glass a reproduction of all of the patterns in the light— discontinuities in luminance and wavelength—that reach the eye and are focused on the retina. In theory, then, by careful drawing and application of pigment on the glass, the pattern of light reflected from the scene to the eye and the pattern of light reflected from the painting of the scene to the eye will be identical.

The fifteenth-century treatises were procedures or rules to teach apprentice painters to make such paintings. Leonardo never claimed that this was how a painter should paint a picture. Once an apprentice mastered the rules for making pictures look exactly like scenes, then he could learn how to create art through controlled variations and viola-tions of these rules. But before considering the violations, I will discuss the rules more carefully.

Leonardo's rules have three critical limitations. The pattern of light reflected to the eye from a scene will match that reflected from a properly painted picture of that scene only if the observer uses one eye (the other eye, because it is in a different place in the observer's head, will receive a slightly different pattern of light) if the observer stands still, and if the observer stands with an eye in exactly the same place in space that was occupied by the painter's eye when the painter made the sketch on the glass. Thus, the rules work only for a one-eyed, motion-less, and properly placed observer.

The perspective theory argues that at least for this, restricted case, the identity of information coming from a scene and from a picture of that scene means that observers can perceive the proper layout of space in pictures by treating the picture of a scene as if it is the scene itself. Nothing extra has to be added.

As far as I can determine, the perspective theory is the only theory ever developed to account for how we perceive the layout of space in pictures. The framework of the theory is the practical application of the geometrical optics of perspective originally proposed by Euclid (circa 300 B.C.) and worked out in detail by Leonardo and his contemporaries nearly two millennia later. In spite of the stature of its founders, it is nearly universally scoffed at. Its most important modern proponent has been Gibson (1951, 1972), although a number of others have embraced it in part or totally.

Perspective theory suggests that whatever information comes to the eye from a scene will also come from a properly painted picture of that scene viewed by a properly placed observer, but the theory does not describe how we perceive scenes. The rules of perspective worked out by the Renaissance painters may well be their invention and not an inherent property of perceivers. Discussion of the rules will be used here as a device to demonstrate my thesis: the similarity between the perception of scenes and the perception of pictures.

My purpose here is to resurrect the perspective theory. I will first enlarge upon it, taking advantage of some modern developments in theory and in research. I will use these to re-examine the objections that have traditionally been raised against the theory.

TRADITIONAL OBJECTIONS TO PERSPECTIVE THEORY OF PICTURE PERCEPTION

Two basic kinds of objections to the perspective theory have been raised, one stemming from the limitation on the observer and the other from limitations on the painter. In brief, no useful theory can demand that we perceivers be one-eyed, motionless, and properly placed observers. We never view pictures this way. What about the other eye? What reality does it see? What about the fact that both eyes can move? What about the fact that we rarely stand in the proper location? Even once these objections concerning the perceiver are resolved, there remain difficulties with the painter. First, even a painter who slavishly follows the rules cannot literally match luminance and color values in representing of the scene. Second, in fact, most painters do not follow Leonardo's rules, yet their layout of space does not appear distorted. Thus, the rules of perspective do not appear to be necessary to account for our accurate perception of the layout of space in pictures. I will consider each of these objections below.

The Station Point Objection

According to geometrical optics, in order to perceive the proper layout of space, the observer must view the picture from where the painter stood. Otherwise, the perceiver will have insufficient or distorted information to map out space accurately. But rarely do we stand in the same place. The correct station point is only one of an infinite number of possible places from which observers can view a picture. In practice, therefore, observers virtually never get the station point perspective of a picture, and if they do, it is only by chance. In this sense, we always have the wrong perspective information coming to the eye. Normally, this is considered the most overwhelming objection to the perspective theory, and most theorists do not go further.

The Nonrepresentational Objection

The perspective theory accounts specifically for the perception of pictures that are constructed in accordance with Leonardo's rules. It also applies to all photographs taken under normal circumstances with an approximately 50-millimeter lens. However, the theory is not designed to account for what probably represents the majority of pictures available for human perception: those pictures that do not meet Leonardo's rules or follow the requisite photographic procedures. Consequently, the objection goes, a theory that fails to account for the majority of viewing experience has little value in explaining human perception.

The Outline and Cartoon Picture Objections

Many pictures are easily and correctly seen in depth even when drawn only in outline form or as cartoons or minimal sketches. Three-dimensional information is minimally provided, yet they are easily seen in three dimensions. It is hard to explain how perspective alone can produce a three-dimensional perception in such pictures.

The Insufficiency of Leonardo's Rules Objection

Even properly constructed representations of pictures or photographs do not capture all of perspective. As Hochberg has shown (Chapter 2 in this volume), the range of contrasts obtainable from pigments in a picture can rarely be more than about 30 to one, whereas with spectral highlights in a real scene, contrast ranges may be up as high as one million to one. Further, the colors are not necessarily rendered accurately—even perspective itself is often reproduced inaccurately. In fact, it has been known for several millennia that natural perspective does not look natural and that perceivers see as more real some distortions in perspective. For example, Leonardo's notebooks contain many procedures for teaching artists how to cheat. The cheating is designed to make pictures "look" more like the scenes they portray, but in most cases, this is accomplished by reducing rather than increasing the identity of the pattern of light being reflected from scene and from picture.

Each of these objections might be considered seriously damaging to a theory based upon perspective. Taken together, they usually relegate the theory to ridicule. As I will now demonstrate, each of the objections is answerable. All that is needed is a new approach to the theory—one based on recent research on perceptual development, perceptual learning, perceptual coding, and perceptual compensation. I will consider these four topics in turn.

PICTURE PERCEPTION AND PERCEPTUAL DEVELOPMENT

Children of all cultures have continuous experience from birth onward viewing real three-dimensional scenes. Children encounter innumerable scenes before they see and react to many pictures. Even when pictures are initially available, as in Western cultures, they usually are not given particular importance. There is no need for children to perceive the three dimensions correctly in a picture or on a TV screen, and they receive neither feedback nor training to do so. The moral of this is that all children have extensive three-dimensional viewing experience before they have to deal systematically with pictures. We do not yet know all of the bases by which adults or children perceive the layout of three-dimensional space in scenes. Some of these are undoubtedly innate; some are probably maturational; and some are explicitly learned. However we come to be able to perceive the layout of space in scenes, we accomplish it before pictures represent an important part of viewing experience.

The most reasonable developmental hypothesis about picture perception would presume that it is based upon scene perception, that is, from the time children can perceive the layout of space in scenes, they presumably use the same processes to do so in representational pictures. Thus, children attribute to pictures the same three-dimensional information, that is, the perspective information in pictures, as if it came from real scenes.

Research evidence suggests that children are slow to develop the two-dimensional reality from pictures. Yonas and Hagen (1973) and Hagen (1976) have shown experimentally that when children are presented with pictures, they seem to have trouble dealing with the two-dimensional realities from them. Particularly, children younger than five or six are unable to adjust or compensate for the distortion introduced when viewing a picture from an oblique angle, an adjustment Hagen (1976) has shown depends upon having available the two-dimensional information from the picture.

Young children have no trouble recognizing familiar objects in pictures, and as Hochberg and Brooks (1962) have shown, an eighteen-month-old can do this without any prior experience of any kind with pictures. It is not known, however, to what extent young children confound pictures with scenes. Do young children think a picture of a scene is really the scene itself, as if it is a window opening out into space? Developmentally, this seems a possibility for very young children.

I recognize that some theorists will treat this developmental hypothesis as putting the cart before the horse. Psychology has too long assumed that because pictures have one less dimension than do scenes that they are that much easier to perceive. Researchers are finding large developmental changes in different aspects of picture perception well into the school years but relatively few further changes in scene perception at these late ages. Developmentally, it is time that we recognized that scene perception precedes picture perception by several years at least, and even thereafter, the time spent looking at scenes accounts for many thousands of hours more than that spent looking at pictures. It seems most reasonable therefore that children approach pictures initially as if they were scenes and that only secondarily do they develop ways of perceiving both of the realities in pictures.

PICTURE PERCEPTION AND PERCEPTUAL LEARNING

One of the traditional objections to a perspective theory is that it will not account for the perception of the layout of space in outline drawings, sketches, cartoons, and caricatures or for pictures in which the perspective information is incompletely rendered. This objection actually constitutes a problem for any theory of picture perception to answer. I will describe several aspects of an answer, aspects that are compatible with the type of perspective theory presented here.

One part of the answer is that we may be able to perceive the layout of space without needing all of the perspective information that Leonardo's rules would provide.

Hochberg (1972, 1978) has proposed the notion of canonical form to account for the easy recognition of objects from outline drawings, sketches, and cartoons. Thus, recognition does not depend upon the full articulation of all of the features and properties of an object but can occur just as easily, or perhaps even more easily, if the object's essential characteristics or distinctive features—that is, its canonical form—are provided.

I suggest an extension of this concept to include canonical depth. There are perspective "features" that can define all the possible three-dimensional relationships in a picture without requiring a full articulation of all perspectives and other depth information. Perhaps, the indication of a vanishing point will be the single most important canonical depth feature. As far as I know, perspective features for depth have never been investigated. If they do exist, these canonical depth features would permit the correct perception of the layout of space from sketches, outline drawings, cartoons, and other incomplete figures.

The presence of canonical depth features may also account for why some two-dimensional drawings and sketches create visual size and orientation illusions. If a few depth features are present, enough to register the three-dimensionality but insufficient in number to cast the whole drawing into depth, then the two-dimensional features in the drawing could be misperceived. This is a restatement of Gregory's inappropriate constancy scaling theory (1966, 1970) and is consistent with the concepts Gregory presents in Chapter 12 of this volume.

The existence of canonical form and canonical depth features does not tell us how perceivers come to be able to use them. Thus, not only do we need research on what these features are but we need to know how perceivers develop the ability to extract and generalize from them. This may involve a process of perceptual learning, or it may turn out that our perceptual systems can extract such features without prior practice and experience with them.

Canonical depth features can be considered a kind of convention or symbolization in pictures that observers use to properly perceive the layout of space. While these kinds of features have not been described before as conventions, a number of others have been.

One of the most important (yet usually overlooked) conventions is the use of lines to represent edges or boundaries in space. Objects in scenes are not surrounded by lines; yet we have no trouble representing and perceiving objects in drawings simply by outlining their boundaries. Kennedy (1974) has argued that this convention is not learned, and certainly the data of Hochberg and Brooks (1962), mentioned before, support him. While it has not been demonstrated, I think it quite likely that the information coming to the eye from the edges of objects in a scene and the lines bounding objects in a drawing are both coded by the visual system in the same way before that information even reaches the cortex.

One way to demonstrate this might be to look at the spatial frequencies represented at the eye from luminance and spectral discontinuities and compare those to the spatial frequencies presented by an outline drawing of the same scene.

A second potentially unlearned convention has been demonstrated in the work of Benson and Yonas (1973). They showed that even young children assume that the source of illumination in a picture comes from the top. Since illumination defines shadows in relation to objects and therefore helps to locate those objects in space, this conventional assumption is an important way of specifying the layout of space.

Other conventions are clearly learned through interaction with pictures. Movement is one of the most important of these conventions, since pictures themselves are static. Movement can be indicated by multiple representations of legs, by a smear drawn behind the object indicating speed, and by blurring edges, to name just a few conventions. Friedman and Stevenson (1975) report some evidence that movement conventions are acquired during preschool and early primary school ages. Examples of other conventions are drawing stars above someone's head in a cartoon to mean the person is "seeing stars" or using big print in a cartoon balloon to mean the speaker is talking in a loud voice. One of the finest analyses of conventions in caricature was done by Goldman and Hagen (in press).

Substantial developmental sequences should be found for those conventions that undergo learning and very little change for those that do not. There also should be cultural differences for many of the learned conventions; in addition, there probably would be individual differences within an age and culture depending upon the amount of experience with pictorial conventions.

Friedman and Stevenson (in press) have provided a detailed, historical, and developmental analysis of the different conventions used to represent movement in pictures. We badly need comparably good analyses for spatial conventions, as well as for affective conventions and for sequential conventions (as used in cartoon strips for example).

Before leaving the topic of conventions, I will discuss them in relation to pictorial art, as distinct from representational pictures. It is critical to recognize that the creative artist's intention is rarely to render a painting or photograph so that it perfectly reproduces the spatial layout of a comparable scene. As I noted earlier, Leonardo's rules were not intended for painters to follow but for painters to know so they could knowledgeably and effectively break them.

An analog to this exists in the creative use of language. One way to define a literary metaphor is as a violation of co-occurrence restrictions imposed by the rules of semantics or syntax. For example, many nouns and verbs in English can be classified as animate or inanimate. English has a rule requiring that an animate noun be used with an animate verb and an inanimate noun with an inanimate verb (Katz and Fodor 1963). Consequently, the juxtaposition of "the clouds cried" or "the rocks laughed," in which inanimate nouns occur with animate verbs, are violations that create a metaphor. One detailed analysis of this kind has been reported by Kypriotaki (1972). Painters, in effect, can use the same technique in creative pictures: the violation of some of Leonardo's rules of perspective may be what makes pictures into art. Cubism, for example, shows many violations of perspective. There is extensive use of parallel perspective, so that lines do not converge to vanishing points. Many objects are portrayed as transparent, so that interposition among objects does not occur, and we have difficulty telling what is in front of what. We can even see the backs of objects. Front and back ambiguity is further enhanced by inconsistent station points in constructing the picture so that we can see around objects. These are all examples of visual metaphors resulting from the controlled violation of the rules of perspective. The critical point is that violations of perspective work as metaphor, and therefore as art, only if both the painter and the observer know the rules and know how to apply them.

Hochberg (see Chapter 2 of this volume) provides a different example of violation—not of principles of perspective but of principles of optics. Because of both the optics and the neural coding networks in the human visual system, each momentary glance at either a scene or a picture will produce a clear percept only for the area straight ahead, with the surrounding parts of the scene or picture being seen as fuzzy and indistinct. Hochberg goes on to show that to perceive an entire scene or picture as a clear panorama requires the observer to integrate information from successive glances as eyes explore the scene or picture. Some painters, however, have capitalized on the tunnellike quality of simple glances. One example Hochberg mentions is found in some of Rembrandt's portraits, in which there is only one area of the picture that is rendered clearly and brightly, with all of the surround in shadow or drawn indistinctly. In this way, Rembrant mimics the optics and neural coding of single glances and defeats integration.

A reverse example comes from many Impressionist paintings, in which the entire scene is depicted indistinctly, as if all of it is being seen out of the corner of your eye. No matter where you look, it is fuzzy. This is again a creative way of coping with a basic perceptual processing mechanism.

CODING OF EDGES: LUMINANCE AND WAVELENGTH

Older versions of perspective theories of picture perception (for example, Gibson 1951) did not recognize that a geometrical optics analysis of perspective would necessarily display some inadequacies. If a painter is concerned only about the boundaries of surfaces and objects in the scene, Leonardo's procedures will enable him or her to reproduce lines on the glass that reflect the same pattern of light to the stationary eye in the proper position as will the boundary edges in the scene. However, in practice, the luminance levels and the wavelength levels will not match. In a picture made up of pigments applied to canvas, or black marks on paper, or the image on a photographic print, no matter what the source of illumination, the ratio of the highest reflectance to the lowest reflectance on the surface will rarely exceed 30 to one and virtually never 50 to one. This is a limitation imposed by the nature of flat reflecting surfaces.

In a natural scene, however, spectral reflectances, the light re-flected from water, mirrors, metal, or narrow edges of almost any object, may be hundreds, thousands, or even millions of times more intense than the light coming from the same source reflected from other surfaces in the corresponding picture. One of the important functions of these spectral reflectances is to define changes in orientation, such as folds in a curtain or a gown or the presence of a knife edge catching the sun. Thus, a painter with pigments on a palette cannot hope to duplicate in a straightforward manner this range of natural reflectances in a picture. Nor can the painter match the contrasts of hues found in a real scene. The brightness of the hues will be muted, and the range of saturation of the colors available on the canvas will be restricted.

The perceptual impact of these contrast restrictions is to make pictures look flatter than the scenes they represent. Natural scenes have a large gradient of saturation and of brightness—surfaces in the foreground appear brighter and have more saturated colors, whereas distant objects appear less bright and less saturated. When this gradient is restricted, as in a picture, then the difference in distance between objects in the near ground and farground will be lessened. Photographs are even more restricted than paintings in each of these respects.

Hochberg (1978; see also Chapter 2 of this volume) describes a number of different solutions worked out by painters to solve this problem, that is, to put the depth back into their pictures. The major techniques involve contrast induction, use of shadows, pairing of complementary colors on adjacent parts of the picture surface, and the use of additive rather than subtractive mixtures of colors. Ratliff (1972) also describes a set of devices based upon lateral inhibitory processes between adjacent areas, which produce larger apparent contrasts than are present on the canvas.

Thus, for the painter to produce a picture that reflects the same pattern of light to the eye as does the scene it represents, he or she has to distort the local color and brightness relationships. In other words, to paint a picture that looks like a scene requires some cheating on the laws of perspective. The apprenticeship of a painter is in part learning how to cheat and get away with it. Failure to cheat in a painting or in a photograph means that the resulting picture will look flatter because the scene depth would be compressed, just as it should according to the theory.

PERCEPTUAL COMPENSATION

Most of my remarks to this point have been designed to answer objections other than those stemming from station point violations.

Since the station point objection has been the one that has sunk the perspective theory over and over again throughout its history, any attempt to salvage the theory hinges on an ability to explain why violating the correct station point does not seem to matter. My explanation rests on the mechanisms of perceptual compensation. The concept of compensation is based on the notion that the particular pattern of light on the retina at any one moment in time is never perceived as such. Rather, it serves only as a source of information from which to construct a representation—a perception. It, in itself, is not a representation of space or anything else. Once this fact is recognized, it is not difficult to understand that the retinal pattern from a picture of a scene may differ from that of the scene itself and yet that both can contain the same information leading to the same perception.

I will briefly describe six different kinds of compensations that the visual system is capable of making so that our perceptions agree with reality of space.

Movement Compensation

When the pattern of light reflected from objects in space and imaged on the retina moves, we do not perceive movement in those objects if that retinal movement is caused by eye movements, head movements, or body movement. In some fashion, therefore, movement on the retina is canceled by information or knowledge that the movement was the result of the perceiver's motion and not of the object's motion in space. This compensation may be the result of feedback from the eye muscles, efferent information coming from the eye movement control systems, afferent information coming from the patterning of changes on the retina, or from combinations of all of these. Whatever the cause, however, the compensation clearly occurs. It is one of the most prominent examples where changes in the retinal image are not reflected in perceptual experience (see MacKay 1973 for a review of this process).

Direction Compensation

We know where straight ahead is regardless of the orientation of the eyes. The layout of space remains oriented in relation to our "Cylopean" eye irrespective of where our movable eyes are looking. This compensation probably works on principles similar to those for motion compensation, though the impact on perception is dramatically different (see Matin 1976 for a review).

Saccadic Blur Compensation

Scenes are perceived by the eye by means of continuous successive samplings, in which the eye makes brief discrete fixations separated by saccadic movements, which occur at tremendous velocities. But we do not see the blur of the retinal pattern during these eye movement velocities. Rather, what we perceive is a continuous stable scene irrespective of the successive samplings that our eye takes by brief fixations on it. Thus, while on the retina, the visual scene is broken up into small slices several times a second, separated by massive blur as the eye shifts position, none of which is reflected or registered in our perceptual experience (see Volkmann 1976 for a review).

Tunnel Vision Compensation

Optical factors produce a sharply focused image with high contrast only over the center of the retina. Further, neural coding is concentrated in this area as well, producing coding of fine detail, color, and contrast only in central vision. Thus, the visual system acts as if our eyes are really a telescopic lens. Yet, the appearance of typical scenes is not of clear centers with fuzzy surrounds but of a panoramic "wide-angle" construction of the world.

In order to construct the panorama, multiple eye movements are required over a scene, with a substantial overlap between a large number of fixations (Hochberg in press). The point is that the panorama itself does not resemble any one of the retinal images but is constructed from the sequence of them. This is yet another kind of compensation, in which perceived experience is not the same as any of the patterns of excitation on the retina.

Binocular Disparity Compensation

When we look at a scene, the two retinal images are not the same. If we saw our images, that is, if they were the basis of our perception, then we would continually have rivalry or suppression between them. Rather, however, we have a Cyclopean image. We construct a perception that uses the disparities from the two retinal images to create a third dimension. The Cyclopean image does not duplicate either retinal image alone but requires a comparison of the two of them. There, again, our perceptual experience does not correspond to what is on the retina, either of them.

Station Point Compensation

The station point compensation naturally follows on the list I have already given. This compensation is the transformations of the retinal images that occur as we move around pictures. These transformations are not perceived because we compensate for our orientation and our distance from the picture surface.

Two-dimensional information precisely defines for us our orientation in relation to the picture and to the wall and our distance from those surfaces. Information that what is in front of one's eyes is flat comes from the frame and the surface texture of the picture on the wall, as well as from motion perspective and binocular disparity. All of these provide powerful sources of information about what is flat and what is in depth.

Pirenne (1970) has proposed a station point compensation hypothesis, but because he did not see how similar this compensation mechanism is to the other kinds of compensations, he argued that station point compensation is learned on the basis of experience with viewing pictures. He would agree that young children would show poor compensation and that, therefore, pictures would have a distorted layout of space when viewed from the wrong station point. But Pirenne would attribute this to young children's lack of experience with pictures, whereas I feel it is due to their poor perception of the two-dimensional reality, which they need to determine the orientation of the picture surface. Specific experience with pictures is unnecessary for station point compensation to occur. What children need is more general experience in processing two- and three-dimensional information about the layout of space and of orientation.

CONCLUSION

Infants and very young children have substantial viewing experience of natural scenes. From some combination of built-in mechanisms, maturation, and learned reactions, they are able to perceive the layout of space from the pattern of light reflected from such scenes to their eyes. When they encounter a picture, they perceive its layout of space from the pattern of light reflected from the picture in the same way as if the light had come from a natural scene. Such perception will be undistorted if the picture is viewed from the proper station point and if the picture was completely and exclusively constructed upon Leonardo's rules of perspective. To the degree that the young viewer is at the wrong station point, the layout of space in a picture will be distorted, because at a young age, a child does not yet know how to compensate through use of information about the distance and orientation of the picture surface. Such distortion will be overcome as the two-dimensional realities of pictures is perceived and then used to compensate for the incorrect station point. To the degree that the picture is not based upon Leonardo's rules, then the application of the three-dimensional perceptual processes from which the child is generalizing will be ineffective, and distortion may occur. This distortion will be overcome as the child learns or somehow acquires the canonical depth features that minimally specify the correct layout of space, or as the child acquires the knowledge of the cultural conventions used in representing space in pictures. Of course, some residual distortion of the layout of space may remain if the picture maker intentionally or otherwise violated some of Leonardo's rules.

The preceding paragraph represents a brief statement of a perspective theory of picture perception that predicts when the layout of space perceived from picture will be accurate and when it will be distorted. The theory in this form is partially anchored in principles of geometrical optics and evidence from experimental psychology. The origins of this theory are found in the fifteenth-century teaching treatises on perspective, since those treatises, especially Leonardo's, implicitly rest on the correspondence between information in light reaching the eye from scenes and from pictures of scenes.

In trying to revitalize a perspective theory of picture perception, I am making explicit that perceiving the layout of space in two-dimensional display is harder, not easier, than in three-dimensional scenes. Pictures may have one less dimension, but they have one more reality with which to contend, and it is reality that has always been hard to perceive.

REFERENCES

Benson, C. W. and Yonas, A. "Development of Sensitivity to Static Pictorial Depth Information." *Perception and Psychophysics* 13 (1973): 361–66.

Friedman, S. L. and Stevenson, M. "Perception of Movement in Pictures." In *What Then Are Pictures?: The Psychology of Representational Art*, edited by M. A. Hagen. In press.

Gibson, J. J. "A Theory of Picture Perception." *Audio Visual Communications Review* 1 (1951): 1–23.

———. "The Information Available in Pictures." *Leonardo* 4 (1972): 27–35.

Goldman, M., and Hagen, M. A. "The Forms of Caricature: Physiognomy and Political Bias." *Studies in the Anthropology of Visual Communication* 5 (1978): 30–36.

Grayson, C. L. B. *Alberti: On Painting and on Sculpture*, translated from the Latin. London: Phaidon Press, 1972.

Gregory, R. L. Visual Illusions." In *New Horizons in Psychology*, edited by D. Foss. Baltimore: Penguin, 1966.

———. *The Intelligent Eye*. London: Weidenfeld and Nicholson, 1970.

Hagen, M. A. "Influence of Picture Surface and Stationpoint on the Ability to Compensate for Oblique View in Picture Perception." *Developmental Psychology* 12 (1976): 57–63.

Hochberg, J. "The Representation of Things and People." In *Art, Perception and Reality*, edited by E. H. Gombrich, J. Hochberg, and M. Black, pp. 47–95. Baltimore: Johns Hopkins University Press, 1972.

———. "Art and Perception." In *Perceptual Ecology Handbook of Perception*, edited by E. Carterette and H. Friedman, Vol. 10, Ch. 10. New York: Academic Press, 1978.

———. "Perception of Successive Views." *Science* (in press).

Hochberg, J., and Brooks, V. "Pictoral Recognition as an Unlearned Ability: A Study of One Child's Performance." *American Journal of Psychology* 75 (1962): 624–28.

Katz, J. J., and Fodor, J. A. "The Structure of a Semantic Theory." *Language* 39 (1963): 170–210.

Kennedy, J. M. *A Psychology of Picture Perception: Information and Images*. San Francisco: Jossey–Bass, 1974.

Kypriotaki, L. R. "There Came a Wind Like a Bugle: From Linguistic Analysis to Literary Criticism." Paper presented at the Southeastern Conference on Linguistics, April 1972, Athens, Georgia.

MacKay, D. M. "Visual Stability and Voluntary Eye Movements." In *Handbook of Sensory Physiology*, edited by R. Jung, vol. 7, pt. 3, pp. 307–31. Berlin: Springer-Verlag, 1973.

Matin, L. "Saccades and Extraretinal Signal for Visual Direction." in *Eye Movements and Psychological Processes*, edited by R. A. Monty and J. W. Sender, pp. 205–20. Hillsdale, N.J.: Lawrence Erlbaum, 1976.

Panofsky, E. *Albrecht Durer*. Vol. 1 Princeton, N.J.: Princeton University Press, 1948.

Pirenne, M. H. *Optics, Painting and Photography*. Cambridge: Cambridge University Press, 1970.

Ratliff, F. "Contour and Contrast." *Scientific American* 226 (1972): 91–101.

Richter, J. P. *The Notebooks of Leonardo da Vinci*. Vol. 1. New York: Dover Publications, 1970.

Volkmann, F. C. "Saccadic Suppression: A Brief Review." In *Eye Movements and Psychological Processes*, edited by R. A. Monty and J. W. Senders, pp. 73–84. Hillsdale, N.J.: Lawrence Elbaum, 1976.

Yonas, A., and Hagen, M. A. "Effects of Static and Kinetic Depth Information on the Perception of Size in Children and Adults." *Journal of Experimental Child Psychology* 15 (1973): 254–65.

Chapter Six

Attached and Cast Shadows

Albert Yonas

A painting is a great many things—a source of aesthetic satisfaction, a cultural artifact, a social statement, historical record, and an economic product. There are as many ways to think about a painting as there are intellectual disciplines. From the psychologist's perspective, a painting may be approached as a tool for understanding visual perception.

It is a paradox that pigments spread on a canvas can evoke in a viewer the experience of objects and scenes that are not present. This discovery must have amazed those who first scratched on cave walls and experienced new objects or shapes. Our understanding of the processes involved has progressed remarkably little since the monumental work of Leonardo da Vinci (Richter 1970). In the fifteenth century, Leonardo described the way in which light is structured by an environment; in so doing, he explored the techniques available to a painter for representing the layout of surfaces on a flat canvas. His work, both literary and artistic, implies that the visual system of the human is able to detect the information presented in a painting. The ultimate challenge for psychologists of perception is to discover the processes and mechanisms that respond to this information as though it were occurring in the real world. This challenge is primarily a problem for the future. My task is to describe information that can be frozen in a picture, to experimentally vary that information, and to assess the effects on the viewer's experience—perhaps by uncovering what skilled painters have known intuitively for a very long time.

Leonardo, in his "Six Books on Light and Shade" (Richter 1970, pp. 67–128), distinguished two types of shadows: the primary or attached shadow, which is inseparable from a body, and the derived or cast shadow. An attached shadow occurs when the shadow of an object is visible on that same object; it refers to the shading on an object due to the differences in the orientation of surfaces of the object relative to a light source. The cast shadow is disengaged from an object; it occurs when the shadow of one object is seen on another object. Cast shadows appear in the absence of light on an otherwise illuminated surface, created by an occluding object. Both types of shadows provide spatial information, but the attached shadow provides information about the shape or relief of a single object, while the cast shadow can show the spatial relationship between an object and other surfaces, particularly the ground.

ATTACHED SHADOWS

Variations in light intensity, the shading on an object, provide us with an important source of information about the three-dimensional shape of an object. As is the case for most processes in vision, our ability to recover shape from shading presents us with a problem. When an image is formed by an eye, a camera, or a realist painter, the intensity of the light at a point in the image is mainly determined by three properties of the corresponding point in the scene: the incident illumination, the surface reflectance, and the surface orientation. A central problem for the visual system is to extract information confounded in the image, that is, a single intensity value could be determined by an infinity of combinations of illumination, reflectance, and orientation.

Scientists in the area of computer-simulated vision such as Horn (1975) and Barrow and Tenenbaum (1978), have begun to design programs that recover from images the orientations and reflectances of surfaces by employing a set of simplifying assumptions. These assumptions may be instructive in explaining how the human visual system functions. By assuming that illumination comes from a single, specified direction, that the illumination does not vary in intensity, and that objects are uniform in reflectance, surface orientations can be recovered from light intensity. These assumptions, derived from research on human vision, allow for careful varying of reflectances of the pigments applied to a surface; as painters do, it is possible to specify the curvature of a surface, such as folds of cloth. A mural preserved in the ruins at Pompeii demonstrates that painters used shading to specify shape as early as the fourth century B.C.

The photograph in Figure 6.1 demonstrates that the visual system assumes that illumination is constant in intensity, comes from a particular direction, and that objects are constant in reflectance. This display was created by photographing a convex and a concave mold within a single surface, with the light positioned so that only attached shadows were created. Because no cast shadows are present in the

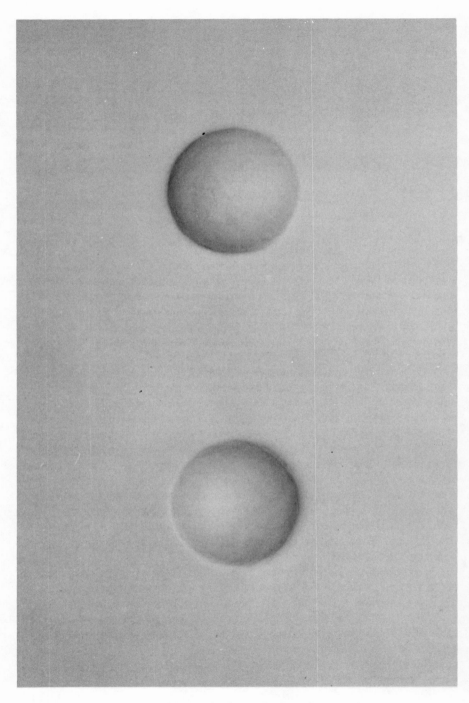

Figure 6.1 Photograph of a convexity and a concavity.

picture, the direction of the illumination is ambiguous, that is, the light could be coming from either the top or the bottom of the picture. When the picture is rotated 180 degrees, the two forms appear to reverse in relief. Apparently, the visual system assumes that the light source is at the top of the picture. Since light generally comes from above in a terrestrial environment, this is not an unreasonable assumption. In Leonardo's "The Practice of Painting," he gave specific advice on the permissible direction of illumination: "Above all, see that your figures are broadly lighted from above . . . for you will see that all the people you meet out in the street are lighted from above, and you must know that if you saw your most intimate friend with a light (on his face) from below you would find it difficult to recognize him" (Richter 1970, p. 278).

There is even reason to believe that this assumption is innate, at least in chickens. Hershberger (1970) raised chicks in a cage in which light always came from below. The chicks were trained to associate a real, convex bump with a food reward. During training, the bumps were carefully lighted so that there were no shadows at the top or bottom of the shapes. After training, the chicks were presented with photographs of forms like those in Figure 6.1. They consistently chose to peck at the form that depicted a convex bump, that is, given that the light was coming from above, they pecked at the form that was bright on top and dark on the lower side.

Benson and Yonas (1973) found a similar sensitivity in three-year-old children. The children first placed one hand inside a curtained box in which a convexity and a concavity were tactually available. They were told to point to the bump, and they were quickly and consistently able to do so. They then were presented repeatedly with a photograph of the shapes and asked to point to the bump. We hypothesized that if they assumed that light comes from above, they would point to the shape with the bright top. In fact, they did so on 86 percent of the trials. Eleven of the 15 children were nearly without error in their choices.

If three-year-olds are sensitive to shading and assume light comes from above, is the same sensitivity present in infants? We have some evidence to suggest that it is. Four-month-old infants were presented with a display containing a pair of actual convexities or concavities lighted from the side (Yonas, Cleaves, and Petersen 1978). They were allowed to look at the shapes for five 12-second periods. Over this time, they looked for a shorter period of time at the shapes, suggesting they became habituated to the display (this was indexed by an observer, looking at the infant's eyes through a small hole between the shapes). The shapes were then replaced by a photograph of the forms, one shape with a shadow on top and the other shape with a shadow on the bottom (see Figure 6.2). If the infants were habituated to a particular three-

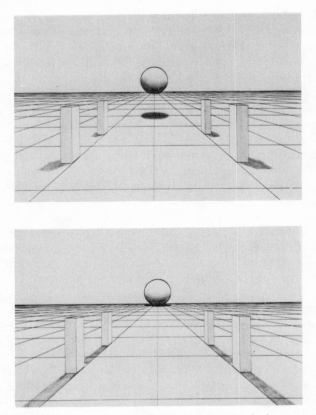

Figure 6.2 Drawings in which the location of the cast shadow is varied.

dimensional shape and recognized that shape in the photograph, we anticipated that they would then prefer to look at the novel shape. Generally, this did occur. (This result should be accepted with some caution, since an attempt at replication was unsuccessful when less habituation was obtained. The study should be repeated using a method that makes certain that the infant is habituated to the first display before the second display is presented.)

But what is it that tells the visual system where "above" is? What frames of reference can specify "above"? We investigated three sources of information for the direction of illumination, using Figure 6.1 as the display and testing children from three to eight years of age (Yonas, Kuskowski, and Sternfels in press). By changing the position of the child's head, rotating the display, and changing the location of the actual source of illumination, we manipulated the relevance of egocentric, environmental, and lighting-specified frames of reference. The rather surprising outcome of the study was that the most effective indicator of the direction of lighting was the orientation of the child's head and not the location of the light illuminating the photograph. (To experience this effect, rotate Figure 6.1 90 degrees, so that the shading is to the right and left sides of the circular forms, and turn your head. Most subjects report that the form that is lighter on the side near the top of the head appears more convex than the other form.) The light frame of reference was less effective than the orientation of the shading, relative to gravity. Nevertheless, we found that each of the three frames of reference can specify the direction of light when the other frames of reference are irrelevant.

Researchers in this area have clearly not exhausted the variables that may influence the interpretation of shading information for relief. Boring (1942) asserted that an entirely *imaginary* light source can also determine whether a form is seen as a dent or a bulge:

> Most psychologists know the photograph of the turret of the monitor *Lehigh,* dented after having been used as a target. The depth, given solely by light and shade, is reversed (dents become bulges), if the photograph is turned upside down or if the direction of the light is reversed in imagination from downward to upward. If both imagination and photograph are reversed together, the depth remains, of course, the same (p. 304).

While a preliminary study revealed that there are wide individual differences in the ability of viewers to reverse the direction of illumination in the imagination, it is clear that many viewers can do so. The cognitive processes involved in moving an imaginary light source over a real picture are a mystery to psychologists. In addition, psychologists have put too little effort into building theories of the complex, interrelated processes that detect direction and intensity of illumination and the orientations and the reflectances of surfaces. Land's (1977) recent work on color vision is an exciting approach to the problem of reflectance, and Gilchrist's (1977) finding that perceived lightness is dependent on perceived spatial arrangement suggests that a proper theory will have to deal simultaneously with all three properties—reflectance, orientation, and illumination.

CAST SHADOWS

Gibson (1950) presented a theoretical analysis of space perception that stressed the importance of the relation between the object and the textured surface of the ground. Gibson argued that a gradient of texture density can specify the slant of a surface, providing a continuum of distance in which the position of objects on that surface is fixed. He also asserted that the size of an object is given by the scale of the textured surface where the object rests on the background. This theory implies that the visual system "assumes" that an object is resting on, and not floating above, the background surface that it occludes. For a moving organism, the accretion and deletion of texture of the occluded surface can specify the relief of an object; however, in the frozen world of the picture, the only information that an object is not in contact with a surface is the character of the shadow cast by the object. Leonardo pointed out in his "Practical Methods of Light and Shade" that "to increase (the) relief of a picture you may place, between your figure and the solid object on which its shadow falls, a line of bright light dividing the figure from the object in shadow" (Richter 1970, p. 278). Trompe l'oeil painters in the nineteenth century, such as William Harnett, were very skillful at using a gap between the objects in the picture and the shadow cast by those objects to make the objects appear to float several inches in front of the surface of the canvas.

Yonas, Goldsmith, and Hallstrom (in press) explored the effects of varying the location of the shadow cast by an object. The displays in Figure 6.2 were presented to three-year-olds, five-year-olds, and adults. The subjects were asked to point to the sphere that was closer to them, higher off the ground, and larger. Half of the displays were drawn with posts casting shadows indicating that the source of illumination was above the sphere; half the displays were drawn without the posts. The presence of the posts had little effect on the results, which are presented in Figure 6.3. Age is presented along the horizontal axis, and percent of correct responses on the vertical axis. Although there was some improvement with age, the subjects generally chose the sphere with its shadow lower on the picture plane as farther off the ground and closer to them. For the youngest subjects, the relative distance of the spheres did not influence perceived size, although distance did function in this way for the older subjects.

In another experiment (Yonas, Goldsmith, and Hallstrom in press), children from three to five years of age were presented with a cardboard circle and an ellipse and trained to consistently point to the circle. They were then presented with the drawings shown in Figure 6.4 and asked to point to the circle. When presented with the drawing on the right, even the youngest children were quite consistent in responding to the ellipse with a shadow continuously connected to it as a circle resting horizontally on the floor. When presented with the drawing on the left, the children tended to see both forms as vertical ellipses.

These studies argue that cast shadows constitute an important source of information for determining the shapes and sizes of objects and for the layout of objects in space. Piaget and Inhelder (1967) have reported that it is not until the age of seven or eight that children can

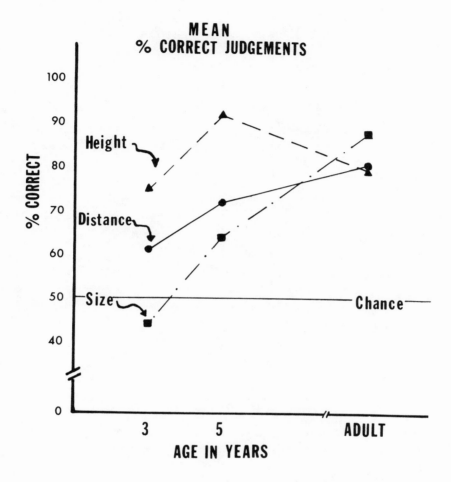

Figure 6.3 Percent of trials in which the subjects chose the sphere with a gap between the sphere and the cast shadow as higher off the ground, closer to them, and smaller.

predict the shape of the shadow cast by a disc placed in various orientations to a light source. While an intellectual understanding of shadow projections appears to be a rather late accomplishment, some sensitivity on a perceptual level to the information that cast shadows provides is apparently present by three years of age.

One may conclude, then, that a gap on the picture plane between

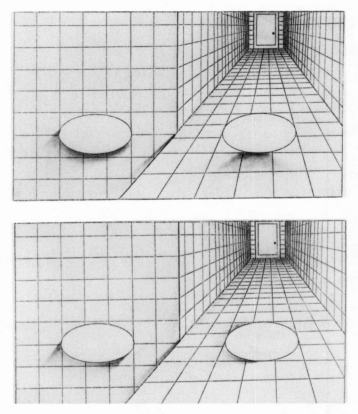

Figure 6.4 Drawings in which the shape of the cast shadow is varied.

an object and the shadow it casts informs the viewer that the object is not resting on the surface. Conversely, a cast shadow that is continuously connected to an object places that object on the surface. When we used drawings that specified that the source of illumination was directly above the object, the location of the shadow cast on the ground rather than the location of the object on the picture plane indicated the object's distance from the viewer (Yonas, Goldsmith, and Hallstrom in press). At present, one unanswered question concerns the sensitivity of the visual system to information for the location of the light source. If we had indicated that the light was behind or in front of the sphere in the drawings in Figure 6.2 would this have altered the perceived location of the sphere, as principles of geometry would require?

Just how finely tuned is the perceptual process that responds to cast shadows? Can the relation between an object and its cast shadow specify the shape of the surface on which the shadow is cast? If an object casts a shadow that is inconsistent with the shape of the object—

for example, if a sphere casts a rectangular shadow—is this immediately detected? Would a three-year-old notice the anomaly? Psychologists need to explore in a systematic fashion the sensitivity of the visual system to the incredibly complex and informative way in which light is structured by the surfaces of the world, and they must begin the difficult task of building a theory of the processes involved.

REFERENCES

Barrow, H. G. and Tenenbaum J. M. "Recovering Intrinsic Scene Characteristics from Images." In *Computer Vision Systems*, ed. A. Hanson and E. Riseman. New York: Academic Press, in press.

Benson, C., and Yonas, A. "Development of Sensitivity to Static Pictorial Depth Information." *Perception and Psychophysics* 13 (1973): 361–66.

Boring, E. G. *Sensation and Perception in the History of Experimental Psychology* New York: Appleton–Century–Crofts, 1942.

Gibson, J. J. *The Perception of the Visual World* Boston: Houghton-Mifflin, 1950.

Gilchrist, A. L. "Perceived Lightness Depends on Perceived Spatial Arrangement." *Science* 195 (1977): 185–87.

Hershberger, W. "Attached Shadow Orientation Perceived as Depth by Chickens Reared in an Environment Illuminated from Below." *Journal of Comparative and Physiological Psychology* 73 (1970): 407–11.

Horn, B. D. P. "Obtaining Shape from Shading Information." In *The Psychology of Computer Vision*, ed. P. H. Winston, Ch. 4, pp. 115–51. New York: McGraw-Hill, 1975.

Land, E. H. "The Retinex Theory of Color Vision." *Scientific American* 237 (1977): 108–28.

Piaget, J., and Inhelder, B. *The Child's Conception of Space*. New York: Norton, 1967.

Richter, J. P. *The Notebooks of Leonardo da Vinci*. New York: Dover, 1970.

Yonas, A., Cleaves, W. T., and Petersen, L., "Development of Sensitivity to Pictorial Depth." *Science* 200 (1978): 77–78.

Yonas, A.; Goldsmith, L. T.; and Hallstrom, J. L. "Development of Sensitivity to Information Provided by Cast Shadows in Pictures." In *Perception*. In press.

Yonas, A.; Kuskowski, M.; and Sternfels, S. *"Role of Frames of Reference in the Development of Responsiveness to Shading Information."* Unpublished paper, 1978.

Chapter Seven

Perspective and Its Role in the Evolution of Dutch Realism

Arthur K. Wheelock, Jr.

Realism is an all-pervading concept in Dutch art, one that lies at the very basis of seventeenth-century Dutch artistic practice and theory. If one were to ask a seventeenth-century Dutch painter what a painting should be, he would probably respond that it ought to appear naturalistic. Van Hoogstraten (1678), one of the few Dutch artists who wrote about his expectations for painting, defined the art of painting "as a science that represents all ideas or notions that the entire visible world can give, and deceives the eye with outlines and colors" (p. 24). He felt that a "completed painting is as a mirror of nature, where things that do not appear seem to appear, and which deceives in an allowably entertaining and praiseworthy manner" (p. 25). Indeed, Hoogstraten was a master of that uniquely Dutch art form, the perspective box, where this mode of artistic representation could be most fully achieved. Looking through a peephole in one of these boxes revealed a world so real in appearance that the interior limits of the box were totally negated by the illusion.

Hoogstraten's concept of realism is somewhat different than that which has been attributed to Dutch artists since the nineteenth century. Fromentin (1882), a great admirer of Dutch realism, wrote that Dutch art attempts to "imitate what is, to make what is imitated charming, to clearly express simple, lively, and true sensations. . . . It has for law, sincerity, for obligation, truth" (p. 135).

I have recently begun to see that such an interpretation of Dutch realism is rather misleading and not at all what Hoogstraten intended by his remarks. Fromentin, for example, would have been very surprised to find that two paintings of a town square in Cologne by Jan van der Heyden (National Gallery, London; Wallace Collection, London), both of which appear to be realistic and topographically accurate, vary extensively in the buildings depicted. Similarly, Fromentin was unaware of the many symbolic and allegorical references that are often hidden within the apparently real interiors of Dutch paintings. Jan Vermeer, for example, depicted a painting of a procuress scene on the back wall of his *Concert* (Gardner Museum, Boston), an obvious allusion to the nature of the musical party enacted below it. Vermeer's painting of an *Artist in his Studio* (Kunsthistorisches Museum, Vienna), moreover, is clearly an allegory on the art of painting, depicting, as it does, an artist dressed in a fanciful costume, painting an image of Clio, the muse of history.

Hoogstraten, in fact, does not recommend that painting copy nature but that it give the *appearance* of having copied nature. Painting, he felt, was a science and was based on a theoretical level beyond that of pure imitation. An interesting example of this aspect of Dutch realism may be seen in a comparison of two interiors by Pieter de Hooch, *The Bedroom* (see Figure 7.1) and *Maternal Duty* (see Figure 7.2). Both of these scenes take place within the same spatial setting, although de Hooch has varied effects of light and the placement of furniture to create different moods that reinforce the respective subject matters. One does not question that these scenes were painted from life, but as with van der Heyden's paintings of Cologne, de Hooch has freely varied architectural components of the rooms, particularly the marble floor in the ante-chamber to further reinforce the focus of his compositions.

Despite the apparently intuitive nature of these modifications, de Hooch has based his representation of this interior space upon a firm scientific foundation—the laws of linear perspective. De Hooch has effectively integrated a single vanishing point perspective system within his naturalistic scene and, in doing so, has followed the example of the most influential early seventeenth-century Dutch perspective theorist, Jan Vredeman de Vries, as shown in Figure 7.3. Vredeman de Vries had demonstrated in his treatise of 1604–5 many ways in which abstract concepts of linear perspective could be applied to problems of pictorial representation. In this illustration, for example, he has shown that the orthogonals of floor tiles, ceiling beams, open doors, and windows should recede to a single horizon. Vredeman de Vries, who insisted that the horizon line should be suitable for a person whose eye level was 5 1/2 feet high, has also demonstrated how every figure in the painting should be placed along this horizon.

De Hooch, because he was dealing with the problem of depicting an actual scene and not an abstract one, was less consistent than Vredeman de Vries and varied the level of his horizon in these two paintings, raising it for the painting with standing figures and lowering it for that with seated ones. As with his attitude toward imitating nature, de Hooch felt free to vary from strict perspective rules to enhance the compositional effects of his painting.

The imaginative way in which Dutch artists adapted the perspective conventions of Vredeman de Vries for their apparently realistic architectural interiors has meant that their dependency on his influence has often been overlooked. Gerrit Houckgeest, for example, began experimenting around 1650 with dramatically expressive viewpoints for his paintings of the tomb of William I (shown in Figure 7.4), which have always been thought to represent a dramatic break with his earlier fanciful architectural scenes. Houckgeest's composition, however, is clearly based on a de Vries illustration (shown in Figure 7.5), which demonstrates how to organize a scene with two vanishing points (Wheelock 1977b).

The Dutch artist with perhaps the most sophisticated understanding of the theoretical principles of perspective was Pieter Saenredam. In his remarkable painting *St. Bavo in Haarlem*, shown in Figure 7.6, he has depicted a view down the nave of the church, emphasizing its deep space through his perspective construction. As with de Hooch and Houckgeest, Saenredam constructed his scene along principles borrowed from Vredeman de Vries, demonstrated by Figure 7.7, to give his realistic portrayal of an interior space a firm and certain foundation.

Paintings like the *View of St. Bavo in Haarlem* and Saenredam's more intimate portrayal of *St. Janskerk in Utrecht* (Centraal Museum, Utrecht) testify to the appeal of perspective traditions inherited from the Italian Renaissance. They are composed so that viewers who properly place themselves at the correct distance and vantage point will experience an extraordinary sensation of belonging to the space depicted by the artist. In such paintings, the vaults, walls, and floor tiles, painted with subtly modulated colors, give one an almost complete illusion of reality.

The character of these two paintings by Saenredam, however, is rather exceptional for this master's oeuvre, and, indeed, for most of Dutch art. Although, as Hoogstraten recommended, Dutch artists generally sought to give the illusion of reality in their works, they recognized that paintings constructed along strict orthogonals often appear distorted when they are not viewed from the proper vantage point. In one instance, we know that van der Heyden actually supplied a viewing device attached to the frame of a painting of *The Dam in Amsterdam* (Uffizi, Florence) to ensure that the perspective did not appear distorted (Wheelock 1977b).

The difficulty that van der Heyden faced with his painting was common to most Dutch artists: their paintings were frequently small, cabinet-size works, whose destination was not known in advance. Both Pieter de Grebber, a contemporary of Saenredam in Haarlem, and Hoogstraten warned artists not to distort perspective effects in their paintings too extensively without knowing the exact location of their eventual placement. Most of Saenredam's paintings avoid this potential hazard by being organized along different principles. He generally established a sense of depth by differentiating scale and by overlapping forms rather than through orthogonals. This type of spatial construction is used, for example, in his *Interior of St. Bavo in Haarlem*, shown in Figure 7.8, and his *Entrance to St. Lawrencekerk, Alkmaar* (Museum Boymans–van Beuningen, Rotterdam), paintings that retain their illusionistic qualities when viewed from many vantage points.

As evident in comparisons of Saenredam's preliminary sketches and construction drawing for the *View of St. Bavo in Haarlem,* Saenredam subtly transformed architectural elements to enhance the two-dimensional, as well as three-dimensional, aspects of his composition (Liedtke 1971; Wheelock 1977a). He adjusted the height and width of the columns, as well as the angles of the arches, to create a more grandiose impression of the scene. The construction drawing for the painting demonstrates how carefully these revisions were made: indications of compass marks and rulers abound on the sheet.

Many of van der Heyden's paintings, as, for example, his *Architectural Fantasy* (National Gallery of Art, Washington, D.C.) or his *View of the Westerkerk in Amsterdam* (Wallace Collection, London) are similarly oriented along the picture plane rather than at opposite angles to it. Even in such an apparently diagonal composition as Emmanuel de Witte's imposing *Interior of the Oude Kerk in Delft* of 1651, shown in Figure 7.9, the space is not very deep, and orthogonals are kept at a minimum. De Witte, for example, has blocked our entry into the painting with a band of choir stalls and has flattened the sense of depth by tangentially relating the large vault on the far side of the crossing with the foreground column.

The intent of these comments has been to suggest both the deep-rooted perspective traditions in Dutch art and the modifications Dutch artists made with perspective to enhance the apparent realism of their scenes. By minimizing the use of rigid orthogonals and deeply recessive spaces, Dutch artists avoided many of the artificial limitations of traditional perspective. Only in occasional paintings by Saenredam, van der Heyden, and in perspective boxes by Hoogstraten do Dutch artists force the observer to view their works from a specific vantage point.

The problems inherent in the relationship between perspective and Dutch realism are even more pronounced in the realm of landscape than in architectural painting. Whereas the diagrams in the perspective treatise of Vredeman de Vries could be adapted by architectural painters for their depictions of actual buildings, the abstract, geometrical nature of traditional perspective theory was not as directly applicable for depictions of irregular aspects of nature. The problems of trying to apply a single-point perspective system to landscape can be illustrated with a drawing by the early seventeenth-century Dutch master, Jacob de Gheyn, shown in Figure 7.10. In this scene of a flat river landscape, the rapid recession of the river, created through strict adherence to a system of linear perspective, prevents the scene from achieving the naturalistic effects sought by artists during the first decades of the seventeenth century.

An interesting drawing by Simon de Vlieger dated 1645, shown in Figure 7.11, is one of the few seventeenth-century documents illustrating contemporary perspective practices. Significantly, de Vlieger, who was a sea painter and thus had to situate different size ships convincingly on the flat surface of the water, experimented with a number of perspective systems, including the use of modules to indicate the relative scales of objects. Later in the century, another seascape painter, William van de Velde II, seems to have recommended a modular system based on Gregorie Huret's treatise of 1670, *Optique de Pourtraiture et Peinture*, which avoided all orthogonals and depended upon proportional relationships of a human module between the horizon and the base line (Wheelock 1977a).

The rarity of such perspective drawings suggests that Dutch artists sought other means to establish a representational space. The geometrical optics of Vredeman de Vries did not address problems of light and atmosphere, so essential to the depiction of a naturalistic scene. According to an early seventeenth-century Dutch critic, Huygens, the ideals of landscape painting were that artists should be able to render "the appearance of trees, streams, hills, and similar things that men see in a landscape, with light, graceful and vigorous lines" (Constantijn Huygens wrote that one of the foremost of these artists, Esaias van de Velde, painted so naturalistically that his works lacked nothing "except the warmth of the sun and the moving of the wind" [Huygens 1911, p. 117]).

Esaias van de Velde and his contemporaries in Haarlem in the early decades of the seventeenth century were, indeed, the first artists to depict naturalistically various aspects of the Dutch landscape. Their prints, drawings, and paintings (see Figure 7.12) are remarkably free from the established landscape conventions of the preceding generation (compare Figure 7.10). They tended to minimize effects of linear perspective and to depict scenes that extend across the picture plane rather than at right angles to it. They also began to explore atmospheric effects of nature and to paint their scenes with subtly modulated tones of brown.

The naturalistic qualities evident in their works have little relationship to the formulas of contemporary perspective theory, but they are not incompatible with an aspect of contemporary perspective practices, specifically with the use of certain mechanical aids.

The most prevalent aid to perspective was certainly the glass frame. Ever since its appearance in Dürer's treatise *Underweysung der Messung mit dem Zirckel und Richtscheyt* in 1525, the glass frame had been popularized by perspective theorists. It played a prominent role in Samuel Marolois' treatise of 1614, and when Hendrik Hondius, another Dutch theorist, described its use, he wrote that it "est practique par les plus excellents maistres ordinairement" (1622, p. 19). Such devices allowed an artist to accurately record the appearance of objects without the necessity of complex perspective projections.

A modification of this device appeared in an earlier book by an English author, John Bate (1635). Bate placed before the squared frame a small glass, presumably a concave lens, as shown in Figure 7.13, which, he explained, helped one depict a wide compass, as, for example, a profile view of a city, in a small space. Esaias van de Velde's *View of Zierikzee* of 1618 (shown in Figure 7.12) resembles the scene depicted in Bate's woodcut, but without any corrobative evidence, it is impossible to determine his artistic procedure. Lenses leave no physical traces on the painting, and only when certain distortions are evident or optical effects present that cannot be seen with the naked eye, is it possible to deduce that an optical device has been used as an artistic aid.

One of the most intriguing artistic aids available in the early seventeenth century was the camera obscura, an optical device Huygens admired for the "beautiful brown picture" it created (Huygens 1911, p. 89). Huygens wrote that the camera obscura "makes admirable effects in painting from reflections in a dark room; it is not possible for me to reveal the beauty to you in words; all painting is dead by comparison, for here is life itself or something more elevated if one could articulate it. As one can see, the figure and the contour of the movements join together naturally and in a grandly pleasing fashion (Huygens 1911, p. 94).

The remarkable similarity in Huygens's response to the image of the camera obscura and to contemporary landscape painting underscores one of the reasons this optical instrument gained such widespread popularity in the early seventeenth century. The naturalistic image it created entirely coincided with contemporary expectations of realism in painting. One even wonders if the stylistic evolution of Dutch landscape painting to a tonal phase in the 1620s and 1630s was at all influenced by the "beautiful brown pictures" Huygens and others saw in the camera obscura. Unfortunately, as with the glass frame or lenses, the actual extent that artists used the camera obscura as an artistic aid is difficult to determine without specific documentation. No physical traces of the use of a camera obscura were left on the painting, and optical distortions created by it could be easily corrected by the artist. The difficulty of pinpointing specific examples of its use has meant that little attention has been paid to role of the camera obscura in the developments of Dutch naturalism. Questions as to its effect on style are difficult to answer without knowing who used it and how it was used (Wheelock 1977a).

Only in instances where artists have sought to exploit the expressive characteristics of optical effects associated with lenses and the camera obscura can one speculate on their use with any assurance. During the early decades of the century, when artists were intent on enhancing the realistic qualities of their landscapes, such interests are not apparent. After mid-century, however, certain artists began to exploit optical effects viewed with these devices that are not specifically naturalistic. For example, Vermeer, in his *View of Delft* (circa 1660), shown in Figure 7.14, painted small diffused highlights on the boat and buildings near the water in a way that resembles the halation of highlights that appear on unfocused images in a camera obscura. Although such diffused highlights do not appear in natural vision, Vermeer apparently recognized how effectively they suggest the movement of the water as it reflects upon the surrounding objects (Seymour 1964; Wheelock 1977a). Ironically, Vermeer has adapted an unnatural optical effect to enhance the apparent realism of his painting.

Carel Fabritius, in his little painting of 1652, *A View in Delft with a Musical Instrument Seller's Stall*, shown in Figure 7.15, seems to have exploited an optical device for a different effect. In this instance, the small, remote appearance of the Nieuwe Kerk, which in reality is very large and quite near the picture plane, and the peculiarly distorted foreground space suggest that Fabritius had been inspired by the wide-angle effects of a concave lens, demonstrated in Figure 7.16. His intent appears not to have been to accurately depict the site, as Bate would have recommended (see Figure 7.13), but to exploit the peculiarly distorted effects for their emotional impact. By juxtaposing the landscape vista with the large-scale figure of the man and his instruments, Fabritius created a dreamlike setting that allowed him to infuse his small painting with the man's melancholic mood (Wheelock 1973).

The concept of realism in Dutch art is thus an extremely fluid one. It varied throughout the century as artists' needs and aspirations changed and matured. It partook of established perspective conventions, but it also recognized the advantages of artistic aids that enhanced the artist's awareness of tonal relationships. In certain instances, artists even chose to emphasize in their paintings effects seen with optical devices that were alien to natural vision. Dutch realism had at its core, however, the desire to enhance the viewer's association with the image depicted, to bring to him the immediacy of an encounter with the physical world.

REFERENCES

Bate, John. *The Mysteries of Nature and Art*. London: T. Harper for Ralph Mab, 1635.

Fromentin, Eugène. *The Old Masters of Belgium and Holland*, trans. Mary C. Robbins from *Les Maîtres d'Autresfois*, published in 1882. New York: Dover, 1963.

Hondius, Hendrick. *Institutio Artis Perspectivae*. The Hague: Hendrick Hondius, 1622.

Hoogstraten, Samuel van. *Inleyding tot de Hooge Schoole der Schilderkonst: anders de Zichtbaere Werelt*. Rotterdam: Fransois Van Hoogstraten, 1678.

Huygens, C. *de Breifwisseling* (1608-1687), vol. 1. Translated by J. A. Worp, ed. The Hague: Nyhoff, 1911.

Liedtke, Walter A. "Saenredam's Space." *Oud-Holland* 86 (1971): 116–41.

Marolois, Samuel. *Opera Mathematica ou Oeuvres Mathematicques traictons de Geometrie, Perspective, Architecture, et Fortification*. The Hague: Hendrick Hondius, 1614.

Seymour, Charles. "Dark Chamber and Lightfilled Room: Vermeer and the Camera Obscura." *The Art Bulletin* 46, (1964): 323–31.

Vredeman de Vries, Jan. *Perspective*. Leiden: Hendrick Hondius, 1605.

Wheelock, Arthur K., Jr., "Carel Fabritius: Perspective and Optics in Delft." *Nederlands Kunsthistorisch Jaarboek* 24 (1973): 63–83.

———. "Constantijn Huygens and Early Attitudes towards the Camera Obscura." *History of Photography* (1977a) 93–103.

———. *Perspective, Optics, and Delft Artists Around 1650*. New York and London: Garland, 1977b.

Figure 7.1 Pieter de Hooch's *The Bedroom* (Washington, D.C., National Gallery of Art).

Figure 7.2 Pieter de Hooch's *Maternal Duty* (Amsterdam, Rijksmuseum).

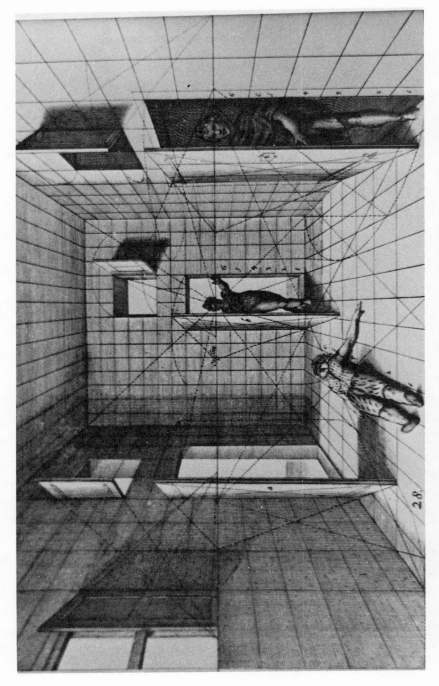

Figure 7.3 Scene from Jan Vredeman de Vries' *Perspective*, engraving (Leyden, 1604-5, pl. 28).

Figure 7.4   Gerrit Houckgeest's *Tomb of Prince William I of Orange in the Nieuwe Kerk, Delft*, 1651 (The Hague, Mauritshuis).

Figure 7.5 Scene from Jan Vredeman de Vries' *Perspective*, engraving (Leyden, 1604–5, pl. 23).

Figure 7.6 Pieter Saenredam's *St. Bavo in Haarlem* (Philadelphia, Philadelphia Museum of Art).

Figure 7.7 Scene from Jan Vredeman de Vries' *Perspective*, engraving (Leyden, 1604–5, pl. 47).

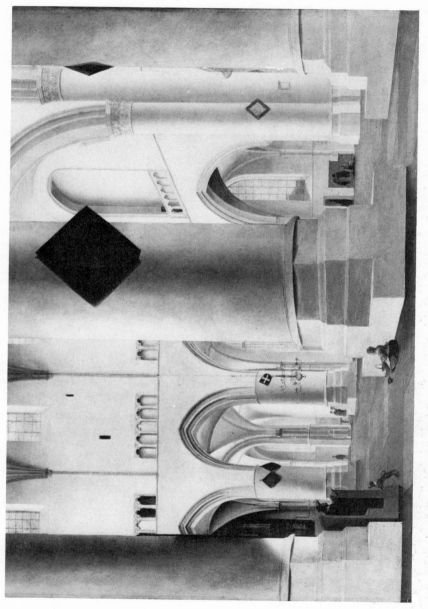

Figure 7.8 Pieter Saenredam's *Interior of St. Bavo in Haarlem*, 1637 (London, National Gallery).

Figure 7.9 Emmanuel de Witte's *Interior of the Oude Kerk in Delft*, 1651 (London, Wallace Collection).

Figure 7.10 Jacob de Gheyn's *Flat River Landscape with a City in the Distance*, 1598, drawing (Amsterdam, private collection).

Figure 7.11   Simon de Vlieger's perspective studies, 1645, drawing (London, British Museum).

Figure 7.12   Esaias van de Velde's *View of Zierikzee*, 1618 (Berlin–Dahlem, Staatliche Museen).

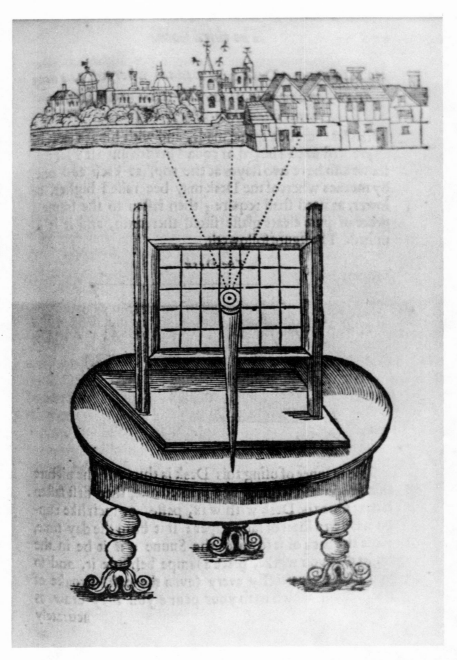

Figure 7.13   Perspective device, woodcut (from John Bate, *The Mysteries of Nature and Art* [London, 1635]).

Figure 7.14 Jan Vermeer's *View of Delft*, ca. 1660 (The Hague, Mauritshuis).

Figure 7.15 Carel Fabritius' *View in Delft with a Musical Instrument Seller's Stall*, 1652 (London, National Gallery).

Figure 7.16 Delft, view of Nieuwe Kerk through a double concave lens in a tilted position (photograph by Jac. P. Stolp).

Chapter Eight

Visual Science and Modernist Art: Historical Parallels

Paul C. Vitz

The central thesis of this chapter is that there are many remarkable but poorly appreciated parallels between modern visual science and modernist art. By *modern visual science* is meant the study of visual phenomena in the nineteenth and twentieth centuries. Examples are the contributions to the knowledge of vision and perception made by Helmholtz, Gestalt psychology, and the recent work of such investigators as J. J. Gibson, Julesz, and Hochberg. Thus, the thesis concerns the scientific study of vision and not science in general. Parallels and connections between visual science and art prior to the modern period are excluded, not because such parallels do not exist—they certainly do—but because restriction is necessary in order to keep the amount of material manageable.

The term *modernist* art refers to the tradition of *avant-garde* art commonly assumed to begin with Manet and the Impressionists. The concept of parallelism is that modernist painting has been fundamentally an investigation by artists into visual perception—an investigation that has developed in parallel with the scientific discoveries and theories

Early forms of this chapter were given as lectures, presented in various courses, at New York University, especially in the author's regular Psychology of Art course, starting in 1973; versions were also given at psychology department colloquia at Columbia University (1973) and the University of Victoria, B.C. (1974). The present chapter, although it contains more text than was read at the symposium, remains a considerably abbreviated and summarized part from a book-length manuscript, entitled *Modern Science and Modernist Art: The Parallel Analysis of Vision.* The parallelism thesis and supporting evidence are developed there much more extensively. The encouragement and intellectual stimulation provided throughout this project by Arnold Glimcher is gratefully acknowledged. Early stages of this work were supported by the Wilfred P. Cohen Foundation and The Shalom Foundation.

of modern visual science. The notion of development in parallel entails the assumption that over the last century, both disciplines have investigated similar perceptual phenomena at about the same time and have arrived at similar conceptual understandings. Evidence for the thesis is of two kinds. The first is evidence from the writings (or comments) of artists and scientists which make it clear that both had arrived at a similar conceptual understanding of similar perceptual problems. This kind of evidence is termed *conceptual parallelism*. The second comes from the discovery of strong similarities between many avant-garde works of art and the visual stimuli constructed by scientists used to investigate or embody some aspect of perception. The physical similarity of images in the two disciplines will be called *pictorial parallelism*. In some recent cases, it is not possible to tell which image is by the artist and which by the scientist.

Parallelism does not necessarily assume that the artist was causally influenced by visual science, for often, the artist appears to have independently arrived at an interpretation that is quite similar to the scientist's and in several cases, the artist's insight appeared in advance of science. The issue of historical causality, therefore, is complex, and although it will be discussed when possible, no single generalization about causality characterizes the parallelism thesis.

The thesis of parallelism starts with the assumption that both visual science and modernist art have been guided by the same general intellectual attitude—one that will be called *analytical reductionism*. The terms *analytic* and *reductionist* refer to a particular manner of thinking which assumes that understanding a given phenomenon requires first the discovery of a new, more important, fundamental level of reality that lies beneath or behind the familiar level of understanding; and second, that this new basic level can be analyzed, that is, broken down into elements, relationships, processes, and so forth, which account for, and explain, the observations at the familiar level.

Analytic and reductionist thought became a dominant characteristic of science in the nineteenth century and has remained so since. (The growth of specialization is a major symptom of the change: see, for example, Whitehead 1925, chap. 6). In physical science, this approach uncovered successively lower levels of reality from chemical substance, to atom and molecule, to subatomic particle, to today's quark. In biological science, the historical sequence starting in the 1830s ran: cell, nucleus, chromosome, gene, RNA, and DNA. The same approach was equally characteristic of the study of visual perception. In this field, the integrated, phenomenological world of natural perception was broken down into a large variety of sensory and perceptual effects, most of which were "explained" in terms of elements and processes at the lower, presumably more fundamental, level of sensory physiology. For example, depth was analyzed in terms of binocular disparity; brightness perception was separated from color and form and analyzed in terms of the relative, rather than absolute, brightness of objects; while perception of color was interpreted as a consequence of the proportional stimulation of three different visual pigments.

The analytic and reductionist approach is very much in contrast to the synthetic and hierarchical pattern of thought of the previous centuries. Instead of breaking apart by analysis, this opposite approach synthesizes and integrates, and instead of reducing explanation to a lower, more specific level, it uses higher, more general concepts in its search for explanation. A major example of this approach is the philosophy summarized under the phrase "the great chain of being." This rather general intellectual position, brilliantly presented in Lovejoy's (1936) classic treatment, represents the dominant world view of the Middle Ages and the Renaissance.

Lovejoy documents the culmination of the static, synthetic, moral, hierarchical "great chain" philosophy in the eighteenth century, followed by its rapid collapse. This collapse started in the latter eighteenth century and was pretty well completed by the first decades of the nineteenth century. It was, of course, supplanted by the familiar modern system, with its emphasis on the dynamic, the analytic, and on lower, amoral material reality as fundamental.

The present thesis assumes that artists adopted the analytic reductionist mentality around the middle of the nineteenth century. (Evidence for this assumption is given below.) In so doing, they were adopting the successful approach of perhaps the most dynamic and dramatic force of their time. Being artists, it also followed that they applied this new mental strategy to visual and perceptual problems. In accepting the new analytic reductionist mentality, artists carried out the well-known, steady reduction in the moral, social, and historical content of their painting. On the other hand, as the parallelism thesis predicts, the sensory, the visual, the perceptual, or the optical character of modernist painting grew steadily as the traditional meanings lost ground.

Artists, critics, and art historians have been quite aware of the analytic and reductionist character of modernist art, with its consequences of flatness and dramatic color (see Greenberg 1960; Rosenberg 1969; Duchamp [1911–12], in Chipp 1968; Courbet, in Reff 1977). Occasionally, the influence of visual science on a particular artist has been noted, but seldom is this influence given prominence, and almost never is it viewed as decisive. However, even more neglected by art historians has been the long-term, intimate connection of visual science to modernist art—an active influence from the start and one still present.

THE ROOD-HELMHOLTZ INSIGHT

Some early important evidence for conceptual parallelism comes from the writings of two physicists, each of whom made important contributions to visual science. Rood (1879) directly influenced many modernist artists—Seurat, Delaunay, and Kupka in particular, according to Homer (1964), Vriesen and Imdahl (1967), Chipp (1958), and Hodin (1968). The other is Helmholtz.* Both made essentially the same observation—although Rood seems to have been the first in print by a few years. Rood (1861, p. 184) starts by noting the fact "that a landscape appears more vivid in color, when viewed by the eyes brought into an abnormal position, as in looking under the arm." He explains this as follows:

> To me it seems that this effect is intimately connected with our perception or non-perception of distance . . . if by any means the mind is prevented from dwelling on distance, it is thrown back on the remaining element, color; and the landscape appears like a mass of beautiful patches of color heaped upon each other, and situated more or less in a vertical plane (p. 184).

Helmholtz had the same insight, but he gives it a lengthier, more informative expression (1867). He writes about the perception of a landscape:

> The first thing we have *to learn is to pay heed to our* individual sensations. . . . By way of illustration . . . the instant we take an unusual position, and look at [a] landscape with the head under one arm, let us say, or between the legs, *it all appears like a flat picture;* partly on account of the strange position of the image of the eye, and partly because, as we shall see presently, the binocular judgment of distance becomes less accurate. It may even happen that with the head upside down the clouds have the correct perspective, whereas the objects *on the earth appear like a painting on a vertical surface* (pp. 7-8) (italics added).

---

*Helmholtz published his analysis in book form for the first time in 1867 *(Handbuch der physiologischen Optik)*. However, according to Boring (1942, for example, p. 124), the work came out in three monograph sections: section 1 in 1856, section 2 in 1860, and section 3 in 1866. Thus, it is possible the above quotes were first published earlier, for example, in section 1 in 1856. The author has been unable to locate any of these rare monographs, hence the date 1867 and the order Rood-Helmholtz instead of Helmholtz-Rood. The quotes are taken from the English translation by J. P. C. Southall, entitled *Treatise on Physiological Optics* (1924). This translation of the third German edition reproduces the 1867 edition, unchanged except for various addenda.

Helmholtz makes the same point as Rood about color when viewed in a manner that breaks our common preconceptions by focusing attention on the "individual sensations." When observed in this manner, "the colours of a landscape come out much more brilliantly and definitely" (Helmholtz 1867, p. 8). And they

> now lose their associations also with near or far objects, and confront us now purely in their own peculiar differences. Then we have no difficulty in recognizing that the vague blue-gray of the far distance may indeed be a fairly saturated violet, and that the green of the vegetation blends imperceptibly through blue-green and blue into this violet, etc. This whole difference seems to me to be due to the fact that the colours have ceased to be distinctive signs of objects to us, and are considered merely as being different sensations (Helmholz 1867, p. 9) (italics added).

Rood and Helmholtz demonstrate their reductionist attitude by providing a mental approach for eliminating the higher meaning of a scene where objects are responded to in terms of their associative meaning and by bringing our attention to the new, visually exciting lower level of pure sensation, where such meaning is absent. Further, they emphasize the breaking apart or analysis of the new sensory experience into separate areas of different colors.

Of major importance is the Rood–Helmholtz observation that such an attitude toward a perceived landscape changes the appearance of the colors, by making them brighter, more varied, flatter, more unusual, and less associated with a particular distance.

Helmholtz' discussion should be compared with a similar but later statement (1889–1901) of the Impressionist Monet (Perry 1927):

> Try to forget what objects you have before you. . . . Merely think, here is a little square of blue, here an oblong of pink, here a streak of yellow, and paint it just as it looks to you, the exact color and shape, until it gives your naive impression of the scene (p. 120).

Monet followed this axiom so regularly that even while observing the body of his dead wife, he reported that he could not help but note in her face the shades of blue, grey, and yellow which death had brought (see Seitz 1960).

A comment, radical in 1890, by the symbolist critic Maurice Denis, expresses the same sentiment: "It must be recalled that a picture, before it is a picture of battle horse, nude woman, or some anecdote is essentially a plane surface covered by colors arrayed in a certain order" (see Chipp 1968, p. 94).

These two scientists, before Impressionism—even before most of

Monet's initial modernist works of the mid-1860s—have nevertheless identified two major changes in visual experience which occur when the observer analyzes that experience in terms of the lower level of individual sensations and ignores the higher meaning of the objects that are present. These changes are a reduction in perceived depth, with a consequent reduction in the meaning of the objects viewed and, also, a dramatic increase in the strength and variety of color. An exploration of these two perceptual changes will preoccupy modernist artists for years—indeed, the development of an artistic understanding of these two effects is often identified as the essential characteristic of modernist art.

PICTORIAL PARALLELISM

The other major type of evidence for parallelism comes from the physical similarity between the stimuli constructed by scientists in their investigations of vision and avant-garde paintings. A large number of these pictorial parallels have been discovered, and some will be presented and briefly discussed to serve as a limited set of examples of this common kind of parallelism.

Georges Seurat is well-known for his pointillist technique of painting, shown in black and white in Figure 8.1([C] and 8.1[D]). What is less well-known is that this technique was directly influenced by Seurat's systematic study of visual science, especially the contributions of Helmholtz, Rood, Chevreul, Blanc, and others (see Homer 1964). Seurat himself claimed he was making painting into a science. The basic theory of his analytic technique (sometimes called *divisionism*) is that small dots of color could be mixed optically, that is, the light reflected from them could be mixed in the eye instead of having the artist mix the pigments on the canvas.

This technique for optical mixing was suggested by the visual theory of his day, especially Blanc (1867), which Seurat studied (compare Figure 8.1[A]). The Blanc diagram and its accompanying text propose optical mixing by painting with dots (or stars) of one color on a background of another. The pointillist idea is also implicit in the work of Chevreul (1839), which was widely known to French artists in the second half of the nineteenth century. Seurat's major source for color theory, however, was Rood's *Modern Chromatics*, which was translated into French in 1881 and became something of a bible for many French painters in the next generation. Seurat picked the colors used in his familiar *Sunday Afternoon on the Isle of the Grand Jatte* from a color wheel of Rood (Homer 1964), thus indicating a deep and direct influence by visual science. In addition, in his painting he constructed what can be

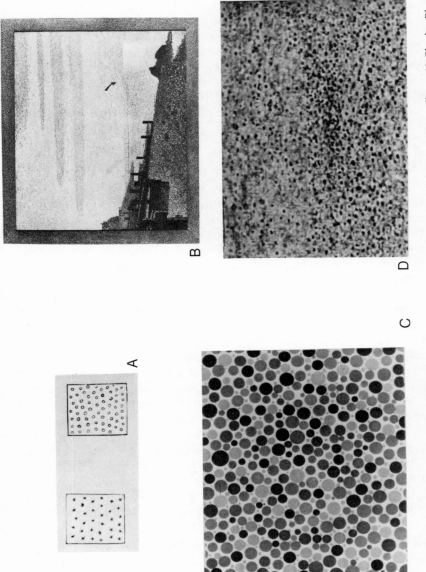

Figure 8.1 Scientific analyses of color based on dot elements and an example of Seurat's pointillism. A) Charles Blanc, *Grammaire des arts dessin.* B) Georges Seurat's *Evening, Honfleur,* 1886 (New York City, Museum of Modern Art). C) Jakob Stilling, pl. 1–1, in *Stillings pseudo-isochromatische Tafeln zur Prüfung des Farbensinnes.* D) Georges Seurat's *Evening, Honfleur,* insert from area marked by the arrow in B).

interpreted as a elementist, or punktat (punctuate), theory of the visual world.

An important but little-known parallel to Seurat are the pseudo-isochromatic charts of Stilling (1878). These charts, published in Germany in the late 1870s, are the first color blindness test plates. They were the standard test for many years—in wide use until about 1920; they have since been forgotten, being replaced by more recent U.S. and Japanese tests. An example from Stilling is shown in Figure 8.1(C) and can be compared to an enlarged insert of Seurat's technique, shown in Figure 8.1(D). The Stilling plates, like Seurat's paintings, can also be described as pointillist or punktat. Furthermore, these plates can be interpreted as a visual expression of the elementist theory of perception, which dominated the German experimental psychology of the time—that is, for both the scientist and the artist, the unified natural world of perceptual meaning was reduced to a field of sensory elements. It is this elementist position that Gestalt psychology would rebel against in the next generation. (The elementist theory of perception is often attributed to Wilhelm Wundt [Boring 1950, pp. 329–30], but Ernest Mach's view of the visual world is probably a purer example of elementism [Mach 1886; Blumenthal 1975]).

Figure 8.2(A) shows a plate from Rubin (1915, 1921) that introduced to science the distinction between figure and ground. Rubin did this by devising examples of stimuli that were ambiguous as to which part was the figure (that is, the object focused on and attended to) and which part was the background. In Figure 8.2(A), it is not clear, for example, whether the white "organic"-shaped figures lie on top of a black background or whether these shapes have been cut out of the black, allowing the white background to show through. Figure 8.2(B) shows a work of the artist, Jean Arp, which is so remarkably similar to the Rubin that it (plus its title) suggests that Arp was also investigating figure–ground ambiguity. Evidence that this is the case also appears in Arp's rather well-known relief *Mountain, Table, Anchors, and Navel* (1925). In this work (not shown), the areas appearing white can be observed only because the artist has cut out the shapes, allowing the white background to be seen. If Arp's construction were viewed from the side, the different flat surfaces would easily show that he was toying with figure–ground principles. A similar technique is shown in Figure 8.3(A) of the now familiar Rubin "claw." In the center area it is not clear which is the figure—the black claw or the white fingers. In Figure 8.3 are two paintings by Matisse that use the Rubin claw form of ambiguity. Indeed, this use of figure–ground is a distinctive, though largely unrecognized, stylistic feature of many later works by Matisse.

Picasso and Braque also incorporated figure–ground ambiguity as a distinctive part of their Cubist works. Picasso's classic *Ma Jolie*

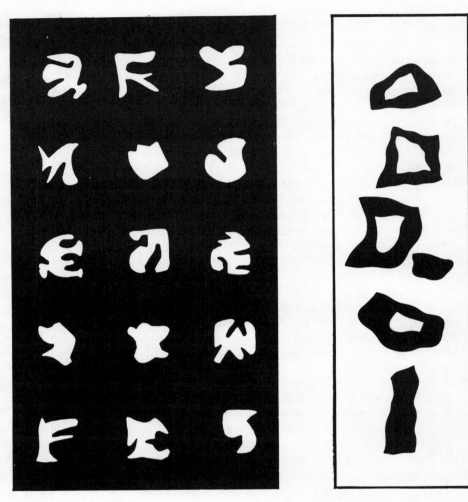

A   **B**

Figure 8.2 Rubin's portrayal of ambiguous figure–ground and works by Arp. A) Edgar Rubin, pl. 1, in *Synsoplenede Figuren*, 1915 B) Jean Arp's *Constellation of Six Black Forms on White Ground*, 1957 collage.

(1911–12), as the art historian Richardson (1971) notes, is filled with continuities and discontinuities that make it difficult for us to separate the figures from their background.

These "Cubistic" relationships, schematically represented by his diagram in Figure 8.4(A), are standard figure–ground ambiguities, which provide much of the visual interest, for example, in Picasso's *Card Player* (1913–14) and in Braque's *Guitar and Clarinet* (1918) (B and D in

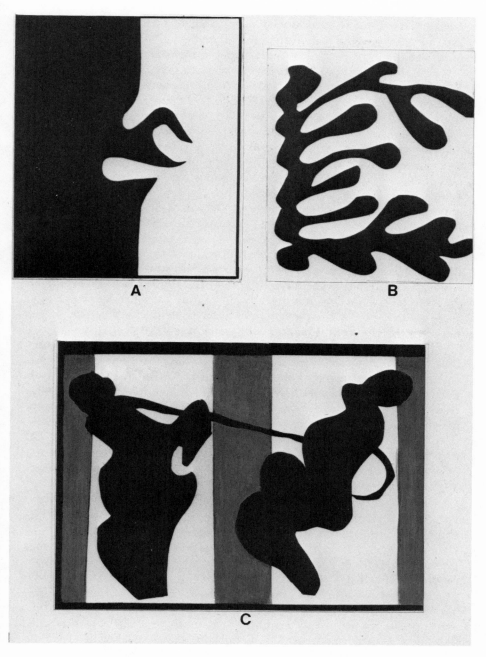

Figure 8.3   Rubin's portrayal of ambiguous figure-ground and works by Matisse. A) Edgar Rubin, pl. 2, in *Synsoplenede Figuren*, 1915 B) Henri Matisse's *1001 Nights*, 1950, insert. C) Henri Matisse's *The Cowboy*, from *Jazz*, 1947 (Museum of Modern Art.)

Figure 8.4). Usually overlooked are Rubin's starkly simple figure–ground stimuli, shown in Figure 8.4(C) and 8.4(D)—yet, they present motifs found in many Cubist works, for example, D and F in Figure 8.4.

Figure 8.5(B) shows a color circle of Helmholtz (1867), and Figure 8.5(A) shows one from Rood (1879). Color diagrams of this kind were studied both by Delaunay and by Kupka (see Chipp 1958; Vriesen and Imdahl 1967; Mladek and Rowell 1975), the artists responsible (with Kandinsky) for initiating and developing nonobjective painting. In addition to contact with Chevreul and pointillist theory, both artists were familiar with the French translation of Rood's book. Delaunay's *Disk* (1912) (Figure 8.5[C]) shows an obvious closeness to the scientists' color circles. Kupka, who also broke through into a nonobjective style, apparently doing so independently of Delaunay, also painted a similar image of his *Disks of Newton* (1911–12) (not shown). In this work, the connection of painting to color science is even stronger. Kupka laid out his colors according to a color table in Rood's *Modern Chromatics* (1879, p. 26) (see Mladek and Rowell 1975). Figure 8.5(E) shows a later Delaunay similar to the many color disks or wheels found in Rood, for example, Figure 8.5(D). However nonobjective Delaunay's and Kupka's paintings were claimed to be, the structure of their color imagery can be attributed to the theoretical diagrams of visual science.

Figure 8.6(A) shows a set of drawings published by Wertheimer (1923). These diagrams, studied by Klee, obviously influenced the forms selected in his paintings, shown in Figure 8.6(B). This example of parallelism was discovered by Teuber (1976), where she insightfully shows that a great deal of the visual vocabulary of Klee was taken from his study of Gestalt psychology and other visual science. She concludes that Klee's work is an investigation into the nature of perception—an artistic investigation which can be seen "as paralleling the developments in psychology and laboratory studies of visual perception (from the late 19th century to 1933)" (Teuber 1976, p. 148).

Figure 8.7(A) shows an example of texture gradients from Gibson (1950). The gradient on the left shows a change in the density of dots, thus suggesting depth, while the gradient on the right has no such change—hence, it does not suggest depth. Figure 8.7(B) is a 1966 painting by Bridget Riley that is almost identical to the simpler Gibson gradient. That Riley was exploring depth effects in texture gradients can be observed by comparing C with D in Figure 8.7. Figure 8.7(C) shows a checkerboard texture gradient that is created by a sharp drop-off to the lower plane on the right. Such a texture gradient was used in a series of experiments by E. J. Gibson and R. D. Walk (1960)—experiments referred to as *visual cliff* experiments. In these experiments, young animals and children were placed on a center board and were observed to see whether they stepped off the center board on either the

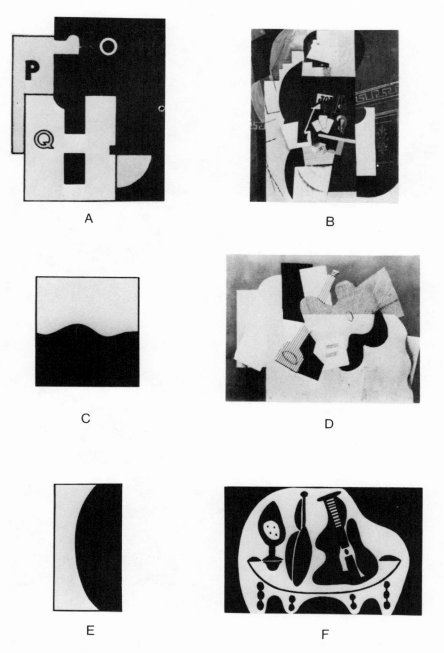

Figure 8.4 Ambiguous figure–ground patterns and Cubism. A) Diagram entitled "Cubistic Relationship," John A. Richardson's *Modern Art and Scientific Thought*. B) Pablo Picasso's *Card Player*, 1913–14. C) Edgar Rubin, pl. 8, *Synsoplenede Figuren*, 1915. D) George Braque's *Guitar and Clarinet*, 1918 (Philadelphia Museum of Art). E) Edgar Rubin, pl. 12, *Synsoplenede Figuren*, 1915. F) Pablo Picasso's *Still Life with Fruitbowl, Bottle and Guitar*, 1925.

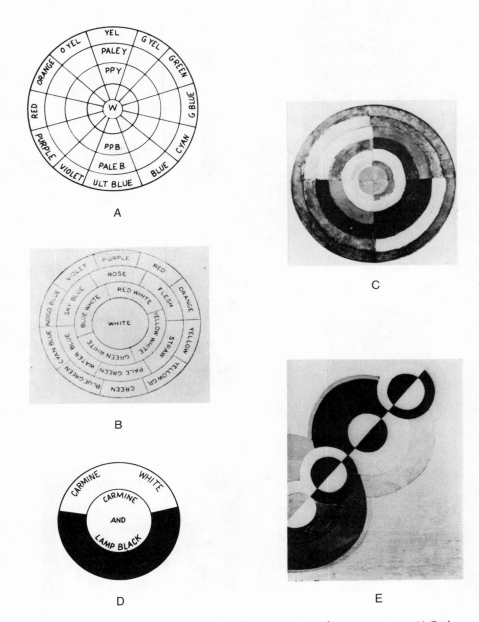

Figure 8.5 Scientific color circles and Delaunay's nonobjective painting. A) Ogden Rood, color circle, *Modern Chromatics*, 1879. B) Herman Helmholtz, color circle, *Handbuch der physiologischen Optik*, 1867. The circle was translated into English and published by Edwin G. Boring, *Sensation and Perception in the History of Experimental Psychology*, 1942. (C) Robert Delaunay's *Disk, First Non Objective Painting*, 1912 (Collection of Mrs. Burton Tremaine, Meriden, Connecticut). D) Ogden Rood, color disk, *Modern Chromatics*, 1879. E) Robert Delaunay's *Rhythms*, 1934 (Paris, Musee National d'Art Moderne).

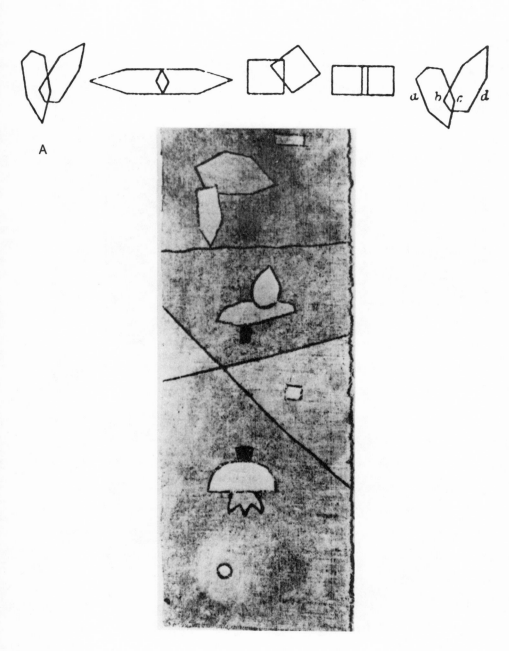

A

B

Figure 8.6 Gestalt psychology principles and Klee. A) Max Wertheimer, partially and completely overlapping planes, *Psychologische Forschung*, 1923, from Marianne L. Teuber, "*Blue Knight*, by Paul Klee," in *Vision and Artifact*, ed. Mary Henle, 1976. B) Paul Klee's *Vegetal–Analytical*, 1932 (Kunstmuseum, Basel).

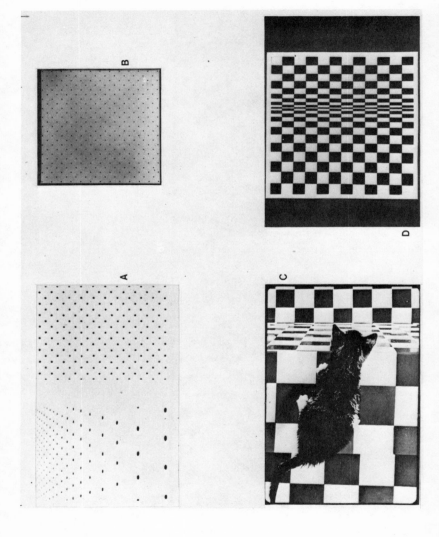

Figure 8.7 Gibson's texture gradients and paintings by Riley. A) James J. Gibson, *The Perception of the Visual Word*, 1950. B) Bridget Riley's *Static 1*, 1966, in Maurice de Sausmarez's, *Bridget Riley*. C) James B. Maas, *Slide Group for General Psychology*, Slide no. 106, from study by E. J. Gibson and R. W. Walk, "The Visual Cliff," *Scientific American*, 1960. D) Bridget Riley's *Movement in Squares*, 1961.

"deep" or the "shallow" side. Riley's work, *Movement in Squares* (1961), shown in Figure 8.7(D), is an obvious artistic investigation of a change in a checkerboard texture gradient giving rise to a sudden increase in depth. Indeed, this work is very like a kitten's eye view of the visual cliff in Figure 8.7(C).

Figure 8.8(A) shows a plate from Vitz and Todd (1971) adapted from an article by Hochberg and Brooks (1960). It presents a large number of two-dimensional drawings that can be seen as three-dimensional shapes. Hochberg and Brooks, like others, were interested in the properties of these flat drawings, which facilitate seeing them in three dimensions. Figure 8.8(C) is a figure from a later Hochberg study (1968), in which he identified the connected corner, shown at the very bottom section, as crucially important in determining the perception of a figure's three dimensionality. In a related experiment, Hochberg (1968) presented the corners of a figure in sequence viewed through a circular aperture (see Figure 8.8 [D]). The subject's task was to recognize the complete shape from the sequence of corners. Figure 8.8(F) is an example from a study by Orbach, Ehrlich, and Vainstein (1963), who studied the ability of a subject to reverse the perceived location of the cube. To control for various factors, the subject was told to fixate on the dot. In the 1960s, then, perceptual psychologists systematically experimented with factors underlying the perception of depth in such two-dimensional drawings.

The paintings of Al Held show a remarkable parallel to this work (see Tuck 1974). In the first Held (Figure 8.8 [B]), done in 1972, one sees an aesthetically organized cluster of various two-dimensional drawings, all of which can be seen in three dimensions. In Figure 8.8(E), shown in 1974, Held has begun to focus on the figures' corners. He even puts one inside a circular "aperture." He also has begun to show gaps in the sides, as though he intuitively understood that the complete sides are not necessary for the viewer to construct the figure—that they are, in a sense, visually redundant. Later in 1974, as shown in Figure 8.8(G), Held has placed further emphasis on corners, dropped out still more of the sides, and introduced small dots or rectangles, which come close to serving as fixation points for the viewer. The Hochberg-Held parallel is very intriguing, since there is no reason to believe that Held knew of Hochberg's work in perception. Instead, the artist's own intuitions seem to have been guided in similar directions in a search for the perceptually informative and visually interesting factors.

In the late 1940s and early 1950s, both perceptual psychologists and artists became particularly interested in the concepts of chance and statistical randomness. In particular, techniques for constructing random visual stimuli were introduced into both disciplines at about this time.

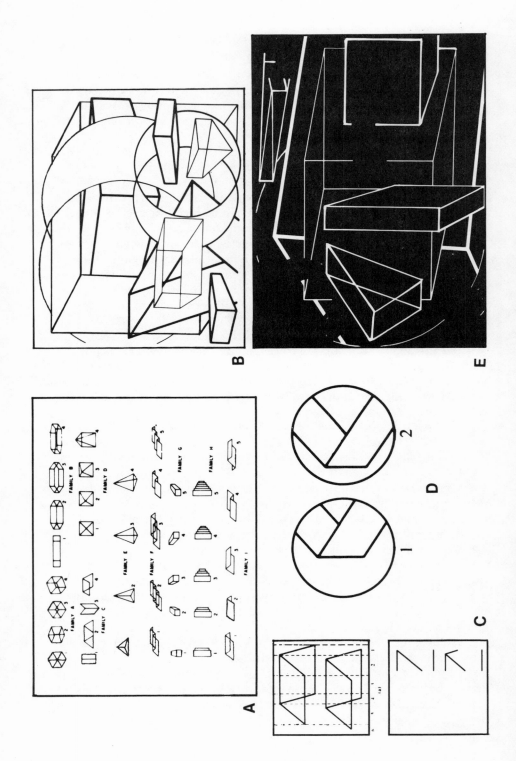

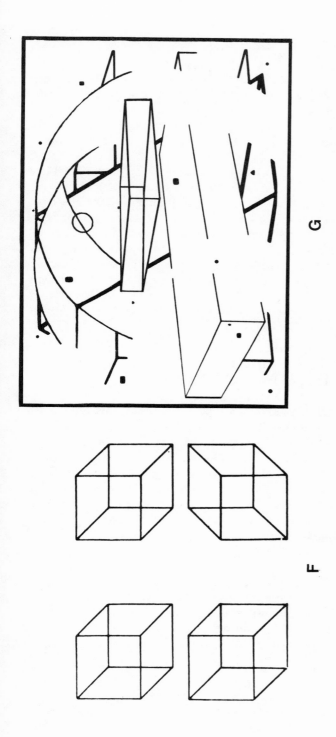

G

F

Figure 8.8 Perceiving the third dimension in two-dimensional drawings: experiments by Hochberg (and others); paintings by Held. A) Paul C. Vitz and Thomas C. Todd, "A Model of the Perception of Simple Geometric Figures," *Psychological Review,* adapted from Julian Hochberg and Virginia Brooks, "The Psychophysics of Forms: Reversible Perspective Drawings of Spatial Objects," *American Journal of Psychology,* 73 (1960). B) Al Held's *Southeast,* 1972, in Marcia Tucker's *Al Held.* C) Julian Hochberg, "In the Mind's Eye," ca. 1966, in *Contemporary Theory and Research in Visual Perception,* ed. Ralph Haber, Fig. 5a, p. 318. D) in *Contemporary Theory and Research in Visual Perception,* ed. Ralph Haber. fig. 7, p. 321. E) Al Held's *Black Nile VI,* 1974, in Marcia Tucker's *Al Held.* F) J. Orbach, Dan Ehrlich, and Ella Vainstein, "Reversibility of the Necker Cube," pt. 3, "Effects of Interpolation on Reversal Rate of the Cube Presented Repetitively," *Perceptual and Motor Skills,* 1963. G) Al Held's *Solar Wind V,* 1974 in Marcia Tucker's *Al Held.*

In Figure 8.9(A) is a set of random checkerboard stimuli constructed by Dorfman and McKenna (1966), which they used to investigate visual preference for such patterns. In Figure 8.9(B) is a similar black and white checkerboard pattern, made in 1951 by Ellsworth Kelly (Goosen 1973). Kelly used a random technique in making this and other works.

Another pictorial parallel is found in Figure 8.9. Figure 8.9(C) is a black and white random square constructed by Julesz (1960). To the right (Figure 8.9[D]) is a print by the artist Francois Morellet (circa 1961), which is indistinguishable from the work of Julesz. I have been unable to find out whether Morellet hit upon the same procedure by himself or whether he took the idea directly from Julesz. In any case, the parallelism is extreme, as is the relation between the "block" face of Abraham Lincoln described by Harmon and Julesz (1973) and a recent self-portrait by Chuck Close (1977). Other examples of the use of random patterns (lines) can be found between Vitz (1966) and Morellet prints of 1967 (see Honisch et al. 1977).

A CASE HISTORY OF PARALLELISM: FROM THE STEREOSCOPE TO CUBISM

One final example of parallelism will be presented because of its historical importance, as well as to show the kind of additional material that often can be brought to support the parallel conceptual and pictorial development in the two disciplines. For centuries, European artists used a fixed, deep homogeneous and Euclidean space. This idealized container of visual experience was routinely accepted as providing a framework within which the painting was constructed. People and objects might be moved as the artist searched for his final composition—occasionally, even unusual angles of vision were used— but the space itself remained constant, homogeneously connected and unaffected by the objects placed within it. It is, of course, commonplace to find avant-garde art breaking up and distorting this previously sacrosanct space. What is not so commonly known is that visual scientists began the experimental and theoretical breaking up of this same space some years before modernist art began.

THE STEREOSCOPE

Ordinary visual experience is of a single, homogeneous visual world similar to that portrayed in traditional painting. At least, this is essentially the case when our gaze is fixed on the scene in front of us. (This is not so when our gaze is moved from one object to another.) It

Figure 8.9 Visual stimuli and paintings constructed using random (chance) techniques. A) Donald D. Dorfman and H. McKenna, "Pattern Preference as a Function of Pattern Uncertainty," *Canadian Journal of Psychology*, 1966 B) Ellsworth Kelly's *Seine*, 1951, from E. C. Goosen's *Ellsworth Kelly*. C) Bela Julesz, *Foundations of Cyclopean Perception*, 1971. D) Francois Morellet's *40,000 Quadraten*, 1961 (from Catalog of Galerie Denise Rene, Paris.)

had long been known that this single, or Cyclopean, visual field was somehow constructed from two visual images—the slightly different views of each eye. The question of how the separation underlying right and left eye views were put together to make one view became rather suddenly a major issue in visual science in 1838. In that year, this long-dormant problem came into prominence when Wheatstone (1838) invented what is known as the stereoscope. This instrument, using mirrors or prisms, enabled the viewer to fuse two slightly different two-dimensional drawings of an object into a single, strikingly three-dimensional view. In Wheatstone's original 1838 work, a major point was that the two eyes have a different image projected on them from the scene or object in view. The dissimilarity, of course, is due to the fact that the left and right eye have slightly different points of view. This disparity between the two images in normal vision is combined in the stereoscope (and in stereoscopic sight) to give a strong, three-dimensional perception. For example, Figure 8.10 shows two pairs of drawings of objects taken from Wheatstone (1838). In each pair, the objects are carefully drawn from slightly different angles of regard. The views, when optically fused, cause the objects to be seen in depth.

The stereoscope fractured the existing visual space in various ways. First and most important for the general public, stereoscopic photographs literally broke the visual space by presenting the viewer with two images taken from slightly different viewpoints. The apparatus, held by the viewer, demonstrated in very concrete terms that the Cyclopean, homogeneous visual world was a construct that could be analyzed into two underlying, separate "flat" views. The breaking of space was represented in even more specific detail to any scientist or photographer engaged in making stereoscopic photographs, for example, if two cameras were used, each one very clearly represented a different view of space.

As an example of complex fracturing of space, Wheatstone in 1852 reports taking a series of photographs of the same portrait bust, all from systematically different distances and angles (described in Brewster 1856). The resulting set of photographs represent the same object from multiple points of view. Considered as a *set*, these multiple view photographs, plus the conceptual framework that generated them, contain the essence or kernel of Cubism and can be considered the first visual expression of the Cubist idea. This set is also very suggestive of the first cinematic multiple views developed later by Eadweard Muybridge.

Some of Wheatstone's photographs violated a correct understanding of stereoscopic vision and, hence, were criticized by more knowledgeable scientists (for example, Brewster 1856, pp. 151–53) as representing "binocular and multiocular monstrosities." (The expression

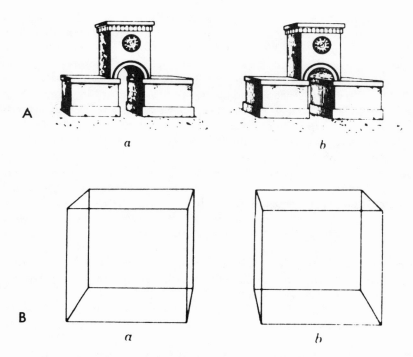

Figure 8.10 Two pairs of stereoscopic drawings from Wheatstone's (1838) article, which first described the stereoscope. Stereoscopic drawings from Charles Wheatstone, "On Some Remarkable and Hitherto Unobserved Phenomena of Binocular Vision," *Philosophical Transactions.*

"multiocular monstrosity" is certainly worthy of the early critics of Picasso.) Whatever their "theoretical" accuracy as stereoscopic views, such images show precisely that not just two but multiple points of view follow naturally from the study of stereoscopic vision.

An additional influence leading to the breaking up of traditional space was the theoretical debate over the exact nature of stereoscopic vision. For example, Howard and Templeton (1966) show the important early theory of space perception proposed by the scientist Hering (1861) not only described the separate view for each eye but also the normal, resultant view first described by Hering and Helmholtz, and later by Julesz, as the "Cyclopean eye." Such theoretical diagrams emphasized the independence, or autonomy, of each eye's view.

EADWEARD MUYBRIDGE: SCIENTIST/PHOTOGRAPHER

In their studies of animal movement, Muybridge and Marey are generally acknowledged as the founders of the cinema (see Hendricks

1975; Scharf 1968). The approach of both primarily involved the analysis of movement in time—but in the case of Muybridge, space was also broken into different points of view.

In Muybridge's famous early photographs, for example, those of the horse in motion (see Chapter 13 in this volume) taken in 1878, he used 24 high-speed stereoscopic cameras placed in series (Haas 1972; Hendricks 1975). The use of the stereoscopic camera technique directly links Muybridge to Wheatstone (see also Figure 8.11). Muybridge's accomplishment was an analytic reductionist one, for this sequence of images broke down the natural perception of animal movement into a series of discrete stills, each existing at a level beneath normal perceptual experience. At the time, this aspect of Muybridge's photographs drew criticism from those who rightfully argued that the discrete, frozen images of moving animals were not correct in terms of natural vision because they show the animal as the human eye could never see it. Such photographs ignored the natural blurred image of movement, mostly due to the persistence of the image on the retina. Instead, they pointed the way to both understanding multiple points of view and the development of cine technique.

At least partly at the instigation of Marey, Muybridge placed the sequences of photographs of the moving horse on a circular glass, which was then rapidly rotated across a narrow opening. This setup, with a light lens, was used to project the series of animal stills on a screen. When presented rapidly, the result was an early form of cinema—one reported to be much smoother than the first jerky movies. The apparatus presenting this early cinema was called the zoopraxiscope. Muybridge's first attempt to devise his zoopraxiscope was based on Wheatstone's reflecting stereoscope. Here, too, he is linked with Wheatstone (Forster-Hahn 1972, p. 71). Later, he abandoned this approach and developed his own instrument, more closely related to the stroboscope invented in 1830 by the French scientist Joseph Plateau (see Boring 1942, p. 589). Muybridge himself claimed his zoopraxiscope to be the prototype for "synthetically demonstrating movement analytically photographed from life" (Hass 1972, p. 26).

MANET

The compositional character of Manet's paintings has from the beginning drawn criticism not only from his detractors but also from staunch supporters. Critics have commented on Manet's "compositional difficulties." Thus, Richardson (1958, p. 12) complains that Manet's works were frequently "badly composed, out of scale, incoherent, especially if the composition involves a degree of recession or indicates two or more figures or groups." I do not wish to take sides in the

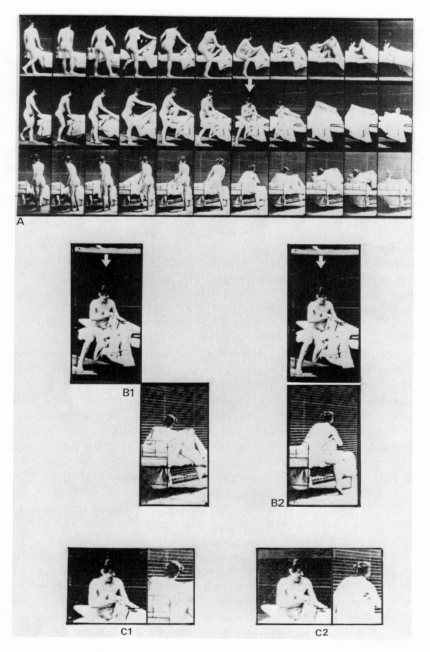

Figure 8.11 Muybridge's sequential photographs from three different points of view plus an illustration of how such different viewpoints can be combined to interpret the composition of Manet's *Bar at the Folies Bergère*. A) Eadweard Muybridge's *Getting into Bed*, ca. 1885 (The University of Pennsylvania series, The Philadelphia Civic Center Museum). B) Enlarged inserts from A. C) Enlarged inserts from A.

evaluative character of this debate; however, it is certainly possible to interpret Manet's intuitive exploration of the new perceptual world with its various points of view as inevitably leading to compositions that would be judged as unsatisfactory by traditional criteria. His well-known *Bar at the Folies Bergere* (1881) is such an example (see Figure 8.12). In this grand painting, the viewer is placed in a spatially or temporally ambiguous situation. The problem is that from the normal point of view, it is impossible for the figures reflected in the mirror to be consistent with the viewer's position in front of the woman. I will propose two closely related interpretations of Figure 8.12 that follow from a Wheatstone–Muybridge type of analysis: interpretation A is that the painting is an integration of one observer's experience at two slightly different points of view, each also at a slightly different point in time. The first view at location one and time one is six or eight feet directly in front of the young woman. At location two and time two, the observer has moved a few feet to the left, allowing the top-hatted man to approach the bar from the right rear. The observer then turns his or her gaze to the reflection of the two figures in the mirror. This analysis argues that the left-hand two-thirds of the painting and the right third are the viewer's two brief glances, which Manet has integrated.

Interpretation B is that there are two observers (or cameras)—one, the man with the top hat, who is standing directly in front of the barmaid, and the other, an observer standing at the left, looking at their reflections in the mirror. In this case, the two viewpoints are of the same moment in time but from different spatial locations—as in taking a stereoscopic photograph. (This argument assumes that the top-hatted man standing in front cannot see his own reflection in the mirror, since it is presumed to be hidden by the young woman.) In either interpretation, however, Manet in a proto-Cubist fashion has integrated two points of view in the same painting.

The conceptual nature of Manet's integration can be understood by noting how multiple points of view are shown in the various Muybridge photographs, for example, the sequences of a woman getting into bed, shown in Figure 8.11(A). Each horizontal series, taken from a different location, is an analysis of time; each vertical column shows the same time from three different locations—while a diagonal grouping of images represents different points of view at slightly different times. Interpretation A of the Manet painting is that of two "diagonal" images—that is, two views from different locations and at slightly different times. The two diagonal images are shown in Figure 8.11(B). (Observe that the top frame in Figure 8.11 [B] is the middle row, seventh frame, in Figure 8.11 [A]—note arrow.) These two forms are integrated in Figure 8.11(C, 1), which should be compared with Figure 8.12. Interpretation B represents the integration of two images from a

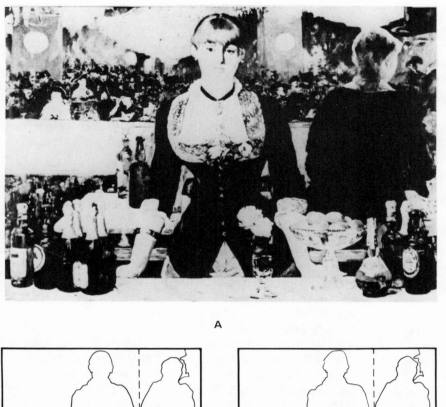

A

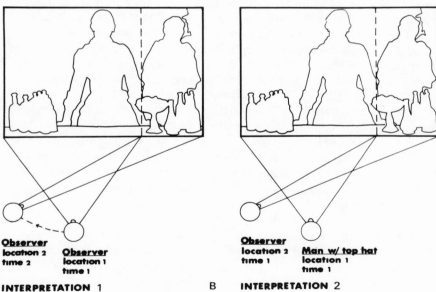

Observer
location 2
time 2

Observer
location 1
time 1

INTERPRETATION 1

Observer
location 2
time 1

Man w/ top hat
location 1
time 1

B   **INTERPRETATION 2**

Figure 8.12   Manet's *Bar at the Folies Bergère*, 1881, and two interpretations of the painting. Each interpretation assumes the integration of two points of view. A) Edouard Manet's *Bar at the Folies Bergère* (Courtland Institute Galleries, University of London). B) Drawings done for the author.

vertical column, Figure 8.11(B, 2) on the right side. Interpretation B starts with the same frame as A (arrow) but then uses a different second frame. These images are taken from two locations but at the same time; they are integrated in Figure 8.11(C, 2) (compare also with Figure 8.12). In any case, the Manet composition can be understood as an artistic equivalent to the space–time analysis of the Wheatstone, Brewster, Hering, and Muybridge tradition.

CÉZANNE

A broken space combining two or more points of view is a familiar characteristic of many of Cézanne's paintings. Excepting Manet's still very tentative work, it is Cézanne who pioneered this type of spatial treatment. Cézanne did it so often and so successfully that it is probably his single greatest contribution to modernist painting and one that proved to be essential to the later development of Cubism. Loran (1943) has identified this property of Cézanne's work with special clarity. Loran's analysis of the *Still Life with Fruit Basket* (in Figure 8.13[B]) is particularly informative: "The first eye level, marked I, takes in, roughly, the front plane of the fruit basket, the sugar bowl, and the smaller pitcher. . . . The second eye level, much higher, marked II, looks down on the ginger jar, and the top of the basket" (1943, p. 76).

The eyes at Ia and IIb represent still two other points of view on the right side of the picture, as though the observer had stepped to this new location. All of this increases the illusion of "seeing around" the object. There is no evidence that Cézanne arrived at these effects through a conscious, scientific approach, but the parallel with Muybridge's multiple views is obvious. The short step from Cézanne's and Muybridge's analyses to Cubism is clearly represented by the sketch of André Lhote (Chipp 1968, p. 193) in Figure 8.13.

Read (1952) noted that although Cézanne never showed any particular interest in science itself (unlike Seurat, for example), his "whole attitude toward nature . . . [was] analytical, experimental, essentially scientific."

We do not wish to detract from recent scholarship, which has emphasized the content of the Cézanne pictures, but Cézanne's great contribution was not in his choice of subject matter, however much it enriched his work. Instead, it is Cézanne's new perceptual understanding that is essential. Cézanne consistently spoke of his preoccupation with a sensory and perceptual experience of nature:

> One must make a vision for oneself . . . one must make an optic. One must see nature as no one has seen it before you—being a painter I attach myself first of all to visual sensation.

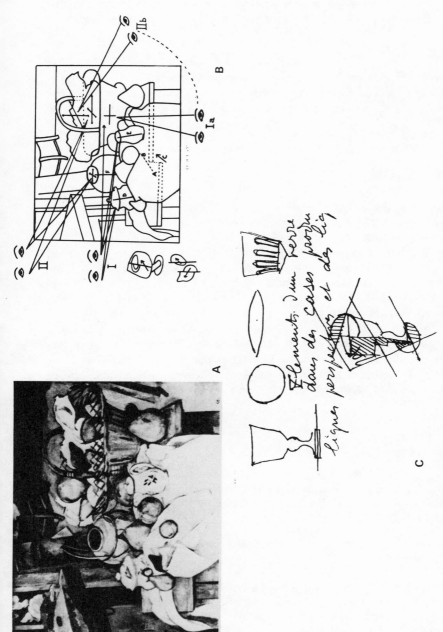

Figure 8.13   Wheatstone-Muybridge multiple viewpoints in a Cézanne painting and a Cubist glass by André Lhote A) Paul Cézanne's *Still Life with Fruit Basket*, 1887(?). B) Erle Loran, *Cézanne's Composition*, 1943. C) André Lhote sketch, 1952, from Herschel B. Chipp's *Theories of Modern Art: A Source Book by Artists and Critics*.

Literature expresses itself by abstractions, whereas painting, by means of drawings and color, gives concrete shape to sensations and perceptions (Chipp 1968, pp. 12–13.)

The French philosopher Merleau-Ponty (see Wechsler 1975, p. 16) in an insightful analysis of Cézanne, interprets his spatial deviations as a rejection of fixed, static perspectives; he writes that Cézanne gives the impression of an object "in the act of appearing"—what better description of the Muybridge photographs?

CONCLUSION

The preceding examples serve to establish the existence of pictorial and conceptual parallelism in the development of visual science and modernist painting. Limitations of space have forced a serious reduction in the number of artists discussed, as well as a reduction in detailed material. Nevertheless, those seminal artists treated here who have been directly affected (for example, Seurat, Delaunay, Kupka, and Klee) make it clear that the scientific study of vision has had a systematic long-term impact on modernist painting. Putting aside the issue of direct influence, the many artists—for example, Manet, Cézanne, Picasso, Arp, Kelly, Riley, and Held—whose distinctive imagery has striking similarities to scientific stimuli support the thesis that both disciplines have been pursuing closely related perceptual studies, more or less in parallel, over the last 100 (or so) years.

REFERENCES

Blanc, C. *Grammaire des arts dessin.* Paris: Renouard, 1867; English title, *The Grammar of Painting and Engraving,* translated by K. N. Doggett. New York: Hurd and Houghton, 1874.

Blumenthal, A. L. "A Reappraisal of Wilhelm Wundt." *American Psychologist* 30 (1975): 1081–88.

Boring, E. G. *Sensation and Perception in the History of Experimental Psychology.* New York: Appleton–Century–Crofts, 1942. (Boring dates the color diagram, on p. 145 as 1860—published in one of Helmholtz' monographs, which preceded the first book edition).

———. *A History of Experimental Psychology.* 2d ed. New York: Appleton–Century–Crofts, 1950.

Brewster, D. *The Stereoscope: Its History, Theory and Construction*. London: Murray, 1856.

Chevreul, M. E. *De la loi du contraste simultane des couleurs* Paris: 1839. This book went through several later editions and is still available in an edition edited by Faber Birren (New York: Reinhold, 1967). The translator's preface to the 1857 English translation by John Spanton, entitled *The Laws of Contrast of Color* (London: Routledge), makes it clear that at that time in England, Chevreul was viewed as the first to scientifically investigate the aesthetic significance of color.

Chipp, H. B. "Orphism and Color Theory." *The Art Bulletin* 40 (1958): 55–63.

———. *Theories of Modern Art: A Source Book by Artists and Critics*. Berkeley: University of California Press, 1968.

Chuck Close: Recent Work. Anon. catalog. New York: The Pace Gallery, 1977.

Dorfman, D. D., and McKenna, H. "Pattern Preference as a Function of Pattern Uncertainty." *Canadian Journal of Psychology* 20 (1966): 143–53.

Forster-Hahn, F. "Marey, Muybridge, and Meissonier—The Study of Movement in Science and Art." In *Eadweard Muybridge: The Stanford Years, 1872–1881*. Palo Alto, Calif.: Department of Art, Stanford University, 1972.

Gibson, E. J. and Walk, R. W. "The Visual Cliff." *Scientific American* 202 (April 1960): 64–71.

Gibson, J. J. *The Perception of the Visual World*. Boston: Houghton–Mifflin, 1950.

Goosen, E. C. *Ellsworth Kelly*. New York: Museum of Modern Art, 1973.

Greenberg, C. "Modernist Painting." In *Arts Yearbook*, (edited by Hilton Kramer) no. 4 (1960).

Harmon, L. B. and Julesz, B. "Masking in Visual Recognition: Effects of Two-Dimensional Visual Noise." *Science* 180 (1973): 1194–97.

Hass, R. B. "Eadweard Muybridge, 1830–1904." In *Eadweard Muybridge: The Stanford Years, 1872–1882*. Palo Alto, Calif.: Department of Art, Stanford University, 1972.

Helmholtz, H. *Handbuch der physiologischen Optik*. Leipzig: Voss, 1867. English title, *Treatise on Physiological Optics*, translated by J. P. C. Southall. Rochester, N.Y.: Optical Society of America, 1924.

Hendricks, G. *Eadweard Muybridge: The Father of the Motion Picture*. New York: Viking, 1975.

Hering, E. *Spatial Sense and Movements of the Eye*, translated by A. Radde. Baltimore: American Academy of Optomology, 1942. (Original German publication, 1861.)

Hochberg, J. "In the Mind's Eye." In *Contemporary Theory and Research in Visual Perception*, edited by R. Haber, pp. 309–31. New York: Holt, Rinehart and Winston, 1968.

Hochberg, J., and Brooks, V. "The Psychophysics of Forms: Reversible Perspective Drawings of Spatial Objects." *American Journal of Psychology* 73 (1960): 337–54.

Hodin, J. P. "Introduction." In L. Vachtova's *Frank Kupka*. New York: McGraw-Hill, 1968.

Homer, W. I. *Seurat and the Science of Painting*. Cambridge, Mass.: MIT Press, 1964.

Honisch, D., Lemoine, S., Imdahl, M., Boehm, G., and Morellet, F. *Francois Morellet*. Berlin: National Galerie Berlin, 1977.

Hoog, M. *Robert Delaunay*. New York: Crown, 1976.

Howard, I. P., and Templeton, W. B. *Human Spatial Orientation*. New York: Wiley, 1966.

Julesz, B. "Binocular Depth Perception of Computer-Generated Patterns." *Bell System Technical Journal* 39 (1960): 1125–62.

Erle Loran, *Cézanne's Compositions*. Berkeley: University of California Press, 1943.

Lovejoy, A. O. *The Great Chain of Being*. Cambridge, Mass.: Harvard University Press, 1936.

Mass, J. B. *Slide Group for General Psychology*. New York: McGraw-Hill, 1967.

Mach, E. *Beitrage zur Analyse der Empfindungen*. Jena: 1886. English title, *The Analysis of Sensations*, translated by C. M. Williams and S. Waterlow (from fifth edition of work). Chicago: Open Court, 1914.

Mladek, M., and Rowell, M. *F. Kupka: A Retrospective*. New York: Guggenheim, 1975.

Needham, G. "Manet, *Olympia*, and Pornographic Photography. In *Woman as Sex Object*, edited by T. B. Hess and L. Nochlin. New York: Newsweek, 1972.

Orbach, J.; Ehrlich, D., and Vainstein, E. "Reversibility of the Neckar Cube," pt. 3, "Effects of Interpolation on Reversal Rate of the Cube Presented Repetitively." *Perceptual and Motor Skills* 17 (1963): 571–82.

Perry, L. C. *The American Magazine of Art* 18 (1927): 119–25.

Read, H. *The Philosophy of Modern Art*. London: Faber and Faber, 1952.

Reff, T. *Manet: Olympia*. New York: Viking, 1977

Richardson, J. *Edouard Manet: Paintings and Drawings*. London: Phaidon, 1958.

———. *Modern Art and Scientific Thought*. Urbana: University of Illinois Press, 1971.

Rood, O. N. "On the Relation between our Perception of Distance and Color." *American Journal of Science* (2d ser.) 32 (1861): 184–85.

———. *Students' Textbook of Color*, or *Modern Chromatics* New York: Appleton, 1879. French translation, *Theorie scientifique des couleurs*. Paris: Bailliere, 1881.

Rosenberg, H. *Artworks and Packages*. New York: Dell, 1969.

Rubin, E. *Synsoplevede figurer*. Kobenhavn: Gyldendalske, 1915. German edition, *Visuell wahrgenommene Figuren*. Kobenhavn: Gyldendalske, 1921.

Sausmarez, M. de. *Bridget Riley*. Greenwich, Conn.: N.Y. Graphics Society, 1970.

Scharf, A. *Art and Photography*. London: Penguin, 1968.

Seitz, W. C. *Claude Monet*. New York: The Museum of Modern Art, 1960.

Stilling, J. *Die Prufung des Farbensinnes beim Eisenbahn und Marinepersonal* (with three plates), Zweite Auflage. Cassel: T. Fischer, 1877. Figure 8.1 (C) taken from plate in *Stilling's pseudo-isochromatische Tafeln zur Prufung des Farbensinnes*, edited by E. Hertel. 17th ed. Leipzig: George Thieme, 1926 (first published in 1878).

Teuber, M. "*Blue Night*, by Paul Klee." In *Vision and Artifact*, edited by Mary Henle, pp. 131–51. New York: Springer, 1976.

Tucker, M. *Al Held*. New York: Whitney Museum of American Art, 1974.

Vitz, P. C. "Preference for Different Amounts of Visual Complexity." *Behavioral Science* 11 (1966): 105–14.

Vitz, P. C., and Todd, T. C. "A Model of the Perception of Simple Geometric Figures," *Psychological Review* 78 (1971): 207–28.

Vriesen, G., and Imdahl, M. *Robert Delaunay: Light and Color*. New York: Abrams, 1967.

Wechsler, J., *Cézanne in Perspective*. Englewood, N. J.: Prentice-Hall, 1975.

Wertheimer, M. "Untersuchungen zur Lehre von der Gestalt." *Psychologische Forschung* 4 (1923): 301–50.

Wheatstone, C. "On Some Remarkable and Hitherto Unobserved Phenomena of Binocular Vision." *Philosophical Transactions* (Royal Society of London) 128 (1838): 371–94.

Whitehead, A. N. *Science and the Modern World*. New York: Macmillan, 1925.

Chapter Nine

Subjective Contours, Contrast, and Assimilation

John M. Kennedy

Today, most theories of perception are "bottleneck" theories: they try to define the unyielding limitations that constrict the flow of activities coursing through the sensory channels. In these conceptions of perceiving and knowing, much goes in but little comes out, and that little is accomplished with considerable effort. These are theories about a sensorium's chronic constipation.

Overshadowed by such theories of limitations, there have been attempts throughout the history of experimental psychology to find and describe productive work by the senses. Researchers sought for clear cases of modifications in percepts engineered by attention and for manipulation of the sensory messages that went far beyond merely grouping, classifying, and interpreting the energy streaming through the perceptual systems. Most of the supposedly clear cases psychology brought forward were simply inappropriate cases, incorrectly analyzed (Kennedy 1974a). But in at least one instance, one where it happens art and psychology are both very active today, there does seem to be a solid reason for believing the phenomena to be the result of productive work by the perceptual machine. The particularly good example is the *subjective contour*.

What is a subjective contour? At this juncture, the answer is best begun with a few demonstrations. Figure 9.1 offers three. One is a line figure, another is a dot figure, and the third is a contour figure, in the sense that expanses of pigment are being used to provide individually distinct real contours, which, in turn, act as a substrate for perceptual effects. In all three, the central region can take on an enhanced brightness in perception. The bright center is generally circumscribed by a distinct division between the inner, brighter region and the outer region. The division is a subjective contour, and the brightness is subjective brightness.

Figure 9.1 The central region in each figure has an apparent brightness greater than the surrounds and is bounded by a subjective contour. The contours and the differences in brightness are not real.

The boundary of the subjective brightness need not always be sharp, and the region bounded by the subjective contour need not always be brighter, as we shall see.

These phenomena have to be included in a modern discussion of painting and representation for several reasons. First, they are popular in one of contemporary art's strongest currents—Op Art and its tributaries. Major painters, such as Victor Vasarely and Bridgit Riley, luxuriate in them. Second, recent perceptual psychology has turned its attention to the effects that can be obtained at the side of a line—the line as divider, as shape (see Figure 9.2)—and the model of that kind of research can readily be borrowed and applied systematically to the end of a line, the bend in a contour, and even the dot, as elements for anchoring visual activity. Many of the effects at the side of a line are representational in kind, and we can expect that many effects at the ends of lines or in dot or contour figures will be representational too. The cave artist uncovered many of the representational effects at the sides of lines, but in this century, we seem to be discovering the pictorial uses of many other kinds of elementary devices. Third, picture perception is bicameral—it is defined as seeing factors like depth and flatness at one and the same time.

The pictured scene is in depth visually while the picturing surface is also, at the same time, seen to be actually flat. Subjective contours may be bicameral too, because the viewer may have them visible as differences in brightness while seeing at the same time that the surface is actually uniform. Hence, subjective contours may be a kind of pictorial brightness perception comparable to pictorial depth perception.

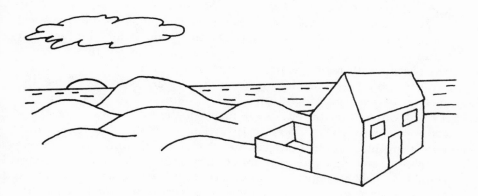

Figure 9.2 In this drawing, lines are used in outline fashion. The sides of the lines are portraying differences in slant (convex and concave corners). Both rounded hills (occluding bounds) and flat foregrounds (occluding edges) are shown. The terminations of the lines are not necessarily significant, since they can "trail off" or be discontinuous with impunity (after J. M. Kennedy, *A Psychology of Picture Perception,* 1974b).

Recent years have seen investigators explain subjective contours in several different ways. Some theories emphasized overlap (Kanizsa 1955; Coren 1972; Gregory 1972; Yonas 1978); others stressed closure (Kanizsa 1974) and figure–ground effects (Bradley and Dumais 1975). Let us consider these theories critically, and begin to sketch an alternative.

OVERLAP

The triangles in Figure 9.1 generally look as though they are resting on top of the inducing elements. Noting this appearance of overlap, some theories propose that stratification in depth is necessary for the production of subjective figures. The foreground surface accounts for the underlying elements by seeming to be an opaque occluder, and the subjective contours are the edges of the occluding surface. The reason for the perception of stratification is that there are depth cues in the display, where a depth cue is defined "as some aspect of a configuration which can be read as consistent with a given spatial arrangement of objects at different relative distances" (Coren 1972, p. 365).

This is a fishy explanation. On the one hand, the definition of a depth cue is very general and rests in a suspiciously circular manner on the impression it is trying to explain. Also, Coren and Yonas suggest that the visual system operates on the principle that "anytime there is a discontinuous black line on a white ground, the discontinuity may be caused by an interposed white figure" (Coren 1972, p. 365). But lines can end for any of a host of reasons! Interposition is just one possibility: a crack, a corner, sheared strata, the actual ending of a shadow, a stick, or a ridge are other possibilities. On the other hand, the fact that stratification accompanies the contours need not mean that it causes the contours. It might be the contours that provide an opportunity for stratification to occur. In figure–ground, real contours enable the viewer to see foreground and background (Rubin 1914; Kennedy 1974b). Subjective contours have many of the properties of real contours (Kanizsa 1955; Gregory 1973; Farne 1979). It is logical that figure–ground depth could be the aftermath of subjective contour formation and not the forerunner. If so, then subjective contours should be able to appear without necessarily being accompanied by stratification—for example, if there was strong information for the relative locations of the inducing elements and their product being at the same depth. This kind of information is provided in three-dimensional constructions—"brightness statues" (see Figure 9.3).

Figure 9.3 is a photograph of a construction, not a flat graphic design (it is not the kind of display where the viewer has had lots of

Figure 9.3 Wooden construction, painted. The central empty area is seen as having a bright circle, sometimes described as like a bright piece of transparent glass, contiguous with the inducing rods (constructed by Colin Ware.)

practice setting aside flatness information as irrelevant and using figure–ground skills to see pictorial depth). In the center of the construction, it is possible to see a vivid subjective contour figure. Viewed directly, rather than in a photograph, with free head movement and binocular vision, there is compelling information for the location of the inducing rods. The viewer can see the induced brightness figure as being at the tip of the rods, coplanar with them, not overlapping.

A number of these displays have been made (Ware and Kennedy 1977, 1978). Both children and adults can see the subjective effects in these brightness statues, and can see the subjective figures as co-planar with the inducing elements. Hence, stratification appears to be unnecessary. (See also Kennedy 1975.)

Finally, a crucial objection to the overlap theory must be raised. The theory has no way of explaining why subjective contour figures are bright. It addresses itself only to the shape of these figures and the location of the edges. If the heart of the matter is the brightness, then this theory has entirely missed the point.

CLOSURE

Kanizsa (1955, 1976) thought that stratification was indeed a secondary factor, and only provided one way to ensure completion of inducing elements with gaps in them (1974, p. 107). He argued that the essential factor is completion of inducing elements. To widen his viewpoint we might ask whether the induced figure should be a complete form. In one respect, the completion viewpoint has been identical to the overlap one. Kanizsa and Coren both emphasize that the reason why completion and overlap operate is to simplify the display, make the inducing display less complex.

Is completion necessary? Will subjective contours arise in figures that do not call for completion of the inducing elements? Figure 9.4 offers an answer (Kennedy 1978).

Figure 9.4 is made of several triangles pointing towards a central open unmarked area. Notice that none of the triangles are incomplete, there are no gaps in the otherwise continuous lines, there are no indications of broken, overlapped or erased inducing elements. Nevertheless, a distinct glow appears in the central region. The subjective brightness does not complete anything; the inducing elements are not completed perceptually in any way. The brightness itself seems to have an indefinite form, though given its surrounds it could have fitted easily as a circle. We might say that it seems like a superfluous vague addendum. To emphasize the point that the subjective brightness is not necessarily (1) something complete, (2) something whose appearance is simple, whole, (3) a means for making the display a less complex Gestalt, consider Figure 9.5.

Figure 9.5 is a display looking rather like a ribbon of paper which has been cut into sections, a series of strips which converge and form a single strip. It is possible to see a subjective contour join the tips of the points where convergence occurs. It is implausible to argue that the extra brightness simplifies the figure, completes some gaps, or is itself a complete figure.

Once again, it should be noted that theories about completion are not just in error, but they may have missed the point; they offer no clue as to why the subjective phenomena are bright. The vagueness of Figure 9.4 may indicate what role completion and overlap theories should play. Perhaps they can help explain the shape taken by subjective

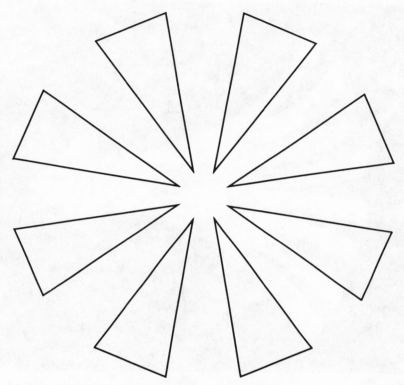

Figure 9.4 Concentric triangles induce a subjective glow in the center, although all the triangles are complete; the glow is an addition rather than a simplification of the figure.

brightness once it appears, induced by other factors. They may account for the vagueness of the perimeters of some effects and the sharpness of the contours of others (Kennedy 1978).

FIGURE–GROUND

Why is the subjective figure brighter than the surround? Bradley argued that the explanation lay in observations made by Rubin (1914). Perceived figures often are more dense in texture, more saturated in color, and more like surface color than physically identical grounds. The white triangular central areas of Figure 9.1 are seen as figures, we might say, and therefore should look more surfacy, more dense, and more saturated (Dumais and Bradley 1975).

This is not a satisfactory explanation, on the face of it. The essential problem to be explained is brightness, and at best, this

Figure 9.5 The tips of the converging strips can be seen as connected by a subjective contour—lighter on the empty side, darker on the side with the strips. The contour adds to the figure rather than simplifying it.

figure–ground account mentions *saturation*, which is not quite the same thing, *surface color*, which is, again, not quite the same thing, and *texture density*, which is very far from brightness. It also fails to account for what might be called the *reciprocal* of Figure 9.1 (Kennedy and Lee 1976).

In Figure 9.6, the elements that might have been missing in Figure 9.1 are shown. Curiously, a shadowy triangle now makes its appearance. It is filmy and insubstantial, weak, but nonetheless something that is seen by adults and children. Also, it is the figure, yet it does not have the properties ascribed to it by Bradley.

Another blow is provided by Figure 9.7.

Here, the figure is now fully presented because lines have been drawn around the triangular perimeter. But the strong brightness has disappeared. The *normal* case does not behave as Bradley would wish, so there is little point in trying to extend a faulty description of it.

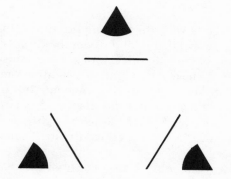

Figure 9.6   Reciprocal figure. The result is a shadowy triangle. In a black–white negative, the shadowy triangle becomes whitish, misty.

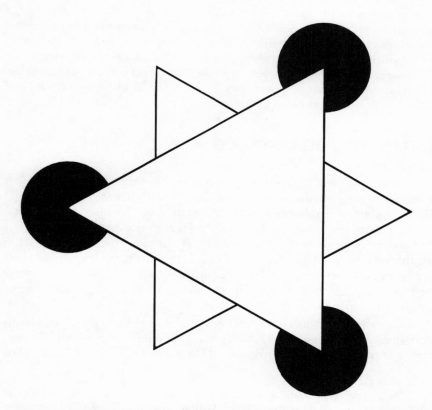

Figure 9.7   When the Kanizsa triangle is drawn with the outline of a triangle, the central region loses most of its strong brightness.

CONTRAST

To grapple directly with the striking brightness in these displays it may be necessary to avoid the kind of depth and form theories above (and other versions of such theories, for example, Ginsberg 1975).* The natural contender then, is some kind of brightness manipulation; one that acts on certain kinds of inducing elements but in a way which is related to aspects of form, so that the shape and clarity of the contours can be considered. One kind of well-known brightness effect that might be of direct relevance is brightness contrast (Brigner and Gallagher 1974).

In its simplest form, a brightness contrast theory is easily refuted. Changes in the luminance of the display have different effects on standard brightness contrast and subjective contour effects (Brussell, Stober, and Bodinger 1977; Dumais and Bradley 1975). Also, brightness contrast increases with the amount of blackness near a white region, but this need not occur in subjective contour formation. Figure 9.8 demonstrates that reducing black solid areas to lines need not diminish subjective brightness and that adding a few more black lines judiciously can reduce the extra brightness to a minimum (Kanizsa 1974).

Something over and beyond simple brightness contrast is called for. I will argue here that both a theory of enhanced brightness contrast and a theory of assimilation are required.

ENHANCED BRIGHTNESS CONTRAST

To account for Figure 9.8, it is necessary to propose that brightness contrast is magnified at the ends of lines (see Figure 9.9). Imagine that there are small brightness buttons attached to the ends of the lines. When these are collected in a central area, the combined effect is massive enough to be visible, though it is not easy to detect the button at the end of a single, solitary line. Two, three, or four lines close together are adequate, however, as Figure 9.10 shows. Hence, as a mass of black pigment is pared down to a series of lines, it grows a set of brightness buttons.

The sharp terminations of lines are not the only features with enhanced brightness contrast effects. Terminations are only the extreme form of a bend (see Figure 9.11)—a line termination is a kind of

---

*The present displays are ones that work well monocularly. Displays that require binocular processes do not always rest on contrast and assimilation effects (Kennedy 1975), and those that do not rely on such effects do not generate brightness differences, although subjective divisions may be produced.

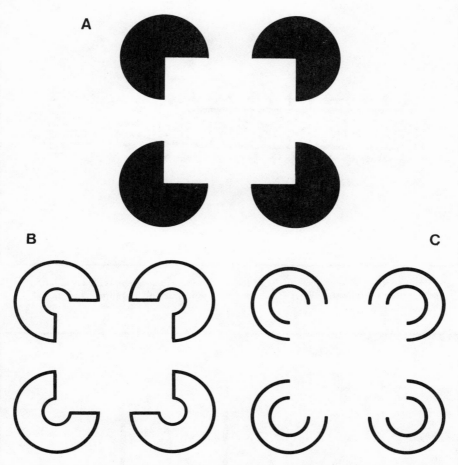

Figure 9.8 Removing most of the black inducing area leaves the central region bright as in C if the inducing elements include the ends of lines terminating in the central region. If the terminations are joined, as in B, and thus turned into corners, the brightness is markedly reduced (after G. Kanizsa, "Subjective Contours," *Scientific American*, 1976).

360-degree bend! Very strong brightness effects can be obtained from quite thick bars (see Figure 9.12) whose perimeters change direction to form bends or cusps rather than points.

Dots can also generate subjective brightness (see Figure 9.13), albeit in a somewhat weaker fashion than displays made of lines. Fading lines work well too—here, a glowing appearance is possible (see Figure 9.14). The dot figures seem to assimilate the interstitial neighboring regions, making them darker, and then the region as a whole acts as a block or stripe or line, depending on its thickness, with enhanced

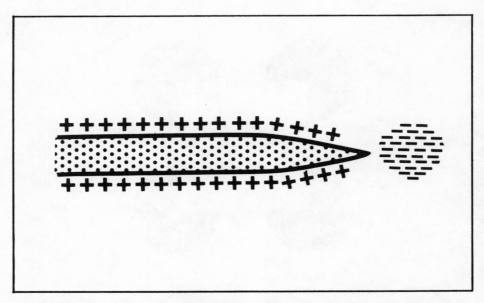

Figure 9.9 A theoretical model of the end of a line, magnified, with assimilation (+) and contrast (–) indicated. There is assimilation alongside and a brightness button at the end.

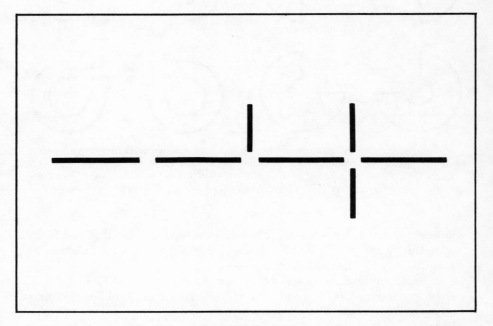

Figure 9.10 Circumscribing a region by line endings induces apparent brightness (see W. Ehrenstein "Uber abwandlungen der Hermannschenn Lelligkeitserscheinung," *Zeitschrifte fur Psychologie*, 1941, and R. Arnheim, *Art and Visual Perception*, 1954.

Figure 9.11 A theoretical model of a bend in a contour with assimilation (+) and contrast (–) indicated. The brightness button is distributed symmetrically on either side of the bend.

Figure 9.12 Strong brightness effect obtained from thick bars with perceptible cusps.

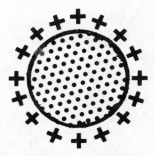

Figure 9.13   A theoretical model of a dot (magnified) showing that it is surrounded by assimilation (+).

Figure 9.14   Sun figure (after J. M. Kennedy, "Sun Figure: An Illusory Diffuse Contour Resulting from an Arrangement of Dots," *Perception*, 1976). Dots are assimilated, forming fading strips, which induce a subjective glow.

contrast acting at the changes in the perimeter of the region. The changes in the perimeter can be changes in direction (bends or cusps) or in reflectance (fading). Elsewhere, assimilation is evident, for example, at the sides of lines, so that there are two dark regions alongside a line, as well as the brightness button at the end (see Varin 1971).

These postulates can account for Figure 9.8 (C). In Figure 9.8 (C), the ends of lines have been removed. What remains are right-angle bends, so that now the brightness buttons are balanced by a darkening effect at the sides of the lines. (In addition, the brightness buttons are not placed squarely and entirely within the central rectangle any longer. Since each button is distributed symmetrically on either side of the bisector of the right-angle bends, a portion of the button is now outside the central rectangle. The difference between the regions outside and inside the rectangle is diminished, compared with Figure 9.8 [B]).

A direct demonstration of the role of brightness buttons at the ends of lines is provided by Figure 9.15. As lines become less and less orthogonal to the area they surround, less and less of the brightness buttons would be included in the central area. Consequently, the difference between the center and the surround would be less marked.

It should be noted that the enhanced contrast theory here is distinct from those contrast theories that emphasize enclosure. Brigner (1969) and Brigner and Gallagher (1974) argue cogently that a region enclosed in an acute angle receives more contrast than a region enclosed in a more obtuse angle. The present theory sees change in direction of a contour as a basis for enhanced contrast. The end of a line, being 360 degrees, is not minimal as an agent for contrast, as Brigner's theory predicts, but maximal, as the present theory predicts. Figure 9.10 favors the present theory over Brigner's.

ASSIMILATION

It is understandable that the dot regions have assimilation effects in their interstices, while lines have assimilation effects alongside. Only where the change in direction in a perimeter is sharp does assimilation give way to brightness contrast. A round dot and a straight or curved line have uniform rates of change of direction—none have cusps. At a cusp in the perimeter, contrast replaces assimilation.

Like contrast, assimilation can produce subjective contours in three dimensions. Figure 9.16 is a black and white construction where the midsection of the bars is white. Most observers, including children, report seeing a mist or film joining the midsections. The mist is produced by assimilation and not just contrast from the exterior black parts of the bars, because if the midsection is painted red, the mist will have a red tinge, if it is painted yellow, the mist will be yellowish, and so

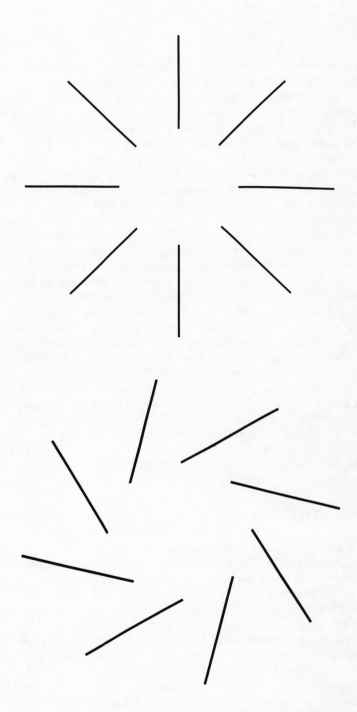

Figure 9.15   As lines become tangents, subjective brightness diminishes because less of the brightness button is interior to the central region.

Figure 9.16 Wooden construction, painted: the central rods assimilate the neighboring regions, inducing a misty appearance. (Constructed by Colin Ware.)

forth. On the other hand, changing the color of the exterior bars has little or no effect on the interior mist. The main effect of the exterior bars is in respect to brightness—if it is made the same lightness as the interior bars, subjective brightness effects are minimized (Brussell, Stober, and Bodinger 1977; Jory and Day in press).

Some authors (Frisby and Clatworthy 1975; Jory and Day in press) suggest assimilation explains the "spreading" of the brightness throughout a large region rather than being concentrated in brightness buttons at the ends of the surrounding lines. An alternative possibility is that the perceived brightness of a region depends on its brightness differences with its neighbors—and a gradual change in brightness across a region will simply not be noticed. (The Ganzfeld experiments of the Gestaltists demonstrate this point of Koffka [1935]). It is evident

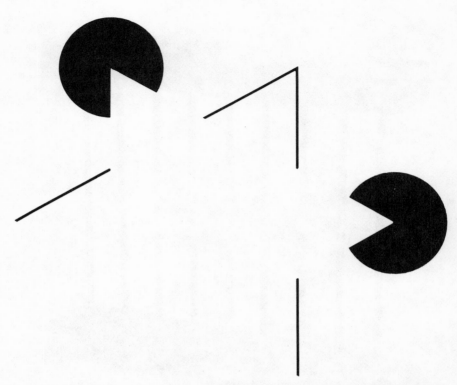

Figure 9.17   When a side of the triangle is deleted, the remainder induces a fading, incomplete triangle.

that there is a gradient of brightness if we erase the base of a Kanizsa triangle (see Figure 9.17). Here, the subjective wedge fades as it narrows. The head of this triangular "comet" does not form a complete figure (it may be added), and the line elements are not "explained" by the presence of the "comet" (as remnants of another triangle).

In sum, there are assimilation effects alongside contours where there are no cusps. At cusps, contrast occurs. Contrast also arises where lines or strips fade, and contrast can follow an initial assimilation of a region of dots.

The contrast and assimilation effects need not be supposed to have sharp borders; indeed, if they are supposed to merge gradually with adjacent regions, this alone may explain how they can seem to affect large regions. How, then, can the sharpness of the edges of subjectively bright forms be explained? For an answer, consider the role of grouping mechanisms.

GROUPING MECHANISMS

Frisby and Clatworthy (1975) argue that enhanced brightness contrast occurs at right angles to the ends of lines. This is unsatisfactory. The brightness effects do not occur in so simple a fashion. Just as the overlap/closure theories miss the point that the brightness must be explained, so, too, some brightness contrast theories fail to recognize that the shape or locus of the effects must be part of the account.

Consider Figure 9.18. The eight concentric line terminations do not vary from the A figure to the B figure, and in both cases, a square is seen. The directions from which the lines come control the perception of the subjective shape. The locus of the brightness effects is not at right angles to the lines, however, in one of the figures. (Also, in simple line figures, such as Figure 9.11, the shapes formed by the subjective brightness vary from circular to square to pincushion. Another figure with varying shapes has been devised by Bradley and Dumais (1975).

The shape of the subjectively bright area depends on the inducing elements and how they are grouped visually in an ensemble.* Thus, the inducing elements surround a square in Figure 9.18 (B). The square can be formed by elements that meet it at any angle, not merely right angles. The square encloses enough of the brightness buttons from the ends of the lines to swell in brightness above the exterior area.

Presumably, the brightness buttons at the ends of lines are just in front of the line. In becoming manifest in perception, they act on either side of divisions between perceived groupings. When there is a division that cuts across the line at right angles, all of the brightness button is on one side of the division (and all of the assimilated darkening alongside the line is on the other side of the division). When the division is not orthogonal to the line, it cuts across the brightness button, leaving some of it on either side of the division. When the division is collinear with the line, the brightness button is equally present on both sides of the division, and no brightness differences between the two sides will remain to produce a subjective contour.

That grouping factors have to be an essential part of any discussion of subjective contours is shown by Figure 9.19. This figure is a series of converging lines that meet at a central dividing line. The divider is quite

---

*Note that questions about what ensures one grouping rather than another are not being addressed here, only the impact of the final grouping at a given time. Gestalt principles, attention, ecological factors, depth indicators, the completeness of the result, the inherent interest of the result, and other factors can all influence grouping (Kennedy 1975, 1976b, 1978). No one factor is necessary. Other approaches to subjective contours have often mistakenly taken one influence on grouping and claimed it to be the sole generating factor.

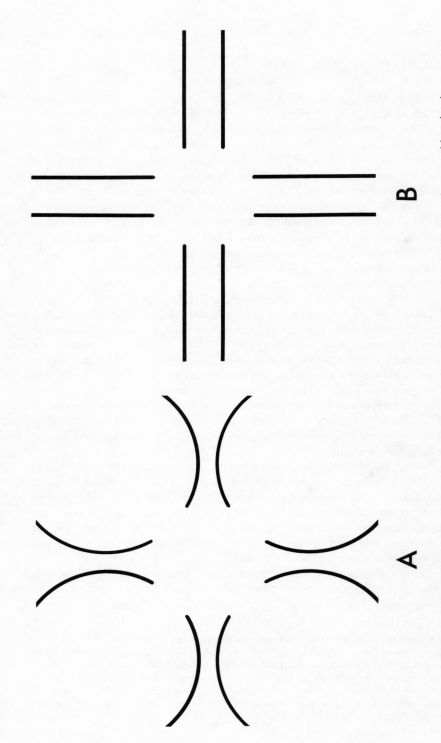

B

A

Figure 9.18   Two similar subjective forms induced by pairs of lines that readily group around a central square, although only one has the lines terminate as normals.

Figure 9.19 A central dividing line: the two regions on either side of the line can be perceived as equal in brightness at the same time as the line is seen.

visible (*modal* in Kanizsa's terms, as opposed to *amodal*, like our sense of the back of an object). Yet, it is not simply a bright strip; nor is it a contour between a dark side and a light side.

If we were to adopt the thesis that enhanced brightness occurs at the ends of lines and at right angles to them, Figure 9.19 would be puzzling. But there are two factors evident here. One is the grouping of the lines' endings along a rectilinear locus and the second is the brightness effects that operate on both sides of the divider. At the tip of one line, the brightness button is mostly to the left; the neighbors have enhanced brightness to the right, while their neighbors have extra brightness to the left, again. The result is a dividing line supported by brightness contrast in a curious, oscillating manner. We see a visible divider, and although it is hard to be sure of its brightness, its location is sharply exact. (Occasionally, subjects are able to say that it is brighter to the front of each line, that the brightness fades away the further from the line endings, that it is darker alongside the lines, and that the division is least clear midway between the line ends.) The line can be made to curve simply by staggering the line ends appropriately. Evidently, then, the grouping factors are of paramount importance, not just a mechanical physiological contrast mechanism operating solely on local line terminations, cusps, and so forth joining them by straight lines.

ENVIRONMENT FEATURES

Contrast and assimilation are traditionally called *sensation* issues. Grouping influences are then held to be higher-order Gestalt factors. A third level of analysis is the ecological. In other words, one asks about energies, then about patterns, and, finally, about meaning. Attempts to find perceived environmental factors in subjective brightness and form have been oversimplifications, so far, and correction is called for.

Gregory (1972), Coren (1972), and Yonas (1978) all call attention to the fact that the visible termination of a line could be the result of occlusion. However, to leap to this particular account is to be blind to the real environment, as well as to be all but circular, because the percept is being used to select only one of many possibilities. The termination of a line can result from a corner, from a surface being wiped clean, from the end of a rod, or from the end of a shadow. A contrast in the light to the eye can be an indication of a pigment change on a surface, a shadow on a surface, an edge, a corner, or a highlight. The surface can be opaque or transparent. It can be a radiant source or a reflector of light. The contrast in light to the eye can be from two abutting surfaces, one surface against a background or empty sky, or it might be just a wire with background on either side. A serious account of the structures or patterns that distinguish one kind of environmental origin from another is only just beginning (Gibson 1966; Kennedy 1974b; Winston 1975). What is clear is that to select one kind of origin and one kind of subjective contour and build a theory on them is to insist that these selections fully represent the other possibilities— which, of course, they do not. Further, it is now sure that conditions like occlusion are not necessary for subjective contours to form.

The underlying conceptions in an ecological approach are that the inducing patterns are sufficiently meaningful and that the percepts are of the relevant environmental origins. Taken baldly, both conceptions are in error, but in both, there is a saving grace, which may prove eminently helpful in the study of perception. Consider the conceptions in turn.

The inducing patterns in subjective contour displays are not always distinctive of particular environmental origins like objects, surfaces, shadows, and so forth. They can be made so detailed that they specify an edge or even a whole object, like a silhouette of a man. But they do not have to be so detailed. A few lines around a central spot suffice. Evidently, these are not supplying ecological information specific to an origin (Kennedy and Ostry 1975). Further, *none* of the subjective contour displays specify whether the environmental object is bright or dark. Yet, perception of particular brightness–darkness relations is consistent across subjects and occasions. (In principle, it would be possible to make the displays so detailed that a brightness relationship was specified, but that is totally irrelevant for present purposes). The factors impelling perception of subjective contours in the figures here are not those relevant to ecological optics. The figures here are artificial, simple displays. They call for a kind of analysis of structure that pertains to what Gibson called *impoverished* displays, although it is better to think of them as displays that maximize and emphasize perceptual factors, such as contrast and grouping, which aid perception but do not operate at the level of meaning or reference or singling out environmental origins.

Nevertheless, just as nonsense syllables can find meaning, so, too, subjective contour figures have remnants of meaning even in their simplified condition. It is not that the perceiver registers a pattern or structure that specifies an environmental origin but, rather, contrast and grouping factors produce a percept that has some characteristics of a percept of an environmental origin. The range of characteristics matches the range of brightness differences in the environment. Brightness differences can arise from opaque surfaces, alike in perceived characteristics to our perception of Figure 9.1. The surface may be luminous, appearing like Figure 9.12 to the eye. The edge of a brightness difference can be abrupt or sharp, appearing like Figure 9.14

to the eye. The surface need not be opaque, in which case it will look like Figure 9.16 (subjective mist). The brightness difference may arise as a result of a shadow, looking like Figure 9.7, or it may be simply a crack, looking like Figure 9.19.

In sum, for each environmental case that constitutes a brightness difference, there is a corollary subjective contour effect. Normally, the relevant percept is only occasioned when there is an adequate ecological optic structure to justify it. But these displays marshal contrast and grouping effects to enforce the percept in the absence of optical information. There are two routes to the percept, it seems.

However, it should not be thought that the percept is necessarily "illusory" or "hallucinatory," in the sense that the perceiver takes it to be real—a point that needs some careful thought.

EPISTEMOLOGY AND PHENOMENOLOGY

Phenomenologically, subjective contours can adopt the various guises to which real contours come wrapped, be they opacity, transparency, shadow, or substance. Were the viewer to take a genuine foreground white object and a subjective contour form to be one and the same, indistinguishable so far as solidity were concerned, he or she would be said to be suffering from an illusion. Without claiming that subjective contour forms are always detectably unreal, let us examine the possibility that it is possible to see subjective contours and see that they are unreal at the same time, in the kinds of displays used here.

My own observations and my informal gathering of other people's impressions are firm and consistent. Asked if they can see "the shape that isn't really there," most naive observers immediately point to Kanizsa's triangle, the sharp dividing line in Figure 9.19, and so forth. It might be conjectured that leading questions, some informal knowledge of Op Art, and contamination with figure–ground effects underlie these judgments. Hence, tests with children are necessary, and the tests should be conducted with displays that do not have distractions, such as pictorial depth, in them. The appropriate displays are three-dimensional constructions, such as Figures 9.3 and 9.16. The results are surprisingly definite.

Children of three to four years can see the same mists and glasslike shapes in brightness statues as adults. They also say that the mists and glasslike shapes cannot be touched and will not be disturbed by putting one's finger or a pencil in them; indeed, some children have expressly said the shapes are made of "nothing" or "air" (Kennedy, Ware, and Magnan-Smith 1977).

What do these results mean? Subjective contours are visible and visibly unreal at one and the same time (just as a picture allows us to see depth and flatness at the same time). The theory we must develop to account for subjective contour should include this fact.

One possibility is that subjective contours are products of extra-foveal activity. We might consider that regions outside the foveal channel in the visual system create subjective contours and that the reason they look unreal is that foveation tells us what is unreal, because under foveation, they disappear.

This is an attractive possibility, but possibly too simple. First, foveation destroys our percept of faint stars and the gradual penumbra of shadows. But we are not lead to the conclusion that stars and shadows are unreal! Second, not all subjective contours disappear under foveation (for example, Figure 9.19 holds at some distance).

An alternative theory can be developed—in a kind of processing model.

A PROCESSING MODEL OF SUBJECTIVE CONTOURS

In the beginning is the real contour, and the real contour is perceived, and the perceiving is of the real contour. The mind gathers the real contours one unto another that they may belong together and yet each have their own place. The mind says unto the contours: be fruitful and multiply.

The mind knows the world and knows that it is good. The mind is wont to say: ho, what manner of contour is this that they may be divided each unto their own kind: one for shadow, one for highlight, one for edge, one for color, one for being luminous, and one for transparency? For the divisions of light are of several kinds. Thus, semblance belongs in perception. Verily, the mind knows semblance, and true division, and multiplying, but the greatest of these is truth. Accordingly, the mind keeps for itself the real contour that it may be compared to the fruit of the contour. And when comparison is done, the mind knows what is true and what is mere semblance.

In other words, inducing contours are primary. These have two kinds of properties. First, there are properties that are dealt with in perception of their brightness characteristics—magnitude of brightness differences and rate of change of brightness. In processing these properties, strictly local contrast and assimilation effects arise at the ends of lines, sides of lines or dots, changes in direction of perimeter, and fading out of strips. Once this kind of processing is complete, a copy is handed on to a more global processing system. Second, there are properties that allow them to be treated globally and grouped, such as shape, location, symmetry, and so forth. Grouping defines divisions between regions. On either side of a division, the global processing system may find the brightness contrast and assimilation factors different enough to be noticeable. The result is a percept that has some properties in common with a veridical percept of opaque or transparent surfaces, luminous or reflecting surfaces, shadowed or illuminated surfaces, edges, corners, cracks, wires, and so forth.

The perceptual system is thus operating with two kinds of properties, as well as a system of classification. The classifying system is provided with two sources of energy, one being a copy of the inducing contours and the second being the upshot of the grouping activity. In the grouping product, there are some extra contours, but since these have no local support in the copy of the inducing contours, they can be deemed to be unreal, despite the fact that they resemble genuine environmental conditions.

PROBLEMS

The theory of contrast and assimilation delineated above is more convincing than any of its contemporary competitors. It handles the three basic phenomena quite well. First, the brightness in subjective forms can be accounted for. Second, the location of subjective contours and divisions is understandable. Third, the inducing elements involved are listed. In addition, some perceptual judgments of the contour's status in reality suggest a processing model.

However, it has loose ends that should not be ignored. At the level of inducing elements, there is something forced in classifying the product of a fading line (or strip) along with line ends and cusps in contours. Why a fading line should give rise to enhanced contrast is not obvious, unless some overlap theory is useful here (see Kennedy 1976b). Also, the claim that assimilation gives way to contrast when the line develops a sharp bend—while well based in phenomenology—needs some further substantiation. Further, some subjects report that the brightness relations in subjective contour displays are reversible (Kennedy 1976b), which is a total mystery at present.

What about grouping? Here, too, there are perplexities. If a brightness button occurs at the end of a dark line, why should its effect be corralled by a grouping which in part cuts across it? The claim, above, was that when a large portion of the brightness button was inside a shape and a small portion was outside, a sharp contour defining the shape would be perceived. The explanation is vague, however, on just *why* the contour is sharp.

On resemblance and ecology, the theory is unclear about why opacity occurs. It seems possible that the Kanizsa triangle could be filmy, but instead, it looks opaque, which is one reason why the overlap hypothesis was advanced in the first place. It seems clear why transparent films would appear in three-dimensional constructions, since the background is visible. But should we simply say that in the absence of information for transparency, surfaces are opaque, and leave it at that?

In sum, the theory faces up to the main issues, but it is less forthright about some quirks. Oddities have a way of suddenly becoming central issues, and it behooves us to be scrupulous about them. It was something of a revolution to replace overlap and closure—shape factors—with contrast factors at the head of the theories on subjective contours. If resemblance becomes a key issue, perhaps a new explanation of the brightness phenomena will be forthcoming.

SUMMARY

Early treatments of subjective contours envisaged them as contradictory to the classic laws of contrast. Closure and stratification were the major explanations in more recent years. Now, it seems that a revised theory of contrast is more satisfactory. The subjective brightness is due to inducing elements, massed within a grouping suggested by the distribution of the elements. The end product resembles one of the range of sources of brightness differences in the environment, albeit a copy of the inducing elements can show the perceptual system where there is no local support for the constructed brightness difference.

Subjective contours are popular in art, instructive to psychology, tantalizing to epistemology, and as curious to the man-in-the-street as to the researcher, and for many of the same reasons, for they call to any inquiring mind. Though our knowledge of them grows apace, our understanding has the look of untried youth—useful, promising, but not entirely convincing.

REFERENCE

Arnheim, R. *Art and Visual Perception*. Los Angeles: University of California Press, 1954.

Bradley, D. R. and Dumais, S. T. "Ambiguous Cognitive Contours." *Nature* 258 (1975): 582–84.

Brigner, W. L. "Theoretical Model for Lateral Inhibitory Interaction in the Human Retina." *Perceptual and Motor Skills* 28 (1969): 119–42.

Brigner, W. L., and Gallagher, M. B. "Subjective Contour: Apparent Depth or Simultaneous Brightness Contrast?" *Perceptual and Motor Skills* 38 (1974): 1047–53.

Brussell, E. M.; Stober, S. R.; and Bodinger, D. M. "Sensory Information and Subjective Contour." *American Journal of Psychology* 90 (1977): 145–56.

Coren, S. "Subjective Contours and Apparent Depth." *Psychological Review* 79 (1972): 359–67.

Ehrenstein, W. "Uber abwandlungen der Hermannschen Lelligkeitserscheinung." *Zeitschrifte fur Psychologie* 150 (1941): 83–91.

Farne, M. "On the Poggendorf Illusion." *Perception and Psychophysics* 8 (1979): 112.

Frisby, J. P., and Clatworthy, J. L. "Illusory Contours: Curious Cases of Simultaneous Brightness Contrast." *Perception* 4 (1975): 349–57.

Gibson, J. J. *The Senses Considered as Perceptual Systems.* Boston: Houghton–Mifflin, 1966.

Ginsberg, A. P. Is the Illusory Triangle Real or Imaginary?" *Nature* 257 (1975): 219–20.

Goldstein, M. B., and Weintraub, D. J. "The Parallel-less Poggendorf: Virtual Contours Put the Illusion Down but Not Out." *Perception and Psychophysics* 11 (1972): 353–55.

Gregory, R. L. "Cognitive Contours." *Nature* 238 (1972): 51–52.

———. "The Confounded Eye." In *Illusion in Nature and Art*, edited by R. L. Gregory and E. H. Gombrich, pp. 48–95. London: Duckworth, 1973.

Jory, M. K., and Day, R. H. "Brightness Contrast and Subjective Contour." Unpublished paper, 1978.

Kanizsa, G. "Margini quasi-percettivi in campi con stimolazione omogenea." *Rivista di Psicologia* 49 (1955): 7–30.

———. "Contours without Gradients or Cognitive Contours?" *Italian Journal of Psychology* 1 (1974): 93–113.

Kanizsa, G. "Subjective Contours." *Scientific American* 234 (1976): 48–64.

Kennedy, J. M. "Perception, Pictures and the Et Cetera Principle." In *Perception: Essays in Honor of J. J. Gibson*, edited by R. B. MacLeod and H. Pick, pp. 209–26. Ithaca, N.Y.: Cornell, 1974a.

———. *A Psychology of Picture Perception.* San Francisco: Jossey–Bass, 1974b.

———. "Depth at an Edge, Coplanarity, Slant Depth, Change in Direction and Change in Brightness in the Production of Subjective Contours." *Italian Journal of Psychology* 2 (1975): 107–23.

———. "Attention, Brightness and the Constructive Eye." In *Vision and Artifact*, edited by M. Henle. New York: Springer, 1976a.

————. "Sun Figure: An Illusory Diffuse Contour Resulting from an Arrangement of Dots." *Perception* 5 (1976b): 479–81.

————. "Illusory Contours Not Due to Completion." *Perception* 7 (1978): 187–89.

Kennedy, J. M., and Lee, H. "A Figure-density Hypothesis and Illusory Contour Brightness." *Perception* 5 (1976): 387–92.

Kennedy, J. M., and Ostry, D. "Approaches to Picture Perception: Perceptual Experience and Ecological Optics." *Canadian Journal of Psychology* 30 (1975): 90–98.

Kennedy, J. M., and Ware C. "Illusory Contours Can Arise in Dot Figures." *Perception* 7 (1978): 191–94.

Kennedy, J. M.; Ware C.; and Magnan-Smith, J. "Illusory Contours Are Perceived by Children and Judged To Be Unreal" Paper delivered at Canadian Psychological Association Conference, June 1977, Vancouver, B.C.

Koffka, K. *Principles of Gestalt Psychology* New York: Liveright, 1935.

Rubin, E. *Synsoplevede figurer* Kobenhavn, Gyldendals 1915.

Smith, A. T., and Over R. "Tilt After Effects with Subjective Contour." *Nature* 257 (1975): 581–82.

————. "Orientation, Masking and the Tilt Illusion with Subjective Contours." *Perception* 6 (1977): 441–47.

Varin, D. "Fenomeni di contrasto e diffusione cromatica nell' organizzazione spaziale del campo percettivo." *Rivista di Psicologia* 65 (1971): 101–28.

Ware, C., and Kennedy, J. M. "Illusory Line Linking Solid Rods." *Perception* 6 (1977): 601–2.

————. "Perception of Subjective Lines, Surfaces and Volumes in 3-Dimensional Constructions." *Leonardo* 11 (1978) 111–14.

Winston, P. H. *The Psychology of Computer Vision* New York: McGraw–Hill, 1975.

Yonas, A. "Comments on Subjective Lines." *Leonardo* (in press).

Chapter Ten

A New Theory of
the Psychology of
Representational Art

Margaret A. Hagen

The development of a perceptually based theory of representational art belongs most properly to the perceptual psychologists rather than to any other of the many types of visual scholars active today. Yet, it must be admitted that despite the obviously necessary and intimate relationship between theories of perception and theories of representation, the field known as the psychology of art is still in its infancy. It is only in the recent past that theoretical writers in psychology have turned their attention to the subject. Likewise, it is only in the last fifteen years that the field of empirical psychology has shown a flurry of research activity on problems of pictorial perception (discussed long ago by anthropologists and child psychologists).

Yet, despite this renaissance of interest in the problems of the psychology of art, no theory of the relationship between perceptual processes and the process of creating and perceiving a representational picture has been forthcoming. Perhaps it is because such a theory of visual perception must be descriptively adequate, ecologically valid, and successfully account for the range of cultural and historical options in representational depiction, which seem on first glimpse to be incomprehensibly diverse.

Currently, the field has offered us three rather different theories of how a representational painting works perceptually. The first is the constructivist theory of Gombrich, the second the Gestalt theory of Arnheim, and the third, the perspectivist theory of Gibson and his students. Gombrich is a constructivist in that in his perceptual theory, he makes the traditional philosophical distinction between sensation and perception within the context of a distinction between sight and knowledge. For Gombrich, seeing is the experience of sensation, while knowledge is the construction of a meaningful percept. Percepts are constructed out of sensory raw material through a process of trial-and-error hypothesis testing. The percepts so constructed are always "theory laden," or conceptual in nature, rather than innocent products of stimulation. In a like manner, Gombrich traces the history of art. The sensory raw material of depiction was given to early man perhaps by patterns of growth or erosion (easily observed in nature). These patterns prompted the development of schemata, or canons of representation, which succeeded for a time, until the images they produced no longer looked convincing. When this took place, the schemata would be modified until convincing images were again generated. Since this theory is intrinsically subjectivist and allows no criteria for what looks convincing outside the reigning schemata, it is extremely difficult to see how development in the history of art would ever have taken place. Yet, according to Gombrich, take place it did and in a clear direction of an evolution toward the depiction of visual sensation—sight—away from the depiction of visual percepts (knowledge). This distinction and development is familiar to many psychologists in the form of the argument which states that children and primitives draw what they know, while adults and sophisticated peoples draw what they see.

Gombrich argues that such an evolution was misguided, and indeed doomed to failure, since all adults experience only theory-laden percepts, not sensations, and are incapable of recapturing the innocent eye assumed to be possessed by babies. Gombrich explicitly denies that his theory depicts art history as a development toward realism, but his treatment both of that history and of perception leads to that interpretation. If realism is removed from his scheme of things as a post hoc mover of development and if nature herself is unavailable to the artist in any objective way, then the history of art given by Gombrich is one of unaccountable mystery. Not only do the adoption and abandonment of various representational schemata occur for no known reasons, but the perceptual relationships among the schemata are also unknown. Since schemata are not generated out of a common perceptual core of visual "truth," no systematic means of discussing similarities and differences among schemata and consequent styles can possibly exist. The interrelationships discussed therefore become geographical and chronological rather than perpeptual. For the purpose of arriving at a perceptual theory that adequately accounts for the history and diversity of art, this is clearly an unsatisfactory state of affairs.

In fairness to Gombrich, however, it must be observed that he is not a perceptual psychologist and that his omissions are therefore a natural consequence of his primary domain of interest. Arnheim, on the other hand, is a psychologist, a Gestalt psychologist, who has done more to establish the field of the psychology of art than any other scholar, living or dead. There are two basic components to Arnheim's perceptual theory: Gestalt principles and the visual concept. The recognition or discovery of the primacy of organizational factors in perception led, of course, to the serious weakening of the constructivist influence on theories of perception and to the establishment of research endeavors designed to identify the laws of organization. These laws are familiar to all perceptual psychologists as the laws of symmetry, proximity, common fate, good continuation, and so on. Arnheim saw in the Gestalt principles of organization a common ground for artist and perceptionist to meet. For Arnheim, the act of perceiving and the act of artistic creation are alike in that their natures consist of the grasping of significant structural patterns. This grasping of structure is the primary function of what Arnheim calls a *visual concept*. According to Arnheim, the simplest visual concept of the object has three important properties. "It conceives of the object as being three-dimensional, of constant shape, and not limited to any particular projective aspect" (1954, p. 90). The nature of the visual concept leads to three different perceptual attitudes: the everyday attitude, the sophisticated aesthetic attitude, and the reductionist attitude. These three perceptual attitudes toward the world also lead to three different artistic attitudes or approaches. The everyday perceptual attitude consists of noticing only the permanent, constant properties of objects, using the momentary variations in appearance as indications only of relative location. The aesthetic attitude reflects the ability to grasp the unfolding identity of an object while appreciating the multitude of appearances presented as the object or observer goes from situation to situation. The reductionist attitude consists of perceiving a given object to be changing its character when its context or appearance changes. The representation of these three attitudes in artistic style is obvious. The *everyday attitude* presumably characterizes the art of children and primitive people, who are concerned primarily with the depiction of simple object identity without attention to momentary appearances. Thus, the objective permanent shape of the object will be reproduced as closely as the medium permits. The *reductionist attitude* is rather beautifully exemplified in the works of the Impressionists, probably most clearly in Monet's work; and the *aesthetic attitude* is found in Western post-Renaissance painting up to the time of the Impressionists.

Arnheim's system and theory is provocative and even elegant, but it has three basic shortcomings. First, it is based on a perceptual theory that has never been shown to have adequate explanatory value for the perception of the ordinary environment. Second, his postulation of a development of perceptual and artistic attitude from everyday to aesthetic or reductionist is belied by both the facts of so-called primitive art and by the art of non-Western cultures; and third, his system really does not give us an organizational framework for discussing similarities and differences among art styles across time and culture. It is really more appropriate as a system for analyzing individual paintings into applications of Gestalt principles.

The third school of thought provides objective criteria and an organizational framework for discussing similarities and differences among art styles and for evaluating development in the history of art. This theory, that of the perspectivists, argues that linear perspective in pictures is a logical, optical, geometrical necessity. Thus, any picture can be evaluated as a representation in terms of how accurately it depicts linear perspective, and historical development of art can be similarly logged. This theory is based on sound scientific and mathematical analyses of the structure of the light striking the eye from scenes and pictures. Its problems, however, have received a great deal of attention in recent years and may be briefly mentioned here.

First, as an optically based system of representation, linear perspective nevertheless has been shown empirically to be inexplicably limited in its applications, as well as in its utility, in accounting for the problem of form perception in pictures. Second, it is completely impossible to account for the representational success of all the nonperspectival drawing systems, past and present using linear perspective as the fundamental criterion of success. Since nonperspectival systems, such as those of the Egyptians, the Kwakiutl Indians, and David Levine, clearly do succeed as representations, there is something wrong with the theory.

What is wrong with perspectivist theory is the same thing that is wrong with perceptual theory in general—too great an emphasis on a single facet of perception. In this case, as with the constructivists, there is too great an emphasis on the importance of the momentary appearances of objects—on the problem of perceiving permanance or constancy in the world in the face of continual change in the stimulus. This preoccupation obsessed perceptual psychologists until James Gibson, who argues that perception has nothing to do with experiencing sensations or integrating momentary appearances to achieve constancy. He writes that picking up the permanant properties of the environment is dependent instead on detecting the formless and timeless invariants in light that specify them. Gibson argues that the business of perception consists of resonating to the invariant properties of the structure in the light to the eye which specify objects, layout, and events in the world while ignoring the momentary or accidental appearances of things on the retina. This theory can also be criticized for having too great an emphasis on a single aspect of the perceptual process. Both Gibson's and Arnheim's emphasis on the importance of structural invariants in perception has seriously underestimated the importance and availability to awareness of the variant or momentary appearances of things, just as the constructivists and perspectivists failed to consider the critical importance of invariant appearance.

An adequate theory must conceive of visual perception as consisting of three interrelated components: first, the ability to pick up the formless and timeless *invariants* that specify the variant properties of objects; second, the ability to attend to and indeed generate the momentary perspective appearances of objects that specify the variant properties of objects; and, third, an awareness of the rule for generating these invariant and variant aspects operating as a conjunction of the permanent properties of the object and the geometrical transformations it can undergo. The entire family of possible perspective views of an object is determined by a rule that specifies the invariant information for the object persistent across its members. Each aspect is available to the perceiver, as are the generative rules governing them.

The psychological availability of such generative rules is evidenced by the facility with which novel views of objects and scenes are perceived—in pictures, in psychological laboratories, and by small children. Ordinary perception is most probably concerned with the business of picking up invariant information from the permanent properties of the environment. But, it also seems true that the perceiver must be aware of the lawful generation of perspectival families and their members for the perception of novelty, change, and location of self. Both the variant and invariant components of optical structure are determined by the common projective rule, which generates them as a function of object character and transformation. Neither has priority logically, developmentally, or artistically.

The representational implications of this generative theory of perception are many. In the first place, it anchors all perceptual components of art into a common core of projective geometry. In visual perception, the projective geometry for an observer at any given station point is given by what is traditionally called *natural perspective*. Natural perspective is the solid angular analysis of the structure of the light coming to the eye and contains such familiar components as the variation in size and occlusion of projected elements with angle and distance of view point. Gibson moved our analysis of natural perspective to a greater level of ecological validity by stressing the structural relationships within natural perspective and changing the unit of analysis from points to relations across time. Nevertheless, the context of nonchange across time is that of change or natural perspective, which characterizes the changing momentary appearances of things. Thus, any adult at any time in any culture will and must experience all three of these components of perception: variants, invariants, and generator. All three components are constantly available to the artist. Therefore, *representationally* speaking, there can be no perceptual development in art across culture or history. This means the aesthetic attitude is always available to the artist and always has been. So, what then is the difference among styles of art, and how can the differences be characterized perceptually? There are only three perceptual ways in which one representational system differs from another and by which it can be characterized perceptually. First, one style differs from another in the station point assumption made by the artist, be it one station point versus many, central versus eccentric, or near versus far. Each artist chooses his or her depiction system. Second, styles differ in their relative emphasis on the variant versus the invariant properties of objects and scenes. Third, paintings and styles can be categorized according to the artist's relative degree of interest in the three- versus the two-dimensional components of the painting, in the problem of what might be called the *depiction of volume versus the creation of pattern*. These three characteristics of style, determined as they are in the constraining context of natural perspective, together create a system for analyzing the representational character of any art style and for placing it within an organizational framework that allows for the determination of the degree of similarity and difference among seemingly diverse styles.

To demonstrate the applicability of this generative system, I will undertake a very brief analysis of two art styles. I have selected rock art and Egyptian art, because historically, scholars have written very different things about them.

Rock art is the earlier style, despite the previous assertion that there exists no perceptual development in representational art. Indeed, it is hoped that the cave art chosen for analysis may itself present strong visual evidence against such development.

This rock art is that found in the caves of Spain. The site chosen for analysis in Figure 10.1 is the cave at Altamira, Spain. These paintings date from 10,000 to 12,000 years of age and have been assigned to the Magdalenian (final) division of the Upper Paleolithic age. It should be noted, however, that this dating is more a function of theory of the evolution of art style than it is of more objective archaeological techniques. Thus, the specific placement of the Altamira paintings within the Ice Age is a matter of some controversy, but for the present purposes, precision of dating is not relevant. The paintings depicted in Figure 10.1 are from the ceiling of a chamber known as the "Picture Gallery." The chamber is approximately 20 yards long and ten yards wide, while the ceiling is only approximately five feet high. A group of about 25 animals was painted on 15 yards of the ceiling. According to Walter Fairservis of the American Museum of Natural History, the animals are not placed in any particular order but are grouped into a kind of rough equilateral triangle, with the base extending along the long axis of the chamber. The paintings, discovered by accident by the

Figure 10.1   Rock art from cave at Altamira, Spain.

young daughter of the archaeologist Marcelino S. de Sautuola in 1879, were copied originally by Abbé Beuil in the early 1900s. There are horses, wild boar, and bison, which are painted in vivid reds, browns, blacks, and blues.

Representationally, Altamira artists were faced with the same three choices that confront the modern artist: of station point option, of the relative emphasis on variant versus invariant features of the depicted contents, and of the relative degree of emphasis on two-dimensional versus three-dimensional components of the picture. The choices they made rouse a striking feeling of familiarity in the modern Western observer. In the depiction of the animals, it is clear that the station point option selected is the most common in present-day Western pictures. The Altamira artists depicted no scenes at all, only objects. Each picture shows a single station point selected, central to the object being depicted and at an intermediate distance from it. Similarly, the relative emphasis on variant versus invariant features of the object strikes a familiar chord in the modern observer, since the balance present is much the same as ours.

The importance to the artists of invariant structural features is evident in the very frequent selection of characteristic aspects and poses of the animals depicted. Specific distinctive features, like horns, tails, and hooves, are clearly present, as are the all-important spatial relationships among the individual animal properties. The placement of the eye relative to the head, the head relative to the body, and the body relative to the legs and tail are clearly preserved and depicted, especially in the pictures of the standing bison. These clear depictions of spatial relationships specific to the animal are an obvious example of the artists' concern with depicting views of the animal that have what Arnheim has called *renvois* (the underlying structure of the animal). The preservation of fundamental structural relationships at the expense of, or without regard to, momentary appearance is also present in the very elegant stylization of certain features of the depicted animals. The curve of the horns, the sketch of the tails, and the lines of hoof and mane all bear testimony to the facility with which the artists captured their essential structures and depicted them with attention only to invariant relationships.

The sense of familiarity with which the modern observer greets these paintings is due not only to the elegant depiction of invariant structural relationships but also to the arresting mastery of the depiction of momentary appearance or variant properties of the object. The attention to variant appearance is frequently considered to be the distinguishing mark of "developed" rather than "primitive" art, so its presence in the paintings of Altamira produced the skepticism that prevented the proper dating of the works for many years. Attention to variant appearances is evident in the range and types of postures selected and the depiction of fleeting detail. The boar is depicted leaping—its stride arrested by the artist's hand. Bison are depicted not only standing, but bellowing, turning, and lying in the curled posture of sleep or death. In contrast with the structural clarity of the standing bull, the curled bison is a geometrical confusion of skeletal relationships, and a picture of astonishing beauty. The curled posture can hardly be considered to be a characteristic view of a bull. It is a view with little renvois but with extraordinary grace of form. The aesthetic perfection of this fleeting uncharacteristic pose rendered so superbly by the cave artist bears forceful testimony to the presence of the aesthetic attitude, even in early man. The arch of the neck of the bellowing bulls, the upward tilt of his tail, as well as the beautifully cocked head likewise bear witness to the aesthetic attitude of the Altamira artists, to their evident concern for capturing the beauty of fleeting form. The capture of momentary appearance is also apparent in the use of overlapping and foreshortening, both of which are accidents of the moment. Similarly, the unstylized use of shading, evident particularly in the musculature of the curled bison, shows a remarkable sensitivity to the particular beauty of the moment or pose.

No one knows what prompted the artistic endeavors of early human beings, but it seems clear from the Altamira cave paintings that aesthetic espression was surely among their many motives. No one knows for sure the function of this early art, but it is clear from this brief analysis that whatever the function, it guided the artist's hand to a balance between variant and invariant feature depiction very familiar to the modern eye. The Altamira artists were as aware as modern artists of the momentary appearances of things, as well as of their persistant properties—and were as ready to depict them both. The Altamira artists seem to differ from their modern counterparts most clearly in relative emphasis on two-dimensional versus three-dimensional aspects of the paintings.

The curled bison represents one figure in which the artist's concern for the depiction of a two-dimensional pattern is evident. Whereas in many others, the preponderance of effort was directed toward the successful representation of voluminous objects. It is worth noting that the picture surface itself, the ceiling of the cave, was frequently incorporated into the representational character of the painting. This was accomplished either by engraving into the rock or by utilizing the hollows and protrusions of the stone to enhance the rising and falling curves of the animal's bodies. When such a semirelief practice is employed, it seems the artists had difficulty attending to the two-dimensional character of the work. All components tend to contribute to a successful depiction of three-dimensional volume.

The second style chosen for analysis is Egyptian art. This style was selected because it is frequently cited as an example of an art style remote from our own art style, but in fact, many similarities exist. The analysis will be broken into two parts: first, a discussion of the problem of the representation of a single object, and second, a discussion of techniques of spatial layout.

Two objects have been chosen to illustrate depiction characteristics: the human figure and the bird. Egyptian artists were confronted with the same three choices that confront their modern counterparts: station point, relative weight on variant versus invariant features of the object, and relative emphasis on two- versus three-dimensional components of the picture. It is probably in the depiction of the human figure that one sees the greatest evolution or change across time in technique but many commonalities span the time frame. The station points selected are distant and central. It is only the multiplicity of station points that appears odd.

In the figures that we consider to be most typically Egyptian, the eye, shoulders, and torso are frontal views; the hips, legs, and face are in profile. In a frontal face, the nose is in profile. The feet are nearly always in profile and seen from the inside. All the aspects assembled in a single subject create a very odd human figure to the eyes of the modern observer, as witnessed in Figure 10.2. At least the figure is not so perceptually incongruent as to prevent us from perceiving the identity of the subject. We know which objects are birds and which are human and which of these are male and female. The multiplicity of station points selected does not interfere with our perception of the object or with the perception of the relationships among the parts of the objects—a factor that I feel is due to the clear depiction of the invariant features of the object. The clear depiction of the invariant features of the object demands attention both to the nature of the object parts and to their structural interrelationships. Egyptian art, perhaps more than any other style, attended to the selection of what Arnheim has called the *most characteristic aspect* of an object part, as well as to its careful placement in a skeletal structure that preserves the spatial relationships among those parts. Both the aspects chosen and their placement have renvois. We perceive properly assembled humans with their clearly human distinctive features.

That the primary emphasis in Egyptian art was on the depiction of invariant rather than variant features is evidenced also in the relative infrequency with which uncharacteristic views were selected and in the almost complete absence of foreshortening and perspective. However, it is too frequently argued that the Egyptian artist was either unaware of, or uninterested in, the fleeting or variant appearance of his subject. This is not the case. It is clear from Figure 10.3 in the many depictions

Figure 10.2 Four New Kingdom depictions of the human figure. Top left from Groenewegen-Frankfort. Bottom right from Capart. Top right and bottom left from Abbate.

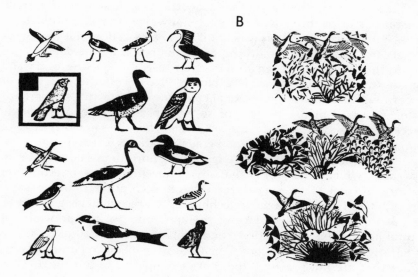

Figure 10.3   Various examples of Egyptian depictions of birds. A) From Abbate. B) From Capart.

of fowl that clarity of invariant feature was a dominant concern, but there are also fowl captured on the wing, almost photographically, sitting with wings furled, shot from below, displayed like an architect's plan drawing, standing with necks upright and bent down to peck and struggling with their wings squashed in the vise-like grip of a slave. Likewise, the human female figures are depicted sitting, standing, bending forward and backward, occasionally wrinkled, overlapped, and even a little foreshortened. There are certainly many views familiar to us that are missing, particularly those with orthogonal lines piercing the plane, but one cannot successfully argue that the Egyptian artist was insensitive to variant momentary appearance.

We come now to the question of the relative emphasis of two-versus three-dimensional form. Were they concerned primarily with the problem of volume or the problem of pattern? It seems obvious that overwhelming concern was with pattern—with the arrangement of forms on a two-dimensional plane or surface. The figures balance and complement each other. They duplicate and triplicate each other. Two small forms weigh down a single large one; a small dynamic figure balances three large but static ones. The picture of the goddess as the enveloping canopy of the night sky is a superb example of the Egyptian concern with form per se, but of course, she is rather unusual. However, the concern with two-dimensional balance, complementarity, and symmetry is commonplace.

This relatively heavy emphasis on the two-dimensional pattern components of pictures does not imply, however, that the problem of three-dimensional depiction was ignored. The assertion that the Egyptian artist did not understand the problems posed by the depiction of corporeality is incomprehensible in the presence of those birds and humans (pictured as so tactilely plump). However, the question of concern with the three-dimensional components of pictures is perhaps better discussed in the context of scene depiction rather than single object portrayal. With scenes, the artist again has the same three choice points: for station point, variant versus invariant features, and two-versus three-dimensional surface layout in more than one way. From my search, which is far from exhaustive, I have found seven techniques that are, in some ways, very different from each other; in other ways, very similar. The most familiar techniques are recognizable and can be seen as the logical consequence of the application of the principles of natural perspective to depiction, for example, preservation of up–down or left–right relationships or of height-in-the plane relations. Techniques that are not practiced today are exemplified in four pictures in Figure 10.4.

The first example is from the Old Kingdom, showing a series of typical scenes from ordinary life observed in life or death by the occupant of the tomb. The scenes are of boating, fishing, herding, and slaughtering. Each is encapsulated and bears no clear relation to any other. From the modern point of view, they are odd for two reasons: first, they bear no clear relation to one another; second, within a scene, all the activity essentially takes place in the same plane. There is very little recession in depth, but this does not render them perceptually incomprehensible.

The second example of an unfamiliar spatial layout technique shows a hunter on a boat hunting birds in a swamp. This picture looks appropriate except for the symbolic pictograms that usually disturb the modern viewer. The oddity is in the size relationships. The modern viewer might well mistake the small female figure to be a child, but to the Egyptian, she was probably a slave. The preservation of visual angle relationships across a scene is not in any way demanded perceptually. It is a consequence of the modern Western assumption of a single station point for the entire scene. When we look at this painting, we make our culturally familiar assumption and conclude with the perception of an anomaly. If the assumption is not made, the anomaly does not occur.

The last two examples of pictures with layout depiction techniques that are very different from present-day techniques are shown in an Egyptian garden scene and a scene of hunting in the desert. The garden is the most striking because it seems the most unfamiliar. It is an aerial view of a pond with trees around it and people standing at its edge. The trees, boat, and people are all presented in their most characteristic aspects, which are usually frontal, and the spatial relationships among the objects are structurally preserved. Arnheim made the point that such a rendering was as perceptually logical as the modern rendering, and this echoes his view. Similarly, the hunting scene is perfectly logical perceptually. Figures are in contact with the ground, and the contour lines of that ground define successive planes in space. The modern viewer is perturbed because the station point is at the same distance for each successive segment. But such perturbation need not take place.

The difficulty the modern observer experiences with Egyptian art is the consequence of the assumption that the eye works as a camera fixed to one point in space. Abandon that notion, and the perceptual validity of Egyptian art is immediately apparent. Remember the station point option selected, the relative emphasis on variant versus invariant features, and the playoff between two- and three-dimensional components.

It was argued by the Egyptian scholar Groenewegen-Frankfort, and by others more familiar to perceptual psychologists, that some styles, like linear perspective, can be understood in terms of reference, of relation to the observer. This is not true. The viewer always has a geometrically determined relationship to the picture; it may be aimed at part of the object, the whole object, or the whole scene; it may be one relationship, or it may be many. The exception occurs when the arrangement of parts can *not* be any possible assemblage of projections. This would make the object or scene unintelligible. We would not be talking of pictures any more but of symbol systems. If a picture cannot be analyzed as facets of natural perspective, then it cannot be perceived as meaningful. "What is it?" becomes the wrong question. It may still be a painting, but it is no longer a picture.

This generative theory is a theory advanced by a perceptual psychologist, not by an artist or an art historian. I wish to make it clear that this is not a theory of art. It is a theory of the nature of the perceptual information that makes successful picture making possible. It solves some old problems; it dispenses with some unreasonable

Figure 10.4 A) A series of scenes from an Old Kingdom tomb painting (from Groenewegen-Frankfort). B) New Kingdom fresco of hunting birds in a swamp (from Abbate).

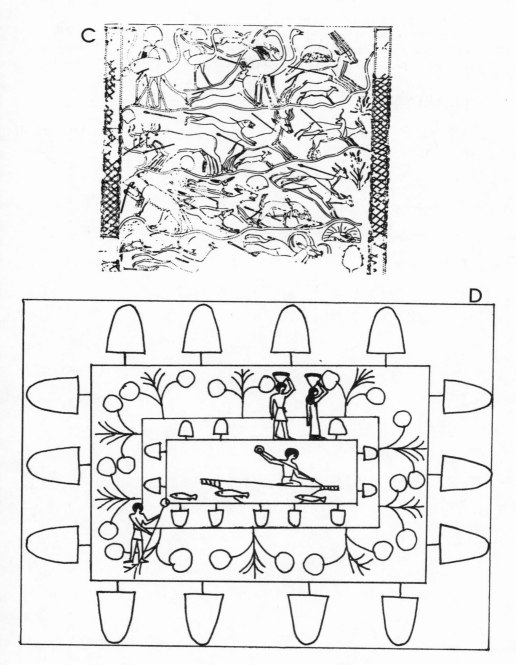

C) Drawing of a desert hunting scene showing successive planes in space (from Groenewegen-Frankfort). D) Drawing of a garden scene in a New Kingdom style of depiction.

assertions about the perceptual components of style. But there is more to art than picture making, and more to pictures than art. A perceptual theory of pictures is one small step toward a true psychology of art.

REFERENCES

Arnheim, R. *Art and Visual Perception: A Psychology of the Creative Eye*. Berkeley: University of California Press, 1954.

———. *Visual Thinking*. London: Faber and Faber, 1969.

Gibson, J. J. *The Perception of the Visual World*. Boston: Houghton–Mifflin, 1950.

———. *The Senses Considered as Perceptual Systems*. Boston: Houghton–Mifflin, 1966.

Gombrich, E. H. *The Story of Art*. New York: Phaidon, 1972a.

———. *Art and Illusion: A Study in the Psychology of Pictorial Representation*. Princeton, N.J.: Princeton University Press, 1972b.

PART III

THE ROLE OF COGNITION

Introduction to Part III

If perception says something about how the way one sees contributes to how one pictures the world, then cognition says something about the way one interprets what one sees. The question raised in the last section was whether an understanding of perceptual processes is sufficient to account for a general theory of pictorial representation. The answer that comes from this section is, no. As we shall see, cognitive processes are not only linked to pictorial representation but, indeed, may play a major role in shaping the way one pictures the world.

Irwin immediately objects to the limits that psychologists and aestheticians impose on the artists' reality. The formers' reality is objective reality. This is an abstraction based on the assumption that reality consists only of a world of objects. Irwin challenges this assumption when applied to questions of human perception and modern art, where process rather than product is the principal concern. Looking at modern art through "objective glasses" distorts the result and changes its meaning. The modern artist seeks modes of expression that go beyond the "frame and plane" orthodoxy of traditional pictorial art. Irwin doubts whether the goals of modern art, which rest on the subjective processes of perception and cognition of the individual, can ever be understood within a conceptual framework that seeks abstract (generalized) truths. Thus, the challenge as he sees it is whether art's critics in science and philosophy can develop a new language to talk about the creative realities of today's art.

Gregory asks, How are pictures seen in three-dimension? and answers that they can be only in the presence of distortions that act as cues for depth, for example, size and shape scaling and the convergence of lines. We have already learned from Wheelock (Chapter 7 of this volume) that seventeenth-century Dutch realist painters skillfully deceived viewers' eyes by exaggerating these depth cues in their paintings. Gregory's explanation of this perceptual phenomenon has a distinctively cognitive flavor to it. Perceptions are formed from hypotheses based on the best sensory data available from the world. Illusions occur when these data are not correctly interpreted and lead to plausible though faulty conclusions and when plausible hypotheses, generated from stored knowledge about worldly characteristics, fill in for insufficient data. The space of pictures is one of these illusions because it is impossible to apply appropriate scales to two spaces simultaneously.

Ward's concern is with how movement is represented in painting, given the fact that the painter is limited to a single "piece" or, at best, several "pieces of the action." The usual answer is that motion is supplied by the viewer. Ward is not satisfied with this answer, however, and calls upon the theories of Arnheim, Gombrich, and Gibson (an unlikely triumvirate) to supply the ingredients for a "new" theory of depicted motion. In essence, Ward proposes that "the depiction of figural movement is dependent upon a clarification of past and potential movement and the fuscation of information for immobility." Ward cites a number of examples from art in which this principle is either successfully or unsuccessfully used to represent motion.

The basis of pictorial representation for Hagen in the last section rested on the pickup of information from the environment (that is, physiological mechanisms of seeing). For Wartofsky, the basis of pictorial representation is picturing which is an acquired (learned) way of seeing the world (objects), using art forms transmitted by the culture (that is, sociocultural, historical mechanisms of seeing). Wartofsky's thesis is that both pictures and paintings are artifacts, that is, products of the human activity that created them. This activity is dominated by human vision, which, he argues, has been shaped not by biological evolution but by a kind of Lamarckian cultural and sociohistorical evolution. Thus, it is the *pictures*, not the eyes, which teach us to see. and what is seen is seen as *intended* to be seen, not what is. This position turns traditional theories of perception upside down, by postulating that human vision is an artifact produced by the very artifacts, pictures, that are being studied and created. Thus, the history of art is as much a theory of vision as are contemporary psychological and physiological theories. Paintings represent because they are made with the intention to represent, and the same argument holds for nonrepresentative paintings or any other visual display. Neither representation, nor, for that matter, beauty, is in the eye of the beholder. Rather, it is in the styles of picturing that have come to be known as representative or beautiful.

Tormey and Tormey ask how pictures and picturing are related to seeing and believing. Can one use art productions as evidence of the way the world is seen and known by the artist? Conversely, does the process of picturing cause the world to be seen and known by the artist as it is (Wartofsky's thesis)? Ultimately, these questions boil down to, What is represented in representational art—truth, convention, habit, style, or value, and so forth? The authors conclude that pictorial representation systems adopt different definitions of realism. These include phenomenal realism, which portrays things the way they are seen or appear; cognitive realism, which portrays things in such a way as to emphasize their most important features; and metrical realism, which portrays things according to their mathematical dimensions. Each of these definitions of reality has a common purpose in the eyes of the artist—"getting the picture right."

Chapter Eleven

Some Notes on
the Nature of Abstraction

Robert Irwin

Modeling our discussion after Gombrich, Hochberg, and Black's
Art, Perception and Reality (1972) as the source of our inquiry seems to
render the question, "What is painting?" one thing, and "What is the
role of perception" quite another. It is naive to assume to use such
weighty terms as *art, perception,* and *reality* unless we intend to pursue all
their implications; here, we can begin by noting that "painting" represents only a fraction of the subject *art,* "visual" only a fraction of the
subject *perception,* and "scientific knowledge" only a fraction of the
subject *reality.*

If at first this seems somewhat obvious, then illusion is a central
part of the problem. For example, begin by considering our apparent
habituation to the deployment of the words *art* and *painting* as if they
were somehow synonymous. Looked at from the historical view of
painting's long and rewarding practice, this illusion might seem a
reasonable one, even a given. Certainly, the young artist is introduced
(educated?) to the rituals and techniques of painting as if there were *no*
questions raised by the requirements (of frame and plane) of this hidden
(right before our eyes) orthodoxy. On the other hand, looked at from
the view inherent in the questions of art, perception, and reality,
painting should be thought of more simply as a tool—a highly stylized
and, hence, productive method. More importantly, it should be considered a contextual (intersubjective) agreement of a not-so-simple series
of conceptual-meaning-games, (for example, historical, social, critical,
aesthetic, and economic) played on reality. Since what other reality does
painting have except the ones we give to it by acting as if its representations, interpretations, and illusions were somehow real? All of these
should more correctly be thought of as games of intersubjective
meaning construction. Nor are such games the exclusive province of
painting: for example, when a mathematician asks you to "Just suppose"

(which he will), what he really means is "Let's pretend," that is, "Let's act *as if*."

What, then, is painting—a perceptual or conceptual metaphor, an icon, a system of signs, a carnal essence, or something else? What is the actual character of its reality? The animals painted on the walls of Lascaux are not there in the same way as the crack or formations, but they are not elsewhere either. When I see in the line and color the distinction that it is an animal, how is it that I do that? When the artist of the Renaissance declared a painting to be a "window on the world" or, more recently, when the color-field artist conceived it to be "flat"— when it is clearly neither a window nor flat—what did they mean?

What is the level of reality when I conceive the contour of an object in a drawing as a line encircling a shape, where there is no such line in nature inscribing the world for our perceptions? In drawing, if one outlines the shape of the figure with a continuous line, one makes of the figure a shape, whereas in the world, the contour is, rather, the limits toward which the sides of the object recede in depth. In drawing, which is the backbone of pictorial painting, it is only with the addition of a conceptualized "reading" that we supply the form and volume of the figure (even to a physical likeness), where, in fact, only a line and plane exist. Such a pictorial reality is derived out of a learned (literate) logic, which has no real parallel in how we perceive nature. So how do I say where the painting is? At what level of reality do all these things— cracks and formations, color and line, shape and animal, window and flatness—live?

Must we now conclude that we have more than one level or kind of reality? If so, how do we distinguish between these levels? What do our distinctions amount to? Is one level more real than another? If so, what would be the grounds for such a stratification?

It is ordinarily assumed that a painting is a representation of something. But just what are the facts of such a pictorial reality? How is a reflection or an image a representation, and what does it mean to represent something? For instance, what are the facts of a "mirror reality" in reflection or painting? The mirror image may be thought of as the best example of an uncluttered representation, such that the image equals its own signification, as opposed to those concepts/images which introduce kinds and degrees of supposed subjective content as form. Yet are there not even here real dimensions missing in such a faithful picturing? How are these lost dimensions accounted for? Is not such a reality a special case, and what it presents, a self-consciousness?

Can every *object* in the world pass from its natural existence, as found in simple experience, and be rethought and appropriated by a kind of objective processing, thereby reappearing as *metaphor* for the purpose of a meaningful intersubjective usage? What is lost and what is gained in such transformations?

(Note how easily our questions are framed with the use of the word *object* to represent the case of reality in conception; of course, *object* as the product of *objective* would certainly seem capable of such a logical cooptation. But can we so simply limit our inquiries through such an obvious presumption? Would the question/answer be the same if we replaced the concept inherent in the use of the word *object* with that in the word *phenomenon*?)

What are the real and hidden consequences (plus and minus) of our use of such radical transformations? Haven't we already habituated to their logic, for example, with the mediacy and level of conviction we give to photographs and the motion picture or the certainty with which we assert that "two plus two equals four" is a concrete fact? Consider *again* what it means to see this page covered with *abstract* marks and marvel at what we are capable of making of them in our ability to gain a certain type of consummation in their social usage. Such conviction must in time not only influence the way we organize our thoughts about the world but also color our perceptions in the world, since what else do perception and reality come to mean here except expectation and fit?

Name all the events in a moment of perceptual experience. Do we have enough words to adequately reflect such a moment's real complexity? How does the system of signs that makes pictures legible differ from that of words? If in your answer you should point to the added visual dimensions of the painting—that is, line, shape, color, and so forth—how do you intend to explain their meaning?

A cloud passes before the sun, trailing its shadow over the landscape, and a chill wind passes. A surface that a moment ago appeared rough is now smooth; something curved, now flat; a bright red, now violet; something in profile, now lost in its environment.

How do we picture such a phenomenon, the weave of its textures? Is it enough to say or picture that a cloud has passed before the sun? If it (red, curved, rough) was real before, is it (violet, flat, smooth) equally real now? Then what do I mean by *reality*? Are neither or both real? Can we disregard these perceptual changes as merely incidental—somehow less than real? While I might walk up to touch the surface of an object to reestablish its roughness, what am I to do about the phenomenon of color, the shift from red to violet?

Certainly, we can say, or picture, that a nameable object—cloud— has passed before another nameable object—sun. But how do we account for the experiential phenomena implicit in such an event? If we say that the cause and effect of the shadow and wind are the cloud and the sun, does such a logical explanation do away with all the perceptual ambiguities?

On the other hand, if one cannot be compelled to accept anything, then we abandon logic and requiredness, since something "concrete," like "two plus two equals four," means nothing to a mind that has negated or relinquished all claims to such a universality. Yet, what kind of a claim for reality does logic make here? What is universal about a logic that cannot account for even a moment in perceptual experience? In the world of lived perception, is not the logic of "two plus two equals four" something of an impertinence?

The degree of certainty with which scientific or aesthetic observers can conclude anything about the experience of any individual human being is based solely on the sureness with which the outward indications—for example, actions, behaviors, and artifacts—can be connected with the individual's inward states of being, and to a critical extent, this depends on how well the observer knows the person being observed. The problem here is that this necessity introduces a sliding scale of intimacy and subjective preknowledge, not to mention the unmentionable objective and subjective interests and biases of the observer—in short, all the messy subjective properties unacceptable to a formal science, all of which individual practitioners tacitly acknowledge, even while keeping up the pretense of acting as if the *social* were, in fact, a *science*.

The alternative, for which all social sciences have opted, is to hold the individual as anonymous, that is, as a typified or ideal type. Such ideal types become the *subjects-made-objects* suitable for the social practitioner's games of interpretive schematization, by virtue of their suscepti-bility to statistical investigation, analysis, measure, summary, and development—that is, how well they not *fit* scientific methods and techniques. Further, as ideal types, they are amenable to the presuppo-sitions needed in developing theoretical meaning–contexts. The quali-ties of such typification can also be obtained, in converse fashion, by distinguishing a goal constituting the ideal objective and thereafter assigning a typical role to fit it, for example, that in Marxism, art has a sociopolitical role. Here, the motive can be postulated as constant regardless of who performs the act or what that person's subjective experiences are at the time—and, further, only the one typical motive is accepted as constituting a typical act.

The construction of an ideal type can thus be taken in two ways: as personal (an ideal type of personal role) or as a material course of action (an ideal type of goal). They are, of course, interrelated. This leads us to the assumption that we can read the "course of action" in the individu-al's performance by attending to the product (object) of those actions relative to the objective meaning–context. Once we are clear as to its meaning, we can then read back to the individual performer and infer the subjective context, that is, the general frame of mind of a performer that would be adequate to such a project.

With the grounds of such an expectation established and joined by a general acknowledgment of all the participants—that is, everyone agreeing to agree on the character, boundaries, rules of thumb, and, even, goals of the game (for example, the requirement of frame and plane in painting and the aspirations to a goal of "high art")—the art of painting now becomes an act polythetically experienced and acted out by a person but conceived and comprehended monothetically by the observer, for example, historian, psychologist, aesthetician, or critic. Anything the observer now permits a "typical ideal type" to report about actions–motives is only hollow prophecy *after* the real events of its meaning have already been deduced.

As quasi-scientists, many art historians, aestheticians, and modern critics have embraced just such a system of evaluation and organization, the operative rationale being the discernment of quality. Art observers so armed now approach the objects of their interests as ideal types (for example, painters who paint, potters who pot, sculptors who cast in bronze, and so forth) or as course-of-action types (for example, figurative, abstract, social purpose, and so forth). This procedure takes for granted the "lower stages" of meaning assignment—for example, individual intentions, subjective input, or simple value distinctions— and pays little or no attention to them. In formalist criticism, it is even currently fashionable, in reaction to previous "romantic excesses," to go so far as to consider any contact with the artist as a corrupting factor. Hence, the observer's goal is *not* to study the creative process, the artist's intentions, or the properties of ideas per se but, instead, to focus attention on the finished work as it relates to the already established historical-social-economic-meaning–contexts—as a fact in a set of facts. In this sense, the individual artist is regarded as having only a predicate meaning, and the artist's actions can be simply classified into appropriate categories.

Interpretations of this kind—whether in the social sciences, criticism, psychology, politics, or in everyday life—may gain the advantages of a neat division of individual actions and give to the observer–activist a "concrete" frame of reference. But it is naive (or Machiavellian) to suppose that the boundaries or goals of any personal act can be objectively determined or demarcated on the grounds of an abstract logic, while the individual person is at the same time considered "free" or "creative." It is essential to the concept of freedom or creativity that the *individual* give meaning to his or her own actions, for meaning here is in the special way in which each individual attends his or her lived experiences. This is precisely the crucial aspect in the process that subsequently elevates experience into action.

Take the all-too-familiar contraction implicit in the word *representation* and recover its critical originary action—re-*presentation*—that is, a radical transformation *in all dimensions* of what was previously known otherwise and, hence, a form of compounded abstraction. It is a *compounded* abstraction, first, because what we perceive is never what is actually out there but is, rather, a transformation in all dimensions, mediated by the intrinsic nature of the neural processes themselves (first-phase processing). This is followed by a transformation, in all dimensions, to conceptual terms of what it is our sentience presents to the thinking mind—again, with the addition of the intrinsic nature, this time, of the thinking processes (second-phase processing). Our mental constructions are in turn followed by a transformation, in all dimensions, from a mental activity into a physical or behavioral activity, whose intrinsic nature now is in our bodily capabilities (third-phase processing). This behavioral action begins the critical transformations from the subjective individual (private access) to the intersubjective community of individuals (public access)—that is, what was up until now subjective gains the features of something objective. This transition underwrites in its turn the transformation of our compounded, individual actions into such intersubjective social schemes, as, for example, language and painting (fourth-phase processing). The critical feature here is in the transformation from process to system, with the resultant gains and losses. (The character of this transaction cannot be rightly described as having an intrinsic nature, since these systems are of our own making and should not be thought of as in any way inevitable.) At this point, we have arrived at a definition of a pure abstraction.

While each phase in this processing of our consciousness has a kind of reality, each new phase of processing must be considered as a compounding in form of the degrees of abstraction in the nature of our consciousness. Thus, the "reality" of such highly stylized systems as pictorial painting is, in fact, the most abstract. This agrees with the root definition of the word *abstract*—"to be derived from or related to"—as in the artist's transformation of feelings or thoughts into a painting or into language, for example.

Now the idea that only those fourth-phase abstractions hold reality or usefulness is the consummate myth of our lives and is especially evident in the attitudes of such formal logics as behaviorism, structuralism, Marxism, logical positivism, and pictorial literate logic, which all too often in their natural thrust toward a conclusiveness claim everything else to be less-than-real, meaningless, abstract, or a mystification and hold even the discussion of human consciousness to be confined to that of cognizant action.

Yet even from the point of view of an objective logic, that is, logical procedure, it follows that such representational systems must be developed *from* something and—this is the critical point—that the nature of that something must be *previously known otherwise,* or how else, why else, could we come to act on them? I suggest that the nature of our perceptions of that something, as that which occurs *in* each of us and *before anything else,* is the real province of art.

The objects of our meaning structures as the focus of a conceptual reality do not exist in a vacuum but rather reside in and depend on a cohesive and reasonably consistent field of perceptual reality. When we open our eyes in the morning, the world presents itself whole, seemingly without our having actively participated in its becoming. Because of its general consistency in our everyday activity, the illusion is created in the cognitive mind that this perceptual field is somehow less real than any particular focus of our thought. But if, for example, this tree I am sitting under while engrossed in writing this chapter were to move or begin to fall toward me, this illusion would be sharply broken, and I would quickly realize that this field is not passing unnoticed. While it is true that thought forms itself out of thought, the discussion or definition of mind, perception, and reality or the questioning of the nature of human consciousness cannot rightly contain itself within such a reductive cognitive bias. We must account for the whole interdependent perceptual/conceptual reality.

In this sense, Marx's formula that "experience determines consciousness," in contradistinction to Hegel's contention that "consciousness determines experience," cannot be resolved or broken off by any definition.

What remains of the actual dimensions of our experience if we surrender to such radical premises as to see "reality" in a pictorial logic, a "solution" in an analysis of form, or something "concrete" in measures of time and space? Does it necessarily follow that reality is then merely the equal of such "meanings"? And if what I perceive does not "mean" anything, what then? Is it now somehow less real? If it is less real, how do I continue to justify my seeing it?

How have we managed to turn the world of "reality" so upside-down as to grant a system of compounded abstraction the status of the *realist* view—so on-its-head that what is determined to be true, universal, or concrete is thought to reside in that which is farthest from what it is we as individuals experience it to be?

Yet, the continuous methodological games of hide-and-seek between propositions of meaning and necessary restrictions of objective form continuously reinforce these myths while holding down our experience. By heaping structure on top of structure, language games on top of image games, and meaning games on top of language games, they have served to catch us all in the turnstiles of their requiredness, and it is this requiredness that isolates our intuition.

For if I should simply look around me, that is *not* how the world looks at all.

What if the artist should try to reduce the image or meaning of painting to a representation of nothing but itself, as some artists already have done? Would this be less about what is real or less about what is thought to be meaningful?

How would we begin to relate to such an idea (phenomenon) of painting? Could someone, an intermediary, be our teacher in this, or would some form of direct experience be required? How would the experience of such a *painting* differ from that of a *picture*? What would be the meaning of such a difference?

For example, what happens to my perception of scale if the figurative reference is removed or to the phenomenon of color when the literate shape is no longer seen to confine and justify its being? When we are confronted by just such a set of circumstances (as we have been in the painting of the Abstract Expressionists or the sculpture of the Minimalists), if we should then ask, "What is it?" or "What does it mean?," what do we intend by these questions? Are we not in effect saying, "Take this potentially new experience directly in front of me and explain what I am seeing by abstracting it from the present and deploying it through a complex referencing to previous constructions (not necessarily my own) that together comprise my learned expectations for what I may now legitimately experience as art?" Isn't all of this substantially a process of literate logic, as opposed to phenomenological receptivity?

Isn't this the real issue raised by modern art? For example, Marcel Duchamp exhibited a urinal and declared it to be art "because I say so and I am the artist." This statement has been popularly misinterpreted as simply the artist expressing himself. But even if we should accept this idea of "expression," what then is *not* an act of expression? The bottom falls out of that shallow conclusion, and we are forced to come to grips with the real issue of Duchamp's statement—that the responsibility for determining what is art is not external, that is, abstract to the individual artist, but intimate to the artist as the perceiving being, as the source of its distinction. In turn, the cultural implication is that this responsibility is carried over to likewise implicate the observer as a direct participant. The critic's only valid function is to clear away the extraneous considerations and return us, naked, to the experience before us.

But can I simply trust myself to experience what it is my instincts tell me? Wouldn't this be shallow hedonism (as are some interpretations of existentialism)? The answer could, of course, be, yes; unless something more is intended in these positions of modern art. Indeed, something is—that the individual, in the moment of creative action, embodies an overlap of both immediate presence and mediated civilization. This most fundamental process of questioning *in* the individual (between what one perceives and conceives reality to be) is the critical action that is called *creativity* and is, more accurately, a process of discovery.

Still, certainly, there can be no general agreement as to whether an experience or feeling is genuine or not. For here, we can prove nothing and claim anything. But what exactly would be the purpose or function of proving, and what would be its legitimate relationship to experience?

Can there really be such a thing as an expert judgment about the genuineness of an expression as it relates to our experience? In seeking this judgment, who would it be proper to consult: psychologists, aestheticians, critics, or artists? If I were to say that on such issues a correct judgment will generally issue from those with better knowledge, how would I then characterize this knowledge—as experiential or cultural? How would I then compare the knowledge and judgment of the social practitioner with that of the creative person? Would the answer lie in how each attends to the nature of his or her perceptions?

From time to time, when an aesthetician, psychologist, historian, or critic gives us a tip, how do we judge *its* correctness? Is it proper to say that what one acquires from aesthetics is a technique for better judgment or better judgment itself? Are there rules here that only knowledgeable people can apply correctly? Unlike rules of calculation, they do not seem to form a stable or proper system. What would a system of aesthetics be like, and what would be its proper relation to art? Wouldn't it somehow be a contradiction in terms? Rules and experience, unlike rules and calculations, intersect in an anomaly. Then isn't the development of aesthetics as a discipline something of a logical mystification, this fantasy that we can discuss and come to understand in objective, literate terms that which has no actual objective properties? Now, does it necessarily follow that we must resort to negative terms (the *via negativa*) when we wish to speak of the ultimate reality of that which is not a thingness? Is this what Wittgenstein meant in the final step of his *Tractatus Logico-Philosophicus* (1922): "Of that which we cannot speak, of that we must be silent." (Logical positivists have interpreted this extraordinary conclusion to mean that that which cannot be logically indicated and accounted for is essentially without worth. Yet, it is clear that we continually run up against contradictions in the present which we do not seem able to resolve through such logical procedures and definitions, no matter how handy—for example, the presence of time/space or the very definition of the word *aesthetics*. Doesn't their interpretation beg the real issue, constituting a sort of blind man's bluff?)

Doesn't the potential conflict arise out of a transgression beyond the intent (limits) that such techniques give to objective meanings? To use such superstructures of meaning to subsume the role of simple human value distinctions, as that action originally informs the beginnings of meaning–structures, is simply not reasonable—especially if we are to give real credence to the idea of a true creative human potential.

This should not be mistaken as suggesting a lack of competence on the part of objective practices per se; rather, it is a questioning of their appropriate use. What are the legitimate grounds for understanding the interrelationships and tasks appropriate to the perspectives of (1) those extending, creative discoveries (in any line of pure inquiry); (2) their subsequent cultural innovation and processing as intersubjective form (in any discipline); (3) their development as social facts, capable of meaningful action (in any practice); and finally (4) their incorporation into a formal substantive structure of working facts, both for the collective whole (historical schematization) and the individual self (memory)?

One thing is clear: when the level or kind of reality resides in the events of perceptual phenomenon, as well as in those abstracted concepts of image transference, such methodologies (tools) as language, script, graphs, photography, and the various games of pictorial, histori-cal, curatorial, and literary analysis and description have only the appropriate limited meaning of their present currency in the world. It is in this sense that modern (so-called abstract, nonobjective) art may seem obscure, as it generates direct questions aimed at each of these seemingly established roles and practices making up the historical distinctions for art.

The loss is clear. Simply consider the sheer beauty of order in a contextual agreement like a painting for the processes of gaining a clarity and true subtlety of intersubjective dialogue—that, for example, each mark or move made in a painting can be eminently compared with and against the whole history of marks or moves by anyone having the knowledge to do so, thus allowing for a continually extending sophisti-cation of understanding and summation, that is, a compounding view of (aesthetic?) quality. So it is only natural that any move outside the boundaries and assumptions of this classic orthodoxy will be seen only in the grossest terms, as antirational, antiart, antisocial, and hence antihuman—or simply not seen at all.

So why and how did modern art and artists ever get themselves into such a predicament? That is, why would anyone in their right mind think to break such an agreement? The overriding fact, however, is that over a period of 150 years, artists have been doing just that—moving through a step-by-step evolution away from the formal logic under-writing traditional pictorial art and thought. Furthermore, the steps taken have been acted out by artists from a wide variety of back-grounds, places, and motives. This history can leave us with only one conclusion: that the questions raised are neither accidental nor inci-dental. The astonishing fact is not so much that the public fails to understand modern art but that psychologists, aestheticians, and even art historians as a whole are unaware of the reasoning of this social phenomenon, which they are living right through. That in itself may be the best illustration of the degree to which modern art is not amenable to their established techniques, which, in turn, only underscores the depth of the change implied.

The fact is that there is no other art in our time but modern art. If we were, even for a moment, to take seriously the questions and consequences implicit in this art—for example, in Cubist painting's concept of "the marriage of figure and ground"—and if we were to play that idea out into the real world, it would necessarily result in the loss of the object as subject. Painting or sculpture as the object of our perception would need, like the figure, to become married to the ground of their circumstances: no longer could they float only in the vacuum of their objective meanings, a form of transcendence. This idea, acted out in early twentieth-century painting and thought, now remains to be acted out in the present by extending the current definition of nonobjective art to be nonobject art. That should raise some nice questions, not the least of which are: Can we live with such a possibility, and if so, how? What are its implications for perceptual consciousness, and what might be its subsequent consequences for social reality?

REFERENCES

Gombrich, E. H.; Hochberg, J.; and Black, M. *Art, Perception and Reality*. Baltimore: Johns Hopkins University Press, 1972.

Wittgenstein, L. *Tractatus Logico-Philosophicus*. London: Routledge, 1922.

Chapter Twelve

Space of Pictures

Richard L. Gregory

Retinal images are pictures as seen from the front of the eye with an ophthalmoscope (which is difficult though not technically impossible), but retinal images are very different from pictures, when considered as the interface between optical stimulation and neural coded signals to the brain. They are not things that we see: they are a cross section of the visual channel, which is the transducer between the object world and our visual world. This forces us to start from physiology.

Physiology makes it clear that perception depends upon signals from the organs of sense. The sense organs are essentially like detecting instruments of science, used to provide information for building and testing hypotheses. This account of perception as being indirectly related to the world and dependent upon signals from monitoring "instruments" is surprisingly new. At any rate, its implications are still not apparent in many current discussions. An important implication is, surely, that perception requires signal-processing strategies—perhaps closely related to the strategies by which instrumental signals are used to select and test hypotheses in science.

If on the other hand, we look back to the Irish philosopher George Berkeley (1709)—and there are echoes of his view of perception in some present-day influential theories—we see that the basis of perception was not regarded as signals from sense organs providing data for guessing the state of the external world: the accepted basis was experience—of red, hard, square, and so on. Perceptions were supposed to be built from the "sense data" of experience, not from signals from the organs of sense. The sensations of color and shape and so on (the *sense data* as they were called in that paradigm) were held to be part of the external object world. So perception was regarded as direct, "intuitive" knowledge of reality. But if perception is given by neural signals from the organs of sense monitoring the world, as now seems obviously true from physiological knowledge, then sensation cannot be the basis of perception. Perception cannot be direct or intuitive knowledge of the world, as held by Berkeley.

The principal founder of the modern experimental study of perception, Hermann von Helmholtz (1821–94), was a great physiologist and was concerned to discover and describe the physiological mechanisms of the eye, the ear, and the other organs of sense. He did not, however, believe that a description of these mechanisms would give a complete description of perception. He held that the central nervous system must be carrying out "unconscious inferences" to make effective use of signals from the sense organs. He regarded perceptions as conclusions of inferences, and he thought that to understand perception, it is just as important to appreciate the procedures of inference as it is to understand the physiological mechanisms. The unconscious inference notion of Helmholtz has, however, always been resisted: initially because inference was associated with conscious processes; possibly now because the extraordinary success of physiology in revealing the fascinating mechanisms of the senses has drawn attention away from the strategies—which, if Helmholtz is right, are necessary for making effective use of the signals they provide. We might regard the study of perceptual strategies as the investigation of cognitive processes; but this is still dubiously regarded by most physiologists, who tend rather to hold that further elucidation of the mechanisms will provide the full story. So, perhaps, many physiologists tend to regard perceptual inference as a paradigm-flouting idea—and so to be rejected if possible. At the same time, it cannot be rejected—so we seem to need a "paradigm revolution."

We see here three rival paradigms of perception. In the first place, Berkeley's direct or intuitive knowledge of reality through experience, which he supposed to be basic data; second, a physiological account in which the sense organs are regarded as transducers providing neural signals, somehow adding up to perceptions of external objects; and third, the Helmholtz notion that perceptions are more or less valid inferences from sensory data. Certainly in this last paradigm, awareness of sensory qualities remains mysterious. Unlike the Berkeley paradigm, sensations are not given any clear "causal" importance, for they are not accepted as parts of reality. To Helmholtz, sensations are not selections of "reality." Perception is accepted as a kind of indirect and fallible knowledge, which somehow we experience. It is the nearest we ever get to reality—except that scientific knowledge may be a better candidate, although it also is dependent upon instruments, assumptions, and inferences. With this view, scientific and perceptual knowledge are esentially similar.

So we come to the notion that perceptions are extrapolations of data—hypotheses—much as in science. It is, strictly, an hypothesis that the sun is a ball of gas, 93 million miles distant with a surface temperature of 6,000 degrees centigrade. We may say further that all the laws and objects of science are but indirectly related to pointer readings, and signals, providing data. There is, surely, a subtle step from signals and pointer readings to what is accepted as data. In the first place, the instruments must be calibrated, and their errors must be corrected; they must be aimed in the right direction and not be overloaded or upset by special conditions (such as a magnetic field upsetting an iron plumb bob), or systematic errors will be generated. Error may be generated not only by the instruments themselves being upset but also by strategies and inferences for deriving data from signals being inappropriate or being carried out with errors. Presumably, it is the task of philosophers of science to reveal the assumptions and steps of inference—from instrumental signals to data and from data to hypotheses—which are the strategies of natural science.

Why did Helmholtz (who was a great physiologist) urge that inference is essential for perception to be possible? Why did he reject a "straightforward" physiological account? It is particularly interesting that he did so before the impact of computers on our appreciation of the power of inference and outside the formal proofs of mathematics and the idealized systems of physics. A vital reason is the simple fact (often ignored) that the senses cannot continuously provide adequate and relevant signals, which would be necessary for direct control of behavior or perception. Behavior follows assumptions, such as that (what appears to be) a table is hard or that a face is smiling with amusement—because we cannot directly sense the table's hardness by vision or sense the person's amusement. We can never sense directly another person's amusement or scorn, although we base our life upon such judgments, such "perceptions." The fact that behavior and perception may continue through gaps in available sensory data is incompatible both with Berkeley's direct knowledge or intuitive account, (which we find in modified form in, for example, Gibson 1950, 1966) and also with the "straightforward" physiological account—including the simple, and possibly at first sight, plausible, stimulus–response paradigm. This we must, however, reject, because behavior may continue with no input, or stimuli, by following predictions. In skills, there is often no delay between stimuli and responses, as there should be if sensory signals control behavior directly, for there is delay in the nervous system (as first measured in 1850 by Helmholtz) but in many cases no delay between input and output—so behavior and perception must be predictive. But prediction requires strategies and assumptions: it is essentially this predictive power of perception that supports Helmholtz' paradigm against all its rivals.

Let us consider the kinds of phenomena that seem to reveal perceptual strategies. Since these phenomena are mainly deviations from the facts of the world, we shall have to regard them as "unnatural" facts. But although not "of the world," they are facts of a kind and are evidence for or against our unnatural paradigm for perception—that perceptions are hypotheses.

POWERS OF PERCEPTION COMPARED WITH POWERS OF SCIENCE

Accepting Sensory Signals as Data. We should regard data differently from the physical signals of nerves or wires. Signals become data when they change probabilities between alternative possibilities. For signals to provide data, the biological or instrumental system must be calibrated.

Calibration. As for scientific instruments, changes in the sensitivity or other performance characteristics of the sense organs, which are neural transducers, must be stable and calibrated appropriately to situations they monitor.

Calibration Corrections. Prolonged experience of systematic errors, as well as comparisons with other sensory data, allows distortions of sensory inputs to be compensated, as for example, after wearing new spectacles.

Recognizing Objects. Object perception always goes beyond the available data to non-sensed features, which have to be assumed or inferred. These assumptions, inferences, and predictions are essential for survival in a world that cannot be continuously or adequately sensed.

Guidance by Conditional Probabilities. Perception is affected, usually appropriately, by context information. In a picture, a vague shape becomes a tree, or a windmill, or a man, by the proximity to some other shape, making "true," or "windmill," or "man" the more likely. Here, we see something like paradigm shifts at work. Probable objects are easier to see than are unlikely objects.

Entertaining Alternative Possibilities. It is tempting to suppose that in perception, as in science, "hill-climbing" strategies are employed, so that a better solution may always be discovered, somewhat against present odds. But this capacity for invention and unlikely discovery involves possibilities of generating and accepting false hypotheses—for such strategies cannot always be appropriate or be infallible. They must sometimes result in error or illusion.

Scaling, According to Assumed Invariances. Instrumental, or receptor, calibrations are not adequate for size or distance scale setting except when their data are *immediately* applicable; but this is seldom so. In perception, scale is evidently set by assumptions (which may be false) of regularities and invariances of the object world. Thus, texture gradients and perspective convergences of contours at the retina, generally related to distance, are accepted for setting perceived size. Further, some perceptual hypotheses carry their own scaling constants—which may be applied "downward" to scale sensory data. Such scale changes are dramatic in astronomy, where a few invariance assumptions may set the scale of the universe. Perceptual scale can also be set by assumed distance invariances. Depth-ambiguous objects (such as wire skeleton cubes) change shape with each depth reversal. These scale changes must be due to perceptual hypothesis changes, for the retinal image remains constant, though apparent size changes with apparent distance (Gregory 1970). (See Figure 12.1.)

Capability of Generating Impossibility. In spite of the power of probabilities in perception, there are situations that produce clearly "impossible" or "paradoxical" perceptions. This can occur also in science when inappropriate strategies or assumptions are followed. We may realize the impossibility of a perception without being able to reject it. But instant rejection of the unlikely could preclude learning and discovery: sometimes, the novel and the seemingly impossible turn out to be true, in perception as in science.

Similarities between perception and science may be seen more sharply if we consider the most unnatural facts of all—errors and illusions.

ILLUSIONS OF PERCEPTION COMPARED WITH ERRORS OF SCIENCE

Failure to Accept Sensory Signals as Data. Signals may be rejected by fixed filters and may be accepted or rejected according to likely needs in particular situations.

Sensory "Calibration" Errors. Sensory calibration errors are those due to adaptation, giving scale distortions, and to phenomena such as apparent movement, intensity, and color changes following intense or prolonged stimulation.

Inappropriate Correction of Calibration Errors. These may produce the same kinds of phenomena as the calibration errors themselves, which they tend to compensate (but are generally *reversed*).

Failure to Recognize Objects (Pattern But Not Object Perception). On our paradigm of perception, this is failure to select a hypothesis—often due to insufficient data.

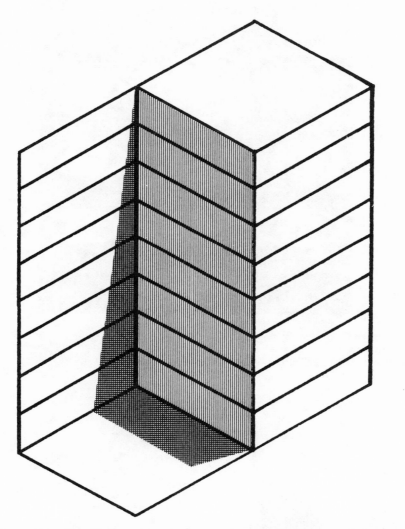

Figure 12.1 This figure reverses spontaneously in depth. The large dark region generally changes in brightness with each reversal—appearing light when it is a plausable shadow (from an overhead light) and dark when it is more likely to be the surface of the wall. This shows that "sense data" are modified by what is accepted as object or (in this case) irrelevant shadow.

Misleading Conditional Probabilities. Misleading conditional probabilities produce inappropriate weighting of sensory data and lead to the selection of false hypotheses. (See Figure 12.2.) This may even create false basic "data," such as "cognitive contours" (see Gregory 1973 and Figures 12.3 and 12.4).

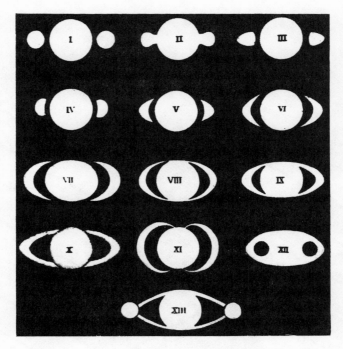

Figure 12.2 The planet Saturn drawn by Galileo in about 1610. He never arrived at the perceptual hypothesis of a globe encircled by a ring. With our present knowledge, it is quite difficult to see Saturn as Galileo drew it, though occasionally, its telescopic image does take these forms.

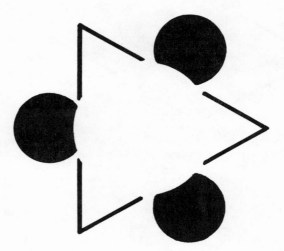

Figure 12.3 The light disc is illusory and could be a serious artifact in practical displays. It seems to be produced as a postulated nearer masking object, as it depends on the gaps being unlikely but forming a likely shape or object.

Figure 12.4 Distinct, potentially misleading lines can be produced (the Ehrenstein illusion).

Spontaneous Changes of Perception with Unchanging Data. Spontaneous changes of perception with unchanging data give perceptual ambiguity, such as figure–ground shifts and the orientation–ambiguity shifts of Necker cubes.

Inappropriate Scaling. This may be upward—from inappropriate data assumptions such as accepting converging lines as retinal perspective (see Figure 12.5), or downward—a false current perceptual hypothesis containing inappropriate scaling data, such as the distortions with reversals of depth ambiguous figures or scale distortion in zero-perspective pictures (see Figure 12.6).

Accepting Misleading External References. Perception of horizontal and vertical are given in part by assuming external features to be horizontal or vertical. This is especially important for pilots.

Accepting and Combining Incompatible Data. Accepting and combining incompatible data generates impossible or paradoxical perceptions. This may occur when the data are preselected ("impossible pictures") or if the organism combines data inappropriately. There are some objects that *always*, from certain points of view, appear paradoxical—impossible objects (see Figure 12.7) when our assumptions of depth are wrong.

CREATING AND DESTROYING SIZE–DEPTH DISTORTION ILLUSIONS

The classical problem of the origin or cause of visual distortion illusions has at least three rival candidates worth serious consideration: (1) neural interactions, such as lateral inhibition, or other neural channel distortions; (2) spatial frequency characteristics of the visual system, associated with Fourier-like transforms, supposedly important for pattern recognition: low pass filter characteristics are held to produce the distortions, especially with converging lines, (3) size scaling, set by perspective features (such as convergence) which when presented on flat picture planes give inappropriate scaling. It has proved surprisingly difficult to distinguish experimentally between physiological channel distortion and more cognitive accounts, though the logical distinctions between these alternatives seem reasonably clear (Gregory 1975).

The present experiments were designed to provide evidence for or against a cognitive account, such as the inappropriate constancy scaling theory, which requires the organism to act on knowledge or assumptions of features of the object world. This theory is, unlike the alternatives mentioned above, a cognitive account because it supposes that the visual system is acting (correctly or inappropriately) from stored

Figure 12.5   Distortion associated with converging lines indicating depth produces illusory expansion. This can occur on electronic displays, where depth is irrelevant.

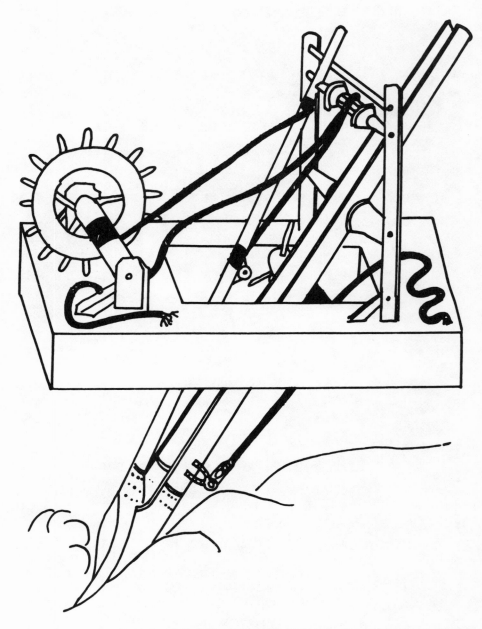

Figure 12.6 Figures or displays showing clearly three-dimensional objects but without perspective are distorted, such that features which are accepted as more distant are expanded. This is a scaling error "downward" from the accepted depth of the object, though this is not explicitly represented.

Figure 12.7 Although this exists as a three dimensional object, it appears three-dimensionally impossible, or paradoxical, from critical viewing positions. (The actual object appears just as paradoxical when viewed directly.)

knowledge of characteristics of the world. The illusion is attributed to applying knowledge to situations inappropriately.

The ways in which the knowledge is stored and used—the physiological mechanisms involved—need not be specified for this to be a legitimate and, for many purposes, adequate account. The first kind of theory, on the other hand, supposes that a modification of a physiological mechanism or channel is responsible. The second class of theory (Ginsburg 1971) makes no such demand or claim on detailed physiological understanding; neither does it call on cognitive processes, involving knowledge of, or assumptions about, external objects.

The three kinds of theory are so conceptually different that the experimenter's difficulty of deciding between them is surprising. Perhaps this difficulty is due to the reasonable biological assumption that even peripheral mechanisms will be adapted to handle typical object situations. We should therefore expect to find crucial differences only in situations requiring stored knowledge of specific classes of objects or visual features. The inappropriate constancy scaling theory does refer to specific classes of features—especially converging of parallel lines by perspective. Retinal perspective (given by optical projection at the retina) used as information for depth, depends on assumptions about the sizes of objects and typical shapes, especially parallel and right-angle features, which hold more generally in some environments than in others. Considerable anthropological data are now available supporting the suggestion that distortion illusions are greatest in "carpentered" environments (Segall et al. 1966; Deregowski 1973). The notion here is that picture perspective is inappropriate to the picture plane—which is flat.

The notion that distortion illusions, such as the Muller-Lyer and Ponzo figures, are perspective drawings goes back at least to Théiry (1896). But Théiry did not realize that typical objects (such as outside corners of buildings, inside corners of rooms, or receding parallel lines) must be accepted as paradigm objects, by inferring depth from retinal perspective. (Théiry's example of the legs of a saw horse is misleading— for the legs could be of almost any angle.) Théiry did not suggest a *modus operandi* relating depth features to distortion on picture planes. This was suggested by Tausch (1954) as size constancy, but was later rejected by him, as depth distortions occur even though depth may not be *seen* in these figures. Gregory (1963) suggested that constancy can be given by size and shape scaling set *directly by depth cues*, even though depth is not seen. This would be somewhat like "releasers" in ethology and would be "automatic" and quite low level in the nervous system.

Two experiments were performed examining size distortions: the first (Gregory and Harris 1975) aimed at testing the notion that perspective produces distortions when the convergence of lines is inappropriate to the depth of the picture or display; the second was designed to explore distortions having a more immediately physiological basis and which do *not* depend on stored object knowledge. Both experiments attempted to *destroy* the illusion—and infer from how they can be destroyed to what their origins may be. It is, also, useful to know how to destroy or remove illusions from displays.

DESTROYING PERSPECTIVE ILLUSIONS

The first experiment was designed to test a specific prediction from the inappropriate constancy scaling theory. We tried to change the significance of the stimuli without changing what in other theories would be considered characteristics that would produce distortion physiologically, as by lateral inhibition. The critical prediction is that the illusory distortions should vanish when the perspective, and the perception of depth, are appropriate. This prediction follows directly from the theory that these distortions are due to inappropriate size scaling. We have said above that scaling is both upward, from certain stimulus patterns typical of depth, and downward, from the prevailing perception (or "hypothesis") of depth—which does not always follow stimulus patterns; thus, they can be experimentally distinguished. We should expect distortions to vanish when both the upward and the downward scaling are appropriate. Downward scaling led us to use stereoscopic projection—to set apparent depth. The importance of upward scaling led us to precisely controlled perspective.

To attain precise perspective and geometrically correct stereoscopic displays, we employ point-source shadow projection, onto a translucent screen, by a pair of horizontally separated miniature lamps cross-polarized to the eyes (Gregory 1964; Lee 1969). They are used to project stereoscopic images of wire models of typical three-dimensional objects. These are right-angle corners, for the Muller-Lyer illusion. The difference in apparent length of the projected verticals was measured with an adjustable comparison line, given by the adjustable line trace of a large-screen oscilloscope (see Figure 12.8).

When the wire models were projected with a single source, they gave two-dimensional perspective figures, which are the usual illusion figures. The usual distortions are observed, and they can be measured. When the wire models are projected in stereoscopic depth (with the pair of cross-polarized point sources), the figures are seen as three dimensional—as though the models were viewed with two eyes directly. So we now have a situation in which both the perspective and the perception of depth are appropriate for these objects. There should therefore be *no distortion*.

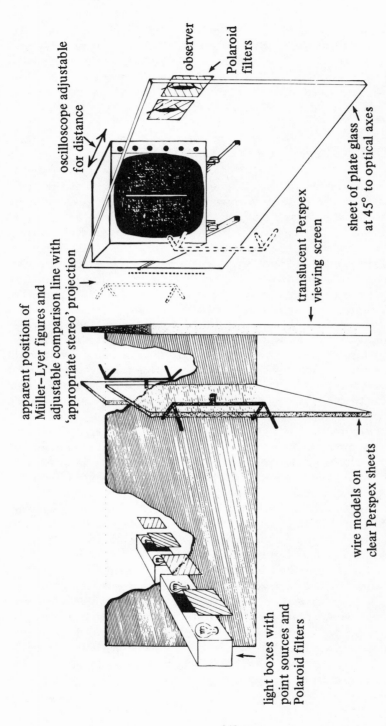

observer

Polaroid
filters

oscilloscope adjustable
for distance

apparent position of
Müller–Lyer figures and
adjustable comparison line with
'appropriate stereo' projection

translucent Perspex
viewing screen

sheet of plate glass
at 45° to optical axes

wire models on
clear Perspex sheets

light boxes with
point sources and
Polaroid filters

Figure 12.8   A pair of point sources, which are polarized orthogonally, can be used to project models in three-dimensional visual space—giving stereoscopic images. Perspective is correct when the projection and viewing distance are equal. Disparity can be controlled by setting the separation of the point sources: thus, the projection can be precisely correct or controlled errors can be introduced.

The geometrical conditions for providing appropriate perspective and appropriate depth perception are easily defined and attained by this shadow projection technique: the projection distance must equal the viewing distance, and the horizontal separation of the projection point sources must equal the observer's eye separation. It is also necessary that the observer has adequate stereoscopic vision, so that he or she does perceive these projections as three dimensional though they lie on the (textured) picture plane of the screen. Other means of attaining accurate depth perception could be used, such as luminous figures with a textureless background, but such alternatives will not be considered here, as stereoscopic projection is readily controlled and most convenient experimentally for giving precise appropriate (or inappropriate) apparent depth.

We had three projection modes: (1) monocular projection, (2) appropriate stereoscopic projection, and (3) reversed (pseudoscopic) stereoscopic projection. Each subject was given five alternative viewing distances (35, 37.5, 42.5, and 45 centimeters), which were adopted to discover effects of slightly inappropriate perspective of the retinal images. The subjects were instructed to match the comparison line to the left-hand (outgoing) or the right-hand (ingoing) figure, as shown in Figure 12.9, following a random sequence.

The curves in Figure 12.10 show an illusion of about 6 percent for the monocular projection and for reversed stereo modes. The illusions (means) at the critical viewing distance of 40 centimeters are, respectively, + 5.5 percent (standard error .67 percent) and 6.1 percent (standard error .7 percent). The appropriate stereo curve is clearly separate from the other curves, and shows zero illusion at the critical viewing distance of 40 centimeters. Thus, our prediction is confirmed.

Pictures are indeed odd because they represent objects in spaces that are different from the (flat) space of the picture plane, which is in

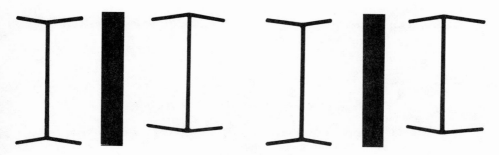

Figure 12.9   The shadow projections. These are seen as three-dimensional corners in the stereoscopic projection mode.

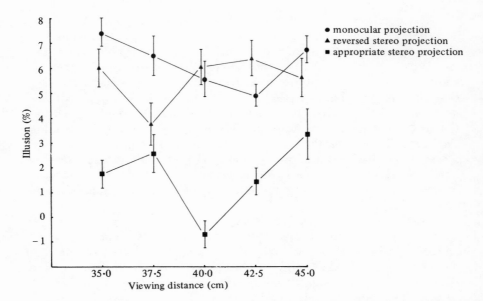

Figure 12.10 The horizontal axis gives the viewing distances. Correct perspective is at 40 centimeters. At this distance, the illusion distortion (shown on the vertical axis) is entirely *absent*; it is insignificant when perspective is nearly correct at the other viewing distances. The illusion is present when the *seen depth* is incorrect (given by monocular or reversed stereo projection)—though the angles of the figure are identical in all three projection modes for each viewing distance. Thus, the distortion could hardly be signal distortion but could be due to inappropriate size scaling (normally giving size constancy set by perspective convergence upward and by the apparent or seen depth downward). The stereo is used to give correct seen depth, though the figure lies on a (textured) display screen, which tends to counter the perspective indication of depth in normal pictures and displays.

no way surprising. However, whether depending upon physiological limitations or specially carpentered environments, it is impossible for space scaling to be appropriate for two different spaces at once. It is hardly surprising then that pictures confound the eye, and makers of pictures employ techniques specially designed to sometimes conceal, enhance, and stimulate us to new ways of seeing and understanding.

REFERENCES

Berkeley, G., "An Essay Towards a New Theory of Vision." 1907.

Deregowski, J. "Illusion and Culture." in *Illusion in Nature and Art*, edited by R. L. Gregory and E. H. Gombrich. London: Duckworth, 1973.

Gibson, J. J. *The Perception of the Visual World.* Boston: Houghton Mifflin, 1950.

———. *The Senses Considered as Perceptual Systems.* Boston: Houghton Mifflin, 1966.

Ginsburg, A. P. "Psychological Correlates of a Model of the Human Visual System." *Proceedings of the IEEE NAECON* (Dayton, Ohio) (1971): 283–390.

Gregory, R. L. "Distortion of Visual Space as Inappropriate Constancy Scaling," *Nature* (London) 199 (1963): 678.

———. "Stereoscopic Shadow Images." *Nature* (London) 203 (1964): 1407.

———. *The Intelligent Eye.* New York: McGraw-Hill, 1970.

———. "The Confounded Eye," in *Illusion in Nature and Art*, edited by R. L. Gregory and E. H. Gombrich, p. 90. London: Duckworth, 1973.

———. "Do We Need Cognitive Concepts?" In *Handbook of Psychobiology*, edited by Blakemore and Gazzinaga. New York: Academic Press, 1975.

———. "Vision with Isoluminant Colour Contrast," pt. 1, "A Projection Technique and Observations." *Perception* 6 (1976): 113–19.

Gregory, R. L., and Harris, J. P. "Illusion-Destruction by Appropriate Scaling." *Perception* 4 (1975): 203–20.

Lee, D. N. "Theory of the Stereoscopic Shadow-Caster: An Instrument for the Study of Binocular Space Perception." *Vision Research* 9 (1969): 1.

Segall, M. H.; Campbell, T. D.; and Herskovitz, M. J. *The Influence of Culture on Visual Perception*, New York: Bobbs–Merrill, 1966.

Tausch, R. "Optische Tauschungen als artifizelle Effekte der Gestaltungspozesse von Grossen and Formenkonstanz in der naturlichen Raunwahrehmung." *Psychol. Forsch.* 24 (1954): 299.

Théiry, A. "Uber geometriscsh-optisch Tauschungen" *Phil Stud.* 12 (1896): 67.

Zeki, S. M. "Colour Coding in the Superior Temporal Sulcus of Rhesus Monkey Visual Cortex." *Proceedings of the Royal Society: Biological Sciences* (London) 197 (1977): 195–223.

Chapter Thirteen

A Piece of the Action:
Moving Figures in
Still Pictures

John L. Ward

Scholarship and research have been little concerned with the study of the depiction of people and animals in motion. In view of depicted movement's important role in the history of art and the engaging questions that it poses, this neglect is surprising. Alternative theories of depicted motion have been presented by Gombrich (1961, 1964) and Arnheim (1954, 1966), but despite the major influence these scholars have had on the psychology of art, neither theory has received much attention. (An exception is Gottlieb [1958] who notes her indebtedness to Arnheim.) Nor have other recent theories of picturing, such as those put forward by Gibson (1971) and Goodman (1968), included a discussion of motion representation. Yet, any comprehensive theory of picture perception must somehow be able to provide an account of the nature of depicted movement, including that of figures. (The term *figure* will be used in this chapter, for lack of a better one, to designate a human or animal form.) The present state of research is summarized in Friedman and Stevenson (in press).

The principal problem to be explained is how movement can be represented when a painter is only able to give us a piece—or, at best, pieces—of the action. How can the movement of a figure, which happens over time, be shown in the timeless medium of a picture? Why do some representations of moving figures appear frozen and stiff, while others are convincingly animated?

One answer is that pictorial movement cannot be directly represented in pictures but must be supplied by the viewer's imagination. The artist can only give the viewer an opportunity to use his or her imagination. This theory has a long history, summarized in part by Gombrich (1964). In a variation that has formed the theoretical basis for most of the research on the experiencing of pictorial movement,

Rorschach argued that a feeling of movement in a picture is based on kinesthetic empathy deriving from memories of past experiences (1921). Arnheim (1954) has pointed out serious weaknesses in Rorschach's theory.

Perhaps the most persuasive apologist for the theory that pictorial movement is supplied by the viewer is Sir Ernst Gombrich. He has argued (1964) that a picture must be observed over time through a synthesis of discrete retinal fixations. Looking at a picture can be compared with hearing music or reading, since in each case, there is an "effort after meaning" that takes into account what one has perceived, is perceiving, and anticipates perceiving. In looking at a depicted action or event, a viewer will tend to "read" it backward and forward in time and space, reconstructing what has happened and anticipating what will happen next. Two qualities will therefore enhance the effectiveness of depicted movement: clarity of meaning (the viewer must be able to understand what is happening in order to understand how it has developed and will develop over time) and unclarity or incompleteness of form, which will arouse in the viewer "the memories and anticipations of movement" (Gombrich 1964, p. 306). Where the subject is recognized, the viewer will tend to fill in the appropriate movement in places where the form has been left vague or incomplete.

In sharp contrast, Rudolf Arnheim regards effective pictorial movement as the result of directed tensions between pictorial forms that have their counterpart in the viewer's brain field. Tension can be produced by such things as unequally proportioned shapes, shapes of the intervals between forms, and the perception of a figure as a foreshortened form in space. It also occurs in deviations from the orientation of the framework, which in a normal rectangular picture takes the form of obliqueness. In any successful picture, this directed tension or movement permeates all of the forms and relationships, not only those that are meant to show physical action.

A figure depicted in motion involves an additional kind of tension, which is related to the memory trace of its normal attitude. The traditional way of depicting a galloping horse with outstretched legs is thus more satisfactory than the gallop as it appears in stop-action photographs, "for only the maximum spread of the legs translates the intensity of the physical motion into pictorial dynamics" (Arnheim 1954, p. 345). This is so not because the position is seen as a momentary phase of an ongoing action, however, but because it embodies the whole character of the action, perceived as a deviation from the horse's stationary positions.

Although Gombrich and Arnheim each develops a theory that offers fruitful insights concerning depicted movement, neither theory appears adequate to explain the effectiveness of movement in specific pictures. Gombrich, for example, suggests that the tendency to read ahead where the form is unclear might account for the increased impression of speed and movement felt by many observers who are shown a photograph of the less legible side view of the *Discobolos* (Figure 13.1) after looking at a photograph taken from the front of the sculpture (Figure 13.2). But the Discobolos's greater sense of movement when viewed from the side appears to result from an increase in *clarity*, not obscurity—clarity, that is, in terms of how the forms will participate in an event. The apparent connection of the left hand to the knee in the frontal photograph makes it seem that only the right arm has any potential mobility, whereas the side view makes visible the twisting movement of the body, the dynamic shift of weight, and the interaction of the various limbs in an integrated, fluid event.

Two simultaneous views of a galloping dog taken by Eadweard Muybridge (Figures 13.3 and 13.4) seem to lend support to this idea. The view from behind, which is less easy to perceive, should offer a greater opportunity for projection. My own experience, however, is that unlike the discus thrower, the dog does not appear to move as convincingly or as fast as in the less-foreshortened view. To be sure, the picture is ambiguous not only in form but also in meaning, and Gombrich might have predicted its failure to evoke motion on the basis of the central role that "the principle of the primacy of meaning" plays in his theory of perception. But the activity of the dog can be understood by comparing it with the companion photograph and, although such a comparison may somewhat increase its legibility and dynamism, I am unable to experience anything like the effect of movement produced by the side view.

Arnheim's theory of depicted figure motion as "directed tension" modified by a memory trace of normal body positions also seems inadequate to account for the success of some depictions of moving figures over others. For example, Géricault's painting of a horse race (Figure 13.5), which Arnheim uses as evidence for his theory, appears curiously locked in place. If motion is expressed, it is that of horses on a low-budget carrousel, mounted on fixed poles that go past the spectator without changing poses, elevation, or relative position. To my eye, at least, Frederick Remington's painting *Indian Warfare* (Figure 13.6), clearly indebted to Muybridge's studies, is far more animated and better conveys the experience of galloping horses, despite the fact that Remington was an artist of more modest ambitions and accomplishments than Géricault.

I would like to offer a different theory to account for the effective motion of Remington's horses and for the experiences of relative movement or immobility that a viewer receives from other depicted figures engaged in action. My theory is influenced by James Gibson's ideas about perception and pictures, although I do not fully agree with them or even fully understand them. My proposal is that the effective depiction of figures in motion is based on the indication of some of the structural properties for motion that provide information for such qualities as its approximate speed, development over time, and the interaction of moving limbs with the ground and with other bodies. But it also depends on the weakening of some of the structural properties of immobility inherent in a still picture. It is theorized that ongoing action will be most effectively depicted when the means by which it arrived at its present position seem clear and when its subsequent movements appear inevitable. Action will appear curiously suspended or awkwardly incoherent when neither past nor future movements or events are clearly indicated or when an alternate action is strongly suggested by the pose. This will be so even when the observer knows or infers from the context (for example, a race track) what kind of action is depicted and even if the picture is a photograph of an actual figure in motion. Specific suggestions of the means by which action can be indicated will be made in the remainder of this chapter.

The properties that Arnheim views as the source of a picture's "directed tension" are here seen to contribute to the quality of effective figure motion to the extent that they specify or suggest some of the properties of motion as it occurs in the ordinary environment. For example, diagonality may create pictorial tension because of its deviation from the orientation of the frame, but its contribution to pictorial motion will be determined by its perceived relation to a depicted space and gravitational field. Diagonality will have a different effect in a diving figure than in a figure with its feet on the ground. In the latter case, a diagonal figure will be seen as falling to the ground in an arc unless the artist either indicates that the figure is somehow braced or that it is moving forward fast enough to offset the pull of gravity. An arm extended diagonally upward may appear as the culmination of a reaching gesture, as part of a downward movement, as part of an upward movement, or as a fixed pose, depending on the context.

I agree with Gombrich that the depiction of action must involve the articulation of past or potential events and thus implies time. But the past or future time that is implicit in depicted figure movement is not usually based on an illusion of real motion in time. It depends, rather, on a general specification or suggestion of the path, character, and speed of the action, which allows events before and after the depicted movement to be visualized only insofar as information is provided for them. The artist's task is not simply to create a projection screen onto which the unguided viewer is invited to project imaginary action but to indicate properties that are specific to the depicted event as well. I also agree with Gombrich that the weakening of structural properties that specify fixed space position by the reduction of clarity or other means may enhance the effect of motion—but only if it does not obscure the indicated development of the motion.

As accounted for by the present theory, Remington's painting (Figure 13.6) depicts the action of galloping horses more effectively than Géricault's (Figure 13.5), because it presents more of the structural properties of a gallop and fewer of the properties of fixed location. The alignment of horses indicates the overall flow of the movement, and the action extends beyond the edges of the picture, so that the implied time and motion is continuous. The complex sequencing of the forms weakens the effect of immobility by obscuring the unchanging positions of figures and parts of figures relative to one another. The horses' legs are organized so as to indicate a flurry of back-and-forth movement, and the raised dust not only indicates the interaction of the hooves with the ground but creates the effect of motion blur.

By contrast, Géricault's picture presents all of the legs in the same position, so that it seems impossible that they could ever move to other positions. Nor would the apparent height of the horses above the ground give them time to gather their legs beneath them before striking it. They therefore hang in a timeless limbo, full of energy but incapable of movement. The quality of motion that the picture possesses is created by the scudding clouds and broken light rather than by the poses of the horses, as can be seen by masking out the sky and the foreground.

It is important to note, however, that the greater effectiveness of Remington's depiction of motion does not arise simply from its greater fidelity to stop-action photography. Although Remington used Muybridge's photographs, he deliberately avoided the more awkward moments in the sequence and altered the poses that he did use. Most significantly, the left front leg of the lead horse should be straight and touching the ground and is therefore as impossible as Géricault's. Because of the difficulty of perceiving this horse as an isolated form, however, its predicament is not evident. What we see is the *overall* flow of the action through space and time and its general properties and rhythms, as we do when watching a group of riders in actual motion.

If the pose of Géricault's horses is as unsuccessful in conveying motion as I have suggested, it may well be asked why the *flying gallop*, as it is often called, has been so widely used in the history of pictures to represent running animals (Lefort des Ylouses 1945). There is probably no simple answer to the question. But the longevity of the pose probably arises in part because it is capable of portraying vigorous forward motion in the proper circumstances. Thus, in Muybridge's picture of the leaping dog (Figure 13.3), a very similar pose is considerably more effective, and it is likely that a clarification of past and future motion (for example, by showing the dog at different points in the action) would greatly enhance this effect. It is in large part the multiplication of the identical pose and the lack of a coherent relationship to the ground that prevents Géricault's painting from appearing to be able to develop in time.

I will now examine several examples of effective depiction of figures in motion to illustrate how motion properties, such as speed, direction, extension over time, and the interaction of forms, can be indicated.

In Michelangelo's drawing of the Resurrection (at Windsor) (Figure 13.7), Christ's eruption upward from the tomb appears to create shock waves that make figures on either side recoil. The interaction of the poses specifies the unfolding of the movements up to the moment shown, but because the poses have approached their maximum extension upward, no further motion is clearly specified. Arnheim has asserted that "every action picture is perceived as representing the maximum movement of the action" and that a picture cannot actually represent the motion of limbs but "only the tension inherent in the deviation from the normal attitude" (1954, pp. 345, 346). But these dual principles, which epitomize what he has written about the depicted movement of figures, do not explain why Muybridge's photograph of blacksmiths with their hammers lifted overhead (Muybridge, 1955, pl. 81) is perceived in terms of a future action (as Arnheim himself claims [1954, p. 345]), whereas Michelangelo's Christ is seen as specifying a past action but not a future one. With the present theory, the difference arises because the blacksmiths' attention is focused on a point that their hammers can easily reach by a simple, easily estimated movement, whereas the risen Christ's supporting leg receives his weight and anchors him to the ground, although the direction of his movement and attention are upward.

In a small scene from the neck of a volute krater, the great but anonymous Greek artist known as the Berlin painter employs the form of the narrow band that encircles the vase to extend the action in time (see Figure 13.8). The women seem to have just appeared, trailing after the combatants and indicating the direction from which they came. There is a crescendo from the smaller steps and slower motion of the women, indicated by their upright poses, to the longer strides and inclined postures of the warriors. Motion and force build toward the inevitable collision in the center. The space between the warriors is charged with tension by the vectors of their potential motion. Each combatant adjusts his moves to the speed of the oncoming opponent, the amount of remaining space, the weight of his own weapon, and its manner of use. This small masterpiece demolishes the familiar claim, recently made again, that in all Greek representation, "each figure remains in a private space of its own" because the Greeks never learned to "coordinate in terms of reciprocal relationships and points of view" (Gablik 1977, p. 14).

According to Gombrich's theory, the symmetrical balance, precise drawing, and clarity of pose should make these figures quite static, yet in fact, every limb is alive with energy. This is so not because we imagine the figures to move but because their postures specify potentialities for action that we see precisely as potentialities, not as projections. It is the perception of events as imminent, not imaginary, which gives this painting its wonderful tension.

Michelangelo's drawing specifies only past motion and the Berlin painter indicates both past and future. A small *Annunciation* by the thirteenth-century Italian painter Guido da Siena (Figure 13.9) begins abruptly with the angel's entrance and extends its action into the future. This future is ambiguous, however, since it is difficult to see how the angel Gabriel can avoid colliding with the Virgin, and her alarmed reaction may be as much a response to his velocity as to his unexpected presence. Guido has specified a rate of movement that is excessive for the dramatic situation but nevertheless convincing. The play of interacting shapes in "directed tension" produces this lively movement by their correspondence to specific structural properties of the action depicted. Although the painter is medieval and the space is not completely determined, there is a sure organization of Gabriel's limbs into a posture that permits him to maintain his balance as his feet push vigorously forward against the ground. The feeling of balance and firm contact with the ground give the heavenly messenger a sense of weight, which increases his momentum. The apparent movement of Gabriel's right knee is enhanced by the pattern of convergent folds, which specify both the deforming pressure of the knee and the backward swing of the drapery. The trees between the figures appear to yield to the air turbulence generated by the angel's headlong charge. Their deformation is greatest at the point opposite Gabriel's outstretched hand and wedge-shaped edge of his left wing, which protrudes from behind his halo. By making visible the forces generated by his approach, the swaying trees give information for the subsequent path of his action, as does the Virgin's timorous response.

All of the pictures considered thus far employ figure interaction to enhance and extend the depicted movement. The dancer on a Mayan pot of the eighth century A.D. (Figure 13.10) is unconnected with other action and remains more or less in place. But here, too, the animation of the figure depends on its relationship to time and space. Past action is indicated by the bands attached to his waist, which swing up on either side, as if he were touching down after a leap, and by the feathers on the headdress, which follow his head in a downward arc. Central to this effect is the presentation of the figure as moving freely through a three-dimensional space. The parts of the body are subtly foreshortened and counterbalanced so as to describe an integrated but complex action. The pose is conceived of as generated by an interaction of muscles and limbs precisely distributed above the toes of the left foot, which is placed so as to absorb the force of the preceding leap and to propel the figure in the direction of the upraised arm.

Arnheim has observed that "works actually intended to show the fleeting moment endow transitory gestures with embarrassing duration or fail to render any activity at all" (1954, p. 346). A comparison of the Mayan dancing figure with some of Muybridge's photographs of galloping horses (Figures 13.11 and 13.12) indicates, however, that it is not the intention to show the fleeting moment that freezes figures in place but the absence of clear indications of prior and subsequent movements. In one picture (Figure 13.11), the horse's rear legs give no indication of whether they are moving forward or backward or moving past each other in opposite directions. As a result, gravity takes over, and the legs hang lifelessly in position. At the same time, the bent front leg appears to have been raised from a position next to the supporting leg rather than to be moving forward, since there is no indication of any movement beyond the positions encompassed by the arc between the lower legs. On the other hand, another photograph from the same sequence is quite successful in specifying the character of the action (see Figure 13.12). The back legs will clearly have just enough time to swing down into position to support the horse as it strikes the ground, and the resulting forward propulsion will keep the horse airborne long enough for the front legs to swing forward, straighten out, and strike the ground in turn.

In this chapter, formal properties, such as line, shape, and pattern, have been considered as providing information for the motion of depicted figures. I have argued that a picture has the quality of an ongoing event rather than a tableau of frozen postures in fixed positions precisely to the degree that these elements or their combination specify some of the properties of movement and interrupt or weaken some of the invariants that specify solid, immobile form. The specification of properties of motion and the weakening of those specifying fixed position are complementary rather than cumulative in effect. The interaction can be extremely complex, as an analysis of Antonio Pollaiuolo's engraving *Battle of the Nudes* (Figure 13.13) may illustrate.

The Pollaiuolo print seems to exemplify Arnheim's recipe for a dynamic composition: the movement of each detail fits into the movement of the whole, and the forms are organized around a dynamic theme that radiates movement throughout the picture. The lively poses are further animated by the undulating line that defines the contours, and the tangle of curving swords, bows, and bodies is echoed in the pattern of foliage behind them. Information for the fixed position of solid figures is deliberately weakened by the complex interlacing of figures, which is exaggerated by the evenness of the pictorial light.

But movement is not merely the result of formless chaos or the tensions generated by the play of abstract shapes and rhythms: sequences of form are also present that, in the general turmoil, function as phases of a continuous movement. Thus, the upper curve of the drawn bow forms a sequence with the two arms in front of it, and the bowman can be seen as an earlier state of the man he follows. These stages are bridged by the lines of the intervening foliage, which create a kind of stroboscopic flicker.

Yet, for all of the energetic movement conveyed by Pollaiuolo's print, as an *event*, it seems to me curiously frozen. It is not the surreal suspended motion of Géricault's horses that I feel here but something more like the activity of an intricate windup toy, in which the figures are capable of only certain fixed, continuously repeatable movements: arms seem capable of hacking and chopping, figures can bend forward or backward, yet the action does not compel conviction as a developing event. The abstract energy generated by line and pattern for the most part do not seem to originate in the depicted action. It is as if we watched a windup toy with complex patterns of shifting light playing over its surfaces—patterns through which we perceived a lurching, repetitive kind of action.

In part, this effect is created by a certain disconnectedness of activity: the man with the upraised ax at the right appears to direct his gaze at a spot on the ground behind the man he seems to be trying to hit. Nor does he notice the arm and sword apparently in the path of his action. But the distribution of figures in pictorial space and the organization of surface relationships contribute even more to the effect of a frozen tableau that the print produces. The combatants are locked into their positions by their approximately symmetrical placement, by the even density of pattern across the picture surface, and by the careful fit of the whole configuration within the picture's edges. All of these properties involve relationships that belong to a closed system, not relationships generated by beings that respond individually to a fluid situation in an unbounded space. Although some of the intermingled forms are arranged in sequences that convey movement generated by the figures and related to the depicted event, others interfere with the action described. Arms and legs merge into other forms that absorb or redirect their movements. As a result, the picture conveys a vivid sense of general activity at the same time that the figures fail to create a coherent sense of ongoing action.

The Pollaiuolo print suggests that an overall, abstract quality of movement can be created without a clearly defined sense of either past or future time. But it also suggests, like the other pictures we have considered, that the depiction of coherent movement generated by figures requires the extension of the action backward or forward in time and space. The effectiveness of this extension depends on the clear articulation of the properties of past and future action—its path, rate of travel, and the submovements of limbs, as well as their interaction with other bodies and surfaces. When this information is provided, a picture can be seen as describing a coherent, ongoing event, not because the figures appear to move but because it is clear what has happened and what must happen next. The viewer is not required to imagine movement; he or she need only recognize the quality of motion and force necessary to achieve the depicted positions and the potentiality for future motion indicated by these positions and the overall situation.

It is theorized in this chapter that the effective depiction of figure movement is accomplished by two complementary means: the clarification of the past and potential movements of the depicted figures and the obfuscation of information for immobility. In this concluding section, some ways of clarifying the depicted motion and obscuring the actual absence of motion are proposed. These suggestions and predictions are derived from my own observations and have not been tested experimentally.

MEANS OF INDICATING PAST AND POTENTIAL ACTION

Pose

The effective depiction of a figure in motion requires the representation of the body parts so that they appear to be engaged in a coherent stage of an action, such as generating motion or preparing to strike the ground, and so that the interacting roles of gravity and momentum, both present and anticipated, are clear. If the actual momentum is misjudged (usually underestimated) by the viewer, the nature of the action is more likely to be misperceived. For example, a figure shown at the last moment before its feet (hind feet in the case of an animal) leave the ground in a forward jump frequently does not seem to have enough momentum to detach itself from the ground and, as a result, looks frozen in place.

In general, there are three requirements for the effective representation of momentum: the depicted pose must appear to have been the consequence of motion in a specific direction, it must appear difficult to maintain, and it must appear capable of clear development in the direction of the apparent previous action. When the action of a figure is mingled with that of a larger group and is not individually discernible, however (see Figure 13.6), the last of these requirements may not apply so strictly. Momentum can be enhanced by a variety of means other than pose. These are discussed in the subsequent sections of this chapter.

A figure that lacks apparent momentum effectively participates in an action only to the extent that its pose appears set to *generate* motion (see Figure 13.1). Consequently, intermediate stages of an action will not convey its full force when momentum is not apparent. Since Arnheim does not admit that momentum can be differentiated from directed tension, he seems to view transitional poses as necessarily less effective representations of actions. But Muybridge's photographs of men throwing the javelin and throwing and hitting baseballs indicate that when intermediate stages of an action contain information for momentum, they may be no less effective in depicting the motion's force than positions at the beginning or the end.

Depiction of Involuntary Consequences of Figure Motion

Inertia of the surrounding medium exerts friction on moving forms and is most apparent in the tendency of flexible parts, such as hair and clothing, to trail behind and specify both the direction and speed of movement. With respect to effects of variable acceleration and deceleration, the appearance of the softer body parts (breasts and buttocks), as well as hair and loose clothing, can indicate that they are momentarily traveling at a different rate of speed than the rest of the body (see Figures 13.9 and 13.10).

Involuntary consequences of figure motion may fail to make the appropriate momentum apparent or to clarify the action if they are unable to suggest a clear continuation of controlled movements that can be reconciled with the figure's pose. In a given picture, effects of friction may be indistinguishable from effects of acceleration.

Direct Depiction of Changes of Position

A direct depiction of changes of position can be created by a streak (blur created by a moving form in which the path of movement is visible)—it is found in photographs in which a figure moves perceptibly during the exposure and is approximated by cartoon "action lines." Or it can be created by stroboscopic imagery or the sequencing of different but visually similar figures engaged in the same action and moving in the same direction (see Figure 13.6). These techniques can provide the most complete information for the path of the action and can enhance the effect of speed. But, except for limited use of streak, they introduce qualities that are sharply at variance with the appearance of the world in normal viewing.

Interaction with the Environment

Subjects that show energy transfer may improve the coherence of the action. Examples would be pictures showing the wake of a speeding boat, a figure reacting to a punch, and a ball thrown into space. But if the interaction leaves the direction of the action ambiguous (for example, if the figure appears to be catching the ball), the action will not appear effective. Other depicted figures' perception of the principal action as indicated by their anticipatory response to it should improve the effectiveness of the action if their response enables the viewer to calculate the path and force of the action (see Figure 13.8). Articulation of the depicted action's goal will make the movement appear more coherent if it provides a clear means of continuation for the action. Varying the ground level may change the appearance of a jump or gallop if it significantly changes the continuations of the event that are available (compare Figure 13.5). Also, the amount of pictorial space shown before or behind a figure in forward motion may affect perception, especially if a point of departure or a goal is indicated by such means as the presence of a pursuing figure, a road, or footprints. The role that such means play in modifying the observer's judgments about the immediate movements of the figure, as well as its long-range activities, is not entirely clear to me. It seems likely, however, that each of them can affect the observer's perception of movement under the proper circumstances.

MEANS OF REDUCING EFFECT OF INFORMATION FOR IMMOBILITY

The means of reducing the effect of information for immobility include the following: (1) reduction in the amount of detail specifying the layout of surfaces in pictorial space; (2) reduction or avoidance of modeling (see Figures 13.10 and 13.11); (3) obfuscation or interruption of the form of the figure (see Figure 13.6) or space (see Figure 13.5) by irregular lighting, overlap, or other means; (4) avoidance of stable background forms that interrupt the flow of action (see Figures 13.1 through 13.13); and reduction in scale. I am least confident of the effects of reduction in scale, but Friedländer (1946) has independently claimed that it enhances motion depiction.

The present theory predicts that the above means and methods will only enhance motion when they do not obscure the nature of the action involved. It is likely that subtle nuances of form may contain essential information to describe the action and that their elimination may destroy the effectiveness of the depicted action.

On the other hand, an increase in information that makes the form more solid and firmly positioned in space without further clarifying the development of the action should reduce the effectiveness of the picture as a representation of motion. A stereoscopic photograph of a figure in mid-jump should appear more frozen than an equivalent single-lens photograph to the extent that it achieves these ends.

REFERENCES

Arnheim, R. *Art and Visual Perception: A Psychology of the Creative Eye.* Berkeley: University of California Press, 1954. New version, extensively rewritten, 1974.

————. "Perceptual and Aesthetic Aspects of the Movement Response." In *Toward a Psychology of Art: Collected Essays,* edited by R. Arnheim. Berkeley and Los Angeles: University of California Press, 1966.

Friedländer, M. J. "Movement." In *On Art and Connoisseurship,* edited by M. J. Friedländer. Oxford: Bruno Cassirer, 1946.

Friedman, S. L., and Stevenson, M. Perception of Movement in Pictures." In *What, Then, Is a Picture?,"* edited by M. Hagen. In press.

Gablik, S. *Progress in Art.* New York: Rizzoli, 1977.

Gibson, J. J. "The Information Available in Pictures." *Leonardo* 4 (1971): 27–35.

Gombrich, E. H. *Art and Illusion: A Study in the Psychology of Pictorial Representation.* 2d ed. rev. New York: Pantheon Books, 1961.

————. "Moment and Movement in Art." *Journal of the Warburg and Courtauld Institutes,* 27 (1964): 293–306.

Goodman, N. *Languages of Art: An Approach to a Theory of Symbols* Indianapolis: Bobbs–Merrill, 1968.

Gottlieb, C. "Movement in Painting." *Journal of Aesthetics and Art Criticism,* 17 (1958): 22–33.

Groenewegen-Frankfort, H. A. *Arrest and Movement: An Essay on Space and Time in the Representational Art of the Ancient Near East.* London: Faber and Faber, 1951.

Johnson, L. F., Jr. "Time and Motion in Toulouse-Lautrec." *College Art Journal,* 16 (1956): 13–22.

Lefort des Ylouses, R. "Les Images du galop ramassé dans l'antiquité," *Revue archéologique,* 19 (1942–43): 18–23.

———. "Le Galop volant." *Revue archéologique,* 24 (1945): 18–36.

Muybridge, E. *The Human Figure in Motion.* New York: Dover Publications, 1955. First published 1901.

———. *Animals in Motion.* New York: Dover Publications, 1957. (First published 1899).

Reinach, S. La Répresentation du galop dans l'art ancien et moderne." *Revue Archéologique,* 36, (1900–1): 217–51, 441–50; 37: 244–59; 38: 27–45, 224–44; 39: 1–11.

Rodin A. *Art.* Boston: Small, Maynard, 1912.

Rorschach, H. *Psychodiagnostik.* Berne and Berlin: Huber, 1921. English title, *Psychodiagnostics.* Berne: Huber, 1942.

Scharf, A. "Painting, Photography, and the Image of Movement." *Burlington Magazine,* 104 (1962): 186–95; reply and rejoinder, 104: 391–92.

———. *Art and Photography.* London: Allen Lane, Penguin Press, 1968.

Souriau, E. "Time in the Plastic Arts." *Journal of Aesthetics and Art Criticism,* 7 (1949): 294–307.

Summers, D. "Maniera and Movement: The Figure Serpentinata." *Art Quarterly,* 35 (1972): 269–301.

Wölfflin, H. *Kleine Schriften.* Basel: B. Schwabe, 1946.

Figure 13.1   Myron's (copy after) *Discobolos* (Munich, Antiquarium)—side view.

Figure 13.2   Myron's (copy after) *Discobolos* (Munich, Antiquarium)—front view.

Figure 13.3   Eadweard Muybridge's *Ike in Rotatory-Gallop*, side view, frame (International Museum of Photography at George Eastman House).

Figure 13.4 Back view of Figure 13.3

Figure 13.5 Theodore Géricault's *Epsom Derby* (Paris, The Louvre).

Figure 13.6   Frederick Remington's *Indian Warfare* (Tulsa, Oklahoma, The Thomas Gilcrease Institute of American History and Art).

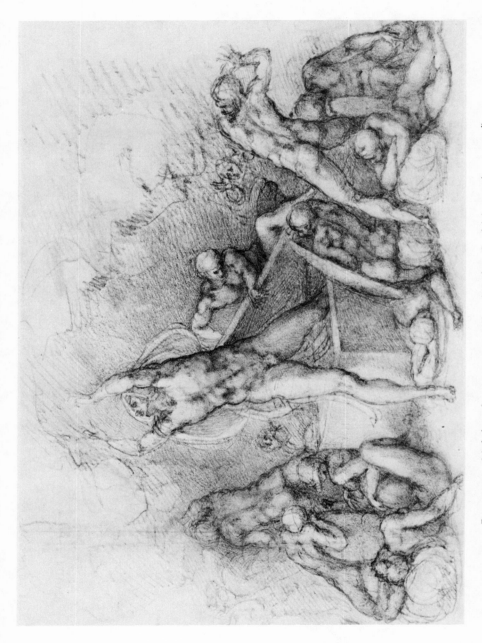

Figure 13.7 Michelangelo's *Resurrection of Christ* (Windsor Castle) (copyright reserved).

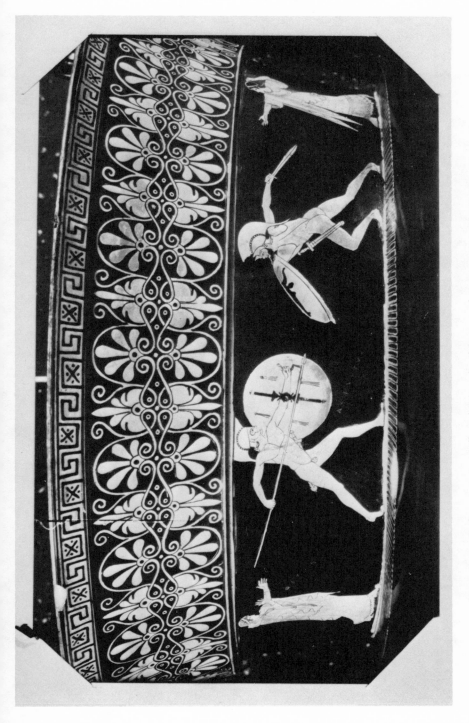

Figure 13.8 Berlin painter's *Achilles and Hektor*, detail from a volute krater (London, British Museum).

Figure 13.9 Guido da Siena's *Annunciation* (The Art Museum, Princeton University).

Figure 13.10 Mayan, Late Classical, *Jaguar Dancer,* on pot, from Altar de Sacrificios, Petén (Ciudad de Guatemala, Museo Nacional de Arqueologia y Etnologia).

Figure 13.11 Eadweard Muybridge's *Bouquet with Rider*, side view, frame 7 (International Museum of Photography at George Eastman House).

Figure 13.12 Later stage of the same action shown in Figure 13.11.

Figure 13.13   Antonio Pollaiuolo's *Battle of the Nudes* (New Haven, Yale University Art Gallery).

Chapter Fourteen

Picturing and Representing

Marx W. Wartofsky

The thesis I want to present in this chapter, although stated very baldly, is: human vision is a cultural and historical product of the creative activity of making pictures. To put it somewhat differently, *human* vision is an artifact, produced by means of other artifacts—for example, by pictures; as such, it is an historically variable mode of perception, which changes with changes in our modes of representation. What follows from this thesis, if it is true, are two radical conclusions—one, methodological, the other, epistemological.

The methodologically radical conclusion is that all theoretical attempts to construct a theory of vision, which presuppose that seeing is an essential, unchanging structure of process; or that the human eye is describable in some generic physiological way, are, if not fundamentally mistaken, then essentially incomplete. For the plasticity of the visual system, if I am right, is such that it requires a historical account of its development and not simply a biological account of its evolution, whether phylogenetically or ontogenetically.

The radical epistemological conclusion is that there is no intrinsically veridical, or "correct," mode of representation, that is, there is no criterion of veridicality that is not itself a product of the social and historical choices of norms of visual representation. There is, therefore, no canon of truth in perception that can be established by reduction to the physiology of vision, or to optics, or to some species-specific biological, or even ecological, account. That is not to say that we do not inherit the mammalian eye, nor is it to say that human vision is not based in an evolved, adaptive structure which develops with the speciation of Homo sapiens. However, truth in perception, as I will argue, is bound to canons of the veridicality of representation; these, in turn, have a history and are rooted in our social practice and in our own activities of picturing and representing. Thus, it is we who *create* the very norms of veridicality by our pictorial practice. Such norms are not arbitrary, though they are conventional; they are not biological but historical.

The larger theoretical enterprise of which the thesis that I propose is a part may be characterized as a historical epistemology. I will present one specific aspect of such a historical theory of vision, which I have begun to develop elsewhere (Wartofsky 1972, 1976). At issue is the question of how representation is possible in the specific mode of representation that we call *picturing*—and, more specifically, in that subcategory of pictures which we call *paintings.*

My argument may be summarized in five points. First, the act of representing something pictorially is a creative act. That is to say, it does not depend on some antecedent notion that something (a picture) "looks like" or "resembles" or "represents" something else (for example, a scene, an object, a person, and so forth), but rather that it is *we* who create the similarity which counts as representational. Similarity is not given, but achieved; made, not discovered. It is invented and created.

Second, the perceptual system—and the visual system in particular—is biologically evolved to take certain things in the visual world as being *like* or *resembling* others, by virtue of the forms of life activity of a given species, that is, the means by which its individual members preserve themselves in existence and reproduce the species life. These canons of resemblance, similarity, or identity are mapped into the neural and neuromuscular structure of the species; they may be said to be coded into its genetic structure by natural selection. The human species, however, has a radically alternative mode of mapping its forms of life activity into structure, and this is by means of canons of visual representation, that is, embodied rules for taking one thing as a representation of something else. Pictures—or rather styles of pictorial representation—exemplify canons of representation, by means of which we come to *see* the visual world as *like* the picture.

Third, the rules of linear perspective in painting and drawing are *not* "correct" representations of the way things "look" but rather proposals to see things the way they are represented pictorially. When they come to look the way they are pictured, it is because we have adopted the rule of picturing as a rule of seeing the world—that is, we *see* by way of our picturing.

Fourth, the alleged paradox of pictures—namely, that the three-dimensional world is represented in a two-dimensional image of the world—is not a paradox; it is dissolved when we recognize that in taking a picture as a representation of the world, we come to take the world as a two-dimensional picture, which is, in *this* respect, like what pictures or represents it. When we are fooled, then the picture is no longer, properly speaking, a picture. However, we are rarely fooled. The argument is this: We say that representational pictures (for example, paintings) "look" three dimensional, that is, they "look like" the three-dimensional objects or scenes which they represent. However, we take the world to "look" three dimensional only by contrast to the two-dimensionality of pictures. The visual concept of "three dimensionality" is thus a constructive concept, which depends upon reference to, or a relation to, the two dimensionality of pictures. We would have no distinctive notion of the three dimensionality of the visual world except for the distinction we come to draw between it and two-dimensional representations of it. In short, the making of two-dimensional representations, or pictures, is what generates the contrastive visual concept of three dimensionality. I would suggest that the geometry which defines the plane projection of a solid is likewise dependent on the more primitive notion of a picture, that is, a representation or configuration in the two-dimensional plane.

Fifth, and finally, modes of picturing change, with changes in form of our social, technological, and intellectual praxis; representation has a history, and thus, in coming to adopt different modes of representation, we literally change our visual world. Human vision is an artifact created and changed by the modes of picturing. Different modes of picturing have different theories. We have *adopted* the theory of linear perspective as our theory of veridical representation. It is not incorrect. But neither is it correct. Veridicality is not a given feature of a mode of picturing. It is defined by the theory of pictorial representation that we come to adopt.

So much for the summary of my argument. Now to the question posed for this volume: "What is a painting?" The question needs to be specified more concretely in order to be answered. It has many answers, depending on what it is that is being asked. A merely ostensive definition—"that's a painting" (pointing at one)—will not do, but it does hide a deeper answer. Namely, paintings are the sorts of things that are *taken* to be paintings. Thus revised, the question becomes, "What is it we take to be a painting?"

I plan to deal with only one aspect of this question here, namely, that of pictorial representation, which is *one* of the things paintings do (or are taken to do). In order to deal with this question, however, there is a more general characterization I want to give to paintings, apart from, but related to their representational capacities, that is, paintings are artifacts, made things, the products of intentional human activity, and insofar as they are representational, they are intended as representations—that is, they are artifacts whose purpose it is to represent something.

The question then becomes, "How do the kinds of artifacts called *pictures* represent?" What is *made* in such a way as to come to represent something else? More specifically, in the case of painting, how do arrangements of lines, areas, colors, and gradients of dark and light on a two-dimensional plane surface come to represent three-dimensional objects, scenes, and persons?

There are several possible answers to this question. I will examine three, but first, I would like to frame my approach so that the context of my considerations will be clear. There are several general points to be made. First, if (as is clear and undisputed) representation has a history and if (as is yet unclear and in dispute) this history is a crucial factor in the historical and cultural evolution of the human visual system, then the history of art becomes an essential component of the theory of vision: alternative modes of representation, the history of styles in painting, the theoretical analysis and reconstruction of the visual concepts of space, objects, and relations, which are characteristic of a given style or period, the phenomenological reconstruction of the modes of intentionality that identify an art-historical epoch, or a school all become essential components of any theory of vision, as crucial as the study of the psychology or physiology of vision and inseparable from these latter inquiries.

Second, since modes of representation are not simply or abstractly visual matters but involve also the larger social, technological, political, scientific, and even ideological contexts of human cognitive practice, a theory of vision is embedded in this larger framework of human social activity. Our seeing is a mode of our activity; just as vision cannot be conceived of simply as an activity of the eye, taken out of its context as part of the mammalian brain, and of the whole organism, so, too, it cannot be conceived of simply as the activity of the visual system, taken out of the context of the form of life in which this system operates, in which it develops, and which it is capable of transforming. To put this another way: it is neither the eye nor the visual system that sees. Rather, it is *we* who see, by means of the eye or the visual system. Similarly, it is not feet that walk. Rather, it is *we* using our feet. I could not walk without feet or see without eyes, but the *I* that sees, walks, talks, paints, argues, and gives papers at symposia is a social being, an individuated member of a life-form which is essentially historical and social. No mode of the life activity of such an individual can be adequately characterized, therefore, by abstractive reduction to the particular organs or apparatus by means of which this life activity proceeds. In this regard, the approach I am proposing is analogous to James Gibson's ecological approach to vision, but it differs sharply from his in that the ecology I am suggesting here is not a natural or biologically defined one but a cultural, or sociohistorical, "ecology." In short, vision, or seeing, is not merely the after-product, the epiphenomenon, of a given apparatus in a given environment or simply the operation of an organ. It is a creative activty that can be transformed and which, in turn, can itself transform a given form of life.

Third, and finally, if vision is a historically variable mode of cognitive practice that changes with alterations in our modes of representation, then the evolution of our visual system, as a cultural artifact, is, in contrast with its evolution as a biological system, no longer Darwinian but Lamarckian. That is to say, in the cultural evolution of *this* artifact, that is, of vision, there is transmission of acquired characteristics from one generation to the next. The mode of transmission is, therefore, no longer genetic but becomes social or cultural. The visual culture of a society or of an age is not inherited by the operation of genetic transmission or by means of the biochemical structures or codes that have been selected out, preserved, and developed by natural selection but rather by means of social structures—in particular, visual artifacts and modes of picturing. To put it simply, the artifact is to cultural evolution what the gene is to biological evolution. Cultural evolution, in contrast with biological evolution, is Larmarckian and not Darwinian. Such a thesis makes it possible to account for the plasticity and also the rapidity of cultural evolution; further, it is directly opposed to the current theoretical approaches to human cognition, as well as to human sociality, which find it necessary to focus on the alleged biological or genetic constraints on, or determinants of, modes of human activity.

To summarize this introductory discussion: (1) we see by way of our picturing—changes in our modes of cognition, in general, and in our modes of vision, in particular, are concomitant with changes in our modes of social practice, in general, and with our modes of pictorial representation, in particular; (2) the human visual system is therefore not simply the biological structure of our species evolution but an artifact produced by our own creative activity of picturing and seeing; thus, its plasticity cannot be defined reductively in biological, that is, physiological or genetic, terms.

Against this larger framework, let me now turn to the specific question, "How is representation possible?" The title of this chapter, "Picturing and Representing," is intended to correct a certain initial tendency to hypostatize: "Pictures and representations" suggests, I think, that we *begin* with certain entities already understood. I want to put in question what it is we understand by such entities and to emphasize that pictures picture and representations represent by virtue of the fact that they are the products of an activity that *intends* them as picturing and representing. That is, for something to *be* a picture, it needs to be *made* as a picture and *taken* as a picture; for something to *be* a representation, it has to be *intended* to represent, and this intention has to be understood in taking it *as* a representation. Nothing, then, is a picture or a representation in itself apart from being made as one or taken as one. There are no entities, then, which may "objectively" be characterized in this way. Instead, things of a certain sort are constituted as pictures and representations by makers and viewers. There is a radical consequence to this view as well: if nothing is intrinsically a picture or a representation, then we cannot ascribe a set of intrinsic properties to something that would identify it as a picture. In effect, *anything* can *be* a picture or a representation if it is made to be one or is taken as one. Let me make clear that I propose this in the strongest way, without qualification, that is, it is not the case that certain things are taken to be pictures or representations *because* they exhibit certain visual properties but, rather, that they come to exhibit certain visual properties *because* they are taken to be pictures or representations.

Now, this flies in the face of common sense—or seems to, for, in fact, not everything *is* taken to be a picture or a representation; in fact, a very narrow range of things is so taken at any given time or in any given culture. However, this narrow range itself *is* variable: some things *not* taken or made as pictures in one context are pictures in another. Moreover, insofar as pictures represent, it would appear that the relation of representing is based on some relation between some properties of the picture and some properties of what it is taken to represent, usually, a relation of resembling, or similarity, or likeness. The pictorial representation is said to be a representation by virtue of being a *likeness*; therefore, a successful representation shares properties with its reference.

My first claim, against this common view, is not original but is shared with Goodman (1976), upon whose more systematic and elaborated argument on this point I will rely. It is that representation requires no relation of resemblance, or likeness, but is rather constituted as an act of reference. My second claim, however, goes beyond this, though it is in the same spirit. It is that likeness, resemblance, or similarity is itself not *given* in our visual perception; it is not a primitive, irreducible relation, as Mill took it to be (in Nagel 1950), but is itself an *achieved* relation, that is, one which is constructed and, therefore, construable (compare Manns 1971). Things come to *be* similar, to resemble each other, be likenesses by virtue of being *made* as similar, or alike, or being taken as resembling each other. Thus, even in the relation of representation in which it is alleged that the representation is *like* what it represents, I am arguing that it is so by virtue of our taking it to be so, in a given respect. It is we who *create* similarity, resemblance, or likeness in those forms of pictorial representation that are said to be based on it. We do so, I would argue, by producing artifacts that are specifically intended to be like other things, to represent them, in this way. The classic story here, of course, is about Picasso's portrait of Gertrude Stein. When told that it did not look like her, he answered: "It will."

On the basis of one interpretation, this may be no more than to say that in making a representation, we imitate what it is that is being represented, that is, we construct something that is similar to what it is to represent—in effect, we make a copy. In this case, then, there should be no surprise that there is resemblance, likeness, or similarity, for is not the representation made expressly to be like what it represents? But this interpretation—the common one—begs precisely the question that it sets out to answer. For in order to make something that is similar to, or resembles, something else, we have to establish *what* the feature is which is being "copied" in this sense, *and* that something else in fact resembles it. Imitating, copying, or reproducing the features of a given object, scene, or relation requires therefore just that creative act of *achieving* the likeness, of establishing that something resembles something else, which is presupposed as a *given* in the standard view. In a second interpretation, one thing may be said to re-present another, not in being like it, or resembling it, in some common properties—for example, same shape, or color, or same relation among parts—but, rather, in causally effecting the same response. Therefore, the representation comes to represent by virtue of bringing about the same physiological response or visual experience as the thing or scene represented, though it does so by means that are dissimilar. So, for example, in this view, paintings of landscapes or figures are pictorial artifacts and, thus, two-dimensional arrays: they are not themselves "like," in this sense, the three-dimensional objects or spaces that they represent. Yet, they are arranged in such a way as to deliver the "same" or a similar light flux to the retina, and thus initiate similar visual responses.

This view, perhaps the most popular psychological theory of representation, retains semblance in the phenomenal experience, or in the response, though it gives up identity or even similarity in the stimulus. In this sense, it presupposes that similarity in the response is passive—a matter of equivalent causal or antecedent conditions, whose equivalence is judged by the sameness of the response.

The faults with this view are many. But let me simply point to one experimental fact: the recognition of pcitures as representations of x ranges over pictures that are obviously *not* similar to each other in any respect one could define as "causally equivalent." Gibson would evade this point by arguing that for all their dissimilarity, such a range of alternative pictorial representations are all alike in transmitting the same higher-order visual *invariances* criteria for object or scene recognition, though through the range of transformations. But such *invariances*, in Gibson's ecological optics, are taken to be objective features of the ambient light, and the organism—in this case, the human one, or, perhaps, the higher vertebrate in general—has so evolved its visual system as to be able to pick up these invariances directly—that is, without processing lower-order variations. The net is woven, so to speak, in order to catch fish of only a certain size (or a higher order) and to let all the smaller ones (or those of a lower order) slip through unnoticed.

This interpretation begs the question in a different way from the first, for it *presupposes* as *invariant* just those features that representations represent—for example, so-called real shape or real size in the case of perceptual constancies—and, thus, does not explain how representation is possible; in fact, it theoretically constructs an explication of *one* kind of representation—namely, that which is constructed in accordance with the rules of linear perspective—that it takes to be canonical. It is no surprise then—in fact, it is inevitable, because circular—that in Gibson's view, what we see is what there is, and representations succeed because they re-present what we see.

If I deny that we have direct access to the way things really *are*, at least as the real objects in our ecological space or the space of our species' life activity, then how else is representation possible? What links representation to *representandum*: how do we have access to the properties of the visual world so that we know how to represent them successfully?

To take a step further, I would propose that we do not come to have visual concepts of the properties of the visual world *except* by such a process of creating representations of it. Nature comes to imitate art precisely because what we make of nature as an object of vision is constituted, in large part, by how we choose to represent it.

Before proceeding with the argument, it may be useful to make explicit some distinctions that have thus far been merely suggested. I have stated that human vision is itself an artifact, produced by other artifacts, namely, pictures. I call something an artifact if it is a product of human activity, in the sense that it comes into being as the result of intentional human making and is made or constructed with an end-in-view or for a use or purpose. This use or purpose defines the artifact as what it is, so that an artifact is what it is made *for*: it is, in short, a teleological entity. It may be odd to talk of vision or seeing in this way, but in fact, it is we who have shaped our vision to certain uses—who have adopted, adapted, and replaced different visual modes in our pursuit of different interests and ends. We have, in effect, learned to read the visual world in different ways, depending on our interests and needs.

One objection to such a view is, obviously, that the physiology of the visual system, though it may be understood as a biological adaptation to a form of life, is not itself the product of our own deliberate design nor is it subject to our intentional manipulation. We cannot be said to "change" our visual physiology as our interests or purposes change, for the structure is a genetically determined one and its evolution to the present species-form is the product of natural and not cultural selection. Within the confines of gross physiology, this is, I believe, evidently true. The adaptive variation of the visual system, in the course of species evolution, is the work of natural selection. But even here, we may characterize this species evolution as the mapping, into the organism's genetic makeup of those features of its life-world and life activity that are requisite for its species-survival. The story is different, however, for the development of vision beyond the species level that is, for the differentiation of visual perceptions which proceed with cultural evolution or with historical changes in the human forms of life. One may go so far as to claim (with Penfield 1966) that the physiological ontogenesis of the neural system in general (and for the visual cortex in particular) is a differentiated one, which maps into the individual's neural structure the specific modes of experience and activity that characterize the life history of that individual. But one need not go so far to see that the visual system as a *way of seeing* is subject to the variability of modes of visual re-presentation.

What then *are* pictures and representations, and specifically, what is a painting? Let me make a distinction between pictures and representations. Pictures are visual artifacts, that is to say, pictures are made to be seen. Many other artifacts, are of course, also visible, but by visual artifact, I mean something expressly made for the purpose of being seen. Pictures, on the other hand, do not exhaust the class of visual artifacts. One may include, here, any marks, signs, objects, or expressions that are expressly made to be seen or any entities which come to be taken principally as objects of vision. So, for example, physiognomic expression, hand signs, sculpted objects, signs or markings of warning, direction, ownership, kinship, and so forth, may be taken as visual artifacts in this sense, that is, that they are intended to be seen and to communicate a meaning visually. Thus, modes of dress, scarification, gestures, and facial expressions are all such artifacts. Pictures, as a special class of such artifacts, I will take to be as those that are made upon a plane surface (thus, not gestures or sculptures for example) and which depend on line or color as their visual means. Not all pictures are representations, though all pictures may be said to have meaning. Moreover, natural objects or scenes may be *taken* pictorially, though they are not made things. Thus, we may see a tree, a sunset, or a cloud *as* a picture when we take it principally as a visual artifact, that is, as a meaningful form or shape seen as if it were on a plane surface. The force of this particular qualification will be seen later, since I will argue that it is by means of our activity of picturing that we come to be able to *see* the world *as* a picture and that the standard theory of vision which underlies constancy theory, in perception, and which proposes linear perspective as the correct representation of the visual world is based on an interpretation of the three-dimensional visual world as a two-dimensional picture.

Pictures, then, are visual artifacts made to be seen—and when understood in this way, seen as pictures. The ubiquitousness of the pictorial in human life leads us to forget that picture making and picture seeing are learned activities of the species. I would go further and suggest that picturing, both in making and seeing, is a fundamental form of the life activity of the human species and, in this sense, I am proposing that it is this activity that shapes human vision and develops it beyond the biological inheritance of the mammalian eye.

If all pictures are not representations, all pictures may be taken to be representations. Visual representations, briefly, are visual artifacts expressly made or understood as referring to something beyond themselves. Thus, there are nonvisual representations that are not pictures, for example, vocal reference in speech or gestural ostension; so, too, there are visual modes of reference that are not pictorial. Representation is symbolic. That is, one thing stands for another, under an interpretation given in a symbol system of which the representation is a part.

There is much more to be said about these distinctions, and Goodman's pioneering work (1976) goes a long way in developing this analysis. I will not pursue it here. But in summary, for the purposes of this chapter, I will distinguish pictures from representations, insofar as there are pictures that do not represent and representations that are not pictorial. More generally still, I will hold that *all* artifacts are putative representations, insofar as the very use, or understanding, or recognition and identification of an artifact as what it is requires that we take it as a representation of the mode of activity involved in its use or in its production. The artifact "represents," literally, in being taken as an imitation of an action, that is, the embodiment of the intentionality involved in its production, reproduction, or use. Thus, for example, a tool or a weapon, such as an ax or a spear, is not only something made to be used for a certain end but is also itself a representation of the action involved in its use and in its production or reproduction. An ax therefore, as a visual artifact, represents the activity of chopping and a spear, the activity of throwing in order to kill in the hunt. Moreover, the artifact also represents the mode of activity involved in its production or reproduction: it is a prototype of its replicas and a model of its own process of production.

What, then, marks off pictorial representations from the wider class of artifacts as putative representations. Again, the emphasis is on intentions, that is, what is intended in the making and taking of such visual artifacts. A spear is made for hunting and also represents the mode of action of the hunt. A spear-picture, on the other hand, is not made for hunting but is made expressly as a representation of a spear. It is principally made as a visual artifact, not a hunting artifact; its very intentionality is distinct in this sense; its purpose is different. Moreover, the representation is detached from use or from production: it functions independently of the activities or contexts of what it represents. Such a relatively autonomous act of representing is made possible by the picture, for it is in the express creation of something as a visual artifact, as something made to be seen, that the separation from other contexts of use becomes possible. It is not that representational pictures have no use but that their intended use is different. The use-value of a picture (representational or not) is in its being seen, whatever other purposes such visual presentation may have, for example, didactic, formal, expressive, informative, and so forth. The use-value of a representational picture is in its visual representation of its referent. It is in this sense that I argued earlier that something is a representation insofar as it is made to be, or taken to be, a representation. The features that come to be called representational will then depend on what is taken to serve this function. Anything can; but not everything, in fact, is chosen to do so. What is chosen to function as representational is a complex question, *not* to be resolved by appeal to physiological (or ecological) optics. Rather, it demands comparative study of what in fact has been taken as representational or what, in various alternative canons, continues to be taken as representational.

Pictures that represent, then, are artifacts which guide or shape our vision of the world, leading us to take *this* as like *that*, to pick out features of the seen world that are referred to by the representations we make, where the act of reference is itself a creative act and not merely a matching of pregiven similarities or identities. One may say, then, that representational pictures are *heuristic* and *didactic* artifacts. They teach us to see: they guide our vision in such a way that the seen world becomes the world scene.

REFERENCES

Gibson, J., "The Ecological Approach to the Visual Perception of Pictures." *Leonardo* 11 (1978): 227–35.

Goodman, N. *Languages of Art.* 2d ed. Indianapolis, Ind.: Hackett, 1976.

Manns, J. W. "Representation, Relativism, and Resemblance." *The British Journal of Aesthetics* 11 (1971): 281–87.

Nagel, E., ed. *John Stewart Mills' Philosophy of Scientific Method*. New York: Hafner, 1950.

Penfield, W. "Comments and Discussion." In *Brain and Conscious Experience*, edited by J. C. Eccles, p. 248. New York: Springer-Verlag, 1966.

Wartofsky, M. "Pictures, Representation and the Understanding." In *Logic and Art—Essays in Honor of Nelson Goodman*, edited by R. Rudner and I. Scheffler, pp. 150–62. Indianapolis and New York: Bobbs-Merrill, 1972.

――――. "Perception, Representation and the Forms of Action: Towards an Historical Epistemology." In *Ajatus* (Yearbook of the Philosophical Society of Finland), vol. 36, *Aesthesis: Essays on the Philosophy of Perception* (1976), pp. 19–43.

Chapter Fifteen

Seeing, Believing, and Picturing

Alan Tormey and
Judith Farr Tormey

One difficulty with interdisciplinary interaction is its tendency to elicit talk at cross-purposes. Because the issues generated by the process and product of picturing have interested artists, philosophers, psychologists, art historians, and others, a cluster of problems has developed around divergent interests and vocabularies, and it is not always clear what questions are being addressed or whether everyone understands the issues in the same way.

It might then be useful to begin with a brief reconstruction of what seems central to the philosophical discussion of picturing. Two issues appear fundamental: the first is a philosophical stepchild of the problem of other minds (not whether there are any but what is *in* them); the second has to do with psychological or other genetic explanations of pictorial activity. These two issues can be raised in parallel pairs of questions:

First, concerning the problem of other minds: What can we know about the way the world is seen from the way it is pictured or depicted, and what can we know about the way the world is believed to be from the way it is pictured or depicted? Second, concerning the psychological origins of picturing or depicting: What is the influence on picturing of the way the world is seen, and what is the influence on picturing of the way the world is believed to be? The first pair are questions of *evidence*, the second of *causality*.

Posing the questions this way, of course, relies on the plausibility of the distinction between phenomenal and cognitive concerns, namely, the distinction (roughly) between seeing and believing. The point is frequently made that there is continuous interaction between phenomenal and cognitive processes and that they are so thoroughly interwoven that the questions posed above could receive no clear answer. Gregory (1970), for example, writes:

> Since perception is a matter of reading non-sensed characteristics of objects from available sensory data, it is difficult to hold that our perceptual beliefs—our basic knowledge of objects—is free of theoretical contamination. We not only believe what we see: to some extent we see what we believe (p. 15).

This is an important claim, for not a few philosophers and psychologists will insist that it is quite hopeless to attempt to *distinguish* systematically between phenomenal and cognitive contributions to our perceptions and to the making and viewing of pictures. If Gregory's hypothesis is correct, however, it should reinforce rather than diminish the need for the distinction between the phenomenal and the cognitive, since if they are not distinct or distinguishable, there can be no sense to the question of the influence of one upon the other, or in Gregory's more picturesque phrase, of contamination of one by the other.

An alternative thesis might be offered here, namely, that the phenomenal is a species of the cognitive (Margolis 1978) and that despite his final emphasis on seeing and believing, that is what Gregory in fact wishes to maintain. The resultant contrast would then be between the phenomenal–cognitive and the nonphenomenal cognitive. The subtleties inherent in variant formulations are not to be dismissed as ultimately irrelevant to an adequate perceptual epistemology, but that there is a need for some such distinction is a thesis that may be maintained whatever its ultimate complications and refinements.

Since our primary concern is an understanding of the relation between phenomenal and cognitive elements of the process and product of picturing and since straightforward attempts to establish either the existence or the boundaries of that relation are apt to meet with precipitate objections, we propose to approach the issue indirectly, first by considering some consequences of the failure to acknowledge any form of the distinction and, then, by extracting the implications of its acceptance.

Negative things first: from the denial that we can separate cognitive from phenomenal contributions to picturing or picture perception, the supposition that there is a single uniform pictorial *purpose* in representational art follows quite naturally. It could be called *the principle of the uniformity of pictorial purpose*. The principle is, bluntly, that representational pictures are always produced with the purpose of *re*producing the way the world looks or appears to the artist, that is, that they are a function of the way the artist sees the world. That there is such a uniformity of pictorial purposes is a natural and predictable consequence of the refusal to distinguish between the phenomenal and the cognitive. This principle may seem remarkably naive, as perhaps it is. It is all the more surprising, then, to encounter it embedded in some very sophisticated discussions. Consider, for example, the following claims:

> Which is the more faithful portrait of a man—the one by Holbein or the one by Manet or the one by Sharaku or the one by Durer or the one by Cézanne or the one by Picasso? Each different way of painting represents a different way of seeing; . . . And we need only look hard at the pictures by any such artist to come to *see the world in somewhat the same way* (Goodman 1960, p. 52) (italics added).

> As a rule in a given cultural context the familiar style of pictorial representation is not perceived at all—the image looks simply like a faithful reproduction of the object itself. . . . [T]he Picassos, the Braques, or the Klees look exactly like the things they represent. . . . As far as the artists themselves are concerned, there seems to be little doubt that they see in their works nothing but the exact equivalent of the object (Arnheim 1954, 117–19).

Finally, "It is true that the varieties of painting at different times in history, and among different peoples, *prove* the existence of different ways of seeing, in some sense of the term" (Gibson 1960) (italics added).

As the quotation from Gibson suggests, we should perhaps expect to find quotes around the word *see* and its cognates in these contexts, but they are perplexingly absent. Indeed, all of these claims seem to presuppose a uniformity of pictorial purpose that is logically linked to the denial of the possibility of distinguishing between phenomenal and cognitive elements in the pictorial process. There may be a powerful additional motivation for making this assumption, for if it were true, it would mean that stylistically variant pictorial systems would provide us with direct or immediate evidence of variant ways of perceiving the world, namely, it would appear to resolve many of the central problems associated with using pictures as *evidence* for the way the world is seen and would thus be a forceful aid in the resolution of the problem of other minds.

This possibility encounters an immediate obstacle in what has come to be known as *the El Greco fallacy*. It takes its name from the naive arguments offered for the view that El Greco must have seen figures in the world as elongated because his pictures contain elongated figures. (In his case, the elongations have been claimed to be evidence for an astigmatism.) But if El Greco had had as his purpose the production of a picture that looked to him the way the world looked to him, namely, elongated, he would not have placed elongated figures in it. He would, rather, have produced a work that looked normal to *us*—his astigmatism distorting *his* view of the picture as it distorted his view of the world. A generalized argument of this form would then suggest that any attempt to argue directly from stylistic peculiarities or from apparent pictorial distortions to a presumed difference in "ways of seeing the world" is logically suspect and that pictures have no evident advantage over language as an immediate reflection of variant ways of apprehending the world. (A Whorfian hypothesis will fare no better with images than with words.)

It is widely known, of course, that a number of these accounts are intended to lead us to an acceptance of conventionalism, namely, to the view that the pictorial systems are themselves conventions analogous to linguistic systems; but at the same time, we are asked to believe that each different way of painting represents a different way of seeing and that the varieties of painting at different times in history, and among different peoples, prove the existence of different ways of seeing. But ironically, if conventionalism *were* true, the evidence offered by different styles of picturing would be *irrelevant* to the question of different ways of seeing. One cannot conclude both that different ways of depicting are conventional, on the one hand, and that they are *necessarily* linked to different ways of seeing the world, on the other hand. One can only argue that differing ways of depicting are *evidence* for differing ways of seeing if one accepts the premise that the way the world is seen is immediately and causally (*not* conventionally) related to the way it is depicted.

In his vigorous defense of conventionalism, Goodman has stated that "realism is relative, determined by the system of representation standard for a given culture or person at a given time. Newer or older or alien systems are accounted artificial or unskilled" (1968, p. 37) and that "reality in a world, like realism in a picture, is largely a matter of habit" (1975). These contentions are surely consistent, though it is not clear that they are the same. Jointly, they are profoundly suggestive and problematic. If, for example, realism in a picture is largely a matter of habit, is it not possible that some persons (or some cultures) may have acquired *bad* habits—undesirable conventions for sorting pictures, for example, the categories of realism and nonrealism. Could the disposition to impose such categories reflect the influence of unfortunate habits rather than of compelling necessity or justifiable choice? If so, then an uncompromising relativism is threatened by the possibility that some systems of representation may exemplify habits or conventions that are preferable to others and whose merits can only be assessed by criteria that are not fully bound by the variables of time and culture.

This does not mean that pictorial realism is, after all, *wholly* independent of variant systems of representation. But it does suggest that even when the force of convention and habituation have been acknowledged, it is still conceivable that some representational systems may permit or encourage more effective, sophisticated, or articulated forms of realism than others; one can imagine a society in which several alternative, disjoint systems are available for the representation of the same class of objects, that is, where the systems are extensionally equivalent—a society whose members are accustomed equally to each system and who yet insist that one of these systems is superior to the others in providing for realistic depiction of its referents. Denying this possibility would amount to taking the most impoverished and the most enriched representational systems to embody equal opportunities for realistic representation, and the arguments for relativism need not, per se, compel us to this conclusion. Moreover, it is surely possible that in some representational systems, realism of whatever sort is not, and was not intended to be, a value and that realistic depiction of the world, however conceived, does not count among the functions of the system.

Consider, for example, Navaho sand painting or the inscriptions on the Mayan stelae, two pictorial systems whose functions would seem to obscure or transcend realism. Thus, even if realism is relative to a system or representation, it does not follow that all such systems must provide for (even) relative realism. Where Goodman contends that "for a Fifth-Dynasty Egyptian the straightforward way of representing something is not the same as for an eighteenth-century Japanese; and neither way is the same as for an early twentieth-century Englishman" (1968, p. 37), it could be argued that for a fifth-dynasty Egyptian, there may well have been *no* straightforward way of representing something, if *straightforward* is taken as meaning "realistic relative to the prevailing system."

In an important subsequent passage, Goodman says:

> Most of the time, of course, the traditional system is taken as standard; and the literal or realistic or naturalistic system of representation is simply the customary one. Realistic representation, in brief, depends not upon imitation or illusion or information but upon inculcation (1968, p. 38).

That is to say, once again, that realism is a matter of convention or habit. But if customary modes of representation then determine what will be taken to be realistic or naturalistic, we shall be hard pressed to explain how comparative judgments concerning the kind or degree of realism attained by various discarded or nonstandard systems is possible. If Masaccio was the discoverer of a "more realistic mode of painting," as the Florentines believed (Scruton 1974, p. 204), then Goodman must be wrong in claiming realism to be relative to the "ease with which information is conveyed." If realism is a matter of habit and relative to the ease with which information issues, then any departure from established styles should initially seem less realistic.

Thus, even if we admit that realism is always relative to some system of representation and that representational systems vary in every conceivable way, it does not follow that realism is simply a function of a preferred representational system. The required and undefended missing premises are that every representational system make some provision for realistic representation and that the principle of the uniformity of pictorial purposes is correct.

These, then, are some of the consequences of assuming that phenomenal and cognitive contributions to picturing and picture perception are indistinguishable or that, correlatively, there is but a single pictorial purpose in representational art, however divergent pictorial styles may be. A further consequence is the admission of but a single type of realism. For if a representational picture is thought always to be an unbreakable synthesis of phenomenal and cognitive elements, there can be no possibility of discriminating between pictures that represent the way the world *appears* to the artist and pictures that represent the way the artist believes the world to *be*. Yet it seems quite evident that there may be differing pictorial systems with which we can associate differing pictorial purposes, and distinct forms of realism as well, if it is granted that realism is relative to pictorial purposes, as well as to representational systems. Moreover, if we recognize that phenomenal and cognitive elements of perception are differentially weighted vis-a-vis varying pictorial purposes, we shall be able to distinguish several varieties of pictorial realism—central though not exhaustive instances of which shall be referred to as *phenomenal, cognitive,* and *metrical realism.*

VARIETIES OF PICTORIAL REALISM

Phenomenal Realism

This is perhaps the sense closest to the way *realism* is used in most ordinary discussions of representation (picturing in general). Put crudely and in an effort to avoid begging questions of resemblance, iconicity, or congruity, phenomenal realism requires the production of a two-dimensional object intended to mimic the appearance of a three-dimensional object from a single perspective or station point: trompe l'oeil or illusionist art, generally. For many, the temptation exists to place all works produced according to Renaissance linear perspective in this category as well, but it is arguable that some of these works can better be understood as a congruence of at least two types of realism when properly read. This will be discussed later.

Cognitive Realism

Cognitive realism is the pictorial portrayal of objects as they are believed to *be* rather than as they simply appear or are seen. Cognitive realism is the result of the attempt to portray objects in such a way that their most important, defining, unique, or essential characteristics are represented. (Even if there is considerable philosophical skepticism about essentialism, that does not mean that those who depict the world may not intend to show an object as they believe it essentially to be.)

One of the most striking examples of this form of realism is found in aboriginal art, as shown in Figure 15.1. A succinct account of the "X ray" art of Australia, Melanesia, British Columbia, and southern Alaska can be found in Adam's (1954) book on primitive art:

> The terms "realistic" or "naturalistic" art are usually applied to work which is done from life and hence is true to nature. But their meaning, though definite enough in sculpture, tends to become ambiguous when applied to the graphic arts. If we speak of a naturalistic painting we mean that it is true to the optical impression of the model as observed at a given moment from a given angle. But in a different sense of the term we may speak of naturalism or realism if an artist represents all the details actually in existence, not only those he can see at the moment, but those he knows are there as well (à la the cubists).

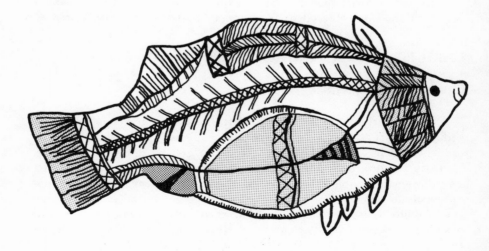

Figure 15.1 "X-Ray" Fish (after an aboriginal cave painting, North-Western Australia).

> *In most primitive arts realism is of this kind;* but we are used to looking on any deviation from our visual impression as artistically inferior, and are inclined to classify this variety of realism as "primitive" in a sense of benevolent indulgence. It might perhaps be called "intellectual" as opposed to purely optical. It reaches its highest development in the "X-ray drawings" of Australia, Melanesia, and the coastal regions of British Columbia and southern Alaska. . . . Here the artist depicts every detail of the body, including backbone, ribs, and internal organs, because he regards these as no less important than the characteristic features of a man's outward appearance (p. 37) (italics added).

It is plausible, then, to content that properties thought to be essential to, or characteristic of, an object are conveyed in these works even though the appearance is not one that normally would present itself, or perhaps could not present itself, to a viewer. (For an example of cognitive realism in children's art, see Gardner and Wolf—Chapter 20 of this volume, Figure 20.4). This reasonable interpretation presupposes the availability of a distinction between seeing and believing.

Metrical Realism

This may be considered a subspecies of cognitive realism that grounds beliefs about the essential characteristics of spatial objects in their mathematical (measureable, metrical) properties and is committed to metrical fidelity in their two-dimensional presentations. As an example, one may cite Dürer's flat depictions of polyhedra, which deliberately sacrifice the way the object looks in favor of presenting those properties metrically essential to it as exemplified in Figure 15.2. In his discussion of Dürer's *Underweysung der Messung mit dem Zirckel un Richtscheyt*, Panofsky (1956) writes:

> At the beginning [of the Fourth Book] Dürer discusses the five regular or "platonic" solids, a problem brought into the limelight by the revival of Platonic studies on the one hand and by the interest in perspective on the other. Whether or not Dürer was acquainted with the work of the two Italian specialists in this field, Luca Pacioli and Piero della Francesca, is an open question. . . . Pacioli discusses, besides the five "platonic" or regular bodies, only three of the thirteen "Archimedean" or semi-regular ones, and he illustrates them in perspective or stereographic images. Dürer treats seven . . . and instead of representing the solids in perspective or stereographic images, he devised the apparently original and, if one may say so, proto-topological method of developing them on the plane surface in such a way that the facets form a coherent "net" which, when cut out of paper and properly folded where two facets adjoin will form an actual, three dimensional model of the solid in question (p. 618).

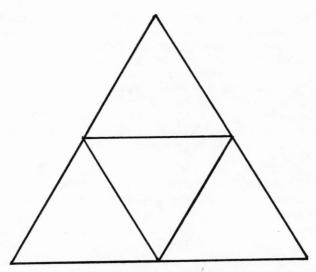

Figure 15.2   "Net" drawing of a tetrahedron

Dürer's "net" is an intentional distortion of phenomenal properties of the figure in the interests of precise metrical information; and this example of metrical realism has an important feature that may be definitive of metrical realism, namely, recoverability. The three-dimensional polyhedron in this case can be constructed without distortion from the two-dimensional depiction. This type of representation, incidentally, comes very close to being a form of notation from which, with an understanding of the relevant rules of metrical construction, the pictured object can be accurately constructed—thus cutting across Goodman's entrenched distinction between notationally and nonnotationally determined forms of art.

As noted in the discussion of phenomenal realism, it might be thought that Renaissance linear perspective provides an excellent example of this type of realism and that is the way it is usually interpreted. It should be recalled, however, that there was passionate enthusiasm among some Renaissance artists and mathematicians not only for the study of principles of perspective in general but for the study of Platonic and Archimedean solids and their relation to perspective. Leonardo not only studied the geometric solids, he also provided illustrations of a number of them for Pacioli's *Divina Proportione* (Venice, 1509), as shown in Figure 15.3, which is a perspectival reconstruction of the Leonardo drawing by Fra Giovanni da Verona.

In light of the forms of realism we have identified, it is worth a brief speculative excursion to explore the possibility that strict principles of projective geometry make it theoretically possible to combine

Figure 15.3 Fra Giovanni da Verona's *Intarsia* (ca. 1525) (Santa Maria in Organo, Verona) (after stereographic drawings of polyhedra by Leonardo da Vinci).

phenomenal and metric realism in the pictorial representation of such objects as polyhedra.

Through an understanding of the geometric principles of projection on which such depictions are based, one can theoretically discover the essential metrical properties of the object and reconstruct the original model. This possibility is not as immediately apparent as it is in Dürer's "net" drawings, but it makes the stereographic representations of the solids more than merely a recreation of appearances. Thus, it may be seen to point the way toward overcoming a notorious problem Plato set for the representational artist (*Republic,* bk. 10, 602–4; see also Gombrich [1973])—that to be true to the "look" of things, the artist must be false to their essential properties, in particular, those properties amenable to measurement. That the Platonic solids themselves should have suggested a solution in becoming models for representations that unite phenomenal with metrical realism is another of those delightful footnotes to Plato.

Realism is not, of course, relative to representational systems and pictorial purpose alone. Once a representational system has been chosen for a particular pictorial purpose, success is no longer a matter of choice, habit, or convention—it is rather a matter of "getting it right." Moreover, a pictorial system may make room for one form of realism and not for another, and two forms may be mutually incompatible. Also, of course, artists may not have a purpose leading to any form of realism at all or, more commonly, they may "modify" otherwise realistic depictions for a variety of reasons unrelated to realism. Thus, as Edgerton (1975) writes of Domenico Veneziano's *Madonna and Child Adored by Saints:*

> The original purpose of this painting was to serve as an icon, a sacred image of the Blessed Virgin to inspire the greatest devotion on the part of the Worshipers. Every aesthetic thought the artist had concerning this holy scene was formed out of his desire to enhance this didactic objective. Linear perspective rules themselves had to be modified or even abandoned if they conflicted with the picture's true purpose in this sense (p. 56).

Finally, then, these are some of the more significant implications of assuming a distinction between the phenomenal and the cognitive and their respective contributions to the structuring and understanding of pictures; we believe that they comprise at least a powerful indirect argument which does greater justice than the alternative to both the complexity of pictorial representation and to the varieties of pictorial purpose.

REFERENCES

Adam, L. *Primitive Art*. 3rd ed. Melbourne, London, and Baltimore: Penguin Books, 1954.

Arnheim, R. *Art and Visual Perception: A Psychology of the Creative Eye*. Berkeley: University of California Press, 1954.

Edgerton, S. Y., Jr. *The Renaissance Rediscovery of Linear Perspective*. New York: Harper & Row, 1975.

Gibson, J. J. "Pictures, Perspective and Perception." *Daedalus* 89 (1960): 216–27.

Gombrich, E. H. "Illusion and Art." In *Illusion in Nature and Art*, edited by R. L. Gregory and E. H. Gombrich, pp. 193–243. New York: Charles Scribner's Sons, 1973.

Goodman, N. "The Way the World Is." *Review of Metaphysics* 14 (1960): 48–56.

———. *Languages of Art*. Indianapolis and New York: Bobbs–Merrill, 1968.

———. "Words, Works and Worlds." *Erkenntnis* 9 (1975): 57–73.

Gregory, R. L. *The Intelligent Eye*. New York: McGraw-Hill, 1970.

Margolis, J. Personal communication, 1978.

Panofsky, E. "Dürer as a Mathematician." In *The World of Mathematics*, edited by James R. Newman, pp. 601–19. New York: Simon and Schuster, 1956.

Scruton, R. *Art and Imagination*. London: Methuen & Co., 1974.

PART IV

UNDERSTANDING PAINTINGS

Introduction to Part IV

This section is concerned with different approaches to understanding paintings. Two approaches are represented. One approach comes from experimental aesthetics and is represented in the first three chapters by psychologists Perkins, Pickford, Kolers, and Smythe. The second approach comes from developmental psychology and is represented in the last two chapters by artist Boretz and psychologists Gardner and Wolf.

Perkins's concern is with the measurement of aesthetic judgments—in particular, value judgments of art works. Do these value judgments have an underlying aesthetic reality? If so, then what is the basis for critical disagreement, which is so manifest in art? Is it because judges use different standards in making value judgments, or is it because the judges are careless and make errors in examining a work of art? To answer this question, Perkins compares the amount of disagreement between value judgments and attribute judgments of the same works of art by different judges, as well as the same judge within. The results suggest that value judgments have little in common with aesthetic reality.

Pickford is concerned with a different kind of aesthetic reality—the concept of universal beauty. Are geometrical figures that rely on curves rather than straight lines judged more aesthetically pleasing than others? Do different cultures share these aesthetic preferences? To answer these questions, Pickford showed geometrical figures believed to be of special aesthetic interest because of their incorporation in abstract and figurative art (that is, the golden section rectangle and figures containing curves after Hogarth's line of beauty), to judges from different cultural backgrounds. The judges rated these figures using ten scales from the Osgood semantic differential. Curved figures were consistently preferred regardless of cultural background.

Kolers and Smythe are concerned with how people "read" pictures and how this type of reading is different from reading printed text. Both pictures and text consist of symbols. The critical difference lies in how these symbols are mapped onto the semantic domain. One type of mapping is the analog, which, following Nelson Goodman's analysis, is defined by the properties of both syntactic and semantic density. Pictures fall under the analog symbol system due to the fact that the pictorial symbols are both conceived and interpreted along unbounded dimensions, where small variations in the symbols change their meaning. A second type of mapping is digital, in which both syntactic and semantic dimensions are more clearly defined and are thus less susceptible to reinterpretation. Text falls under the digital symbol system because words refer to discrete semantic categories.

Having made these distinctions, Kolers and Smythe show through experimental studies how skill and practice with a symbol system enhances interpretation of symbols whether they be pictorial or linguistic. They also examine the role of mental imagery in the interpretation of symbols and conclude that it is the pictorial analog to language.

The developmental approach is introduced in Chapter 19 by artist Bortez, who traces her experiences with art back to her childhood. Her purpose in doing this is to understand the process of how reality, that is, *observed* reality, is translated into her paintings. In tracing the development of her art, she finds herself questioning the concept of reality as defined by her teachers. She objects to their solution, which is to conventionalize reality, and paints her own versions of reality out of view of her teachers. She finds support for her position in the work of other artists (to reinforce her philosophy of painting). Boretz then shows how she uses this philosophy to create an underlying reality for her abstract paintings.

Finally, Gardner and Wolf in Chapter 20 trace the evolution of drawing skills in children and relate them to developing perceptual and cognitive competencies. Their review of the developmental stages in artistry is eclectic, drawing on such well-known authorities as Arnheim, Kellogg, Lowenfeld, and G. H. Luquet, plus their own longitudinal research studies. The authors outline eight stages—from the prescribble stage to the critical capacities stage—and show parallels between drawing capacities and perceptual–cognitive development.

Chapter Sixteen

Are Matters of Value
Matters of Fact?

David N. Perkins

In art, are matters of value matters of fact? That is, does a work of art in principle submit to classification as better than, worse than, or about on par with another, much as a stone submits to classification as heavier than, lighter than, or about the same weight as another? That is, can questions of critical appraisal be said to have answers, even though finding the answers may sometimes be difficult? Or that is, can we find in our perceptions and preferences and ponderings a sound basis for value judgments of art?

The question arises because we often behave as though matters of value were matters of fact. We maintain in our discourse a distinction between goodness and preference: to say work A is better than work B is to make a claim with at least the pretense of general validity, while to say one prefers A over B is simply to report a personal choice. We also organize our looking at and talking about art as though there were something there to be seen rightly and settled surely: We try to look carefully and alertly, to be thoughtful and open-minded. We check our tentative perceptions and evaluations with peers and experts. In short, we behave as though a proper resolution were there to find. Whether value judgments really ought to be construed this way is a matter of contention among aestheticians. But the important distinction between goodness and preference and our efforts to deal reasonably with questions of value are recognized features of critical behavior (on all

The research reported here was conducted at Project Zero of the Harvard Graduate School of Education, operating under National Institute of Education grants G-00-3-0169 and G-78-0031, and support from the Spencer Foundation. The opinions expressed here do not necessarily reflect the position or policy of the supporting agencies, and no official endorsement should be inferred. It is a pleasure to thank Marvin Cohen for his collaboration in designing, conducting, and analyzing some of the studies.

this, see Beardsley 1958, chapters X and XI; Beardsley 1970, pp. 11–15; Ecker 1967; Kennick 1964).

If all went well with these efforts, there would be no issue. One would not question the soundness of labelling some works of art good and some bad, any more than one would question labelling some pieces of furniture tables and some chairs. But with works of art, all does not go well. People disagree about value judgments alarmingly often. They disagree in casual dialogue, from professional reviewer to reviewer, across the field of scholarly criticism, and of course, over the centuries as taste and fashion have shifted.

Disagreement is a frequent fact not only of everyday experience but of psychological research in aesthetics. There is disagreement within and systematic disagreement between groups of students, artists, professional critics, and lay individuals, persons from various cultures, those of different personalities, children versus adults, and so on (see, for example, Getzels and Csikszenmihalyi 1976; Kreitler and Kreitler 1972; Pickford 1972; Richards 1929).

Then in light of this difficulty, are matters of value matters of fact? That depends on how critical disagreement is construed. In fact, two extreme ways of understanding critical disagreement relate to the competing positions about the possibility of sound value judgments.

One of these ways might be called the *different standards theory of critical disagreement*. This theory holds simply that standards vary from person to person. These standards covertly or overtly guide an individual's value judgments. Accordingly, value judgments reflect idiosyncratic preferences more than any universal underlying aesthetic. The distinction in our language between goodness and preference should be viewed as mere pretense.

A competing view about critical disagreement might be called the *error theory*. This view holds that critical disagreement is simply a sign of error. When individuals disagree in their value judgments, just as when they disagree about who discovered America or any other matter of fact, one party, or the other, or both must be mistaken in some respect. Perhaps the work has not been correctly perceived, or standards have been misapplied, or the wrong standards are held. (However, the error theory does not claim that finding the resolution will be easy nor that truth lies in consensus. After all, neither of these holds in general for ordinary matters of fact, even though disagreement certainly indicates error there.)

The error theory draws quite a different recommendation from the phenomenon of critical disagreement than does the different standards theory. Critical disagreement becomes not an excuse to abandon efforts to make sound judgments, but a spur to redouble those efforts, looking more carefully, comparing notes more thoroughly, and so on.

These theories claim that critical disagreement comes about in contrary ways. One can test how critical disagreement does come about only by examining more carefully the perceptual encounter with the work of art and how evaluations arise from it. The following pages will describe several psychological studies which attempt to do that. One by one, several sources of critical disagreement in the perceptual encounter with the work will be discussed.

Then, to anticipate the conclusion, can matters of value be considered matters of fact—yes or no? Maybe. Unfortunately, the findings reveal most clearly the inadequacy of normal perceptual practices in establishing a firm basis for critical judgment. But viewers of art could adopt much better practices. The last section will consider where this leaves the question.

THE "SEEING IS BELIEVING" FACTOR

One factor contributing to critical disagreement is that value judgments of particular parts or aspects of works of art typically appear spontaneously in consciousness. There is no extended reasoning nor attending deliberately to particular critical principles. For instance, while looking at a painting, usually one simply sees value-laden qualities such as grace or clarity. It simply strikes one that the work appears graceful or clumsy, clear or obscure.

In a moment, evidence for this will be given. But first, why would such circumstances promote critical disagreement? Because critical agreement requires doubting and sometimes dismissing first impressions as idiosyncratic or superficial. To reach a sure and general appraisal of a work, one often must seek alternative apprehensions of the work oneself and check one's own judgments against another's. But the way in which value judgments emerge makes this difficult. Because value-laden qualities are so easily and unintentionally perceived, they seem given by the work. "Seeing is believing" the adage goes. The same holds for seeing that a work is graceful or clumsy as much as for seeing that it is red or blue. Once a viewer experiences the compelling reality of a quality in a work, it is hard for him to credit another's contrary perception as anything but peculiarly inept or misguided. If another has not disagreed, it is all the more difficult for him to doubt the rightness of his own perception.

But is the above characterization of the perception of value-laden qualities sound? The reader can examine his own experience for casual evidence. More formal evidence derives from several process tracing studies of poets and artists at work, studies which disclose how the maker exercises critical judgment in the process of making. In these studies, established and novice poets and artists were asked to think aloud as they worked. They were trained in a method of thinking aloud designed to be minimally intrusive. The participants almost always adapted quickly to the reporting and became absorbed in their endeavor as they continued to talk. Their speech was tape-recorded and transcribed. The work of the artists was documented with videotape and color photography. The results already have been considered from some perspectives (see Perkins 1977 a, b), and are still being analyzed from others.

The protocols revealed that extended episodes of reasoning about, or in any way puzzling over, critical judgments were very rare. This did not mean that the protocols disclosed a mindless process from which the work flowered spontaneously. On the contrary, in developing a line of poetry or part of a work of visual art, a subject often formulated aims, passed through two or more steps, discarded alternatives, modified first efforts, and in general displayed a directed problem-solving process. But this was rarely so for critical appraisals of the developing work or its parts.

Note how this finding reverses the every day conception of creative process. Criticism tends to be considered the rational, deliberate, objective, analytical side of making, whereas the production of parts of the work tends to be considered the spontaneous side. These findings disclose just the opposite. Criticism is the more spontaneous aspect and production the more directed, deliberate one.

The protocols also showed that the artists and poets rarely scrutinized the work with particular critical principles in mind. A maker might examine the work with a general intent to locate weaknesses and strengths, but not very often to test particular matters—the rhyme scheme, clarity of meaning, balance, the layout of colors, and so on.

Showing criticism to be a rather spontaneous process, these points might suggest criticism to be essentially an irrational one, where judgments emerged without any conscious reasons for them. But the protocols disclosed that this was not so. A sample of evaluative remarks was taken from each of four different process-tracing studies. Each judgment was classified in two ways. First, did the judgment make reference to a particular aspect of the part of the work appraised—for instance, to meaning, meter, rhyme in poetry or to color, form, texture in the visual arts? Second, did the judgment make reference to any evaluative principle—clarity, unity, balance, for example? Either sort of reference or both might be offered as a reason in critical discourse about the merits of the work.

One researcher scored all the samples and another scored a subset. Interjudge agreement was 85 percent. Table 16.1 displays the first scorer's results. As the table indicates, better than half of the evaluations included reasons mentioning either some aspect of the work, some principle, or both.

TABLE 16.1

Percent of Evaluative Remarks Mentioning Aspect and/or Principle: Process-Tracing Study

Process–Tracing Study	Neither	Just Aspect	Just Principle	Both
Poetry writing	52	10	17	22
Poetry editing	17	20	24	39
Logo design	17	29	2	51
Painting	35	29	10	26

Source: Compiled by the author.

Accordingly, the data disclosed a critical process with little reasoning or deliberate direction, but with reasons aplenty. Apparently, the reasons emerged as part of the perception of the work. For instance, to see a particular form as graceful would be simultaneously to find value in the work and to know the sort of value one had found.

Such reasons help the artist to develop a work further and the audience member to understand a work. Also, they provide the experiential basis for public criticism. They are the raw materials out of which reasoned critical argument can be constructed. They make possible intelligence critical discourse. But because the reasons are given by direct experience of the work, they are hard for the viewer to doubt and hence they promote problems of critical disagreement.

ATTENTION IS NEITHER COMPREHENSIVE NOR COMMON

The second factor to be discussed is that attention is neither comprehensive nor common. Different perceivers base their evaluations on a subset of the parts and aspects of the work and the applicable principles, and the subsets differ from person to person and occasion to occasion. Clearly, such divergence would promote disagreement in overall critical assessments of a work. It is as though different individuals were regarding different works.

In one study, I attempted to measure these problems of attention. The data were gathered from the novice and established poets mentioned earlier. Each subject was asked to criticize a 50-line poem as if for a peer or a student. These critiques were recorded and individual evaluative remarks classified according to line addressed, to aspect addressed (rhyme, meter, meaning, and so forth) and according to any critical principle invoked (clarity, unity, and so forth).

Subjects averaged only 8.75 focussed remarks, ranging from two to seventeen. Focused remarks were comments appraising parts of the poem rather than the poem as a whole. Comments addressed one to five lines at once, with a mean of 2.6. For a 50-line poem, this certainly could not be considered close criticism. Such data showed the individual critical appraisal not to be comprehensive.

Could this finding have been misleading? Possibly all the subjects commented on the very same few things—those most important to the poem's worth. In fact, this did not occur. The three classifications of each comment—according to lines, aspect, and principle—allowed comparing how much one average critic addressed the same matters as another. It was found that 65 percent of the time, one average critic would be commenting on the same line as another. Only 31 percent of the time would the same line be considered with reference to the same aspect. Only 13 percent of the time would the same line be evaluated with reference to the same principle (no matter whether positively or negatively). It should also be noted that these measures overestimate common attention, since two parties might consider the same aspect of the same line with reference to the same principle and still be addressing different parts of the line, nuances of the aspect or variants of the principle. Some further details appear in Perkins (1977c).

The problem of comprehensive and common attention seems due to at least three causes. First, the complexity of works of art leads to sparse perceptual sampling. People miss a lot because there is a lot to miss. Nelson Goodman (1968) has stressed the density and repleteness of aesthetic objects. Roughly speaking, it is symptomatic of the aesthetic that slight variations carry significance and that many dimensions of the aesthetic object—for instance, the texture, blackness, thickness of a line—all count. This circumstance makes both real comprehensiveness virtually impossible and detection of important but often subtle features a considerable challenge.

Second, there are differences in what different parties are able to perceive. For example, the expert may register features to which the novice is blind, or features upon casual scrutiny which the novice could only perceive if they were pointed out explicitly.

Third, one must remember that what a person values will influence not only whether a given attribute will strike him or her as good or bad but whether it will weigh at all or, indeed, even register at all. That is, as well as sampling affecting evaluation, values will affect sampling. Especially when the person has an intent to evaluate, features that for him or her are value-laden are likely to stand out and others recede.

Thus, so far as values do differ, the problem of comprehensive and common attention would reflect in part the involvement of values in the perceptual process. The present data do not allow separating this cause from the prior ones.

IS COMPREHENSIVE AND COMMON ATTENTION THE SOLUTION?

An optimistic interpretation of the above results would emphasize difficulties of sampling and detecting rather than value, and would predict that people would agree more if they were helped toward a more comprehensive and common perception of the work. This notion recalls a familiar idea in arts education. It is often suggested that if only people could be taught to look at art thoroughly and sensitively, values would take care of themselves. There would be no need to impose values on the viewer.

Though I myself have favored this idea (see Perkins 1977c), some experimental results are, frankly, discouraging. One study of mine used four pairs of drawings. The drawings of each pair were slight variants of one another, variants designed to have aesthetic significance. The pairs were selected from the *Meier Art Tests* (Meier 1963), part 2. There were two groups of twelve subjects each—a control group and a treatment group. Subjects from the control group simply considered each pair and chose the ones they thought to be the best artistically. Subjects from the treatment group first undertook to write a list of reasons why one of the sketches was better. Then they did the same for the other sketch. They were encouraged to involve themselves in the task as much as possible, role-playing a defense of both sides. In addition, the instructions for each pair of pictures mentioned two or three dimensions along which comparisons might be useful.

Trial and error had convinced the experimenters that this treatment among several alternatives was most likely to acquaint the viewer with multiple aspects of the work and different perspectives on it. The prediction was that the viewers in the treatment group would agree more among themselves than the viewers in the control group. The prediction was not confirmed. In fact, more diverse opinion was found in the treatment group than in the control group.

A second study attempted to check this result with a somewhat different procedure, hoping for a higher significance level. In this study, twenty subjects made snap judgments for a pair of sketches. Then half of the subjects undertook the debate procedure as described above. The other half simply listed as many contrasts as they could between the two sketches. As before, four pairs of sketches were used.

The analysis compared agreement in snap judgments with agreement after treatment, by groups. If the trend of the prior experiment continued, the debate treatment and perhaps the comparison treatment would produce more disagreement after treatment. Also, the analysis compared agreement across the two contrasting treatments. Since the experimenters had thought the debate treatment to be the stronger one, perhaps, in keeping with the prior finding, it would yield the most disagreement. In fact, no trends even approaching significance appeared.

Involving a relatively small number of subjects, and only four judgments per subject, these experiments were not sensitive measures of the effects of more thorough acquaintance with works of art. For instance, in the second study, the treatments led subjects to change their initial judgments about 25 percent of the time, that is, in about 20 cases. Accordingly, a trend toward more or less agreement after treatment would need to be strong to reach statistical significance. These findings can be taken as evidence against dramatic effects of close viewing of art but not against moderate effects.

Research reported in 1964 by Irwin Child asked a slightly different question, but offered as much statistical sensitivity as one could want. Child examined not enhanced perception of individual works, but enhanced awareness of what features were important to works of art in general. Hundreds of students of several ages were the subjects. All students would see and judge a pair of slides displaying works of art. In one experiment, groups were then told which of each pair was best, and why, according to informed critical opinion. In another study, groups heard no explicit talk of values. However, there was an explanation of stylistic and other features exemplified by each contrasting pair and significant to art in general. Each program continued for several weeks, presenting up to 900 pairs of slides. Changes in agreement with informed critical opinion were assessed by comparing subjects' judgments of a series of initial slides and of the same series repeated at the end. Child noted that the subjects did not simply remember and repeat their initial judgments. In both experiments, there was substantial change of opinion between pretest and posttest.

Child found that the explicit training in evaluation yielded significant effects. At the beginning, subjects tended to disagree systematically with the experts, but by the end their judgments tended to agree with informed opinion. However, no systematic effect on value judgments resulted from the treatment designed to acquaint subjects with important features of art.

These experiments all showed that treatments which one might think would lead to more comprehensive and common attending did not yield more evaluative agreement—agreement with one another in the first two experiments, and with experts in Child's experiment. Why the treatments failed, however, remains ambiguous. Perhaps seeing the work more thoroughly cannot shift viewer's idiosyncratic values, at least not toward consensus or expertise. However, one should not assume that the treatments forced comprehensive and common attending. Certainly, the treatments would prompt somewhat more thorough viewing of the works. But with works of art so complex, a more extensive sampling still might not be that comprehensive nor common from viewer to viewer. Thus, these experiments show critical disagreement to be more intractable than one would hope, while not selecting among alternative explanations.

PERCEIVED ATTRIBUTES MAY BE CONTRADICTORY

There is yet another factor promoting critical disagreement. Evaluations aside the attributes detected by one party may directly contradict those perceived by another. In principle, this contrasts with the earlier emphasis on problems of attention, where different individuals address different parts and aspects of the work. In practice, the contrast with problems of attention is not always so sharp, as will be seen.

An analysis of contradiction drew upon the data gathered in the first experiment described in the prior section. Data from the second experiment could be treated similarly, but this remains to be done. It will be recalled that two or three relevant dimensions of comparison were suggested to the debate group for each pair of sketches considered. Two judges independently scored whenever a subject used any of these dimensions in his argument corresponding to his final judgment. Initial interjudge agreement was 81 percent; all disagreements were quickly resolved by discussion. The results revealed contradictions between different subjects' descriptions of the sketches.

Table 16.2 displays the findings. The relevant numbers appear in the upper right quadrant. The two groups represent subgroups of the 12 subject debate group, subgroups receiving somewhat different pairs of sketches. Each number is a measure of the likelihood of two average subjects disagreeing on a typical dimension they both had used. A one, meaning maximum likelihood of disagreeing, would occur if the population split 50–50. A zero would mean perfect consensus. The figures as they are identify a significant problem of contradictory perceptions. They indicate that more than half as much disagreement occurred as could have. Furthermore, for technical reasons the tabulated numbers underestimate the actual disagreement.

However, one qualification is needed. These figures do represent contradictions concerning which sketch manifests a property, but often a property attributed to different parts of the two sketches. For

TABLE 16.2

Proportion of Disagreements between Subjects and within Subjects on Values and Attributes of Sketches

Group	Values	Attributes
Disagreement between Subjects		
Group 1	.76	.52
Group 2	.66	.72
Combined	.72	.62
Disagreement with Self		
Group 1	.77	.23
Group 2	.64	.36
Combined	.71	.29

Source: Compiled by the author.

example, one subject might praise sketch A over B for its clarity—the clarity of the lines. Another might praise sketch B over A for its clarity—the clarity of contrast between figure and ground. This really is more like a problem of attention.

On the other hand, some contradictions were not of this sort. For instance, one pair of sketches represented a young woman. Some subjects characterized the woman in the second sketch as more emotionally neutral. But others described the woman in the second sketch as deeply troubled and disturbed. Apparently, the sketch allowed either perception, some viewers seeing it one way and some the other.

In summary, these findings show that viewers very often contradict one another in the properties they think a picture manifests. However, the findings do not reveal how often such contradictions represent divergent perceptions of the very same parts of the pictures, and how often attention to different parts. At least, it seems clear that both of these contribute to disagreement—neither can be dismissed.

ATTRIBUTES MAY BE VALUED DIFFERENTLY

The final source of critical disagreement to be discussed relates to the different standards theory mentioned in the introduction: individuals may value an attribute of a work of art differently. For example, one of a pair of sketches represented a graceful, elegant stone idol-like figure. The other of the pair rendered the idol in a robust and rough-hewn manner. Some subjects praised the one and some the other in terms leaving no doubt that the subjects were discerning the same characteristics.

Disagreement about values was measured in the same manner as disagreement about attributes. The suggested dimensions of comparison were employed again and the valued end of each dimension was tallied whenever the dimension was mentioned. The results appear in Table 16.2, the upper left quadrant. The figures represent the likelihood of two randomly selected subjects disagreeing just as before. Again, the figures show that more than half the possible disagreement in fact occurred. Again, the figures are underestimates.

A comparison of the two columns in the top half of Table 16.2 discloses an important point: There was nearly as much disagreement on attributes as there was on values. Roughly speaking, what the picture really looked like was about as uncertain as how its looks were valued. None of the small differences between the columns approached statistical significance.

This finding contradicts common sense and subjects' expectations specifically. Subjects considered what the pictures looked like to be more certain than what attributes were to be valued. This was apparent from the arguments subjects had with themselves. It will be recalled that subjects in the debate group made cases for both choices before announcing their actual judgments. Thus, one could analyze how a subject disagreed with himself in arguing the two sides. The bottom half of Table 16.2 presents the results.

As before, the figures represent likelihoods of disagreement on attributes and on values—this time disagreement between subjects' pairs of opposing arguments. Here there was direct competition between agreement on attributes and agreement on values. When a subject used the same dimension in both his arguments, he either had to change which end of the dimension was valued, or which end of the dimension was to be attributed to which sketch, but not both, in order to produce arguments favoring opposite choices. As the table shows, subjects by far preferred to maintain their attributions and shift their valuations in arguing alternate sides of the case. Though not perfect, the trend was highly statistically significant. Thus, subjects manifested much more reliance on their descriptions than their valuations, a reliance in fact unwarranted by the data in the top half of Table 16.2.

THE DIFFERENT STANDARDS AND ERROR THEORIES ASSESSED

Initially, two accounts of the nature of critical disagreement were introduced—the different standards and the error theories. The research reviewed allows assessing how well these accounts characterize the sources of critical disagreement.

The different standards theory proposed that critical disagreements arose because individuals held idiosyncratic standards. However, the research disclosed several quite different sources of critical disagreement. The "seeing is believing" factor promoted disagreement by locking one into evaluations that might be short of one's own best judgment. The problem of comprehensive and common attending behavior might reflect differing standards in part, but it might also reflect difficulties in sampling perceptually the dense and replete work of art. Finally, what descriptive attributes a work was said to have proved about as inconsistent as how those attributes were valued.

The error theory proposed that critical disagreement simply indicated error by one or both parties. Any results that found evaluative disagreement to derive from resolvable descriptive issues about the work would favor the error theory, because they would remove the problem from the realm of subjective values and relocate it in supposedly decidible questions of appearance. Thus, the difficulties of comprehensive and common sampling, which arose in discussing both attention and disagreement about attributes, supported the error theory.

However, in other respects the error theory did not fare so well. Disagreements were not reduced mostly to matters of attribution. On the contrary, disagreements appeared to derive about equally from divergent attributions and differently valued attributes. So the error theory still would have to face the problem of deciding among contending values. Furthermore, some of the disagreements documented allowed no obvious resolution. Different people responded in contrasting, but seemingly entirely sensible, ways in attributing and valuing attributes.

The difficulty is fundamental to the error theory: to speak of errors at all requires that there be a right answer—a correct attribution or valuing of attributes. But the work of art may be ambiguous, allowing alternative apprehensions. Hobsbaum (1970) argues that disagreements in literary criticism often have stemmed from this cause. Further, it is at least possible that different persons would not even be able to achieve a common perception in such cases, however much they tried to defer questions of value and clarify to one another their respective understandings of the work. Instead, with art dependent as it is on matters so delicate as nuances of facial expression, a kind of radical ambiguity might sometimes prevail, where there could not even be a non-evaluative description of the work with significant inter-subjective validity. (See Perkins 1978, for a fuller discussion of possible degrees of ambiguity in art.) In no way do the present studies decisively demonstrate this sort of radical ambiguity, nor hint that it is prevalent. However, the possibility must be noted.

In summary, the "different standards" theory simply is inadequate. It does not take into account the complex circumstances of critical disagreement. The error theory is more in limbo. It has not received as much encouragement as it might have, and stands at risk before the problem of radical ambiguity.

ARE MATTERS OF VALUE MATTERS OF FACT?

It might be thought that the research reviewed had answered this question. So many were the sources of disagreement that surely no common reality could be teased from the diversity of perceptions and evaluations. Or at least, no common aesthetic reality of significant scope. Of course, there would be some agreement about some things. But for the most part, one could not expect questions of how work is to be valued to be resolvable.

However, such a conclusion is not warranted. The error theory— essentially equivalent to matters of value being matters of fact—was consigned to nothing worse than limbo. None of the results showed that the sources of disagreement were ultimately intractable, for instance because of radical ambiguity. Perhaps with effort and practice, common perceptions and evaluations of works of art could be achieved. Perhaps the more fully and sensitively works were observed, the more evaluations would turn out to converge.

The real lesson is rather different: the usual encounter with a work of art provides a poor basis for intersubjective descriptions and evaluations of art. The sources of disagreement at once analyze the problem and make strategic recommendations. For there to be any hope of finding, or, one might better say, constructing, a common aesthetic reality, viewers would need to look more carefully and thoroughly at works, trust initial perceptions less, cross-check them more with other individuals, attempt alternative perceptions of the work, determine from others what significant features might have been missed, locate and recognize as such ambiguities of a work's appearance, set aside first conclusions that turn out to be attributable to personal idiosyncracies, and so on.

Such strategies rely heavily on communication between individuals, and that points to another difficulty. Not only the individual encounter with the work, but discourse about works suffers from many problems which interfere with constructing an aesthetic reality. For instance, people often neglect to answer one another's points, do not clarify whether evaluative claims assert goodness or preference, fail to pursue claims back into reasons supporting them, deliberately censor their points or adopt defensive attitudes. All these, and other factors too, confuse talk about art. Elsewhere, I have discussed problems of communication in detail, along with some of the difficulties described here (Perkins 1977c). Again, better strategies appeared possible.

So is an aesthetic reality there to be discovered? To resolve the question, we would need to improve our usual habit of scrutiny and discourse. The answer to the question, "Are matters of value matters of fact?" comes down to this: We know what to do if we want to find out.

REFERENCES

Beardsley, M. C. *Aesthetics: Problems in the Philosophy of Criticism*. New York: Harcourt, Brace & World. 1958.

———. *The Possibility of Criticism*. Detroit: Wayne State University Press, 1970.

Child, L. "Development of Sensitivity to Esthetic Values." Mimeographed. Cooperative research project, no. 1748. New Haven, Conn.: Yale University, 1964.

Ecker, D. N. "Justifying Aesthetic Judgments." *Art Education* 20 (1967): 5–8.

Getzels, J. W., and Csikszentmihalyi, M. *The Creative Vision: A Longitudinal Study of Problem Finding in Art*. New York: Wiley, 1976.

Goodman, N. *Languages of Art: An Approach to a Theory of Symbols*. Indianapolis and New York: Bobbs–Merrill, 1968.

Hobsbaum, P. *Theory of Criticism*. Bloomington: Indiana University Press, 1970.

Kennick, W. F., ed. *Art and Philosophy—Readings in Aesthetics*. New York: St. Martin's Press, 1964.

Kreitler, H. and Kreitler, S. *Psychology of the Arts*. Durham, N.C.: Duke University Press, 1972.

Meier, H. C. *The Neier Art Tests*, pt. 2, *Aesthetic Perception*. Iowa City: University of Iowa, Bureau of Educational Research and Service, 1963.

Perkins, D. I. "A Better Word: Studies of Poetry Editing." In *The Arts and Cognition*, edited by D. Perkins and B. Leondar. Baltimore: Johns Hopkins University Press, 1977a.

——— "The Limits of Intuition." *Leonardo* 10 (1977b): 119–25.

———. "Talk about Art." *Journal of Aesthetic Education* 11 (1977c): 87–118. Also in S. Madeja, ed. *The Arts and Aesthetics: An Agenda for the Future*. Saint Louis: CENREL, 1977.

———. "The Significance of Interpretive Disagreements for Cognitive Theories of the Arts: A Response to Anita Silvers." In *The Arts, Cognition and Basic Skills*, edited by S. Madeja. Saint Louis: CENREL, 1978.

Pickford, R. W. *Psychology and Visual Aesthetics*. London: Hutchinson Educational, 1972.

Richards, I. A. *Practical Criticism: A Study of Literary Judgment*. New York: Harcourt, Brace & World, 1929.

Chapter Seventeen

Semantic Differential Judgments of Geometric Figures of Aesthetic Interest

R. W. Pickford

In a previous work (Pickford 1976), I described an experiment using Osgood's (1957) semantic differential technique. There, Scottish and Japanese subjects made various judgments about 16 simple geometric figures. It was hoped that this technique would lend itself to making a series of cross-cultural studies on aesthetic judgments and preferences, especially when ratings proved culturally dependent. The following experiment was carried out with U.S., Scottish, and Pakistani students, using the same geometric figures and scales as before in order to identify which among the figures were most highly rated in each culture.

SUBJECTS AND FIGURES USED

The U.S. students were a psychology class of 9 men and 14 women (aged 18 to 22) at Hiram College, Ohio. The Scottish students were a class of 18 men and 9 women (aged 19 to 22) in the psychology department, University of Glasgow. The Pakistani children were a group of 14 boys (10 to 15 years of age) and 7 girls (9 to 17 years of age) who were recent immigrants to Scotland.

Geometric figures were projected from 35 mm slides one at a time. Instructions and meanings of the scales were translated into Urdu for the Pakistani children. The Pakistani children were young and unaccustomed to experimental work, and therefore, delays were encountered, owing to the need for translation and verbal explanation in Urdu. To avoid fatigue leading to error, this group saw only the first 8 of the 16 figures. (The results, to be given later, show a surprising conformity with Scottish judgments and support the view that translation into Urdu and seeing only 8 figures made no material difference.) The U.S. and Scottish students saw all figures.

Each subject completed a set of semantic differential items for each figure. While only six of the figures were considered of importance in the present experiment, it was desirable that figures in addition to those of special interest be included, so that the subjects' attention could be distributed over a number of items. It was hoped that the set of 16 might form a series suitable for other people to use, and this is being done now by several experimenters. The geometric shapes were as follows, and are illustrated in Figure 17.1.

The special interest of the six figures required explanation. The golden section rectangle is of special interest because there is the unequal division of a line in such a way that the shorter part bears the same relation to the longer part that the longer part bears to the sum of the two parts (Huntley 1970; Valentine 1962; Osborne 1970; Pickford 1972). It has been known since Greek times and has a unique geometric or algebraic relationship. Fechner (1876) made ten rectangles varying from a square to an oblong with rectangle sides in the ratio of five to two; one of these rectangles had sides in the proportions of the golden section, namely, 1 to (almost) 1.618. He showed that subjects asked to pick out the most pleasing rectangle most frequently chose the golden section rectangle. Angier (1903) showed that subjects asked to make the most pleasing but unequal division of a line tended to divide it into golden section proportions. Other workers, like Eysenck and Tunstall (1968) have supported Fechner's results. Benjafield and Adams-Webber (1976) and Benjafield and Green (1978) have found additional intrigue with the memorial relationship in that if persons are asked to classify their acquaintances into two groups, one inferior in some way and the other superior, they tend to do so in the proportions of the golden section, giving the smaller proportion to the inferior group. The golden section has played a certain part in architecture, as shown, for instance, by Le Corbusier's work (1954). The part played by the golden section in pictorial art is discussed in the *Oxford Companion to Art* (Osborne 1970), but it seems to be relatively limited. I have measured a considerable number of rectangular pictures and found that only about one in twenty were golden section rectangles.

It seems that the golden section is a unique mathematical proportion and that it has excited the interest of mathematical and mystical thinkers since Greek times; however, it may not be as closely related to visual art as frequently assumed. Its inclusion in the present series of geometric figures was intended to test whether it would be preferred to other shapes according to culture.

The root ten rectangle, one side being of ten units in length and the other the square root of ten units, was included because McCulloch (1960) claimed that this rectangle, much more elongated than the golden section rectangle, took the place of the golden section rectangle

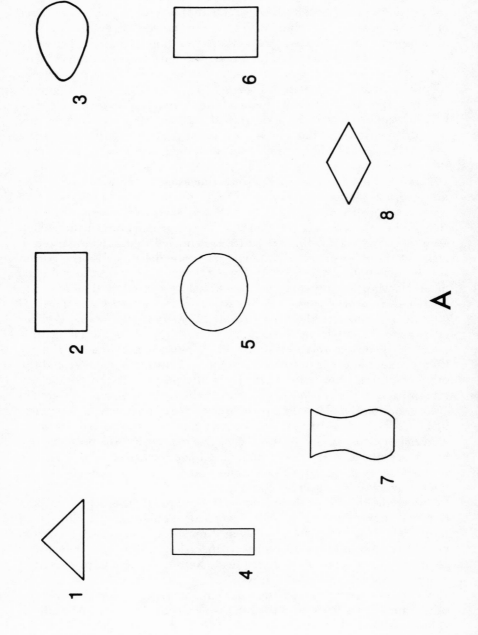

A

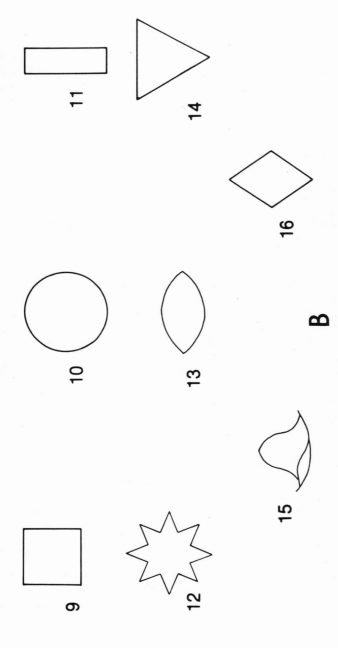

Figure 17.1   A) The first eight figures, including the golden section rectangle (2 and 6), the root ten rectangle (4), and Hogarth's line of beauty in the "vase" figure (7). Geometric figures used were (1) right-angled triangle, resting on hypotenuse; (2) golden section rectangle (horizontal); (3) egg shape; (4) root ten rectangle (horizontal); (5) ellipse (horizontal); (6) golden section rectangle (vertical); (7) vase shape (showing Hogarth's line of beauty on each side); and (8) diamond shape (horizontal). The Pakistani children saw only the first four of these. B) the second eight figures, including the root ten rectangle (11) and Hogarth's line of beauty in the "hat" figure (15). Geometric figures used were (9) square; (10) circle; (11) root ten rectangle (vertical); (12) star with eight points; (13) double lip shape; (14) equilateral triangle, resting on point; (15) hat-shaped figure (incorporating Hogarth's line of beauty three times); and (16) diamond shape (vertical).

319

in Indian (Hindu) art. It was hoped that if Eastern subjects could be induced to do the experiment, this preference might emerge.

Hogarth's line of beauty (Osborne 1970; Pickford 1972) is considered to be an important feature of Western art. It is a special double curve, illustrated in the vase figure of the present experiment, and might be the basis for preferred curves in the human figure, in landscapes, and in abstract designs. It might not have the same interest or be valued so highly in other cultures; it was included in the present series to test it against other geometric figures.

THE SEMANTIC DIFFERENTIAL SCALES

Semantic differential scales each consist of a pair of bipolar adjectives separated by seven dots to show the steps from one limiting adjective to the other. Ten pairs were chosen to include Osgood's three factors, namely, evaluation, potency, and activity. The direction (positive to negative) of the scales was varied on the forms given to the subjects, so that the positive or negative limit was sometimes on the right and sometimes on the left. They are, however, given all in the same direction below, namely, positive to negative. The numbers in brackets indicate the random order in which they were presented to the subjects on the forms to be completed. These can be seen in Table 17.1.

Scoring was accomplished in the following way. The ratings were added for each factor for each of the figures of interest. The mean ratings, standard deviations, and standard errors were then calculated, and comparisons of mean ratings were made by the t-technique, assuming $p < .05$ as a statistical criterion of significance of the differences between means.

The complexities encountered in the analyses precluded summaries on the major dimensions of evaluation, potency, and activity. In order to make understandable summaries, therefore, the numbers of times each figure was given a higher rating than any other figure by men than by women and by women than by men were tabulated and, also, the numbers of times each figure was given a higher rating than any other figure for each of the semantic differential factors irrespective of sex differences.

It is striking that the hat figure produced higher ratings by men than any other figure by either men or women and that the only other noticeable difference was that the root ten rectangle (horizontal) was given more higher ratings by women than by men. It is inevitable that any attempt to interpret such data must be speculative and is necessarily fraught with dangers, owing to the small size of the sample (seven men, nine women).

There can be little doubt that the hat figure, favored highly by men,

TABLE 17.1

Semantic Differential Scales Used in Studies of Geometric Figures

Evaluation

Good–Bad (scale 2)
Beautiful–Ugly (scale 3)
Artistic–Inartistic (scale 6)
Pleasing–Unpleasing (scale 8)
Interesting–Uninteresting (scale 10)

Potency

Hard–Soft (scale 4)
Masculine–Feminine (scale 5)
Strong–Weak (scale 7)

Activity

Rhythmic–Unrhythmic (scale 1)
Dynamic–Static (scale 9)

Source: Compiled by the author.

is clearly a form of feminine sex symbol in terms either of Jungian or of Freudian psychology, and would, in consequence, be expected to be judged highly by men. Similarly, the root ten rectangle is the nearest any of these figures come to being a phallic symbol, and it would be expected to attract women, as, in fact, it did.

NUMBERS OF HIGHER JUDGMENTS: U.S. STUDENTS

In order to clarify the data more fully, it seemed a good plan to show the results in terms of the numbers of judgments for each figure that were significantly higher in accordance with the statistical technique and standards already mentioned. These data are given in terms of the three semantic factors in Table 17.2.

The data in Table 17.2 show that the vase and hat figures share the highest number of judgments of figures for evaluation and the second highest number for activity. The golden section rectangle (vertical) and the root ten rectangle (horizontal) share the second highest number for potency. The golden section rectangle (horizontal) and the root ten rectangle (vertical) received the lowest when all ratings were totaled.

It is possible that the advantage of the vase and hat figures may have been partly due to their somewhat representative character, as

TABLE 17.2

Numbers of Higher Judgments: U.S. Students—
Studies of Geometric Figures

Figure	Evaluation	Potency	Activity	Total
Golden section rectangle (horizontal)	1	3	0	4
Golden section rectangle (vertical)	0	4	2	6
Root ten rectangle (horizontal)	2	4	1	7
Root ten rectangle (vertical)	0	1	0	1
Vase	5	1	4	10
Hat	5	1	4	10

Source: Compiled by the author.

they suggested real objects, which could excite associated feelings not directly related to their geometric shapes alone. This point will be mentioned again below. The curved figures are also much more closely associated with the human form, with animal forms, and with the attractive shapes of flowers, trees, and landscapes, as Hogarth indicated.

SEMANTIC DIFFERENTIAL RESULTS: PAKISTANI CHILDREN

No reliable differences were found between Pakistani girls and boys for any of the semantic factors for any of the figures (12 comparisons). Taking girls and boys together, no reliable differences for evaluation or activity were found between the figures. For potency, the golden section rectangle (horizontal) was given higher potency (in the sense of being harder, more masculine, and stronger) than the root ten rectangle (horizontal). The golden section rectangle (vertical) and the vase figure were also both given higher potency (in the same sense) than the root ten rectangle (horizontal). These data show that the root ten rectangle, at least in its horizontal form, was less satisfactory, in the sense of being softer, more feminine, and weaker, than the golden section rectangle or the vase figure. They do not support the possible view that in Eastern cultures, the root ten rectangle might replace the golden section rectangle of Western cultures as a basis of art forms.

RESULTS IN TERMS OF ESTIMATION

The mean ratings in terms of *estimation*, namely, the ratings on the ten scales, pooled and all measured in the same direction, for the six figures of special interest, and for the three groups of subjects, are shown in the "total" column of Table 17.2. The ratings for the vase and hat figures were higher than all others.

Thus, the vase figure, incorporating Hogarth's line of beauty, was the most highly estimated by all groups. The hat figure received a similarly high rating from the Glasgow group. The golden section rectangles (vertical and horizontal) came lowest for the U.S. students, but second (vertical) and third (horizontal) for the Pakistanis and fourth (horizontal) and fifth (vertical) for the Glasgow group. For the Pakistanis, the root ten rectangle (horizontal) was lowest, while this rectangle (horizontal and vertical) fell in the two lowest positions for the U.S. students and third (vertical) and sixth (horizontal) for the Scots.

While no sex differences were found for the Glasgow group of 18 men and nine women students, it was interesting to observe as found earlier, that the men showed a tendency to give higher average ratings to the vase figure, while the women gave higher ratings to the root ten rectangle (vertical).

DISCUSSION

The Pakistani group's results do not support the possible hypothesis that the root ten rectangle might be valued more highly in Pakistani culture than the golden section, as McCulloch claimed for Hindu art, or more than Hogarth's line of beauty. The root ten rectangle (horizontal) was, in fact, given less potency than the other three figures by the Pakistani children.

It is interesting that no differences between the figures in the evaluative or the activity factors were found for the Pakistanis. This apparently reflects a low sensitivity to these qualities. However, it is striking that the vase figure was highest in their estimation, as it was for the U.S. and Glasgow groups, showing uniformity across cultures. Such uniformity could not be due to home influence or education, because these children had emigrated to Scotland from various sections of Pakistan only a few weeks before the testing and could not yet understand English.

With regard to the U.S. students, it is clear that the two figures incorporating Hogarth's line of beauty were given the largest numbers of high ratings for the evaluation factor compared with any other figures, and the second highest in the activity factor, a number that they shared with the root ten rectangle (horizontal) and the golden section rectangle (vertical), which had the same numbers for the potency factor.

In estimation (mean ratings on combined scales), the two curved figures were again highest for the U.S. and Scottish students. The golden section and root ten rectangles scored lower, showing a high degree of cross-cultural uniformity.

When constructing the figures, the vase was drawn quite unwittingly, so that its width and height exactly correspond to the dimensions of the golden section rectangle (vertical). This fact was not uncovered until all the experiments, so far reported, were completed and their results tabulated. On the strength of this fact, it might be thought that the unintended choice of these dimensions for the vase shows the tendency of the golden section proportions to enter into aesthetic figures and to make them more satisfactory, especially as the vase was the most highly estimated among the figures used. However, the golden section rectangle (vertical) was lowest in estimation by U.S. students and the second lowest by Glasgow students, while it was the second out of the four in the Pakistani children's results. The inadvertent use of golden section proportions for the vase figure would therefore seem to have been, if anything, a disadvantage, because when seen by itself, it was given lower ratings.

The problem would be best handled by replacement of the vase and hat figures by other figures made on the basis of Hogarth's line of beauty and not more representational than the star figure, for instance, not in the proportions of the golden section, and exactly the same whether horizontal or vertical. Suggested figures for this purpose are shown in Figure 17.2. These figures have already been used in one experiment, but the data have not been analyzed.

Another interesting problem that might be examined is the effect of temperament and personality differences. Eysenck and Tunstall (1968) have shown that Fechner's work could be repeated, and when subjects were given a personality inventory, introverts tended to prefer thinner rectangles than extroverts. Similar studies with a variety of geometric figures might reveal interesting differences. For instance, Hogarth's line of beauty is obviously an intermediate double curve, and a series of similar curves could be made leading toward thinner curves in one direction and more voluminous curves in the other. Not only might there be a temperamental difference in the preferences for such curves within a given culture, but in different cultures, where a slender type of human figure is idealized, thinner curves might be preferred and given higher evaluation, potency, or activity. In cultures where stoutness of the human figure is idealized, a more voluminous type of Hogarth's line of beauty might be more highly appreciated.

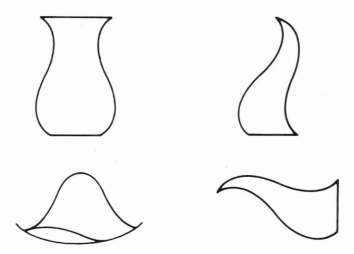

Figure 17.2   The vase and hat figures (left side) with suggested nonrepresentational substitutes (right side).

Mathematical and mystical explanations have been offered by various thinkers as to why the golden section should be a preferred proportion, but the present experiments do not support the view that such explanations have important bearings on art. It is still tempting to speculate further about the most general implications of this experiment. For all that has been said in favor of the golden section or the corresponding rectangle, and of the root ten rectangle also, it seems clear that these figures are less highly estimated than curved figures based on Hogarth's line of beauty.

Architecture may be the form of art most suitable for rectangular treatment, and perhaps this is why it appears to have been the art that was most affected by the application of the principles of the golden section. Would it not be fair to say, however, that Le Corbusier, a great advocate of the golden section, was largely responsible for promoting a geometric kind of architecture that has disfigured most of our cities in the last half century, with its vast blocks of concrete? Surely, the linkage is tenuous between his claim to make a geometric analysis of the human form and the ideal living space of human beings in their buildings, which are essentially machines for living in.

Even "abstract" art frequently draws heavily on curves, and a purely rectangular abstract art, however brilliantly inventive it might be, will not be likely to dominate over art that uses curves and flowing lines. The golden section rectangle may be preferred to other rectangles, and the golden section may be a proportion readily identified, selected, and judged, but they are not as highly appreciated as curved lines and shapes and therefore, cannot play more than a minor part in art.

SUMMARY

An experiment was carried out using 16 geometrical figures, 6 of which were believed to be of special aesthetic interest. They were judged by U.S., Scottish, and Pakistani subjects, using 10 semantic differential scales, grouped into Osgood's 3 semantic differential factors, namely, evaluation (5 scales), potency (3 scales), and activity (2 scales).

The analysis in terms of semantic differential judgments showed that the curved figures incorporating Hogarth's line of beauty were given higher ratings by U.S. students and the Pakistani children, while a further analysis in terms of total ratings for each figure, called *estimation*, showed that the curved figures, again, were most highly judged, this time by all 3 groups; no important age differences were found.

The results do not support the possible theory that the golden section rectangle would be the most preferred among the 6 figures, or even that it would be consistently preferred to the root ten rectangle in Western culture, or that the root 10 rectangle might be preferred to it by Pakistani children, which had been claimed for Hindu (rather than Muslim) culture.

In most general terms, therefore, the experiment would suggest that the golden section rectangle is not a more highly appreciated figure than the root ten rectangle and that curves based on Hogarth's line of beauty are much more likely to be essential.

Three interesting sex differences emerged: U.S. men gave more favorable judgments to the hat figure than did men or women to any other figure—this figure may be seen as a feminine symbol. Similarly, the root ten rectangle (horizontal), which might be viewed as a phallic symbol, was given the next higher number of favorable judgments— this time by women. Similarly, in the Glasgow group, the vase figure, a possible feminine symbol, was more highly estimated by men than by women, and the root ten rectangle (vertical), a possible phallic symbol, was more highly estimated by women than by men.

REFERENCES

Angier, R. P. "The Aesthetics of Unequal Division." *Psychological Review, Monograph Supplements*, 4 (1903): 541–61.

Benjafield, J., and Adams-Webber, J. "The Golden Section Hypothesis." *British Journal of Psychology* 67 (1976): 11–15.

Benjafield, J., and Green, T. R. G. "Golden Section Relations in Interpersonal Judgement." *British Journal of Psychology* 69 (1978): 25–35.

Eysenck, H. J., and Tunstall, Olive. "La Personalité et l'Esthetique des Formes Simples." *Sciences de l'Art* 5 (1968): 3–9.

Fechner, G. T. *Vorschule der Ästhetik*. Leipzig: Breitkopf and Härtel, 1876.

Huntley, E. H. *The Divine Proportion*. New York: Dover, 1970.

Le Corbusier. *The Modulor: A Harmonious Measure to the Human Scale Universally Applicable to Architecture and Mechanics*, Translated by P. de Francia and Anna Bostock. London: Faber 1954. Also *Modulor 2*. McCulloch, W. S. *Embodiments of Mind*. Cambridge, Mass.: MIT Press. 1960.

Osborne, H. ed. *The Oxford Companion to Art*. Oxford: Clarendon Press, 1970.

Osgood, C. E.; Suci, G. J.; and Tannenbaum, P. H. *The Measurement of Meaning*. Urbana: University of Illinois Press, 1957.

Pickford, R. W. *Psychology and Visual Aesthetics*. London: Hutchinsons Educational, 1972.

———. "A Comparison of Scottish and Japanese Judgments about Geometrical Shapes." *Psychology Quarterly* (Lahore, Pakistan) 10 (1976): 1–10.

Valentine, C. W. *The Experimental Psychology of Beauty*. London: Methuen, 1962.

Chapter Eighteen

Aspects of Picturing

Paul A. Kolers and
William E. Smythe

This chapter is meant to pay homage to the picture, or, at least, to the notion of the picture. We do so in the face of disagreements about what a picture is and how it works. Conventional wisdom defines as "picture" some object whose identity is given by a spatial layout of figures, objects, and marks, and pictures have been put in contrast to words and sentences. The nature of the contrast has, however, not always been made clear, partly because the definition of picture has not always been clear. Our chapter is concerned with an elaboration of the notion of picture, and an evaluation as to how different types of pictures may function in perception and cognition.

PICTURES AND TEXTS

An assertion that is often encountered emphasizes what is said to be a fundamental difference between pictures and text—the notion that in their being perceived, pictures are processed holistically, all at once, in parallel, whereas text is processed in a piecemeal, detailed, serial fashion. These notions are found in the public consciousness, expressed by McLuhan (1962) in respect to various media and by many psychologists working within the framework of theories of representation of knowledge. To take one well-known example, Paivio (1971, p. 180) has argued in detail that pictorial experience has a parellel encoding scheme underlying it, whereas language is "specialized for serial processing."

Preparation of this chapter was aided by Grant A7655 from the National Research Council of Canada to the first author. The second author was aided by a postgraduate scholarship from the National Research Council of Canada. The chapter is adapted from a larger analysis by the same authors of some aspects of symbolizing.

No one denies the reality of the difference between word and picture, and even children can distinguish between them (Gibson and Levin, 1975); what is at issue is the basis of the difference. In many ways, they are processed in similar fashion; one of these is the way that eyes move to acquire information from text and picture. Examining the available evidence reveals clearly that both picture and text are sampled across time; movements of the eyes across the surface of the picture, as well as fixation of the eye upon different regions, are common to looking at pictures and to reading text (Kolers 1977). The notion that a picture is processed (apprehended) all at once is simply wrong.

We can be excused for the confusion when we realize that it is difficult to define what is meant by *picture* and even harder to identify the processes constitutive of their perception. Two distinguished contemporary scholars disagree substantially on the way pictures are perceived. Arnheim (1974), without altogether denying a cognitive component, emphasizes the structural organization of the picture and argues that much of its meaning depends upon the apprehension of its intrinsic forces. Gombrich (1960), without denying the importance of organization and layout, emphasizes the interpretative or cognitive role. For Arnheim, the picture is principally a set of marks on a surface, arranged in such a way as to reveal forces, and perception is a matter of the direct pickup of these arrangements. For Gombrich, the picture is a symbol, made up of marks but requiring a reading and interpretation for the marks to be given meaning. Our own view is closer to Gombrich than to Arnheim, and we shall argue that not only are pictures to be seen as symbols but that they encompass different kinds of symbols, whose interpretation is crucial to a significant interpretation of the picture.

ASPECTS OF SYMBOLIZING

The most informative work that we know of on the nature of symbolizing is Goodman (1968), and we shall rely on that as a guide for our discussion. The work is richly detailed and invokes an elaborate technical apparatus for its expression that is well beyond our needs here. We choose two features for discussion: the contrast between continuous and discrete media and the contrast between the structure of symbols and the semantic domain that is mapped onto them.

To begin at the beginning, the word *symbol* refers to any object that properly defines or denotes another. The structural or syntactic aspect of symbols refers to the symbols as such; the semantic aspect refers to the domain that the symbols map. Orthogonal to this classification is one that contrasts the dense with the discrete. That is, dense versus discrete in the syntactic domain has to do with how one interprets the symbols, whether they are interpreted as members of clearly distinguishable atomic categories (discrete) or whether any arbitrarily small difference along some dimension can cause them to be identified as something else (dense). In the semantic domain, the dense/discrete distinction refers to how the domain referred to by the symbols is conceived of, whether it can be described as partitioned into separable units (discrete) or whether it is continuous and without gaps (dense). One illustration of the use of these is Goodman's analysis of the analog/digital distinction. An analog symbol system is defined by the properties of both syntactic and semantic density, whereas a digital symbol system is discontinuous in each of these two ways. An example would be a landscape painting as an instance of analog in both the syntactic and semantic domains, and a musical score or a printed poem as instances of digital. This analysis removes some of the confusion from the distinction and helps clarify the concepts of analog and digital in a way that will be relevant to some points raised later in this chapter. As Goodman has remarked, "Plainly a digital system has nothing special to do with digits, or an analog system with analogy" (1968, p. 160). For the present we are concerned with the implications of this sort of analysis for the contrast that is commonly drawn between linguistic and pictorial symbol systems.

Perhaps one of the most critical arguments of this analysis is directed at the notion of resemblance. Both among aestheticians and psychologists, similarity of appearance receives a special weight in the development of theory; pictures are said to represent the objects they symbolize just to the degree that they look like or resemble them. In Goodman's (1968) analysis, any object can symbolize any other that it denotes or refers to; resemblance or similarity of appearance is a nonstarter as a criterion. In fact, in order to establish that some one thing is similar to or resembles another, one must have a theory, or at least a criterion, against which the aspects of similarity or resemblance are to be judged; the reason is that objects are like each other and different from each other in an infinite number of ways, and only if some theory is applied as a basis can the judgment of similarity be made (Goodman 1972).

The difference between a landscape painting and an architect's plan of a landscape illustrates the difference in the way that pictures may function as analog or digital symbols. In a landscape painting, as Gombrich has shown in his discussion of Constable, for example, all aspects of the painting inform it: brushstroke, coloration, arrangement of lines, and so on, and the geometry of the painting need have no precise relation to the geometry of the scene that serves as the painter's stimulus. The components of the painting may blend and merge into each other in such a way that a change of any component changes the object of which it is part; for example, changing any part of a drawing of a tree creates a different tree. In short, there is no prescribed way of assigning identity between symbols and marks on the surface of a painting.

The architect's plan of a landscape, in contrast, serves as a set of instructions: typically, instructions regarding the geometry of object placement. Whether the placement of an evergreen tree is drawn with a pencil or a pen, whether it is on soft paper or hard, or even whether it is a photocopy are all irrelevant to this usage. The reason is that there is a prescribed way of assigning identity to the symbols drawn and of assigning interpretations to them. In both cases (looking at a painting or at an architect's plan of a landscape), we are looking at pictures; but in one case, the picture functions within analog symbol scheme, and in the other case, it functions within a digital symbol scheme. Hence, picturability or picturing does not by itself identify how a picture may function as a symbol, nor the kind of symbol it may be, analog or digital.

Therefore, the contrast that is often maintained between the pictorial and the linguistic, which is said to accurately characterize two different ways of symbolizing knowledge or information, is misguided. We have just shown that in some circumstances, pictorial symbols may function as discrete symbols in a notational system. We now show that in some cases, the referents of words may fail to function notationally. Words such as *red*, *large*, and *beautiful* are made up of marks that function digitally in the syntactic domain, but because the referents of words are poorly differentiated in the semantic domain, natural language does not function as a digital symbol system. Hence, the contrast between the pictorial and the linguistic does not form a difference between two kinds of symbol system.

SKILL IN SYMBOLIZING

We have shown so far that it is not the medium that carries the message, but ways of interpreting and using symbols in different media that marks performance. We want to show now that skill constitutes an important aspect of using symbols and that skill in their use constitutes a form of knowledge. The demonstration comes from an experimental test (Kolers 1974).

In this case, three different groups of students examinined 56 sentences of connected discourse and then were faced with 56 pages on each of which appeared one sentence from the passage and several alternatives. The task was to identify the sentence from the passage.

One group of students saw the passage, in Sanskrit, written in the unfamiliar Devanagari alphabet. A second group saw the Sanskrit passage transliterated to the English alphabet. The third group saw the passage made of sentences partly in French and partly in English. Whereas the first two groups of students knew neither Sanskrit nor the Devanagari alphabet, the third group was English–French bilingual. It is not surprising therefore that the first group operated at chance level, the second group somewhat better, and the third group better still. As an additional condition, however, and more interesting, is the fact that the students repeated the tests four times. Although they were uninformed for the first trial that their memory would be tested, four subsequent trials with the very same material on each were clearly presented as tests of memory. The data of Figure 18.1 show that even when the students knew what they would be tested for, their ability to identify the sentences they had examined depended upon their having a symbol system appropriate to the encoding. The Devanagari script could be examined and encoded only as so many marks; transliterated to the English alphabet, the letters formed readily identified symbols. Expressing sentences in French or English, the symbols were interpreted semantically as well. Hence, under equivalent exhortations to improve performance, they were unable to achieve equivalent degrees of learning. People's available techniques for encoding the symbols were part of their processing of them. The point can be appreciated by examining Figure 18.2. One of the sentences in the lower part is contained in the upper. The person unfamiliar with the Devanagari script encounters considerable difficulty in finding it. The task is far more easily carried out when the accompanying transliteration to the English alphabet is examined.

The point of this demonstration is to show that mere picturing or imaging by itself was not sufficient to carry information; the people who did not know the Devanagari script could not recognize sentences written with it even when the people were apprised of what to look for. Their coding schemes were probably restricted to the lines, bars, and curlicues that make up the letters. When faced with the same words in the English alphabet, however, patterns and sequences emerged that were more easily recognized at a later time. When the marks carried a semantic content as well, as they did for the bilingual students, performance was better still. Hence, the finding is that for people who are familiar with it, a symbol system serves to capture and incorporate knowledge and acts as an aid to memory. What people remember, they remember not by virtue of any direct apprehension of pictorial qualities but by virtue of skills and practice in using a system of symbols. We believe that this must be as true for pictorial symbols as it is for linguistic ones.

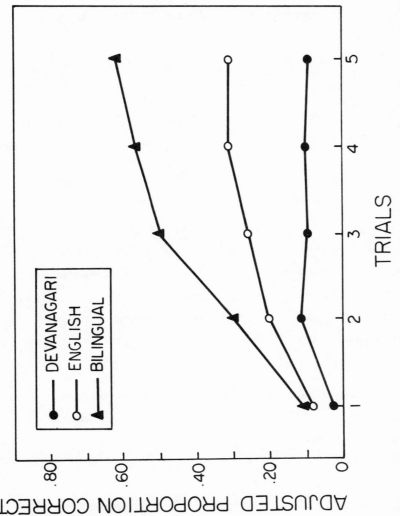

Figure 18.1   The results of tests in which different groups of students first examined a Sanskrit text in the Devanagari alphabet, or in an English transliteration, or in a text partly in English and partly in French. The figure shows the likelihood of correctly identifying a sentence in a subsequent memory test.

इतश्चारि तस्यामेव मनुजगतौ नगर्यामिगृहीतसङ्केता नाम ब्राह्मणी । सा जन-
वादेन नरपतिपुत्रज-मनामकरणवृत्ता-तमवगम्य सखीं प्रत्याह । प्रियसखि प्रज्ञाविशाले
पश्य यच्छ्रूयते महाश्चर्यं लोके यथा कालपरिणतिर्महादेवी भव्यपुरुषनामानं दारकं
प्रसूतेति । ततः प्रज्ञाविशालयोक्तं । प्रियसखि किमत्राश्चर्यम् । अन्यद्भूमेरुद्भूतम् ।

A

1. प्रियसखि प्रज्ञाविशाले पश्य यच्छ्रूयते महाश्चर्यं लोके यथा कालपरिणतिर्महादेवी
   भव्यपुरुषनामानं दारकं प्रसूतेति ।

2. समाकर्णय ।

3. भद्राः शृणुत ।

4. समस्तगुणभारभाजनमेष वर्धमानः कालक्रमेण भविष्यतीति ।

B

Itascasti tasyameva manujagatau nagaryamagrhitasamketa
nama brahmani. Sa janavadena narapati putrajanmanama-karanavr-
ttantamavagamya sakhim pratyaha. Priyasakhi prajnavisale pasya
yacchruyate mahascaryam loke yatha kalaparinatirmahadevi
bhavyapurusanamanam darakam prasuteti. Tatah prajnavisalayoktam.

C

1. Priyasakhi prajnavisale pasya yacchruyate mahascaryam
   loke yatha kalaparinatirmahadevi bhavyapurusanamanam
   darakam prasuteti.

2. Samakarnaya.

3. Bhadrah srnuta.

4. Samastagunabharbhajanamesa vardhamanah kalakramena
   bhavisyatiti.

D

Figure 18.2 An example of Sanskrit texts in the Devanagari alphabet and in
approximate English transliteration. In each case, the same one of the four indicated
sentences in the lower part appears in the text above.

ON MENTAL PICTURES

This volume is largely concerned with pictures on the wall, but these are not the only kinds of picture people may experience. Another commonly encountered type is the "picture in the mind," or mental image. Mental imagery has attracted a great deal of interest in the recent past from philosophers and psychologists; in the belief that the remarks we made above about symbolizing apply equally to mental pictures and to physical ones, we will discuss some work on imagery.

What do we mean by imagery? Examples will explain. Suppose you are given two times: 8:22 and 9:15. In which case do the clock hands form the greater angle? It is supposed that the ability to perform this task without looking at the face of a clock requires the use of imagery (Paivio 1978), and many people performing the task report having a vivid pictorial experience, or a "picture in the mind," of a clock face.

On the basis of two independent experiments, the adequacy of the "picture in the mind" metaphor can be called into question, however, for they showed that imagery could be successfully used even when the object imaged was not fully picturable. In an experiment by Metzler and Shepard (1974), people tried to rotate three-dimensional images to match a standard; they were able to use the image successfully even when its rotation caused it to pass through a plane that reduced its dimensionality. Such a reduction would of course destroy the pictorial resemblance of image to object. In an experiment by Neisser and Kerr (1973), people created images as aids to memory. Whereas in one condition of the study, the objects of the image were to be visible in imagination, in a second condition, some objects were imagined as contained within other objects and so were not picturable in the image. Rated vividness of the images was greater when all its objects could be pictured, but the efficiency of the images as aids to memory was identical in the two parts of the study. Hence, picturability itself need not be an informationally important aspect of the image.

Perhaps it was with such considerations in mind that Shepard and his colleagues (Shepard and Chipman 1970; Cooper and Shepard 1973; Shepard and Podgorny 1978) put forward the notion of image as mental analog rather than mental picture. For the purpose, they distinguished "first-order isomorphism"—the structural identity of brain pattern and physical object—from "second-order isomorphism"—a presumed structural and functional similarity between imagined and perceived objects. Along with the other authors we have discussed, Shepard and Podgorny (1978) argued for an extensive sharing of mechanisms between the processes of perceiving and of imaging, even to the point of maintaining that theories of the two should be "cut from the same cloth" (p. 61). The similarity extends beyond a metaphorical description to a belief that the two processes, imaging and perceiving, not only share mechanisms but have structurally isomorphic inputs, the difference between them only that the input is from visual mechanisms responsive to the object itself, in one case, and to a surrogate of the object, in the other.

In this view, a strict division is presumed between the mechanisms that do the perceiving or imaging and the inputs to those mechanisms, between, that is, perceptual or imaginal process and representation on which the process operates. This division is analogous to that which in computer science distinguishes between data and program. This distinction is widely maintained in current psychological theorizing both by "propositionalists" (Anderson 1976; Kintsch 1974; Norman and Rumelhart 1975) and by "pictorialists," but there are some who have maintained that it is not warranted (Kolers 1968), and some recent developments in the study of artificial intelligence seem even to blur the distinction (Winograd 1972).

It is useful to discuss the basis on which some of these claims are made by Shepard and his colleagues. Perhaps the most widely known of the experiments is that of Shepard and Metzler (1971), in which people were shown two-dimensional drawings of three-dimensional objects and were asked to say whether the drawing shown was the same figure as a comparison standard shown at the same time but in a different orientation. The reported finding was that the time needed to respond correctly (to say yes) increased linearly with an increase in the angular misorientation of standard and comparison figures. The "lure" or comparison standard to which the subjects should have said no correctly was always the enantiomorph (mirror image) of the orientation used for a correct positive report.

In a second test, people were shown capital letters in various orientations and were required to say whether what they saw was a letter in normal orientation or its enantiomorph (Cooper and Shepard 1973). A variable of the study was the kind of information provided prior to exposure of the letter that named the letter, or described its orientation, did both, and so on. The main finding was that time to respond correctly was at a maximum when the letters were upside down, increasing monotonically with either clockwise or counterclockwise rotation of the letter from zero. Hence, the same sorts of results are found whether the comparison is between the simultaneously presented figures that are misaligned or whether one figure is presented and compared to a linguistic description or memory image. Moreover, Metzler and Shepard (1974) extended their results with drawings of three-dimensional shapes and found that, as with letters, shapes too could be compared with their memory.

On the basis of these results, the claim is made explicitly that the mental image rotates in mental space in a manner exactly analogous to the way that a perceived object would be seen to rotate in physical space. In this, they have elaborated upon the suggestion of Howard and Templeton (1966, p. 320), "If [the memory image of a shape and another shape] are differently oriented, then the image and the second shape will not even approximately match unless some internal operation takes place equivalent to rotating the memory image." It is this correspondence of perceptual and imaginal that is referred to as second-order isomorphism. Indeed, Shepard and Podgorny (1978, p. 59) write, "We have taken this similarity of results to indicate that the same kinds of internal processes are operative in both cases," the results referred to being the outcome of experiments comparing perception and imagery. Reasoning from similarity of ends to similarity of means or from similarity of outcomes to similarity of causes is, of course, wholly fallacious. The similarity of mechanism might be put forward as a proposal to be tested but hardly can be accepted as a confirmed result. In the study of perceiving, it is well-known that similar perceptions can be elicited by widely divergent conditions (for example, Kolers 1972). If that is so within the domain of perceiving, how much less true the postulated equivalence must be in respect to the comparison of perceiving with imaging.

The results of Shepard and his colleagues, moreover, seem to depend upon the particular methods of measurement that were used. In other experiments, in which people named letters or read texts in various orientations, the commonplace finding has been that mathematically equivalent 180-degree rotations of the materials around the horizontal, vertical, or depth axes, as in Figure 18.3, produce markedly different times to respond (Kolers and Perkins 1969). It has long been known among students of visual perception, in fact, that rotation of objects around their vertical axes creates particular problems for perception and for memory of shapes (Sutherland, n.d.; Kolers and Perkins 1975). On analyzing the results of tests in which people named isolated letters that were presented in various orientations, Kolers and Perkins (1969) found that rotations around either the vertical or the horizontal axis resulted in marked increases in time needed to name letters, whereas rotation around the depth axis had less effect, but the increases for the first two rotations were found to have different bases. The increase in time to name x-rotated letters (inverted letters, that is, rotated around the horizontal axis) was said to be due to the difficulty in activating the appropriate pattern-analyzing mechanisms, but the increase for T-rotated letters (mirror-reflected, that is, rotated around the vertical axis) was said to be due to their ambiguity, to the absence of good pattern-analyzing procedures for telling them apart. Hence, the question of particular interest in respect to the work of Shepard and his

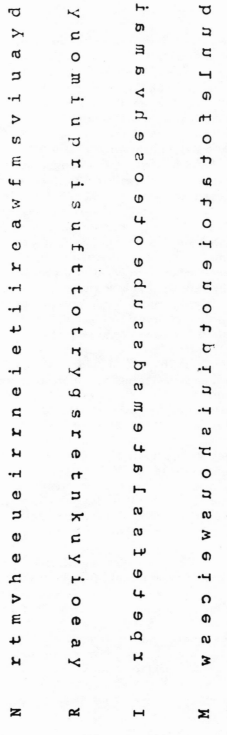

Figure 18.3 Examples of letters rotated around the three principal axes of space: N, normal orientation; R, rotated around the depth axis; I, rotated around the horizontal axis; and M, rotated around the vertical axis

colleagues would ask what there is about their method of measurement, in particular, the use of enantiomorphs as distracters, which produces their results. For the moment, we must reserve judgment on their generality and, therefore, on the generality of those legitimate conclusions that can be derived from them.

SYMBOLIC NATURE OF IMAGERY

One of the confusing elements in the study of imagery is the word *analog*, which Shepard, among many others, takes to have the meaning of similarity of imaginal and perceptual experience. In an earlier section, we argued that the proper use of the term *analog* refers it to a symbol system and not to any analogy or resemblance. The word alludes to the density or continuity of a medium and of the symbols that refer to it. In a similar way, we said that resemblance is not a requirement between symbol and object symbolized. Our assertion is that as true as these remarks are for physical pictures and physical symbols, they are equally true for mental pictures and mental symbols. Any resemblances that are found between symbol and object symbolized depend not on the process of symbolizing but on the purposes to which the symbols are put. For example, in an architect's plan for a landscape, one is likely to find a careful correspondence between metric properties of the sketch and metric properties of the area referred to. The correspondence is not due to a necessary property of picturing but to a requirement about the use of the drawing: it is intended as a model or plan of a particular area.

The same sort of remark can be made about mental imagery in which people report features of similarity of appearance of image to object imaged. We believe that when the image is featurally similar in this way to the object imaged, it occurs because of the instruction given the imager or the use to which the image is put. In other cases, the imagery may be without ready correspondence to physical fact or be bizarre. Hence, the notion of analog in respect to imagery is *wrong* when it is used to refer to similarity of image to perceptual experience. Moreover, there is no requirement with respect to similarity of appearance in imaging and perceiving.

In our view, imagery can best be regarded as an internal representation of experiences that are described in pictorial form; it is the pictorial analog of prevision and anticipation that is also carried out in language, as when we ready ourselves for some upcoming event. We use the metaphor of a mental sketch pad to capture this property of prevision and trial. An important difference distinguishing a mental from a physical sketch pad, however, is the nature of the inscription. On a physical sketch pad, a symbol has both a physical identity as a mark and an interpretation assigned to it; on the mental sketch pad, it has only the status of a symbol, for there is no mind-stuff on which the symbol is inscribed. Distinctions between the linguistic and pictorial certainly fail to capture the main features of what an image is; indeed, making a distinction between the linguistic and the pictorial may actually becloud issues that are better understood in terms of the operations of symbol systems. Our analysis of some issues in respect to symbol systems helps to answer the question of what an image is and the ways in which this pictorial experience is similar to, and different from, the perception of a picture on the wall.

REFERENCES

Anderson, J. R. *Language, Memory, and Thought*. Hillsdale, N.J.: Erlbaum Associates, 1976.

Arnheim, R. *Art and Visual Perception*. Berkeley: University of California Press, 1974.

Cooper, L. A., and Shepard, R. N. "Chronometric Studies of the Rotation of Mental Images." In *Visual Information Processing*, edited by W. G. Chase, pp. 75–176. New York: Academic Press, 1973.

Gibson, E. J., and Levin, H. *The Psychology of Reading*. Cambridge, Mass.: MIT Press, 1975.

Gombrich, E. H. *Art and Illusion*. New York: Pantheon, 1960.

Goodman, N. *Languages of Art*. Indianapolis, Ind.: Bobbs-Merrill, 1968.

———. "Seven Strictures on Similarity." In *Problems and Projects*, edited by N. Goodman, pp. 437–46. Indianapolis, Ind.: Bobbs–Merrill, 1972.

Howard, I. P., and Templeton, W. B. *Human Spatial Orientation*. London: Wiley, 1966.

Kintsch, W. *The Representation of Meaning in Memory*. Hillsdale, N.J.: Erlbaum Associates, 1974.

Kolers, P. A. "Some Psychological Aspects of Pattern Recognition." In *Recognizing Patterns*, edited by P. A. Kolers and M. Eden. Cambridge, Mass.: MIT Press, 1968.

———. *Aspects of Motion Perception*. Oxford: Pergamon Press, 1972.

———. "Remembering Trivia." *Language and Speech* 17 (1974): 324–36.

————. "Reading Pictures and Reading Text." In *The Arts and Cognition*, edited by D. Perkins and B. Leondar, pp. 136–64. Baltimore: Johns Hopkins University Press, 1977.

Kolers, P. A., and Perkins, D. N. "Orientation of Letters and Their Speed of Recognition." *Perception and Psychophysics* 5 (1969): 275–80.

————. "Spatial and Ordinal Components of Form Perception and Literacy." *Cognitive Psychology* 7 (1975): 228–67.

McLuhan, H. M. *Gutenberg Galaxy*. Toronto: University of Toronto Press, 1962.

Metzler, J., and Shepard, R. N. "Transformational Studies of the Internal Representation of Three-Dimensional Objects." In *Theories of Cognitive Psychology: The Loyola Symposium*, edited by R. L. Solso, pp. 147–201. Potomac, Md.: Erlbaum Associates, 1974.

Neisser, U., and Kerr, N. "Spatial and Mnemonic Properties of Visual Images." *Cognitive Psychology* 5 (1973): 138–50.

Norman, D. A., and Rumelhart, D. E., eds. *Explorations in Cognition*. San Francisco: Freeman, 1975.

Paivio, A. *Imagery and Verbal Processes*. Toronto: Holt, Rinehart and Winston, 1971.

————. "Comparisons of Mental Clocks." *Journal of Experimental Psychology: Human Perception and Performance* 4 (1978): 61–71.

Shepard, R. N., and Chipman, S. "Second-Order Isomorphism of Internal Representations: Shapes of States." *Cognitive Psychology* 1 (1970): 1–17.

Shepard, R. N., and Metzler, J. "Mental Rotation of Three-Dimensional Objects." *Science* 171 (1971): 701–3.

Shepard, R. N., and Podgorny, P. "Cognitive Processes That Resemble Perceptual Processes." In *Handbook of Learning and Cognitive Processes*, edited by W. K. Estes, pp. 189–237. Hillsdale, N.J.: Erlbaum Associates, 1978.

Sutherland, N. S. "Shape Discrimination by Animals." In *Experimental Psychology Society Monograph no. 1*, n.d.

Winograd, T. "Understanding Natural Language." *Cognitive Psychology* 3 (1972): 1–195.

Chapter Nineteen

The Reality Underlying Abstraction

Naomi Boretz

In thinking about the topic "What is a Painting?," I have become aware of many questions for which I have few answers. I will make suppositions and speculate about phenomena (visual and otherwise), to which I, as an artist, have access. I will, as this chapter proceeds, present a number of these observations, suppositions, and speculations, questioning more than answering and, perhaps only circling the periphery of the central concern.

"The Reality Underlying Abstraction" reveals my supposition that painting is based, ultimately, on an *observed* reality. The artist, "seeing," subsequently chooses to *do* something about that observed reality: an artist produces a physical fact, with which a viewer (if interested) must deal on the artist's terms; an artist's perceptions, as demonstrated by physical production, are exposed, become material, and are subjected to analysis.

As an artist, I perceive reality, and I, also, *later*, see those physical productions that reveal my perceptions to the public view; as an artist–teacher, I perceive the perceptions of beginning art students, in which they (unwittingly) reveal to me their senses of reality; in addition, I have access to the perceptions of nonartist viewers, since (unusually, if not exceptionally, for an artist) I also instruct in art history through slide lectures; *these* student–viewers do not, themselves, produce, although they perceive.

As an artist who produces so-called abstract art, I observe, later (that is, after the fact of the physical production) that my artwork, in the personal and public views is, indeed, not obviously related to an everyday visual "reality." I know, for myself, that my perceptions–artwork "changed" into these "abstractions" via a rather long development.

Although to the sophisticated viewer-and-gallery-goer, it may seem that modern art is an accepted thing today, the truth is that it is not. Even today, I am still asked: "*Why* do you paint that way? *Do* you see that way? Are you *able* to draw realistically?" I do not believe I can answer the "why," although, here, I may be able to indicate "how"; if I really did "see" that way, I could not find my way to the bus stop; and yes, I am "able" to draw realistically (if that really matters).

"Why do I paint that way?": the unanswerable question arises, "Is There a *Zeitgeist* or only a '*Selbstgeist*'"? Would it have been conceivable for me as an artist in sixteenth-century Florence to produce art like I do? Since I was not there at the time, I cannot answer the question, but a secondary subquestion might reveal something about the nature of such perceptions: Did, for example, Leonardo (see Figure 19.1 [A]) regard figurative representation with the same objectivity as, for example, Klee (Figure 19.1 [B]) or the author (Figure 19.1 [C]).

I suppose, given my awareness of my own perceptions and the manner (the how if not the why) in which they are then materialized, that Leonardo, and then Klee–and–I, did *not* perceive those muscles and bones *in the same way*. My point is that I, as an "abstract" painter, am interested in observing with great accuracy the reality presented by physical phenomena, but I then choose, later, to use those observations which are concerned with reality for something beyond mere reproduction. Clearly, there is a cultural conditioning: a crush of cultural–artistic history superimposed on my original "seeing-eye" view. Leonardo certainly observed reality with accuracy and artistic interest, but he *used* it differently from me. Today, I, as an abstract artist, do not think of that reality as an end in itself, as a *self-contained* and completed vision. I see that reality as a beginning, an impetus for an idea which will be developed in some manner *other* than its initial impression. My perceptions of shape, rooted in real objects and figures, are transformed into something quite different.

For example, analogously, it seems unlikely that the "people" about whom Charles Dickens wrote and the "people" about whom James Joyce write were "real" to them or to their readers *in the same way*. The difference in the surface–texture (of language or of painting) certainly creates a different set of stimuli to which the artist and viewer respond.

What, then, is the significance, and "bite," of cultural–artistic conditioning? I know now (although not earlier) that my work looks different from the everyday reality that I observe. But the nature and thrust of this cultural conditioning still evades me. The question, Do I see that way? is closely related to the question, Why?, and I will relate its answer partly to the cultural conditioning of which I have already spoken and partly to the question, Am I Able (that is, as an abstract artist) to draw realistically?

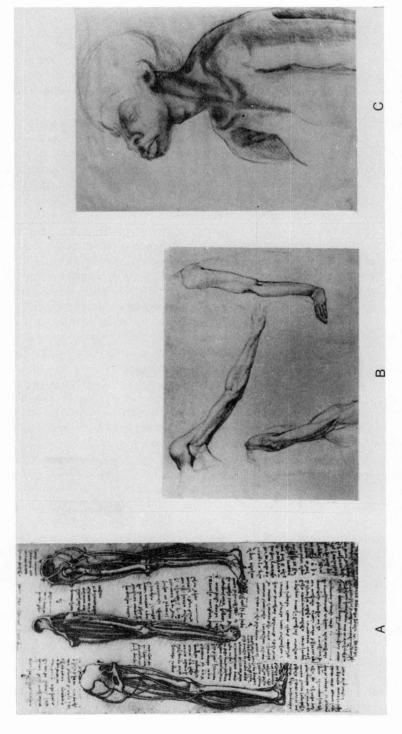

Figure 19.1 A) Leonardo da Vinci's *Anatomical Drawing* (Royal Library, Windsor Castle). B) Paul Klee's *Pencil Study* (Bern, Kunstmuseum). C) Naomi Boretz's *Anatomy Study*.

Would Monet have been able to paint the series of water lilies with such sensitivity if he had not, earlier, painted "realistically" (see Figure 19.2 [B])?

Klee is known as a teacher of art through his *Pedagogical Sketchbook*, a page of which with its little formulas and squares (Figure 19.3 [A]) explains something about Klee's own creative approach (Figure 19.3 [B]). However, Klee, in his own early training, drew muscles and people and flowers, as did Leonardo and Monet. Klee urged his Bauhaus students to observe reality with attention to every detail, for example, a flower, a twig, a leaf, or a stone were to be drawn with an intertwined scientific–artistic accuracy; the artist–observer was to bring something of the naturalist into the drawing of observed "things."

Kandinsky, too, the so-called originator of Western abstract art, taught his Bauhaus students to deal with an observed reality, that is, the "abstract" was drawn *from* the "real" and was, ineluctably, based on it. In the first-semester class, a still-life setup was to serve as the model for the student–artists (Figure 19.3 [C]). They were to draw, to analyze, to geometrize. However, whatever came later, "reality" came first. Without it (and this may sound simplistic), without that reality, nothing could be drawn, analyzed, or geometrized. Thus, abstraction grew out of reality in the first-semester class. This way of "looking" was to serve as the basis for subsequent production; the students' conditioning in perception had begun, and in the beginning were real object–shapes.

How far back can such conditioning begin? Clearly, adult students, who arrive in a studio class preparing to do battle with pencil and paper, do not see with "innocent eyes," or *do* they?

I read that television has lowered the visual orientation of our younger generation. It is claimed that the visual barrage has desensitized contemporary youth and that they see less than did their counterparts before the television era. Others (some of my colleagues in the humanities) have complained to me that it is the verbal capacity that has been lowered and that *I* am fortunate to be teaching art at this time, since television has fostered visual sophistication at the expense of verbal (their students "recognize" only pictures).

After having taught hundreds of studio students over many years, I believe that neither claim is particularly reflected in students' studio work. Twentieth-century American teen-agers, who drive cars, operate computers, watch television, and take photographs with Polaroid cameras, draw figures (as did their counterparts before the television era) in which frontal eyes invariably appear in profile faces and human bodies exhibit those orthopedically distraught positions familiar to us (though ever so much more elegantly conceived) in Egyptian wall paintings. Some mysterious racially unconscious force appears to be guiding their inexperienced hands. Students also take little note of the

B

A

Figure 19.2 A) Claude Monet's *Water-garden at Giverny* (Paris, The Louvre). B) Claude Monet's *Portrait of Mme. Gaudibert* (Paris. The Louvre).

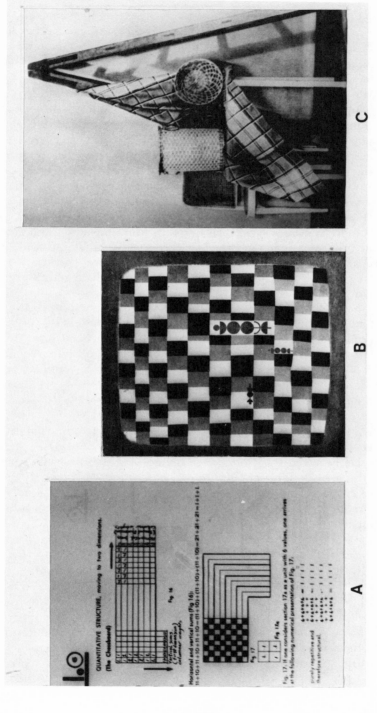

Figure 19.3 A) Page from Paul Klee's *Pedagogical Sketchbook*, trans. S. Moholy-Nagy (New York: Praeger, 1953) (originally published in 1925). B) Paul Klee's *Superchess* (Kunsthaus, Zurich). C) W. Kandinsky's Still – life model, Bauhaus drawing (Illustration from H. Wingler, *The Bauhaus* [Cambridge, Mass.: MIT Press, 1969]).

four-sided format of paper or canvas, which is setting the constraint for their artistic efforts. Yet, these people have been looking at a four-sided television screen since infancy, and they have all looked through four-sided camera lenses—the twentieth-century-Renaissance-perspective-"window-on-the-world."

Studio art and art lecture students alike respond most positively to paintings in which Renaissance-type perspective is utilized; they claim it makes things look "real." They appear to perceive something about Renaissance perspective that they judge to be "correct" and "realistic." Nonstudio and studio students alike laugh at the "wrong" perspective of Byzantine and medieval art, claiming it looks "ugly" and "unrealistic." Is this cultural conditioning? I ask that, since *once in the studio*, these same students who have watched television (a four-sided window-on-the-world), taken photographs (through a four-sided camera lens), approved of Renaissance-type paintings in the museum, laughingly hooted at the "inverse perspective" in early medieval illustrations; and chuckled at the oddly shaped figures in Egyptian wall paintings find themselves unwittingly, and unhappily, drawing in that same "wrong," "unrealistic," "odd" way.

Cézanne, "the father of Cubism," illustrated among other things, an asymmetrical bottle (see Figure 19.4 [A]). Cézanne, like Leonardo, Monet, and Klee could draw "realistically." Yet, he chose, later, to do something about that still-life object—to make it look odd. Approximately 1,800 years earlier, an artist in Herculaneum also did a similar thing to a still-life object; and in the 1970s, a beginning art student made a similar effort (see Figure 19.4 [C]). In each case, the Renaissance perspective has been "tampered with."

Now, we can assume that Cézanne knowingly did something unconventional. Did that ancient artist knowingly make a similar compromise between the "conceptual image" and the observed shape? The results are similar, yet the intent, the desire, was probably quite different from that of Cézanne's. The inexperienced art students, struggling for what they think of as "correct," based on Renaissance-type perspective paintings in museums and photographs they have seen (and taken), unwittingly, unhappily, and invariably produce supposedly archaic results.

Which of these works is an example of cultural conditioning, or a *Zeitgeist* or a *Selbstgeist*? Or are these perceptions "natural," having little to do with conventionalized artistic tradition, the theory of relativity, or the "invention" of Cubism by "intellectual" painters. Are they so natural that variations on this theme appear in most representational artwork and with almost every beginning art student?

Cultural conditioning of perception (some of the time) is so strong that the "self" appears to have been lost in the morass of societal

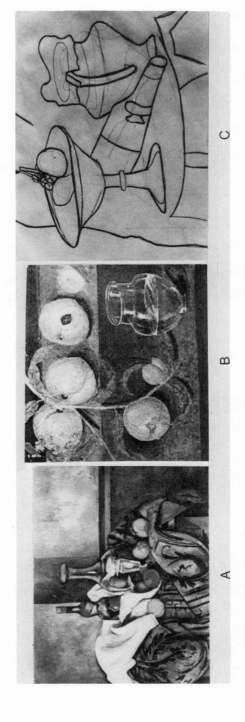

Figure 19.4 A) Paul Cezanne's *Still Life* (National Gallery of Art, Washington, D.C.). B) *Still-life*, Herculaneum wall painting, ca. 50 A.D. (Museo Nazionale, Naples). C) Student's pencil drawing, *Still-life*, detail, 1977.

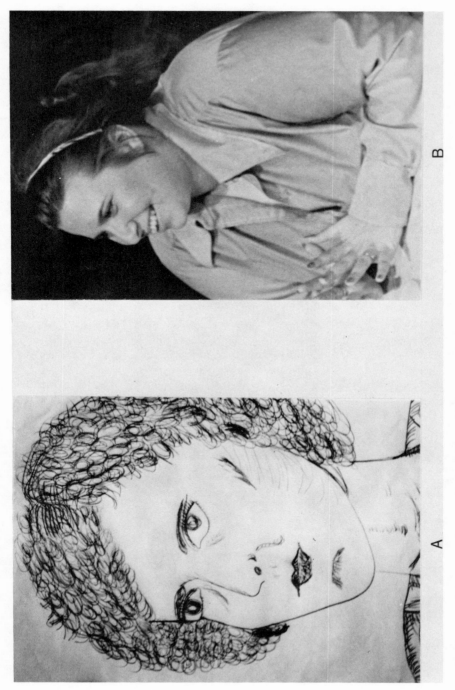

Figure 19.5 A) Student's pencil drawing, *Self-portrait*, 1977. B) Photograph of student in A.

demands upon the individual. Perception of observed reality, in this case (Figure 19.5 [A]), was lost in the "desire" of the inexperienced art student, drawing a required self-portrait, to be acceptably attractive in the twentieth-century–American–Thin-world (Figure 19.5 [B]). She claimed that the drawing looked exactly like herself, except for what she termed the *technical* problem of being unable to accurately represent her new hairdo.

What about an experienced, talented artist? In the nineteenth century, the new European interest in the artwork of exotic-and-past civilizations encouraged artists and copyists to travel, and to draw, for the information of scholars (as well as for the public) supposedly accurate pictures of newly discovered treasures. When we, today, compare some of these copies with the originals, the differences and inaccuracies appear shocking. Several well-known art-historical blunders were made at that time by trusting scholars, who based their suppositions solely on drawings of archaeological finds, which were sent to them by post, and which they had not seen in physical reality. Many drawings of Byzantine and medieval figures were reinterpreted for the contemporary taste. Stiff, hieratic stances, staring eyes, and noncurvilinear physiques were not appealing to the nineteenth-century eye: the stance and limbs of Justinian, shown in Figure 19.6 (A), were considered more attractive than those in Figure 19.6 (B).

Did these copyists actually "see" the original mosaics as reproduced? Were they incapable of truly seeing these figures as we suppose ourselves to be truly seeing them? Or did they make those changes knowingly, with the consciousness in which a talented artist is trained? Did they, like Monet, Cézanne, and Klee, knowingly reinterpret the observed reality, or was the thrust of cultural conditioning so strong that they believed they were accurately representing the artwork as it actually was?

I asked earlier, How far back does this (supposed) cultural assault on the perceptions begin? I should express that rather as, At what point do we become aware that something has happened?

It has been fashionable since the Bauhaus days for artist–teachers to include examples of their students' work in published pedagogy tests. Examples of that kind are *not* helpful for what I am discussing here, since the examples included would be the achieved–accomplished works of "talented" students: naturally, teachers choose what is regarded as the best examples of their kind to reflect and represent their good teaching methods. Books of this kind—whether of the "how-to" variety or of the more sophisticated Bauhaus type—never show examples of the "mistakes" that even talented students make (*talent* here defined, in our society, as the ability to draw in Renaissance

Figure 19.6   A) *Justinian*, mosaic (detail), ca. 526–47 A.D. (S. Vitale, Ravenna). B) *Emperor Justinian*, engraving, *Munchener Bilderbogen* (serial) 1861–90 (illustration from translated edition).

perspective-style realism) or of the work of nontalented students. That early, formative stage in an artist's development is not given sufficient critical attention. Yet, it is from these beginning stages of both talented and nontalented students that *I* acquired most of the information I have about perceptual problems.

For example, it interests me to observe that even "attention," "desire," and the "wish for illusion" appear to be of little help to the "nontalented" art students. With all the contemporary examples (in museums and photographs), as well as societal pressure to draw "realistically," they can not exorcise the "conceptual image." However, their perceptions of others' artwork (Leonardo's, Monet's, Cézanne's, Klee's) seems to function separately from their perceptions, as evidenced in the physical fact of their own artwork.

They *are* aware that Cézanne's perspective seems "off kilter," that the Herculaneum glass is "crooked," that a painted Egyptian figure is "oddly" constructed, yet, when *they* try to draw in perspective, it is more Cézanne-like than it is Leonardo-like—*their* glass pitchers are as up-ended and asymmetrical as is the first-century artist's—and they cannot seem to avoid the conceptual imagery of the human body evidenced in those (elegant) Egyptian wall paintings.

Most of them avoid drawing the overlaps and overlays that might hinder their descriptive-explanatory conceptual image drawing of objects of figures. They draw as a simultaneity what could actually be seen only from different angles at different times. Perhaps, like the Herculaneum artist, perhaps like Cézanne, they are explaining and describing their visual world in a manner closely related to the "explanatory" conceptual-image drawings they had made as very young children.

I have attended major retrospective exhibitions and looked through research studies and picture books on individual artists. Rarely were the earliest efforts of these artists (extant or) exhibited. I often wondered if the earliest efforts—that of the five-year-old artists—evidenced "talent" at that age or whether they drew, and perceived, like all other kindergarteners. Could what society accepts as talented influence the child–artist that early? Does the very important approval of a particular kind of talent encourage the "talented" individual to continue doing more (and better) of the same? It appears to me that it is at this early stage that the pressure of cultural conditioning is most significant. For example, within a Muslim culture, the talented artist would be one who had superior abilities in calligraphy and nonfigurative design; in our Western culture, the standard for talent is recognizable ability in figural representation and Renaissance-type perspective.

The only artist to whose youthful attempts I had access was myself. Trying to gather supporting evidence for points to be made in this chapter, I asked my mother if she had kept any of my childhood artworks. So, one gray afternoon, my mother and I dug out of an antediluvian closet a brown Macy's shopping bag containing about a dozen pictures from my artistic infancy; we looked through them with the suppressed excitement of archaeologists sifting through crumbling artifacts. For reasons best understood by lady schoolteachers in the depths of Brooklyn, Eskimo and Chinese culture was considered especially relevant for six-and seven-year-olds in the classrooms of that era; therefore, many of these productions, whether taken from schoolbook photographs or from suggestions by the teacher were of figures from civilizations at least 1,000 miles away—and not seen by me or part of my "reality."

How am I to judge, and analyze, these works, in the light of my later development? Do they show evidence at this stage of later abilities?

A drawing done when I was five, shown in Figure 19.7 (A), may manifest an incipient understanding of a perspective view within a four-sided compositional format. Was this culturally induced? The farmer is standing in a foreground, and his smaller house is in a

B

A

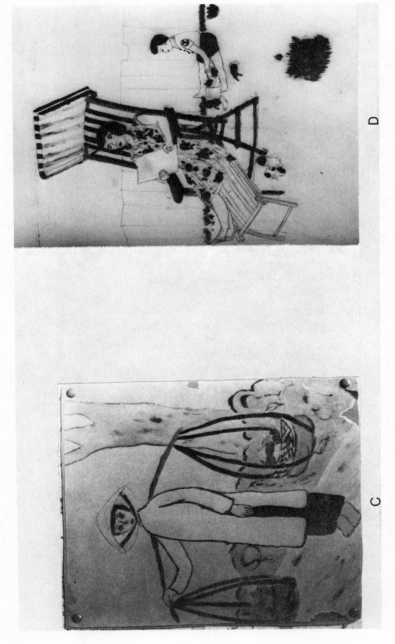

Figure 19.7 Naomi Boretz's childhood art work. A) *Farmer*, crayon drawing, age five. B) *Eskimos*, crayon drawing, age seven. C) *Chinese Girl*, paint on paper, age eight. D) *My Mother and Brother*, paint and pencil on board, age ten.

C

D

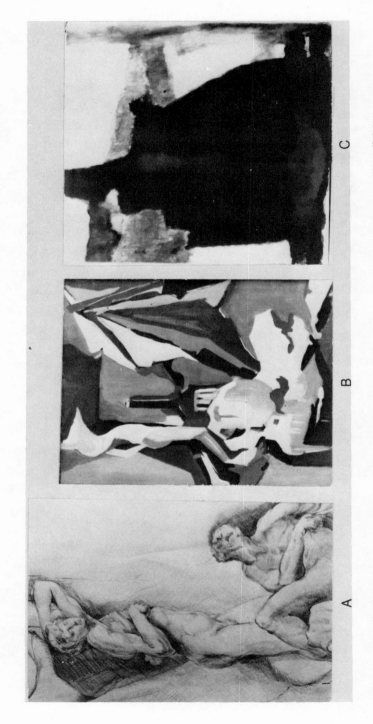

Figure 19.8 Naomi Boretz's art work. A) *Figure Studies* (plaster casts), pencil on paper, age 15. B) *Still Life*, casein on canvas. C) *Earthflame*, acrylic on canvas.

background; there is an implication of distance and a horizon line. The farmer would be larger, hierarchically, but the relative sizes of bush, flowers, and dog, in the foreground, and the house, in the background, contradict that hierarchical view. I have read and observed that children at this age do draw figures and objects in hierarchical sizes, according to order of importance to them, rather than the "true" size. If that is so, then something different was manifest in *this* five-year-old's perceptions about sizes and space. By ages seven and eight (Figure 19.7 [B] and [C]), my two-dimensional figures had acquired bulk and "presence," and the implication of a deeper space, achieved partly by overlaps, was even more clearly depicted. By age ten, I could observe "reality" and individualize shapes and contours with accuracy and sensitivity, placing figures in a more defined, "sophisticated" spatial setting, as shown in Figure 19.7 (D). By age 15, I could draw in the manner shown in Figure 19.8 (A).

Now most of my early art teachers were very "academic," that is, what they called *reality* was defined by a Renaissance-type surface; abstract artworks were regarded by them as the extravagances of a lunatic fringe. Most of my teachers were of the confirmed (if unconfirmable) opinion that abstract painters could not draw and produced such wildnesses only to shock the bourgeoisie. They (the teachers), being pure in heart and talented in drawing, did not have to resort to such pranks, and a "good" student was one who followed in their figurative, and literal, footsteps.

However, the more experienced I became at representing reality "realistically" in the studio classes, the more I seethed at the restrictive constraints. At home, outside the class atmosphere, I did things otherwise. In painting, I had impulses to paint around the edges of the stretched canvas, and drawn objects and figures took on an increasingly "tampered-with" appearance. "Reality" began to look rather more like Figure 19.8 (B) to me.

I would like very much to claim that an epiphanous lightning bolt had struck and had catapulted me and my artistic sensibility into a new, creatively original artworld. But that is not how it happened. First, my teachers disapproved of my rebellion, so I worked on many of these drawings and paintings at home, in a kind of guilt-ridden dead-of-night discomfort. Second, I was not sure myself just where this new "vision" was taking me. Instead of clarifying lightning, I felt, rather, that I was on a bumpy, unplanned ride through a carnival fun house tunnel. Occasionally, the *mise-en-scène* represented "reality"; then, often, through my window-on-the-world, I saw as shown in Figure 19.8 (C).

However, once I accepted the surface difference and the sudden swerves in the tunnel ride became less vertiginous, I decided consciously that I had to use what I saw in a distinctive manner. Although it

358

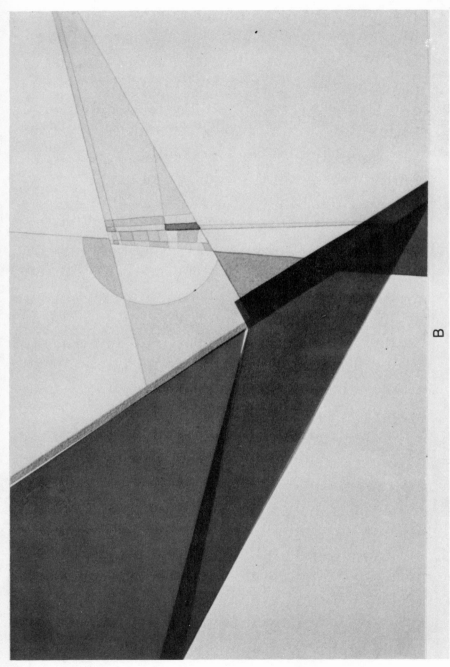

B

Figure 19.9 A) Naomi Boretz's *Landscape 6*, watercolor on paper, 1973. B) *Transparencies VII*, watercolor with acetate on paper, 1976.

might appear that I eschewed and rejected all the representational reality I had formerly observed, the truth is that I was, and am, consistently aware that everything I "know how to do"—all of those earlier observed realities, as well as their materialization in physical fact—were what allow me to produce that which I am now producing.

All that "seeing" of the "real," now acting upon what I can do, means, for me, the creation of a new surface. Those early, materialized perceptions revealed themselves, later, into things like those found in Figure 19.9 (A) and 19.9 (B).

What I get is what I see, and what I see is reality.

Chapter Twenty

First Drawings: Notes on the Relationships between Perception and Production in the Visual Arts

Howard Gardner and Dennie Wolf

INTRODUCTION: THE CHASM BETWEEN ARTISTIC PERCEPTION AND PRODUCTION

That the skilled practitioner can integrate a variety of mental processes and behavioral capacities has become a virtual truism in contemporary psychology. Be it the billiards player, the chess master, the scientific experimenter, or the pianist, the fluent individual appears in decisive control of all relevant sensory and motor processes, handling them in a highly automatized manner yet, at the same time, capable of rearranging, revising, or even totally scuttling a particular skill when exigencies so demand. Few individuals in our society are more skilled than practiced painters, who have had, for many years, to make fine discriminations of shape, color, form, and texture, realize these distinctions in their own works, revise basic schemata in the light of the requirements of specific undertakings, and capture in art works their own feelings (even as they are so often able to arouse feelings of a powerful form in those who contemplate their work). Indeed, in nominating an individual who examplifies the integration of such key psychological processes as making, perceiving, and feeling, one does well in selecting the visual artist.

In light of these considerations, it is astonishing that scant attention has been paid to the interaction of perceptual and performatory capacities in the art work of young children. Indeed, while increasing

This chapter was prepared for presentation at the symposium, "What Is a Painting?," held in Philadelphia, April 17–19, 1978. The research described in this chapter was supported by grants from the Spencer Foundation and the National Institute of Education (G-00-3-0169 and G-78-0031).

(and increasingly enthusiastic) attention has been paid to the productions made by children and while a whole literature (usually written by art educators) describes stages of children's drawings, there has been a virtual conspiracy of silence on the contributions made to such youthful artistry by the child's developing perceptual powers. This conspiracy has not been in one direction. On the contrary, those concerned with the development of perceptual powers (usually psychologists) have traditionally shown little interest in the relationship between youngsters' perceptions of the world and the actions they undertake in representing the visual world through drawing or painting. It is almost as if one had at work two disembodied and unconnected systems—one involved in looking, the other in marking—whose effects on one another were unrelated.

A few voices have broken the quiet surrounding this issue. There have been some general discussions of the relationship between making and perceiving in the visual domain and even occasional works that comment on this issue within the arts (Goodnow 1977; Maccoby and Hagen 1965; Olson 1970). The general claim has been that children's perceptions outrun their performance by a considerable degree; this lag is taken as a sign that the two systems are working primarily at their own pace or, less drastically, that a healthy decalage exists between what children see in the world and the way they capture that knowledge in their own artistic products. Why this should be so has itself stimulated some controversy.

Certain other possibilities also merit consideration. It might be, for example, that what the children draws is unrelated to what he or she can see—hence, supporting that the well-known phrase that "children draw what they know, not what they see." It is also possible that children's perceptions actually follow in some sense upon their productions; this seems to be the impulse underlying Gombrich's comment (1961) that at least in the visual arts, making precedes matching. It might even be the case that the visual arts exemplify the scheme described by Vygotsky (1962) with reference to language, namely, that perception and production initially begin as separate streams but come together at a certain point in development and, henceforth, exert powerful influences upon one another.

As is often the case, no single position can be completely vindicated. One can cite evidence that drawing and perception have little relationship, that one precedes or prompts the other, and that their developmental origins, while different, are eventually supplanted by their increasingly complementary nature. What has seldom been done, however, is to take seriously the possibility that integral ties obtain throughout development between drawing and marking, ties that change over time but which remain perennially crucial in the understanding of each activity. Because few such schemes have even been hypothesized, there remains little evidence available with respect to the plausibility of this notion. Yet, as a result of our own efforts and those of other investigators, it may be possible to lay out a developmental scheme in which the possible mutual influences between perceiving and making in the visual arts can be stated, and, eventually, subjected to empirical test.

In undertaking such an effort, we will begin with a brief review of the developmental stages in artistry, as they have been proposed by principal authorities in the field (compare Arnheim 1974; Kellogg 1969; Lowenfeld 1947; Luquet 1917). Then, invoking the results of our own longitudinal research (Gardner 1976a, 1976b; Shotwell, Wolf, and Gardner in press; Wolf and Gardner in press a), as well as other empirical work in the field, we will return to each of the stages for a more careful look. We will, in each case, sketch the principal cognitive milestones, the chief advances found in children's drawings, those events in the perceptual realm that may possibly be related to the advances we have described, and the major challenges which the child will be confronting at that period. When appropriate, we will also mention linguistic milestones and relevant individual differences.

As is usual in developmental studies, the ages cited will be approximate from our viewpoint: what is important is the *sequence* of the stages and not the age at which each is attained. Much of our discussion will focus on tasks or situations in which the child copies a drawing (or a model producing a drawing), for in such instances, the relations between perception and production can be seen with stark clarity. We will not offer an account of why drawing advances when and in the manner that it does, for our purposes here are primarily descriptive and comparative, not explanatory. A brief summary of the points that we wish to stress, as well as a survey of the entire trajectory of artistic development, can be seen in Table 20.1.

STAGES OF DRAWING DEVELOPMENT: A PREVIEW AT "FAST FORWARD"

Children's drawings have been so frequently studied by different researchers working in a variety of cultural settings that the overall outlines of this process are no longer controversial. Researchers concur that children begin by making large marks or scribbles, which seem motivated primarily by the enjoyment gained from the exercise of their musculature. These scribbles come under increasingly precise motor control and gradually differentiate into far more specific forms: straight lines, curvy lines, single dots, and dense patches. By the beginning of the third year of life, most children are capable of producing more

TABLE 20.1

Drawing Milestones in Relation to the Child's Overall Development

Stage	Approximate Age	General Milestones	Language Milestones	Perceptual Competences	Drawing Capacities, Including Copying
Prescribble	0 to 1	Circular reactions; attachment bond	—	Recognize objects, persons	Marker as objects
Scribble—the first phase	1 to 1 1/2	Incipient tool use	First words	Notice smaller changes in detail	Copy only grosser motor acts; simple scribbles; motor act primary
Scribble—the second phase	1 1/2 to 2	Object permanence; correlated sense of time, space	Naming; two- to three-word sentences	Ready picture recognition; noting shapes in block games	Variety of scribbles examine marks; no motor features of model; paper surface seen; draw near others' marks.
Basic forms and aggregates	2 to 3	Flowering of symbolic capacities (gesture, number, language); individual differences highlighted	Varied linguistic output	—	Forms include circles, squares, crosses, and their combinations; copy more complex actions; place features correctly (number, orientation, romancing); repeat and vary forms

					made by self, others, without model present
First symbols: tadpole and basic objects	3 to 5	Prototypes organize concepts; medium influences expression of knowledge	Storytelling; first songs	Confusion of left and right and diagonals; perception of objects in terms of focal points	Forms of objects; schemata for familar objects; cannot accommodate schemata to specifics of objects; no representation of third dimension
Flowering of expressivity	5 to 7	Apparent artistic highpoint; language regulates behavior	Decline in verbal egocentrism; writing and reading start	Increasing interest in how aesthetic and other effects are rendered; decline of visual egocentrism; ability to integrate forms	Ability to draw scenes, groups of objects; incipient accommodation of schemata to models; simple presentation of spatial relations
Visual realism	7 to 12	Concrete operations; reversibility; literalism in all art forms decline of spatial egocentrism; mapping activities	Written expression usually replaces drawing; language still concrete	Frequently a decline in psychological tasks; efficient scanning	Frequently a decline in drawing; heightened desire to draw realistically; ability to render certain effects, particularly unfocused conditions; spatial knowledge increases

TABLE 20.1 continued

Stage	Approximate Age	General Milestones	Language Milestones	Perceptual Competences	Drawing Capacities, Including Copying
Critical capacities	12 and up	Formal operational thought; preoccupation with personal identity	Language explores hypothetical possibilities; can use abstract symbolism	Smooth interaction of perceptual and performatory skills	Perspective, other more complex effects can be rendered; special tasks not necessary to elicit attention to rendering; interest in decorative effects; drawing may stop

articulated forms: a circle, a cross, rectangularly shaped forms, juxtaposed patches of color, and the like.

The third and fourth years of life are devoted to gaining precision in the production of graphic displays. Not only do children become able to make accurate circles and squares, but they are increasingly able to combine these forms, producing radials, Greek crosses, mandalas, and other combines, aggregates, and hybrid forms. Finally, some time in the third, fourth, or fifth year, the child produces the first forms that are unambiguously recognizable attempts to depict objects in the real world. This representational milestone is considered by many experts the decisive achievement in early drawing; having unlocked the key to graphic symbolization, children are now free to draw upon the arsenal of schemata at their disposal in order to depict the variegated objects, persons, and scenes with which they come into contact.

What happens after the achievement of graphic symbolization remains wrapped in controversy. From one point of view, the children enter a golden age, in which their works are seen as expressive, spontaneous, and enchantingly artistic. Other authorities, while conceding the charm of children's works, find less aesthetic significance in these activities, for they feel that children are now in control of their gifts. But there is general agreement that the child continues to draw unabatedly for a time, producing works of greater richness, interest, and complexity until at least the start of school.

Within our cultural context, drawing activity tends to decline after the child enters school. Not only do children fashion fewer pictures, but what they draw tends to become more stereotyped, less flavorful, more slavishly oriented toward the literal duplication of photographic reality. There is, at the same time, a heightened interest in the drawing conventions used by others, as well as frequent attempts to master such conventions in one's own drawings. Once again, experts do not concur on the causes of this shift in artistic involvement, nor do they know whether the oft-noted decline is a necessary aspect of development or simply an artifact of growth in a certain type of society. But for whatever reasons, artistry declines during the middle childhood years, revives only sometimes in adolescence, and is for many an activity chiefly engaged in during the early years. Even as we can find in all children their "first drawings," we observe in many preadolescents their "last drawings."

There is, to be sure, an end-state of artistic development: that mastery of pictorial schemes, that ready commerce between perceptual and performatory capacities which we sketched at the start of this chapter. It is this end-state that we must bear in mind as we now review at a less hurried pace the major stages of artistic development, focusing on the interplay between perceptual and productive capacities and peering at children's drawings through their own eyes. Yet, it must be said that our end-state is more nearly an idealized description: for only in the accomplished artist do perceptual and performatory capacities combine into a seamless repertoire.

THE RELATIONS BETWEEN PERCEPTION AND PRODUCTION: A STAGE DESCRIPTION

The Year Before Drawing: Age Zero to One

Perceptual capacities, already considerable during the newborn period, are developing at a remarkable rate in the months following birth. Indeed, by the end of the first year of life, infants are performing many of the discriminations made by adults: they readily recognize objects and individuals, they notice variations (discrepancies from schemata) in familiar entities, they honor the various perceptual constancies, and they even seem cognizant of certain properties of graphic depiction (Strauss, DeLoache, and Maynard 1977) (though they of course lack a means of capturing this knowledge, apart from their performance in contrived experimental situations).

The discrepancy between perception and production is never greater than in the first year of life. Indeed, this period provides evidence for what we have coined the *Vygotskian position*: perception and production can be seen initially as two separate developmental streams. Yet, it is clear that events in the first year of life are setting the stage for subsequent drawing performances. To begin with, as the child's motor schemata and circular reactions develop, there is increasing intercoordination between the "visual" and the "practical" space. Whereas at first, the child's actions are primed to go off with little support from, or monitoring by, the visual system, by the beginning of the second year, constant intercalation characterizes such activities as reaching, grasping, ambulating toward targets, and the like.

Other important milestones are also apparent. Children are forming strong attachment bonds to the most valued others in their worlds. These bonds will confer significance upon individuals, who will, in turn, become the modelers of drawing activity, the individuals whose actions are copied, and the audience toward which the scribbles of later stages will be proudly displayed. The challenge confronting one-year-olds is to direct their attention not only to objects but also to their potential consequences: unless they take note of what markers can do, they will never direct their perceptual discrimination—already well developed with reference to the productions of others—to their own fledgling productions.

Scribbling—the First Phase: One to One and One-Half

During the first year of life, markers may well be noticed or grasped, but they are not seen as a source of marks. Rather, like other manipulanda, they are touched, rolled, squeezed, placed into the mouth, and, if not tasty, thrown eventually upon the ground. But in the second year of life, the child becomes capable of incipient tool use. Like apes, who can use a stick to secure some wanted object, children become capable of using objects as means of acquiring some desired end: the marker soon becomes a primary instrument for securing pleasurable consequences.

Around the first birthday, the child will discover new pleasures in manipulating the marker. He or she will bang it against a surface, shake it back and forth, flail with it, and drag it across a wide surface. These initial actions reflect the child's favored gross and fine motor acts and the pleasures secured from certain tactile and auditory forms of feedback. Children at this stage begin to notice the creation of some marks when they hold the marker in a certain way, but they are not yet aware of what *causes* the marks: they simply find these marks an added source of visual stimulation and so, somewhat magically, are motivated to redouble their scribbling activity. When a model makes marks in front of them, they may well imitate the gross properties of the motor action (including sounds) without even looking at the products of this activity: at this point in development, such displays by others are often mimicked for their own sake. The integral relation between the child's (or the model's) motor activities and the resulting marks on the page is not yet appreciated.

Scribbling—the Second Phase: One and One-Half to Two

A critical change occurs at about the age of eighteen months, when the child discovers that the actual placing of marker to paper leaves a graphic trace. The crucial aspect of marking is now the mark, rather than the sounds or the sheer activity of earlier times. This discovery is signaled by a number of indices, as children at this stage will run to fetch a marker when given a blank sheet of paper, turn the marker upside down when it is not writing properly, squeeze with special delight when heavy or colored markers are given to them, and throw away a marker that has faded: these oft-cited phenomena have now been documented in formal studies, where children select the "working" marker from equivalent ones that make no mark or which leave only white marks (Gibson 1969).

Concomitant with the discovery of the capacity for marking are a number of other advances in the graphic sphere. The children at this stage strive increasingly to remain on the page (or surface) in front of them and to exude sufficient pressure to keep the marks coming. The disparate scribbles become increasingly controlled, and one can now discern scribbles that are circular from those which are angular. Marks made by someone else become a seductive target for the child, who frequently will make a mark near or upon them. By the same token, the child, now aware of the source, attends much more compulsively to the marking activity of others and tries to imitate the motoric aspects of this activity (though not yet, however, the marks themselves). Often, this interchange occurs in the context of simple social games, and the delight at "taking turns" seems as important a motivation as the pleasure at imitating zigs, zags, or various patterns of dots.

These advances occur at a time when the child is achieving re-markable progress in a number of other areas. The children's newly acquired sense of object permanence, as well as other aspects of developed sensory motor intelligence, no doubt contribute to their certainty that the marker will produce marks and their ability to fetch a marker in appropriate circumstances. The children's emerging lan-guage capacities help them to label the objects crucial to drawing and attract their attention to marks made by themselves and others. Perhaps most crucially, children at this age become engrossed with pictures—those in books, those in the environment, those on commer-cial products, and those on television. While previously some awareness of this pictorial realm could be demonstrated, sensitivity has now become rampant. Children at this stage gravitate to these depictions and name them at least as accurately and as enthusiastically as real objects, even when they apparently have had little exposure to the principles of depiction (Hochberg and Brooks 1962; Kennedy 1974). By the same token, the children are beginning to recognize visual forms, not only those associated with "real-world objects" but also those abstract forms featured in block building and in simple puzzles. We see, then, the challenge facing children on the eve of their second birthday: to convert the disparate scribbles of which they are now capable into forms of the sort that they are now able to recognize in their play in the world.

Basic Forms and Their Aggregation: Two to Three

During their third and fourth years of life, children host a dizzying variety of symbolic advances. Their language become fluent and articu-late; they begin to hum simple melodies; they are interested in stories and can relate to others what has happened to them; they enjoy gesturing and can dance somewhat by themselves. Nearly everything—

including the most arbitrary forms and figures—becomes invested with meaning. It is the time *par excellence* of symbolic play, where forms in the environment are treated as other objects—where blocks come to stand for people and where events and situations are replayed over and over again in the realms of play, dreams, and fantasy.

It is perhaps somewhat paradoxical, therefore, that true graphic symbolization has not yet occurred. In terms of Vygotsky's model, the two streams are still separate, though their eventual confluence can be readily foreseen. Perhaps the best evidence for this comes from the activity, universal among the children we have studied, termed *romancing*.

At this time, the children have come to produce discrete forms or enclosures in their drawings: circles, squares, crosses, and, by the end of the third year, various aggregations of these forms, including the vaunted (and much speculated about) mandala. To our eyes, and (as far as can be ascertained) to the child's intentions, these forms are not representational. The children seem driven by the desire to work out this graphic language on their own terms rather than by a need to depict the world about them. Yet, often without prompting, and even more often at the behest of prompting, the children will name these forms: they will call a circle "a man," "a dog," or "a tree"; they will call a cross "a man," "a sun," or "an elephant." The term *romance* seems apt here, because there is little apparent intention (and still little capacity) to achieve an actual correspondence between marks and referent; rather, the children seem almost to be "wishing" the graphic symbolization into being. Alternatively, the labeling may also represent a way of keeping track of marks or even of "giving" them to certain persons or objects.

At this age, then, children cannot generate the basic form or schema that will designate to others familiar objects and events. Yet, given some help, children can move a considerable way toward graphic depiction. Supplied with a half-completed form, for example, a human body, even two-year-old children have little difficulty in placing elements in the appropriate place: the legs will be drawn (or named) near the bottom of the form, the head at the top, the arms at the side, and the eyes (usually two of them) placed inside the head. The resulting marks can also be described with some accuracy: "a big leg," "a little leg," "a fat leg," "Daddy's leg"—here, in these aided exercises, the children seem to be moving toward accurate depiction and away from pure romancing. Of course, one must acknowledge the possibilities that the experimentally induced and the spontaneously produced marks seem equally accurate to the child or, alternatively, that they are both mere romancings. Yet, since our end-state entails the production of forms that can speak for themselves, the distinction between highly romanced forms and ones for which some rationale is grounded in the graphic depiction seems justified.

The child's copying also exhibits significant advances. Particularly if children have opportunities to watch adults, they are likely to fashion fairly accurate copies. Children readily copy their own forms and can sometimes even copy simple forms contrived outside their lines of vision by adults. More complex forms, like intricate scribbles or criss crosses, may prove possible if the child has the opportunity to observe the model in action.

Individual differences in drawing approach can now be discerned. Some children engage in a great deal of romancing, irrespective of whether it has any justification: they are likely to make a solitary mark and then relate a lengthy story. These *dramatists*, as we have called them, excel in storytelling and other "event-structuring" activities. They are readily differentiated from *patterners*—youngsters who engage with greater enthusiasm in block building and drawing activities and who are intrigued with the visual possibilities of forms, exploring them at great length, systematically varying their physical parameters, discovering a wealth of graphic possibilities, and engaging much less readily, perhaps only with prompting, in romancing activities.

Whether patterner or dramatist, whether endless visual experimenter or casual scribbler, neither group of children at this point has crossed the Rubicon into graphic symbolization proper. Their making activities still precede their matching—their perception of a pictorial world has not yet been brought into line with their activity in the realm of markings. The challenge facing them at this point, of course, is to relate their treasure trove of forms and aggregates to entities of the world with which they are already so familiar.

First Symbols—Tadpoles and Basic Objects: Three to Five

At some point during the preschool years, a decisive step occurs in the evolution of graphic symbolization. In a series of efforts that can be differentiated with some confidence from romancing, the child begins to combine forms so that they bear a visual resemblance to objects in the world or, perhaps more properly, to the way these objects have come to be depicted in a two-dimensional medium. In nearly all cases, the first physical object immortalized in graphic symbolization is the human being, and in nearly all cases, the form consists of a circle (or two) and two lines protruding from its base—hence, the phrases "the tadpole man" and *"l'homme tétard"* (and, for us, the tadpole stage).

Perhaps in itself, this event is not stunning. After all, the children have been making and combining forms for a number of months, or even years, and many of those have looked as much (or as little) like a tadpole as the one that they so anointed. Similarly, the children have also been naming—or romancing—numerous forms, and they have termed many of them *Mommy*, or *baby*, or *Susie*. What distinguishes this stage is the discreteness of the activity—the children make the marks, then stop, then name them; the order of events, whereby the children increasingly come to announce what they will do before they do it; the consistency, where the term *man* only comes to accompany tadpolelike forms; the ability to produce the form on request; and the undeniable resemblance between these basic forms and the objects they are intended to represent. Paradoxically, early "genuine" representations may receive more general names than the prior romancings; while a three-year-old romances "an igloo," the four-year-old announces "a house."

This milestone unleashes, for children at this stage, a universe of possibilities. Armed with their knowledge of the world and their arsenal of forms and aggregates, they now have the opportunity to depict most any entity in the world. Slowly but surely, they do this, arriving on their own (or with some help) at serviceable schemata for other human beings, animals, houses, items of clothing, and, indeed, any other element of importance in their world. For several years, these depictions are schematic: the same basic form comes to stand for all horses, all houses, and every man. Nor will individuating features and details be added unless they are prompted by others. Here we see at work a more general characteristic of the preschooler's cognitive structures—for their conceptual world seems to be organized around basic objects or prototypes, kinds of generalized or modal examples that prove serviceable in representing (or standing for) a range of members of the category (compare Rosch et al. 1976). Yet, it must be said that these children are far more capable of discriminations in their visual perceptions: while producing a tiny set of schemata to represent houses, horses, and human beings, they can make impressively fine discriminations among exemplars of these categories encountered in real or pictorial worlds.

Why this disjunction between what these children can perceive and what they can capture in their own drawings? Simply to claim a continuing decalage between perceiving and producing does not resolve this question. Indeed, under closer scrutiny, a more complex picture arises. Consider, for instance, the attempts by investigators like Olson (1970) and Golomb (1973, 1974) to define the child's knowledge of such basic entities as the human figure or the diagonal. These investigators cannot specify a point in the early years of life where the child arrives at the concept of a human figure. Indeed, the reverse turns out to be the case. If you provide children with a form and ask them simply to point out features (or, if the form is unfinished, to add the missing features), one finds by the third year of life evidence for considerable knowledge of the human figure. If, on the other hand, one requires children to draw from scratch, offering no help, the figure demonstrates significantly less knowledge. This latter finding cannot, however, be interpreted as representing the child's actual understanding, for if the features are dictated or if a copy is provided, the child will suddenly exhibit far greater mastery of the visual concept in question. Clearly, one's knowledge of visual configurations is arrayed on a sliding continuum—how much is evoked will depend on the nature of the task.

Nor can we assume that the preschool child, however skilled at recognizing birds, makes of car, or strangers (Lorenz 1961), is perceiving the world the way that we are. A myriad of experimental investigations (compare Braine 1972; Elkind, Koegler, and Go 1964; Gollin 1960; Kagan 1965; Mackworth and Bruner 1970; Pick and Pick 1970; Vurpillot 1976) document striking deviations in their performance. Preschool children scan figures differently; they are much more rigid and idiosyncratic in their processing; they fail to note important details; they are insensitive to incongruous figures; they cannot integrate parts or complete incomplete figures; they confuse left with right and diagonals in one orientation from those in another orientation; and they are (so far as we can tell) completely insensitive to aesthetic features, like style and composition. They excel at single-object recognition—the kind of picture naming stimulated by Western picture books. Thus, the gulf between perception and production—while it does exist—should not be overestimated. Indeed, as we shall see, once children learn to examine pictures in terms of their manner of depiction, they may show a surprising capacity to capture this knowledge in their own visual depictions.

In one sense, the child's symbolic capacities have come together. Complementing their ability to tell a story, sing a song, or enjoy picture reading, they are now capable of graphic representation in the plastic media: they can draw, sculpt, or model recognizable forms; they can label these appropriately; they can even engage in clever metaphoric renamings, as when they note an expressive physiognomic similarity between some lines they have sketched and some object or situation in the world (Winner 1978). But as we have stressed, these capacities are still rather limited and tied to specific instances: the children draw primarily single objects, each in its own space, with no consideration of dimensional, spatial, or individualizing features.

The Flowering of Expressivity: Five to Seven

What is most striking about the artistic products of children—at least within our culture—is their charming expressiveness. Drawings of the kindergarten or first grade child are vibrantly alive: they offer an exciting mixture of colors and shapes; they convey a range of moods (though skewed toward the positive end of the affective spectrum); and they depict events, situations, and stories of significance to the child, often revealing in the process what prompted the child to make the drawing. There is a special and lovely balance: each object has its place, there is no crowding, and yet a sense of unity and harmony often pervades the production. This is the age where children can make literally hundreds of drawings of a theme that excites them, be it a yellow submarine, Cinderella, Mickey Mouse, *Star Wars*, a trip they have taken, or a friend they have made. Each of these drawings will explore a somewhat different aspect of the experience; taken together, they constitute a powerful brief on the meaning of this experience for the child. Indeed, it is during this period—which we have elsewhere viewed as an "artistic stage"—that graphic (and other artistic) media may well offer the child a more effective means of expression than any other (Gardner 1973; Wolf and Gardner in press b).

By this age, children are able to copy with some fidelity what other individuals have drawn; they no longer need to observe the model at work. By the same token, they already will display an incipient interest in ways to achieve certain effects, for example, how to draw a moving horse or one object hidden behind the other. Yet what remains striking is the extent to which the children continue to be propelled by personal developmental considerations. Though they can be shaped or trained, they do not seem to want (or need) such direction. So they will arrive (along with millions of children elsewhere) upon their own solutions to graphic problems, designing X-ray (see through) figures, showing all four sides of an object, combining profiles and front-face views, and the like (compare Arnheim 1974; Kosslyn, Heldmeyer, and Locklear 1977). These children are still working on their own to create a graphic language that expresses what they want to express, without worrying too much about the extent to which this language reflects culturally approved standards.

This tendency was well illustrated in an interchange with my seven-year-old daughter. Pressed on whether people's arms really protrude outward from the middle of the torso, she conceded that they did not and drew a more accurate version, with arms extended from the shoulders. Then she said, "But that's the way I want to do it," and blithely reverted to the more symmetrical version she had previously favored.

By now, fairly pronounced differences are apparent in children's approaches to, and competence in, visual depiction. (See Figures 20.1 and 20.2.) Some children, often those earlier labeled *dramatists*, do not draw very much; they still allow their narration to carry the day and

Figure 20.1   Drawing by a three-and-one-half-year-old patterner. The child made the drawing without comment but with rapt attention to each detail. As he connected the dots, he counted them.

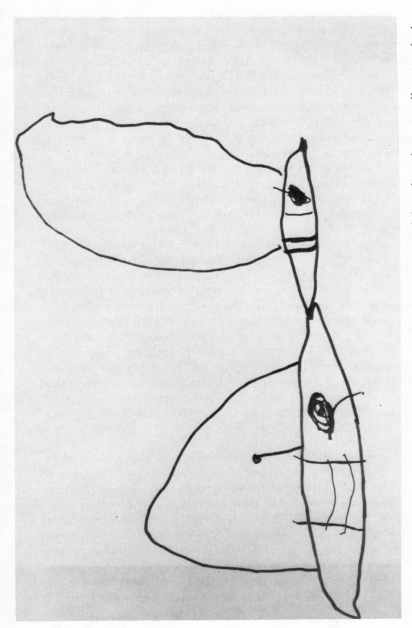

Figure 20.2   Drawing by a three-and-one-half-year-old dramatist. As he proceeded, graphic and narrative effects were freely combined: "Once upon a time, there was a little fish" (draws oblong on the right), "and he had a mommy fish" (draws larger oblong shape on the left). "Once the little fish went swimming away" (draws loop above the little fish). "The mommy chased after him" (draws the loop above the larger fish). "'Bad, bad, you,' she said. 'I'm going to have to put a gate on .'" (draws the stripes on top of the little fish). "I will have one too" (adds stripes on the larger shape), "and I want eyes to see you" (adds eyes on both the fish).

remain tied to a small family of schematic forms. For these children, the depicted object still seems to adhere to its basic schematic form. Other youngsters, often those we have termed *patterners*, are much more involved in the rules, possibilities, and limitations of graphic depiction; invest far more time and energy in the exploration of graphic options; do not depend on narration; and exhibit a far greater variation in their schemata. By the age of five or six, these children are able to take the features of a given model into account: the horse, house, or person drawn will vary, depending upon the physical properties of the model, and they will prove quite resourceful in adapting their still limited resources into a recognizable rendition of the model.

It may be that for some youngsters, the basic schemata function like an alphabet: they know one proper way to draw a person and rely upon it canonically, but they seem unaware that lines can be altered in specific ways to capture any kind of contour—in their efforts, they are simply juxtaposing fixed forms. Other children have apparently made a crucial transition where in addition to invoking frozen schemata, they can actually vary lines in order to capture more faithfully the form of a given object. This difference is well illustrated in the attempts made by two four-year-olds to copy a toy car. (Compare Figures 20.3 and 20.4). One child made a genuine effort to follow the boundary and produced a copy bearing some resemblance to the contours of the model, whereas the second child simply drew a graphic equivalent of each of the parts, in the order in which she listed them, without capturing their spatial interrelations or the overall shape of the model. It is not clear whether the first youngster is at a later stage of development or whether the two youngsters are simply following different routes to graphic maturity. In any case, achieving some control over the resource of line is a milestone through which all children must pass in their graphic evolution.

A second issue at this stage concerns the artistic expressiveness in the child's work. While it is now fashionable to enthuse—as we have—about the artfulness of children's drawings, it remains an open question whether children themselves are in control of this gift. An analogy may be helpful here (compare Gardner, et al. 1978). It has often been reported that youngsters produce a high incidence of figurative language—effective similes and metaphors—in the years preceding school. Whether one chooses to call these *true metaphors* will probably depend on whether the children have any intention to produce these literary instances; whether they have any consciousness (and enjoyment) of the fact that he has done so; and whether they can place themselves into another person's perspective and anticipate that individual's reactions (compare Korzenik 1972; Krauss and Glucksberg 1969).

Figure 20.3   Effort by a four-year-old to copy a toy car. This child made a concerted attempt to capture the model's characteristic contours and to locate features in a visually coherent way.

Figure 20.4   Effort by another four-year-old to copy a toy car. This child produced a "collection" of prominent features—sides, wheels, and circular window—which are grouped together. The child lists the essential features of the car without attempting to organize them in a unified view.

Visual Realism: Seven to Twelve

At this point, our sketch must confront a fundamental issue in the development of drawing. We have arrived at an age where differences among children become overwhelming. Some continue and even accentuate their drawing activities; many others—certainly a majority in our society—draw much less, and perhaps cease altogether, preferring to express themselves through linguistic (including writing) channels. Among those who continue to draw, a number of motives may be operating: some want primarily to illustrate their stories; others become preoccupied with maps, diagrams, and other visual records; still others like to experiment with written scripts; and of course, some are interested in more purely aesthetic or expressive purposes. Unfortunately, there are not enough data (nor sufficient space) to describe each of these optional courses—and their resulting end-states. And so, even at the acknowledged risk of ignoring important differences, we will continue to generalize about the development of drawing.

School-age children differ fundamentally from the youngsters who produced mandalas, tadpoles, and expressive canvases. They are much more interested in the world of facts; they are obsessed with accuracy; they like things to be just what they appear to be, no more, no less; they even want words to remain close to their dictionary meanings and so reject metaphor, fairy tales, and other fantasies (though perhaps not science fiction). Their egocentrism has declined to the extent that they become very interested in how things look to other persons and what others think of their own efforts. Capable of "concrete operations," they are able to reverse states—to take things from what they were to what they will become and back again, to observe two facets of a situation at the same time, and to make systematic comparisons, inventories, and classifications.

These events have clear ripples within the realm of children's drawings. No longer intent on following their own artistic promptings, children at this age become intent on drawing objects and scenes accurately. They strive for realism, in terms of either photographic resemblances or of conventions embraced by their culture: they prefer realistic works by others and often scorn those that deviate significantly from representationality. They want to know how to achieve graphic effects like motions, how to render things in perspective, how to capture spatial relationships accurately, and how to achieve convincing likenesses of people. Far from ignoring models and lessons, they actively seek them, and usually prove to be quick learners, particularly in areas where they have strong interest. They are, in other words, intent on becoming technical craftsmen—in capturing on the canvas everything that they can see in the real world, in wedding finally their perceptions to their productions.

What of their more purely artistic development? To what extent are children aware of artistic facets—such as style, composition, harmony, color blending, tone, balance, and the like—and how do they feel about including these elements, consciously and intentionally, in their own drawings? To state the question so baldly is to suggest a degree of knowledge that does not exist and perhaps is only confronted explicitly by certain aestheticians (and by certain artists!). Yet, on the more general issue of aesthetic awareness among schoolchildren, we can offer a few impressions.

At the age of eight, nine, or ten, most children become quite interested in how effects are rendered in drawings. They will examine a drawing in a book to see how shadowing and texturing are achieved or how machines or landscapes are drawn; they then will strive on their own (or with help) to duplicate this effect. At least in this sense, they are attuned to problems (and solutions) of rendition. Still, in most cases, children remain unaware of those aspects of canvases that we might consider aesthetic. They do not on their own note and comment upon style, composition, expressiveness, and the like.

At this point, however, intervention by others can make a difference. Children may well notice (without being particularly aware that they are noticing) the graphic elements on which these aesthetic effects depend. So, with a reasonably brief amount of tutelage, the average ten-year-old can become sensitive to features like style, expressiveness, and composition (compare Carothers 1978; Gardner 1972a, 1972b; Silverman, Winner, and Gardner 1975). Moreover, as can be seen in Figure 20.5B, they can also enter with some accuracy into the spirit of different styles. The sensitivity displayed will depend not only on individual differences but also on the particular contrasts introduced and instructions offered: stylistic differences between Renoir and Rembrandt are sufficiently pronounced to make such discriminations easy, but more challenging discriminations naturally result in apparently lower aesthetic awareness. Yet, accumulating evidence suggests that an interest in rendering—the capacity to view a drawing as an achievement in the graphic medium—is readily elicited in children of this age. Moreover, unless the particular effects make excessive technical demands upon the children, they will prove able to capture and present these effects in their own drawings (Carothers 1978; Friedman and Stevenson 1975; Ives 1978). Perceiving and producing are now operating in close synchrony with one another.

Critical Capacities: 12 and Up

For those children who are still drawing with some regularity and some enthusiasm, another crucial developmental milestone occurs at the beginning of adolescence. Concomitant with the advent of formal

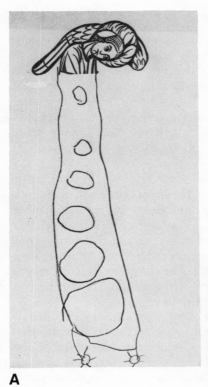

A

B

Figure 20.5 (A) Attempt by a preschooler to complete a stylized angel. Note schemas typically used by this child and other children. (B) Attempt by a primary school child to complete the same stylized angel. Note the matching of dimensions of head and body, attention to postural cues, continuation of quality and uses of line.

mental operations, children experience a decisive increase in their own critical powers: in their ability to anticipate (and monitor) all the possibilities in a work of art, to effect comparisons across a wide range of examples, and to capture in verbal propositions the key aspects of their understanding. This is a dizzying set of capacities, one that may indeed sometimes overwhelm: for if, in considering what others (including peers) can do, one's own works prove too deficient, the possibility arises that one will cease artistic production altogether.

There is also great opportunity. Having survived the press for literally accurate depictions, the adolescent can now try out a range of styles, including ones that minimize representational fidelity. Other pivotal changes in the emotional and affective realm offer to the youth new areas for expression, including ones that depart dramatically from the depiction of mundane events and allow the exploration of a range of emotions and psychological states. Indeed, for children with gifts—and in our society, only such children continue publicly to draw—the years of adolescence offer the opportunity to wed their technical skills— which have already developed significantly—to those personal and expressive facets that have to some extent been muted since the flowering of the preschool years.

CONCLUDING REMARKS

Throughout our survey of a child's artistic development, we have observed the important, and often determining, role of perceptual capacities. In infancy, the child's coming to know the world of persons and objects serves as a necessary prerequisite for handling markers, for noting their effects, and for observing those valued individuals who will introduce the child to the graphic world. By the second year of life, children's perceptual activities are already guiding their initial efforts at marking; and this intercalation of what one sees and what one does will continue throughout their graphic history.

For awhile, nonetheless, drawing seems to lag behind perception; even as children are already appreciating visual depictions of some complexity, their marking is restricted to nonrepresentational scribbles, forms, and aggregates. Yet, the impulse to pictorialism can be observed in children's romancing, in their capacity to place features in the proper locus, and, especially in the case of patterners, in the systematic ways in which the possibilities of lines and forms are explored.

Perceptual and productive capacities come together decisively during the initial phases of graphic symbolism, where the child begins to depict intentionally the objects of the world. For awhile, this depiction is still rigid, as children at this stage cannot yet accommodate their schemata to the specifics of a model. But increasingly, attention to the model can result in a production that captures salient features of the specific entity being portrayed.

Bringing what one can see and what one can draw into close alignment becomes the raison d'être of drawing in the early school years. The children's full graphic energies are marshaled as they exploit resources of line, color, and shading in order to produce an accurate rendition of what they see. If anything, perception and production at this point become too closely yoked: so intent are the children on visual fidelity that they may ignore the dictates of their own personal emotional life and spurn the expressiveness possible through deviations from strict representationality. At the same time, however, the children are learning to look in a different manner at canvases, to see not only the objects depicted but how they have been depicted and how such aesthetic effects as balance or composition are achieved. And, with surprising efficiency, many children can incorporate these insights about rendition into their own canvases. They are on the verge of attaining the artist's capacity to see a painting in terms of its production—how it was made, how it might be altered, why it works the way it does—and to act on the basis of this knowledge.

The development of sufficient production powers, of a gifted repertoire of "graphic moves," gains particular importance because of the advent at the time of adolescence of powerful critical capacities. So overwhelming can the critical perception of adolescents become that they may well come to despise their own efforts, to stop them altogether, and, for the first time, to become but passive participants in graphic activity. This risk—greater possibly in our culture than in others—may stand as a powerful signal of the importance of keeping in balance throughout the course of development one's perceptual and productive capacities. An excessive reliance on production, at the expense of sensitive monitoring and correcting, can result in works that are autistic and devoid of meaning for others. By the same token, excessive reliance on one's perceptual capacities may thwart the development and expression of productive skills, culminating in individuals who see what others have done but remain unable themselves to capture in the graphic realm those deep emotions and understandings that constitute the justification of both child art and great art.

REFERENCES

Arnheim, R. *Art and Visual Perception: A Psychology of the Creative Eye . . . the New Version*. Berkeley: University of California Press, 1974.

Braine, L. G. "A Developmental Analysis of the Effect of Stimulus Orientation on Recognition." *American Journal of Psychology* 85 (1972): 157–88.

Carothers, T. "The Emergence of Aesthetic Production and Perception in Children." Undergraduate thesis, Harvard University, 1978.

Elkind, D.; Koegler, R. R.; and Go, E. "Studies in Perceptual Development;" pt. 2, "Part—Whole Perception." *Child Development* 35 (1964): 81-90.

Friedman, S. L., and Stevenson, M. B. "Developmental Changes in the Understanding of Implied Motion in Two-Dimensional Pictures." *Child Development* 46 (1975): 773-78.

Gardner, H. "Style Sensitivity in Children." *Human Development* 15 (1972a): 325-38.

——. "The Development of Sensitivity to Figural and Stylistic Aspects of Paintings." *British Journal of Psychology* 63 (1972b): 605-15.

——. *The Arts and Human Development*. New York: Wiley, 1973.

——. "The Acquisition of First Symbol Systems." *Studies in the Anthropology of Visual Communication* 3 (1976a): 22-37.

——. "Promising Paths to Knowledge." *Journal of Aesthetic Education* 10 (1976b): 201-7.

Gardner, H., et al., "The Development of Figurative Language." In *Children's Language*, edited by K. Nelson. New York: Gardner Press, 1978.

Gibson, E. J. *Principles of Perceptual Learning and Development*. New York: Appleton-Century-Crofts, 1969.

Gollin, E. S. "Developmental Studies of Visual Recognition of Incomplete Objects." *Perceptual and Motor Skills"* (1960): 289-98.

Golomb, C. "Children's Representation of the Human Figure: The Effects of Models, Media, and Instruction." *Genetic Psychology Monographs* 87 (1973): 197-251.

——. *Young Children's Sculpture and Drawing: A Study in Representational Development*. Cambridge, Mass.: Harvard University Press, 1974.

Gombrich, E. H. "Meditations on a Hobby Horse." In *Aspects of Form*, edited by L. L. White, 209-22. Bloomington, Ind.: Midland Books, 1961.

Goodnow, J. *Children's Drawings*. Cambridge, Mass.: Harvard University Press, 1977.

Hochberg, J., and Brooks, V. "Pictorial Recognition as an Unlearned Ability: A Study of One Child's Performance." *American Journal of Psychology* 75 (1962): 624-28.

Ives, S. W. Unpublished research. Harvard University, 1978.

Kagan, J. "Impulsive and Reflective Children: Significance of Conceptual Tempo." in *Learning and the Educational Process*, edited by J. Krumboltz. Chicago: Rand McNally, 1965.

Kellogg, R. *Analyzing Children's Art*. Palo Alto, Calif.: National Press Books, 1969.

Kennedy, J. M. *A Psychology of Picture Perception*. San Francisco: Jossey–Bass, 1974.

Korzenik, D. "Children's Drawings: Changes in Representation between the Ages of Five and Seven." Ph.D dissertation, Harvard University, 1972.

Kosslyn, S. M.; Heldmeyer, K. H.; and Locklear, E. P. "Children's Drawings as Data about Internal Representations." *Journal of Experimental Child Psychology* 23 (1977): 191–211.

Krauss, R. M., and Glucksberg, S. "The Development of Communication: Competence as a Function of Age." *Child Development* (1969): 255–66.

Lorenz, K. "The Rose of Gestalt Perception in Animal and Human Behavior." In *Aspects of Form*, edited by L. L. Whyte, pp. 157–78. Bloomington, Ind.: Midland Books, 1961.

Lowenfeld, V. *Creative and Mental Growth*. New York: Macmillan, 1947.

Luquet, G. H. *Les Dessins d'un enfant*. Paris: Alcan, 1917.

Maccoby, E., and Hagen, J. W. "Effect of Distortion upon Central vs. Incidental Recall: Developmental Trends." *Journal of Experimental Child Psychology* 2 (1965): 280–89.

Mackworth, N. H., and Bruner, J. S. "How Adults and Children Search and Recognize Pictures." *Human Development* 13 (1970): 149–77.

Olson, D. *Cognitive Development*. New York: Academic Press, 1970.

Pick, H. L., and Pick, A. "Sensory and Perceptual Development." In *Carmichael's Manual of Child Psychology*, edited by P. H. Mussen, Vol. 1., pp. 773–847. New York: Wiley, 1970.

Rosch, E., et al. "Basic Objects in Natural Categories." *Cognitive Psychology* 8 (1976): 382–439.

Shotwell, J.; Wolf, D.; and Gardner, H. "Styles of Achievement in Early Symbol Use." Paper presented at Symposium on Fundamentals of Symbolism, July 1977, Burg Wartenstein, Austria. In press.

Silverman, J.; Winner, E.; and Gardner, H. "On Going Beyond the Literal: The Development of Sensitivity to Artistic Symbols." *Semiotica* 18 (1976): 291–312.

Strauss, M. S.; DeLoache, J. S.; and Maynard, J. "Infants' Recognition of Pictorial Representations of Real Objects." Paper presented to Society for Research in Child Development, March 1977, New Orleans.

Vurpillot, E. *The Visual World of the Child*. New York: Basic Books, 1976.

Vygotsky, L. *Thought and Language*. Cambridge, Mass.: MIT Press, 1962.

Winner, E. "New Names for Old Things: The Emergence of Metaphoric Language." Paper presented at Stanford University Child Language Research Forum, Stanford, Calif., April 1978.

Wolf, D., and Gardner, H. "Style and Sequence in Symbolic Play." In *Early Symbolization*, edited by M. Franklin and N. Smith. Hillsdale, N.J.: Erlbaum Associates, in press a.

———. "Beyond Playing or Polishing: The Development of Artistry." In *Arts Exemplars Models*, edited by J. Hausman. In press b.

Name Index

Subject Index

texture gradient: 58, 105, 144, 232
themes: 74, 76–77
thinking: abstract, f; constraint of, f; language and, f; perceiving and, f; perceptual bases, f; productive, f; visual, f
three-dimensional form: 207, 209; in scene, 25
three-dimensional world represented in two-dimensional image: 273; as two-dimensional picture, 281
three dimensionality as constructive visual concept: 274
transparency of a medium: 14, 15
trompe l'oeil painting: 17, 19, 22–24, 32, 38–39, 106, 289; architectural, 24; artists, 58; vs. optical equivalence, 18;
tunnel vision compensation: 95
two-dimensional form: depiction by children, 372; reality of, 88, 97; vs. three-dimensional components of a painting, 201, 203, 209; vs. three-dimensional, problem of volume, 207–208
two-dimensional image: 273
two-dimensional representation: 274; of three-dimensional forms, 275
two-dimensional object intended to mimic three-dimensional object: 289

unconscious: f
unconscious inferences: 2, 29
universal beauty and aesthetic reality: 299

value: distinction between goodness and preference, 301; and perceptual process, 307
value judgments of art: basis of, 301; validity of, 301; disagreement with, 302, 305, 308–09, 311; and perceptual sampling, 306; training and effects on aesthetic judgment, 308
value-laden qualities: perception of, 303
vanishing point: 89, 91; scene with two vanishing points, 112
variant features (properties): 59–60;

199–200, 203–05; vs. invariant properties of objects and scenes, 201, 203
vectors: 68; path of eye, 69, 77
veridical painting: 23
veridicality in art: (see also, representation and perception); 70, 274
View of the Westerkerk in Amsterdam (van der Heyden): 113
viewing act and painting act: 45
viewing device for perspective: 112
viewing distance and pictures: 35–36
viewing place: 65–66
vision: f, 50; as artifact, 272, 274; central, 29; peripheral, 29–30, 33–34, 38–39; and Impressionism, 35, 38; parafoveal viewing, 30, 33; technical facts, 31; scientific approach, 61, 72; cone of, 62; characteristics of, 69; normative, 70; computer-simulated, 101; as cultural and historical product of making pictures, 272; historical theory, 273, 275
visual: ability, f; aid, f; acuity, 34; angle, 208–09; concept, 59–198; content, 69; cues, 65; culture, 72; dynamics, 69; field, 31; information, 21; metaphor, 92; organization, f; phenomena, 58; pigments, 136; science and color theory, 22; space, 154; truth, 197
visual cliff experiments: 144, 149
visual concepts and properties of the visual world: 279
visual distortion: causes of, 236–241
visual phenomena and the artist: 342
visual properties in pictures and representations: 277
visual realism as a stage of children's drawing: 380–81
visual representation: criterion of veridicality as a product of social and historical norms, 272
visual re-presentation: variability of modes, 280
visual science: 135–137, 139, 144; and modern art, 134, 162

About the Editors
and Contributors

Nodine, Calvin F., *Psychologist*, is Professor of Psychology and Educational Psychology at Temple University. He is interested in the relationship between perception and visual representation in art, as well as image-processing systems in medicine. His interest in art has led to visual search studies, using eye movements, of how people find NINAs in Al Hirschfeld's drawings. This work is related to more applied questions in radiology concerned with identifying perceptual causes of error in diagnostic interpretation. He is currently working on how pictorial composition (notably that of Cézanne) influences the way people look at paintings. He has published extensively in the field of experimental psychology.

Fisher, Dennis F., *Psychologist*, is a researcher at the Behavioral Research Directorate of the U.S. Army Human Engineering Laboratory. His interests are in the area of visual perception with emphasis on information extraction characteristics of readers of text and viewers of pictures. Particular emphasis is placed on eye movement characteristics in determining salient cues and features as they pertain to development and acquisition skills. He is a frequent contributor of articles and chapters on these topics and coeditor of *Eye Movements and Higher Psychological Functions* (Hillsdale, NJ: Lawrence Erlbaum Associates, 1978) with J. W. Senders and R. A. Monty.

Arnheim, Rudolf, *Psychologist*, is Professor Emeritus of the Psychology of Art, Harvard University. He now lives in Ann Arbor, Michigan. It is a rarity to attribute a text as standard, but that is what *Art and Visual Perception* (Berkeley and Los Angeles: University of California Press, 1954 & 1974) has become. No less exciting are *Toward a Psychology of Art: Collected Essays* (Berkeley: University of California Press, 1966) and *Visual Thinking* (Berkeley: University of California Press, 1969), the basis of the foreword to this volume. His most recent book is *The Dynamics of Architectural Form* (Berkeley: University of California Press 1977) He has published other books on film, radio, Picasso, and natural order. His primary interests are seeing, the psychology of art, art education, and the creative process.

Boretz, Naomi, *Artist*, has exhibited her paintings and drawings in museums and galleries in the United States and England and is represented in many private and public collections. She has taught in university art departments and delivered public lectures on her work, including one from BBC Radio in 1972. She has also written critical and analytical articles, most recently for *Leonardo*. She has received awards for her work and was a resident Fellow of the Virginia Center for Creative Arts (1973, 1975) and the Ossabaw Foundation (1975). Since 1974 she has devoted herself almost exclusively to works on paper and drawings and painting in watercolor and mixed media.

Danto, Arthur C., *Philosopher,* is Johnsonian Professor of Philosphy at Columbia University. He has written books on Nietzsche and on Sartre, but his main literary achievement is three volumes: *Analytical Philosophy of History, Analytical Philosophy of Knowledge,* and *Analytical Philosophy of Action,* published in 1965, 1968, and 1973 by Cambridge University Press. He is currently working on a fourth volume in that work, *Analytical Philosophy of Art,* and, in general, on the concept of representation.

Day, Larry, *Artist,* is an exhibiting artist and Professor of Painting and Drawing at Philadelphia College of Art. He has exhibited widely and is represented in many private and public collections, including the Philadelphia Museum of Art. He was, until 1960-61, a nonfigurative painter. Since that time he has been involved in representational painting, but does not consider himself a "new realist." He has written numerous articles and catalog forewords, his most recent being a foreword for a catalog of American figure drawings shown in Australia.

Finkelstein, Louis, *Artist,* is Professor of Art, Queens College, City University of New York. He has shown his work at many one-man exhibits in New York and Rome and participated in numerous group exhibits in the United States and abroad. He contributes frequently to art publications such as *Art News* and *Magazine of Art* and is presently working on a book *Painting, Perception and the Mind.* His particular interest is in the role of perception in art. He has his work represented in the Philadelphia Museum of Art, Yale University Museum, and the Metropolitan Museum of Art.

Gardner, Howard, *Psychologist,* is codirector of Project Zero, Harvard University and staff member of the Veterans Administration Hospital, Boston. He has published four books: *The Quest for Mind: Jean Piaget, Claude Levi-Strauss and the Structuralist Movement* (New York: Knopf, 1973), *The Arts and Human Development* (New York: Wiley, 1973), *The Shattered Mind* (New York: Knopf, 1975), and *Developmental Psychology: An Introduction* (Boston: Little Brown, 1978), as well as numerous articles in psychological journals concerned with development, vision, aesthetics, symbolic competence, and neuropsychology. His interests in the field of art are: development of the creative process, aesthetics, aphasia.

Gregory, Richard L., *Psychologist,* is Professor of Neuropsychology and Director of Brain and Perception Laboratory, Department of Anatomy, University of Bristol, England. His interests vary widely—from the study of blindness, human engineering, and applied psychology to basic perceptual processes and art. He is presently editor of the journal, *Perception,* and has published numerous journal articles, book chapters, and books. He is author of *Eye and Brain* (New York: McGraw Hill, 1966, 1972) and *The Intelligent Eye* (New York: McGraw Hill, 1970) and coauthor of *Illusion in Nature and Art* (New York: Scribner, 1974) with Sir Ernst Gombrich.

Haber, Ralph Norman, *Psychologist,* is Professor of Psychology and Visual Science at the University of Rochester. He has contributed numerous articles to technical journals on topics related to his interests in visual perception as it applies to imagery, eye movements, memory, reading, and pictorial and textual processing capabilities. Among his books are *The Psychology of Visual Perception* (New York: Holt, Rinehart and Winston, 1973) with M. Hershenson; *Contemporary Theory and Research in Visual Perception* (New York: Holt, Rinehart and Winston, 1968); and *Information Processing Approaches to Visual Perception* (New York: Holt, Rinehart and Winston, 1969).

Hagen, Margaret A., *Psychologist,* is Assistant Professor of Psychology at Boston University. She describes herself as a developmental psychologist, a perceptionist, and a Gibsonian (after James J. Gibson). She has published extensively in psychological journals and is editing a volume entitled *What, Then, Are Pictures? The Psychology of Representational Art* (New York: Academic Press, in press). Her primary interest is children's ability to pick-up information in pictures and differentiate them from real scenes.

Hochberg, Julian, *Psychologist,* is Professor of Psychology at Columbia University. His interests are in perception as it applies to art, cinema, reading, and eye movements. He has contributed numerous articles and chapters like those found in *The Handbook of Perception* (E. C. Carterette and N. Friedman, Eds., New York: Academic Press, var.) and *Experimental Psychology* (J. W. Kling and L. A. Riggs, Eds., New York: Holt, Rinehart and Winston, 1971). He is author of *Perception* (Englewood Cliffs, NJ: Prentice Hall, 1968, 1978) and coauthor of *Art, Perception, and Reality* (Baltimore: Johns Hopkins University Press, 1972) with Sir Ernst Gombrich and Max Black.

Irwin, Robert, *Artist,* is an exhibiting artist living in Los Angeles. He has given numerous shows and exhibits throughout the United States and abroad. His works are represented in many museums, including the Philadelphia Museum of Art. His interest is in perception, and his painting has evolved from the more characteristic modernist style to a conceptualization that painting must transcend the traditional bounds of the two dimensional canvas and be part of the whole environment. This concept led to a unique exhibit at the Whitney Museum of Art in 1977.

Kennedy, John M., *Psychologist,* is a Professor of Psychology at Scarborough College, University of Toronto. He is the author of *The Psychology of Picture Perception* (San Francisco: Jossey Bass, 1974). His interest in perception includes illustrations for the blind, active-passive distinction, cross-cultural factors in the perception of pictures, prosthesis for the senses, and the development of perspectives of the kinds of brightness paradoxes discussed in chapter 9 of this book.

Kolers, Paul A. *Psychologist,* is Professor of Psychology at the University of Toronto. He has authored numerous technical articles in perception and cognition, has written *Aspects of Motion Perception* (New York: Pergamon Press, 1972) and coedited *Recognizing Patterns* (Cambridge, Mass.: MIT Press, 1968) with Murray Eden and *Processing of Visual Language* (New York: Plenum, 1979) with Merold Wrolstadt, Anthony Cohen, and Herman Bouma. His recent work is concerned with understanding and reading text and pictures.

Perkins, David N. *Psychologist,* is codirector of Project Zero at Harvard University. He has special interest in the creative process, critical abilities, errors in thinking, visual perception, and rhythmic capabilities. He is coeditor with Barbara Leondar of *The Arts and Cognition* (Baltimore: Johns Hopkins, 1977). He has published extensively in psychology, aesthetic, and communication journals.

Pickford, R. W., *Psychologist,* has been retired since 1978, after having spent a long and illustrious career in the Department of Psychology, Glasgow University. He has published numerous articles on experimental, social, and clinical psychology topics, as well as eight books, among which *Human Senses and Perception* (Toronto: University of Toronto Press, 1964) with G. W. Wyburn and R. J. Hirst, and *Psychology and Visual Aesthetics* (New York: Crane Russak Co., 1972) are most recent. In addition to numerous honors and society presidencies, he was a founder of the International Society for Experimental Aesthetics.

Smythe, William E., *Psychologist,* is a doctoral student in psychology at the University of Toronto. His interest is in the area of perception, particularly in understanding pictures and text.

Tormey, Alan, *Philosopher,* is Professor of Philosophy at the University of Maryland, Baltimore County. He serves as an editor of the *Journal of Aesthetics and Art Criticism.* He has authored many book chapters and articles on philosophical psychology and the philosophy of art, and he has published *The Concept of Expression* (Princeton University Press, 1971). He feels his interest in art and aesthetics is due in part to an early, turbulent career as a professional musician.

Tormey, Judith Farr, *Philosopher,* is Assistant Professor of Philosophy, Temple University, and a member of the Institute of Aesthetics. She has contributed many articles and chapters to volumes and journals in line with her major interests in art and ethics.

Vitz, Paul C., *Psychologist,* is Associate Professor of Psychology at New York University. He has published numerous articles related to psychology and art. His chapter in this book is taken from portions of a book-length manuscript coauthored with Arnold Glimcher, *Modern Art and Modern Science: The Parallel Analysis of Vision.* He is on the editorial board of *Scientific Aesthetics—Science de'l Art.*

Ward, John L., *Art Historian/Artist,* is an Associate Professor of Art at the University of Florida and is an exhibiting painter. He has recently completed his doctorate, which is concerned with pictorial space and picture perception, under the tutelage of Margaret Hagen, Marx Wartofsky, and Samuel Edgerton. He has published in the areas of Flemish Painting, the perception of pictorial space, and photographic criticism.

Wartofsky, Marx W., *Philosopher,* is a Professor of Philosophy at Boston University. His interests are in the areas of aesthetics, perception, representation, and understanding pictures, with particular emphasis on historical epistomology. He is a frequent contributor of articles and chapters and is coeditor of a series *Boston Studies in the Philosophy of Science* (Boston: Reidel, var.) with Robert S. Cohen, and editor of the journal *Philosophical Forum.* His books are *Conceptual Foundations of Scientific Thought* (New York: MacMillan, 1978), *Feuerback* (Cambridge: Cambridge University Press, 1977), and *Models: Representation and the Scientific Understanding* (Boston: Reidel, 1979).

Wheelock, Jr., Arthur K., *Art Historian,* is Curator of Dutch and Flemish Painting, National Gallery of Art, Washington, D.C. He has written and lectured extensively on these topics, in addition to forming many exhibits on Dutch painting. He has published *Perspective, Optics, and Delft Artists Around 1650* (New York: Garland Press, 1977).

Wolf, Dennie, *Psychologist,* is an Educational Psychologist in Human Development and Research Associate at the Harvard Graduate School of Education and Project Zero. Her interests are in the development of cognitive abilities and symbolic competence in children. She is coeditor of a series *Ourselves, Our children* (New York: Random House, 1978) and coeditor of a special volume on developing symbolic skills, (*New Directions in Child Development,* March 1979) with Howard Gardner.

Yonas, Albert, *Psychologist,* is a Professor at the Institute for Child Development and Center for Research in Learning at the University of Minnesota. His major area of speciality is perceptual learning and development emphasizing infant through adult skills and pictorial and depth perception. He is a major contributor of articles and chapters to publications in these areas.